Theories of
Human Learning

Kro's Report

3rd Edition

Presented to the Koron Space Exploration Department
Division of Behavioral Sciences

Prepared by Kro 59 (M-III 611-848-789 CAN)
(Transmitted by Sonarduct in the Sixth Androneas Time Cube,
49th Hexalog, 378th Point)

Theories of
Human Learning
Kro's Report
*3rd Edition**

Guy R. Lefrançois
The University of Alberta

*parts of which are taken from a 1972 book, Psychological Theories and Human Learning: Kongor's Report, *obviously written by Kongor himself (or herself—we were never quite sure); and parts of which were borrowed from a second edition I was forced to write by myself—almost at gunpoint—in 1982. This third edition is Kro's.*

Brooks/Cole Publishing Company

I**T**P™ An International Thomson Publishing Company

Pacific Grove • Albany • Bonn • Boston • Cincinnati • Detroit • London • Madrid • Melbourne
Mexico City • New York • Paris • San Francisco • Singapore • Tokyo • Toronto • Washington

Sponsoring Editor: *Marianne Taflinger*
Senior Promotions Specialist:
  Jean Vevers Thompson
Editorial Assistant: *Virge Perelli-Minetti*
Production Editor: *Marjorie Z. Sanders*
Manuscript Editor: *Chris Kelly*
Permissions Editor: *Elaine Jones*
Interior and Cover Design: *Roy R. Neuhaus*
Interior Illustration: *Gloria Langer*

Cartoons: *Harry Briggs*
Cover Illustration: *Erin Mauterer*
Art Coordinator: *Lisa Torri*
Photo Editor and Researcher:
  Robert J. Western
Indexer: *James Minkin*
Typesetting: *Weimer Graphics*
Cover Printing: *Phoenix Color Corporation, Inc.*
Printing and Binding: *Quebecor Printing/Fairfield*

For more information, contact:

BROOKS/COLE PUBLISHING COMPANY
511 Forest Lodge Road
Pacific Grove, CA 93950
USA

International Thomson Publishing Europe
Berkshire House 168–173
High Holborn
London WC1V 7AA
England

Thomas Nelson Australia
102 Dodds Street
South Melbourne, 3205
Victoria, Australia

Nelson Canada
1120 Birchmount Road
Scarborough, Ontario
Canada M1K 5G4

International Thomson Editores
Campos Eliseos 385, Piso 7
Col. Polanco
11560 México D. F. México

International Thomson Publishing Gmbh
Königswinterer Strasse 418
53227 Bonn
Germany

International Thomson Publishing Asia
221 Henderson Road
#05–10 Henderson Building
Singapore 0315

International Thomson Publishing Japan
Hirakawacho Kyowa Building, 3F
2-2-1 Hirakawacho
Chiyoda-ku, Tokyo 102
Japan

Library of Congress Cataloging-in-Publication Data

Lefrançois, Guy R.
    Theories of Human learning : Kro's report / Guy R.
Lefrançois.—3rd ed.
      p.   cm.
    Rev. ed. of: Psychological theories and human learning. 2nd ed.
c1982.
    Includes bibliographical references and index.
    ISBN 0-534-23202-7
    1. Learning, Psychology of.   I. Lefrançois, Guy R. Psychological
theories and human learning.   II. Title.
LB1051.L567   1994   94-30411
153.1'5—dc20   CIP

Credits continue on p. 385.

This book is dedicated to my blip, Wangor, of Koros in the Androneas system, to my cousin, Kongor M-III, and to Marie, Laurier, Claire, and Rémi Lefrançois of the planet Earth in the Solar system.

(Doctor L said, "Don't thank me." So I won't.)

Kro, January, 1995

Brief Contents

Contents

Chapter 3   Thorndike and Hull: The Effects of Behavior   60

Chapter 4   Skinner's Position: Operant Conditioning   88

Chapter 5   Conditioning: Contiguity, Information, and Biology   128

Part 3   A TRANSITION   **147**

Chapter 6   **Hebb, Tolman, and the Gestaltists: From Behaviorism to Cognitivism   148**

Chapter 8   Neural Networks: The New Connectionism   226

Chapter 9   Learning and Remembering: Models of Memory   246

Chapter 10   Motives: Behavior's Reasons and Causes   274

Part 5   The Last Word   297

Chapter 11   Analysis, Synthesis, and Integration   298

Read This First

. . . not just because it's at the beginning of the book, but because if you don't read it, you won't know what's going on. This opening part is like a preface, a prologue, and an explanation all in one.

Let me get right to the point: The most unusual thing about this book is that it wasn't written by one of us. Truth is, it was originally written by Kongor M-III, 216, 784, 912, LVKX4 and has now been updated, corrected, polished, and perfected by his cousin, Kro. Only this preface, a short prologue, the epilogue, and some footnotes—all identified by my initials, GRL—were written by me, a human person. I swear it.

It all started more than two decades ago. I still have the notes I made at the time, right here in this size 9½ shoe box. Looking back at the very first entry, I see that it had rained during the early part of that spring evening. "A gentle, refreshing, mistlike rain," I wrote in my cramped handwriting, running the lines up the margins to save paper, adding some poetic but irrelevant thoughts about the reflections of the city's lights on the river and soft breezes playing with them.

It seems that I had been sleeping on the riverbank. So when I felt a gentle tugging on my toe, I wasn't certain whether this was really happening or whether it was just part of a dream. Even when I opened my eyes, I still couldn't be certain I wasn't dreaming because what I saw was a little, blue-skinned bit of a creature with bulbous eyes, mobile ears, and pink tufts of hair on its chest and above its ears. What would you have thought?

"Hi," this thing said (I swear it; I have that, too, written in one of these old, yellowed journals). "My name is Kongor M-III 216, 784, 912, LVKX4." As you can imagine, I didn't believe a word of it at the time.

But Kongor, as we came to call him, was—is—real. He's a behavioral scientist. As part of his training, he'd been sent from Koros, a planet in the Androneas system, to explore Earth and to report on the dominant life form thereon.[1] He was my guest for about a year, during which time he prepared a series of reports for his superiors. One of them summarized the then-current state of our knowledge about learning. When he was recalled to Koros, he left that report with me with his permission, in writing, to do whatever I wanted with it. It was published in 1972 under the title *Psychological Theories and Human Learning: Kongor's Report.* That was the first edition of this book.

A decade later, I realized that much of what Kongor had originally written was misleading, inaccurate, or irrelevant. Also, he had promised to sonarduct back some of his other reports so I could put together some outstandingly useful texts. But the so-and-so never did, so I was forced to update and revise the first edition all by myself. The result was the second edition, published in 1983. I removed Kongor's name from the subtitle.

Almost a decade after that (about a year ago now), I was down on the south quarter checking out beaver damage and looking for mushrooms and choke-cherries when—I'm quoting almost directly from my journals here—I heard a "kerplumf!" in the beaver pond behind me. I thought, shoot, there goes another dang beaver. And sure enough, when I turned and looked, I could see the ex-panding circle of ripples where the beaver had smashed his tail down on the water.

But it wasn't a beaver at all. It was Kro, Kongor's cousin. "Oops. Missed," he spluttered as he dragged himself onto the beaver dam. In his hand he had a sodden photograph of a younger, less distinguished *moi*, which he now stared at in apparent bewilderment.

"You're not the guy Kongor called 'the good doctor'?" he asked. It was more an expression of disbelief than a question. I said, "Yes, I am that person. It's been a couple of years, you know." But I had almost as much trouble persuading him that I was Guy Lefrançois as he had convincing me he was Kro 59, Kongor's younger cousin.[2]

Kro had been sent here to update Kongor's original report. It seems that missions of this kind are a sort of primitive *rite de passage* for behavioral scientists on Koros. "You're supposed to help me," he said—rather presumptuously, I thought—leaning to one side and pounding the opposite side of his head to spill the slough water out of his ears.

"What?"

"Well, Kongor said you would," he added, "For a price."

It turns out that the price he had in mind was a billion Koronian credits, which I'm told is nothing to sneeze at. Unfortunately, at this moment I can't even use them to paper the walls of my bush cabin, because they're just a gizmo in a computer somewhere. But if I ever get to Koros, you can bet I won't be hunting mushrooms or selling chokecherries for a living.

---

[1] That Kongor was (is) male has never been clearly established, in spite of my grandmother's strong suspicions following his disappearance with Sylvia during the dance that one Saturday. Nor do we have any convincing reason to believe him female, though, and *it* is somehow demeaning. Hence the male appellation. (GRL)

[2] We had the same problems determining Kro's gender (if any) even after my aunt Lucy, a quite good chicken sexer, attempted to examine him. Kro once claimed to be all sexes but could not easily prove it. (GRL)

"It's a deal," I said, "as long as you also write up a version of your report for human readers, and you give it to me and I can use it any way I want." Even then, I was thinking about you. Honest.

"Deal," he agreed. "You can even pretend you wrote it yourself." Of course I wouldn't do that. I like to give credit where credit is due.

So Kro, who bears a definite family resemblance to Kongor, moved into the little bush cabin up above the beaver dam. But he didn't stay there very long, because there was (and is) no power and no telephone up there; he was anxious to hook into the university library system so he could do his research. "I have to get this done and get the Dickenses back home," he explained in his force-learned, quasi-idiomatic English. So he moved into our house, which was OK except for the dog and cat, who couldn't figure out what to think. Also, Kro broke a lot of stuff, which gets a little tiring after a while. But that's water under the bridge.

In any case, he was with us for most of this past year. And, true to his word, he did update Kongor's learning book. Then he changed the title—absolutely insisted on it—*The Best Learning Theories Book on Earth: Kro's Report*, is what he called it. I tried to explain how inappropriately presumptuous this was.

"Hey," says he, never dangerously modest, "I'll call it what it is!" But we couldn't let him do that, editorial wisdom being what it is.

So here's the version Kro wrote, and entitled, just for you—but with a less presumptuous title.

WHAT'S IN THE THIRD EDITION?

This book is a survey and interpretation of some of the important theories and findings in the psychology of learning. It describes and evaluates behavioristic and cognitive theories, looks at connectionism (neural net models), examines memory and motivation, and concludes with an overall summary and synthesis. The emphasis throughout is on clarity of presentation, relevance of topics, and maintenance of high interest—hence the liberal use of practical illustrations and the occasional use of humor.

The book is written primarily for students of human learning, teachers, counselors, social workers, industrial psychologists, nurses, social psychologists, numismatists, physicians, lawyers, dentists, engineers, housewives, farmers, judges, fishermen, tree planters, glass blowers, vagabonds, poets, and all others—in that order. And, of course, it was written for Korons.

ACKNOWLEDGMENTS

Kro wanted me to pass on his appreciation to Stephen R. Coleman, Cleveland State University; Jim Grubbs, Simpson College; David Hogberg, Albion College; Todd Schachtman, University of Missouri; Mike Selby, California Polytechnic State University–San Luis Obispo; Ron Stephens, Western Kentucky University; and Lenore Szuchman, Barry University.

Kro also wanted me to indicate that he is not responsible for any errors and misinterpretations that remain in this text. "If any errors creep in," said he, "it'll be the fault of reviewers, editors, and other publishing types." That, of course, is absolutely untrue. Kro is fully responsible for any weaknesses in the book.

Guy R. Lefrançois

ABOUT THE COVER

Kro insisted there be an explanatory note about the flag on the cover. It's really just a bit of rag I first saw when Kongor planted it near the beaver dam (close to the southwest corner of the northwest quarter of Section 15, Township 48, Range 23, west of the 4th Meridian). It's made of synthetic fibers and boasts both a pig rampant and a turkey glissant on a field of flowers that look suspiciously like dandelions.

Aunt Lucy said Kro's undershorts boasted the same design.

Part 1

Preamble: Science and Theory

1 Human Learning: Science and Theory

Chapter 1

Learning: Science and Theory

It ain't so much the things we don't know that get us into trouble. It's the things we know that just ain't so.

Artemus Ward

Preliminary Note to the Human Reader: Chapter 1 Objectives

Hi. Call me Kro, and if you don't mind, I'll just call you "reader," like some of your textbooks do. Lefrançois asked me to write a note in front of each of the chapters of this report. "Explain clearly what you're doing and why," he said (which is easy for *him* to say).

Other than for these preliminary notes, reader, this whole book is almost identical to the report I'm sending back to my home Behavioral Science Division—except, of course, that this version is in English, French, Spanish, and German instead of in electronic code. Also, most of the examples are human illustrations because you wouldn't understand Koronian ones. Lefrançois helped me a little with them.[1]

The entire report, organized into 11 chapters, summarizes what your planet's psychologists know and believe about learning. It presents a historical view of the development of psychological theories related to human learning, describing the major principles and applications of each theory and evaluating its main strengths and weaknesses.

This first chapter is a bit of a preamble; it defines important terms and sets the stage for what is to come later. When you finish studying this chapter, you should know the following with stunning clarity:

- What is meant by the term *learning*
- What psychological theories are
- How theories are developed
- How theories can be evaluated
- What the principal information-gathering methods are in psychology
- Some of the advantages and weaknesses of these methods
- How to stew a rabbit

If you don't know these things when you finish, read the chapter again. Or ask your grandmother.

SIXTH TIME CUBE, 49TH HEXALOG, POINT 211

As a preamble to my official report, let it be recorded that I've landed on the planet and that I followed exactly the coordinates set by Kongor M-III—which put me smack in the middle of a beaver slough, up to my personal private one in mud! I'm certain cousin Kon did this on purpose, which proves our conclusion that he was on the verge of going crazy as an aquatic bird when he was here. When I return, I'll file a full report witnessed by Doctor Lefrançois's thumbprint and

[1] A lot. (GRL)

signature. He was there and almost had to save my life. I would hope that Kongor's punishment will be appropriate, unless he gives me back all the stuff he borrowed from me.

I moved into the little cabin by the beaver pond and set about familiarizing myself with the dominant species (and a few others less dominant). I didn't have to start right from scratch, of course, having read cousin Kon's original report and having access to his dictionary.[2] However, it turns out that much of that report was misleading or, worse, dead wrong. In this updated report, I plan to set things straight once and for all.

PSYCHOLOGY AND LEARNING

Let me begin at the beginning. Here on earth, **psychology**[3] is the science that studies human behavior and thinking. It looks at how experience affects thought and action; it explores the roles of biology and heredity; it examines consciousness and dreams; it traces how people develop from infants into adults; and it investigates social influences. Basically it tries to explain why people think, act, and feel as they do.

This report is limited to psychological theories that deal with human and animal learning, with an emphasis on human learning. Reports 2 through 74 deal with other facets of psychology.

Learning

Ask some grandmother (or father) what learning is and the most likely answer will have something to do with the *acquisition of information*. If I tell you that Star Hegel is 48 billion years old and you can then repeat that it's 48 billion years old, I might infer that you have learned something. In this case, the nature of the information that you've acquired is obvious.

Some Examples

In many cases, though, what is acquired during learning isn't so obvious. For example, Toch and Schulte (1961)[4] used an apparatus (a stereoscope) to present police recruits with a split-second glimpse of a different image for each eye— one neutral and the other depicting some form of violence. Almost invariably, third-year trainees saw the violent pictures significantly more often than did novices. Why? What had they learned? What specific information had they acquired? They had apparently learned something, but the learning didn't involve regurgitating information; instead, behavior changed.

Psychologists therefore usually define learning as *a change in behavior*. To illustrate: When I first went over to the Lefrançois house, their dog reacted in a

---

[2] *Kongor's Dictionary: A Koronian guide to Earth English*. Hungry Coyote Publishing: Sixth Androneas Time Cube, 48th Hexalog, Point 654.
[3] Boldfaced terms are defined in the glossary at the end of the text, starting on page 331.
[4] In this text, references are cited in the style approved by the American Psychological Association (APA), with the name of the author(s) is followed by the year of the relevant publication. The bibliography at the end of the book provides complete information about the source. (Kro)

very peculiar and embarrassing way. As I moved toward the back of the house, the dog followed, her nose to the ground and her tail wagging in excitement. Whenever I stopped she would raise her paw, stretch her nose to within an inch of my personal nose, raise her tail high in the air, and remain rigid until I moved again. I didn't much like this.[5] Eventually the dog realized that I was not a new species of game bird and abandoned her attempts to "point" me. This change in behavior is an example of learning.

But consider the case of the student who after taking LSD finds that the fire hydrants have become deranged turkeys; in response, he runs madly down the street, shouting "Help!" Here is a striking change in behavior, but to say that this change is an example of learning is to stretch the inclusiveness of the term beyond reasonable limits.

Behavior changes that are the temporary results of things like fatigue, injury, or drugs don't define learning. Similarly, changes that are mainly determined by biology (like physical growth or sexual maturation) or that result from injury or disease (especially of the brain and other parts of the nervous system) are not examples of learning.

Definition

To summarize, **learning** is generally defined as *all relatively permanent changes in behavior that result from experience but are not attributable to fatigue, maturation, drugs, injury, or disease.*

Performance versus Learning

Changes in behavior that define learning aren't always obvious. In a classic experiment, Buxton (1940) left rats in large mazes for several nights. These mazes had start boxes at their beginnings and goal boxes (without food) at their ends. After a few nights in the mazes, there was no evidence that the rats had learned anything at all. Later, however, Buxton gave the rats a small taste of food in the goal boxes, then placed them in the start boxes. Now more than half of them ran directly to the goal boxes without making a single error! Clearly they had learned a lot during the first nights in the maze, but their learning was **latent** rather than actual. It was not evident in their **performance** until there had also been a change in their **dispositions**—that is, in their reasons for going through the maze.

So learning may involve changes not only in capability (the *capacity* to do something) but also in disposition (the *inclination* to perform). For example, if in a classroom a student successfully learns how to perform some complex action, then there is clearly a change in the student's capabilities. However, unless there is later an opportunity and a need to perform this action, the change may never be apparent—a fact that makes it no less real.

---

[5]If truth be told, at first Kro (who stood only about 4 feet on tiptoes) was quite terrified of this harmless—and useless—hunting hound. But eventually he came to like her. That's another example of learning. (GRL)

THEORY

Behavior is a complicated thing; there are all sorts of factors at play in determining what you do. The principle task of the learning psychologist is to understand behavior. From understanding comes the ability to predict and sometimes the ability to control, both of which are useful and important functions. For example, teachers' predictions about how well students are likely to perform are critical for decisions relating to teaching and evaluating.

To understand something as complicated as behavior, psychologists need to simplify, to discover regularity and predictability, and to invent metaphors (comparisons). Man looks for order where there is none, said Francis Bacon, perhaps not yet realizing that woman is as guilty of this as man. And Bacon may have been correct that humans would look for order even if there were none, that they seem to have a need to find order. But the fact is (as we Koronians have long known) that there is considerable regularity and predictability in the world. Discovering this regularity and then trying to explain it is, in a nutshell, what theory building is all about.

Humans like to build theories, says Stagner (1988). Years ago they devised theories about the lights in the sky, about why babies look like their parents, about the shape of the earth. Often, these theories were expressed as metaphors: the sun is a chariot, racing across the sky; dreams are the adventures of souls walking parallel worlds while the body sleeps. Modern scientific theories, too, can often be explained and understood as metaphors: the heart is a pump; the brain is a computer; the eye is a camera. In Chapter 6 I look in more detail at metaphors in psychology.

Theories, Laws, Principles, and Beliefs

A scientific **theory** is a collection of related statements whose main function is to summarize and explain observations. In a simplified sense, theory building works something like this: Theorists begin with certain assumptions (unproven beliefs) about human behavior, perhaps based partly on their observations of regularity or predictability in behavior. As a result, they develop tentative explanations for what they observe. This leads them to believe that certain relationships exist, that *if* this, *then* that. These if-then statements, or educated predictions, are called **hypotheses**. Now the theorist gathers observations (data) to test the validity of the hypotheses. If the evidence supports the hypotheses, then the theorist can make **generalizations**, statements that summarize relationships and that become part of the theory. Some of these statements might be principles, and others laws; some might simply be beliefs.

Principles are statements that relate to some predictability in nature or, more pertinent for psychology, in behavior. Principles are generally agreed-upon conclusions that are thought to be true because they are based on solid evidence. They are nevertheless somewhat tentative and open to doubt. With new evidence, principles are subject to change.

Laws are statements whose accuracy is beyond reasonable doubt. That is, they are conclusions that are based on what seems to be irrefutable evidence and flawless logic. A statement like $E=mc^2$ is an example of a law. Laws should not be confused with *truth*, however, since any law can be refuted given sufficient contrary evidence. By definition, truth can never be found to be untrue.

Beliefs describe statements that are more private and more personal than are principles or laws. Beliefs, too, attempt to describe observations and, unfortunately, are often treated as though they were as universal as principles or even laws.

Beliefs and Bubba Psychology

Because people are very interested in themselves and in the behavior of others, societies have developed large bodies of commonly held beliefs about human behavior. These beliefs are part of what Kelley (1992) calls **bubba psychology**; *bubba* means grandmother. Hence the term indicates an intuitive sort of folk psychology, one that is also termed *implicit* or *naive* psychology (Grippin & Peters, 1984).[6]

The beliefs of folk psychology are often correct. If they weren't, people would constantly be surprised at what others say and do. Most people know enough about human behavior to be able to predict that, for example, those who are sad might cry, those who are overjoyed might smile and laugh, and those who are outraged might do something outrageous.

Quite often, however, the beliefs of folk psychology are at least partly wrong. For example, it might seem obvious that many people don't dream, that some women are more likely than others to give birth to sons, and that most people are altruistic enough to try to help someone being raped, mugged, or beaten. In fact, however, all normal people dream, although not all can remember doing so (Cartwright, 1977); it is the man's sperm, not the woman's ovum (egg), that determines the infant's sex; and some studies indicate that many people will not try to help someone in need, even if that person is being killed (Darley & Latané, 1968).

Because they are often misleading or flatly incorrect, personal beliefs can be very dangerous in science. Yet even educated and trained professionals are often victims of false beliefs. For example, many nurses believe that childless couples who adopt are likely to have a child of their own, and that more infants are born during a full moon. Both these beliefs are wrong (Gilovich, 1991).

Functions of Theories

The principles and beliefs that make up a psychological theory have a number of important functions. As mentioned earlier, one of these functions is to simplify and organize observations. If a theory is successful in so doing, it should also lead to prediction. A prediction based on a theory is called a **hypothesis.**

---

[6]My references to bubbas and grandmothers are never derogatory; they are merely explanatory. I like grandmothers. (Kro)

For example, Lefrançois's grandmother's has a theory that spells out relationships among different kinds of fertilizers and the growth of different plants. If her theory reflects these relationships accurately, it should allow her to hypothesize (predict) with greater accuracy what will happen to her garden when she uses different fertilizers. In much the same way, the usefulness of a theory in psychology has much to do with how accurately it predicts. Thus a theory that tries to explain how humans learn should lead logically to suggestions for arranging experiences in such a way that behavior will change (or not change) in desired ways.

In addition to these practical considerations, theories also serve to suggest which facts (that is, observations) are most important, as well as which relationships among these facts are most meaningful (L. M. Thomas, 1992). Because theorists may have dramatically different ideas about what is important, however, a large number of theories may emerge in the same area of investigation. And although these theories may be quite different, none will necessarily be totally incorrect, although some may be more useful than others. In the final analysis, a theory cannot easily be evaluated in terms of whether it is right or wrong. Instead, it must be judged mainly in terms of its usefulness.

Evaluating Theories

How, then, should a theory be judged? L. M. Thomas (1992) suggests a number of important criteria. First, a theory should reflect the generally agreed-upon facts in a field. And because facts do not always stand still in the social sciences, this criterion is especially relevant for psychological theory.

Second, a good theory should be clear and understandable. One of the functions of theories is to simplify—to impose order on chaos. Hence theories should not be so complex as to be difficult to understand. More precisely, they should be **parsimonious**. A parsimonious statement is the simplest and shortest statement that adequately covers the fact. Accordingly, a parsimonious theory is one that describes all important relationships in the simplest but most accurate terms possible. Theories that are unnecessarily detailed and complex are said to lack parsimony.[7]

Third, as indicated earlier, a theory should be useful for predicting as well as for explaining. Thus it should have practical applications in the real world—for example, in education or in therapy.

Fourth, theories should not be based on a very large number of unverified **assumptions** (beliefs that are accepted as fact but are not tested). Although all theories are based on some assumptions, the better theories are those whose assumptions are evident and lead to predictions that can be tested.

---

[7]The human preference for parsimony and simplicity seems to me highly revealing. Of what? Of intellectual limitations evident in a widespread inability to understand chaos and a natural aversion to detail and complexity. It says something, as well, of the human's problems in separating reason and emotion. "Simplicity and parsimony *feel* better," said Lefrançois when I asked him. "Complexity can be so *frustrating*." Strange, hunh? (Kro)

TABLE 1.1   Criteria of a good theory, applied to Grandmother Francoeur's fertilizer theory. This theory holds, in part, that horse manure stimulates potatoes and carrots, that chicken droppings invigorate cabbages, and that dried cow dung excites flowers.

Criteria	Grandmother Francœur's theory
Does it reflect the facts?	Yes, if carrots, potatoes, and other plants behave as expected under specified conditions.
Is it clear, understandable, and parsimonious?	It is less parsimonious than might be, long-windedness being a family characterstic. But it is quite clear except to the very stupid, who are seldom asked to judge theories.
Is it useful for predicting as well as explaining?	Very. We can predict in the spring what will happen in the fall. But will we be correct? Only if the theory fulfills the first criterion.
Is it based on many untested assumptions?	Perhaps, but its predictions can easily be tested.
Is it satisfying and thought provoking? Does it have heuristic value?	Oh yes, very satisfying! But is has not been very research provoking; hence it lacks heuristic value.

Finally, a good theory should not only provide satisfying explanations, but it should also be thought provoking—or, perhaps more important, *research* provoking. Theories that have the greatest impact on a field are often those that give rise as much to opposition as to support. Such theories typically lead to research designed to support, to refute, or to elaborate on them. They are said to have high **heuristic** value in the sense that they lead to new research and to new discoveries.

These criteria are summarized and illustrated in Table 1.1.

PSYCHOLOGICAL THEORIES AND SCIENCE

As we saw, common sense doesn't always make sense. Many highly cherished beliefs are wrong, even though they are remarkably pervasive. Gilovich (1991) points out that there are about 20 times more astrologers than astronomers in North America, a fact that my cousin Kongor had mentioned but that I had not believed. Also, more people believe in ESP than in evolution. Yet there is no good evidence that these beliefs are the least bit valid!

One of psychology's important tasks is to determine what does make sense—to sort fact from fancy. How can psychology determine whether a belief is correct? The answer is simple: **science**.

What Is Science?

Science is both a collection of information and a way of dealing with or obtaining it. As a collection of information, it is illustrated by the content of such disciplines as chemistry, physics, astronomy, and psychology. As a way of dealing with information, science is evident in (a) an attitude toward the search for knowledge that emphasizes replicability, objectivity, and consistency; and (b) methods for gathering and analyzing observations that are designed to ensure objective and generalizable conclusions. Science is psychology's most powerful tool for separating fact from fiction.

An Illustration

There is a story told by one of my Koronian teachers to illustrate the precision and rigor with which psychologists approach their subject.[8] It tells of a brilliant young investigator who conditioned a flea to respond to the command "Jump" and then experimented with variations of the procedure. He wanted to discover the relationship between the removal of a flea's legs and its response to the command to jump. At every step of the experiment he made careful and detailed notes in his lab book:

> *Time.* 1:30.7
> *Procedure.* Held flea gently in left hand with thumb underneath the abdomen. Grasped flea's two hind legs securely between thumb and forefinger of right hand. Removed both legs simultaneously by means of sharp pull. Placed flea on the conditioning table at 1:32.8 in position 3-Y, facing north. Said "Jump" once in a normal tone.
> *Observation.* The flea jumped.

Apparently the experimenter "delegged" the flea in three stages. After the first two pairs of legs were removed, it still jumped vigorously in response to the command "Jump." But after the last two legs had been pulled off, the flea remained quivering on the table even when the command was repeated. The last recorded observation was this:

> *Conclusion.* When a flea has all six legs removed, it becomes deaf.

This illustration suggests that the validity of conclusions does not always follow from careful experimental procedures, although it is certainly true that such procedures increase the likelihood that inferences will be accurate.

Rules of the Scientific Method

As noted above, a useful way of looking at the meaning of the term *science* is to think of it as an attitude rather than simply as one of several bodies of knowledge or as a series of recipes for acquiring and systematizing knowledge. As an

---

[8]This is not quite true. In fact, I'm the one who first told Kro the story, in an entirely different context. (GRL)

attitude, science insists on objectivity, precision, and replicability; it accepts as valid only those observations that have been collected in such a way that they can be repeated by others under similar circumstances.

This view of science leads logically to certain prescribed methods for gathering information. These methods collectively make up what is often referred to as the scientific method, which can be simplified in terms of four steps:

1. Ask the Question

Do people who are most highly rewarded always work hardest? Is punishment effective in eliminating undesirable behavior? Are adoptive parents more likely to have children of their own? There is no shortage of questions in the study of learning and behavior. As a method, science makes no judgments about whether questions are trivial or important; it simply insists that they be clear. And its initial conclusions are always tentative.

2. Develop a Hypothesis

These tentative conclusions often take the form of a prediction—an if-then statement—which, as we noted, is labeled a *hypothesis*. In a sense, hypotheses are statements that appear to be reasonable conclusions based on what the researcher already knows or suspects. Their function in the development of science, and of theories, is that they can be tested.

3. Collect Relevant Observations

Testing hypotheses requires making relevant observations so as to determine whether *hypothesized* state of affairs actually exists in real life. Scientific study always begins with observations.

Science suggests a number of different ways of gathering observations. The most powerful of these is the **experiment** (discussed shortly). Experiments sometimes make use of **surveys**, which are ways of making observations concerning the behaviors, beliefs, attitudes, and other characteristics of a sample representing some population. Surveys often use **questionnaires** (lists of predetermined questions to which subjects respond), **interviews** (where investigators question participants), or different kinds of tests and measurements (such as intelligence or personality tests, or measures of weight and height).

4. Test the Hypothesis

The reason for gathering observations is to determine whether the hypothesis is valid. The whole point of the exercise is to answer the questions that inspired the research in the first place.

If conclusions are to be valid, not only must observations be accurate, but it is also necessary to determine their meaning. Doing so is not always very simple. Science is very concerned that observations might just be *chance* occurrences. Accordingly, a series of mathematical procedures have been developed to help researchers separate chance events from those that are **significant**.[9]

In scientific research, conclusions usually take the form of accepting or rejecting the hypotheses that have guided the investigation. Sometimes, of course, the results are unclear or are contrary to what is expected. Research outcomes suggest another question rather than an answer, another hypothesis rather than a firm conclusion. Sometimes, too, a series of unexpected observations may lead to major changes in theories.

Experiments

The **experiment** is science's most powerful tool for reliably determining cause-and-effect relationships. It allows the investigator to control important variables systematically in an attempt to determine what causes what. Consider, for example, an experiment designed to test Lefrançois's grandmother's belief that obese people are more "picky" eaters than skinny people.

Sampling

The first step in carrying out this experiment is to select two groups: one obese and one not. This requires a clear definition of obesity (for example, 20% above "ideal" body weight as determined by this planet's American Medical Association).

In an experiment, it is very important that participants be selected at **random** from the population to which the investigator wants to generalize. Random selection means that everybody has an equal chance of being a participant. Common *nonrandom* ways of selecting participants are to have them volunteer or to select them from institutions or classrooms.

The problem with nonrandom selection of subjects is that systematic biases may be introduced. For example, people who volunteer for experiments may be more adventurous than those who do not, and the investigator's conclusions might then be valid only for those who are adventurous. Similarly, students may be systematically different from nonstudents (and institutionalized people from noninstitutionalized people) in terms of interests, motivation, background, and other characteristics.

Having selected participants, the investigator then assigns them *randomly* to groups. Random assignment increases the likelihood that subject biases will even out. Some subjects are probably more intelligent than others; some are more aggressive, more tired, or hungrier. If subjects are assigned to different groups at random, some of the bright ones will be in each group, as will some of the tired, the hungry, and the aggressive. In this way, the investigator tries to make sure that groups are as similar as possible in all important ways.

---

[9]These *statistical* procedures help human scientists determine the chance probability of what they observe. Many scientific conclusions are based on the assumption that observations that would rarely be expected to occur by chance must have some other (often identifiable) cause. (Kro)

One way of reducing systematic biases among groups of subjects is to select *large* random samples. Observations of the sexual behavior of ten college students from one little town is not likely to lead to conclusions that can confidently be applied to students in the whole state.

When an investigation involves a sufficiently large sample drawn at random from the population, the researcher may be highly confident that the sample will be representative of the entire population. If 52% of the population of obese individuals is male, then about 52% of the sample should also be male; and if 22% is highly aggressive, then about 22% of the sample should be aggressive.

Experimental and Control Groups

Next, subjects are randomly assigned to **experimental** or **control** groups (sometimes also called comparison or no-treatment groups). The groups are as identical as possible, except that experimental group members are exposed to some *treatment*; members of the control group are not. Without a control group, it might be impossible for the investigator to know for certain that observed changes following treatment are actually caused by the treatment and not by some other uncontrolled factor.

Independent and Dependent Variables

An experiment is a situation where the investigator systematically manipulates important aspects of the environment to determine the effect of so doing. What is manipulated is the **independent variable**; the effect of this control or manipulation is reflected in the **dependent variable**.

Identifying dependent and independent variables is a relatively simple matter when an experiment is phrased as an *if-then* statement. The objective of an experiment is to uncover cause-and-effect relationships—to determine whether it is true that if A occurs, then B will occur. The "if" part of the equation represents what is controlled or manipulated (the independent variable); the "then" part represents the consequences or outcomes (the dependent variable). Virtually any hypothesis can be phrased as an if-then statement.

An Example

Fat people are finicky, claimed Lefrançois's Grandma Francœur. Decke (1971) phrased it differently, saying that *if* something tastes good rather than bad, *then* obese individuals will eat relatively more of it than normal individuals. To test this hypothesis, Decke selected obese and normal subjects, randomly assigning them to an experimental condition in which they were presented with either a very good milkshake or one to which had been added a dash of quinine (which makes a milkshake taste rather bad). Taste, which was under the investigator's control, was the independent variable; (the cause); the amount eaten, which was the outcome being studied, was the dependent variable.

The results? As shown in Figure 1.1, obese subjects consumed about 35% more of the good-tasting milkshake than did normal subjects, but drank only about a third as much of the bad-tasting milkshake. Under some circumstances, then, obese individuals appear to be more finicky than nonobese people. But that is far from the whole story.

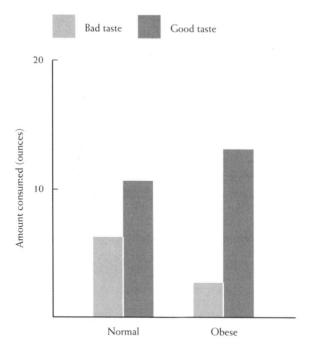

FIGURE 1.1 In Decke's experiment, obese and normal participants were allowed to drink as much as they wanted of either a good- or a bad-tasting milkshake. The obese group drank more of the milkshake when it tasted good, but far less when it tasted bad.

Thinking Critically about Psychological Research

One of the important limitations in psychological investigations is that observations are not always incontestable facts. It is a fact that apples fall when they become detached from trees. And if a lazy person (perhaps named Newton) is sleeping below the tree directly under the apple, it *will* hit him on the head. But is it a similar fact that 6-year-old North American children have a 3000-word vocabulary? Is it a fact that 3-year-old boys love their mothers, and 7-year-olds their fathers? On Koros, yes; on Earth, maybe. The point is that human behavior is subject to tremendous variation. Not every 6-year old would have a vocabulary of 3000 words if that were the average. Some would know far more words; some far less. The characteristics of apples, on the other hand, are far less variable—and their behavior far more predictable.[10]

---

[10]It shouldn't be inferred from these comments that physical facts are more "factual" than psychological facts. Indeed, in this chaotic and relativistic world, the word *fact*—be it physical or psychological—is a statistical concept of varying probability. Kro's point is that although it's simple to observe an apple falling, it's less easy to ascertain children's vocabulary or their attachment to mothers. (GRL)

Psychological investigations are also limited by the amount of control that can be exercised over relevant variables. Two rats reared in identical cages and subjected to the same daily routines from birth may reasonably be assumed to have had highly comparable experiences. The same assumption can't be made as confidently about two children who are raised in different middle-class homes; their parents, friends, siblings, and peers are all different. Thus the concept of *control* in psychological experimentation should take into account relevant differences among subjects.

Consider Figure 1.1:

Problem. To determine the relationship of rest to problem-solving behavior.

Subjects. All students in a private school are selected for the study. They are randomly divided into two groups.

Hypothesis. Well-rested subjects will perform significantly better on a problem-solving test.

Method. One group is allowed to sleep as usual; the other is kept awake all night. In the morning, the test is administered to all subjects and results for the two groups are compared.

Results. The rested group does significantly better.

Is the conclusion that rest is related to problem-solving ability warranted? The answer is "yes," *providing that a number of other relevant variables have also been controlled.* If, for example, the rested group were on average more intelligent, all male or female, or had had previous training in problem solving, these variables could also account for differences in test performance. It would then not be logical to conclude that rest is the significant factor. But because participants were assigned at random to either of the two groups, there is a greater chance that they are similar on each of these important variables. As we saw earlier, random selection is one way to control for relevant variables. Another is to match the groups on these variables. If subjects in each group are similarly intelligent, balanced by sex, and have the same amount of previous training, then the conclusion is more justifiable. Because it is usually impossible to account for all relevant variables in psychological experimentation, however, the possibility that results may be influenced by unidentified factors remains a limiting feature.

It is because of problems and limitations such as these that science insists upon critical thinking; things don't always mean what they seem to mean. The following are some important questions you should ask yourself when interpreting and evaluating psychological research.

Have I Committed the Nominal Fallacy?

Luria (1968) reports the case of S, whose memory was so remarkable that he could remember completely accurately the most trivial of details—not just for minutes, hours, or days, but for decades. He seemed never to forget even the most meaningless of sounds, the most nonsensical of words. "Yes, yes," he would say when Luria asked him to remember some jumbled paragraph or a complex table of digits he had been asked to learn years earlier. "Yes, this was a series you gave me once when we were in your apartment. . . . You were wearing a gray suit and you looked at me like this" (Luria, 1968, p. 12).

Why did S remember so well? Do you suppose it was because he had what is popularly called a photographic memory, or because he was a professional mnemonist (that is, memorizer)? Neither. These are simply labels for someone with a good memory; they don't explain why his or her memory is so good. The assumption that names are explanations is the *nominal fallacy*. Nominal fallacies are quite common. For example, if you think some children have difficulty learning because they are mentally retarded or learning disabled, you are guilty of a nominal fallacy. To say that children have difficulty learning because they are learning disabled or mentally retarded is not to say anything at all about *why* they have difficulty.

Have I Committed the Gambler's Fallacy?

There is a simple classroom demonstration where an instructor asks students to predict the outcome of a sequence of coin flips and to keep track of their predictions. He flips: "Heads," he says. He flips again: "Heads." Of course, he doesn't let anyone actually see the coin, but they trust him; he's their professor. Seven or eight flips in a row, he announces "heads," lying as often as he needs to.

Remarkably, following an unbroken series of heads or of tails, a majority of students continue to commit the *gambler's fallacy*: They make the opposite prediction. Gamblers are easily convinced that if a "one-armed bandit" has not paid off for a while, chances of it doing so on the next pull are much greater. But the outcome of a turn on the one-armed bandit, like the outcome of the flip of a coin, is unaffected by prior events. The probability of a *fair* coin coming up heads or tails is no different on the 1st than on the 100th flip; it is exactly .5 (one out of two times, on average) no matter how many times it has just come up one or the other.

Is the Sample Representative?

The samples on which conclusions are based have to be representative of the groups to which they are generalized. So investigators try to select *unbiased* samples (that is, samples whose characteristics are much the same as those of the general population), using random selection whenever possible. Research is sometimes limited, however, to groups such as students, institutional inmates, or housing complex residents. In such cases, to ensure that a sample represents a larger population, it is necessary to compare the two on important variables like age, sex, and educational background. If the sample is biased (that is, different from the population), conclusions might apply only to the sample upon which they are based.

Can Subjects Be Believed?

Sometimes research runs into memory problems. How well can participants remember their fourth birthday? Do they remember the age of their first menstrual period? Their first ejaculation? Do they remember what the thief was wearing? What about how they felt on their first date? The color of her eyes?

Sometimes the problem is one of honesty. Questionnaires that probe into highly personal areas are especially vulnerable to deliberate distortion. And if there is something to be gained or lost by presenting a certain image, that also must be taken into account by the critical consumer of research.

Is There a Possibility of Subject Bias?

In a historic study, Roethlisberger and Dickson (1939) tried to increase the productivity of a group of workers at Hawthorne Electric by changing aspects of their work environment. Over a series of experiments, they did things like increase or decrease the number of work periods, shorten or lengthen breaks, increase or decrease illumination, and provide or take away bonuses. No matter what the experimenters did, production increased. It seemed that subjects were simply responding to the knowledge that they were being studied.

Although the **Hawthorne effect** is not often apparent or usually very large (see Rice, 1982), it may nevertheless be an important factor in some psychological research. Participants in experiments are often anxious to please the investigator; consequently, their responses may occasionally be misleading. To guard against this possibility, subjects are often not told that they are members of experimental groups, or they are compared with others who also think they are part of the experiment but actually are not.

Is There a Possibility of Experimenter Bias?

Margaret Mead, the well-known human anthropologist/sociologist, had a profound belief that cultures shape people. Her studies of isolated inhabitants of New Guinea uncovered three very different tribes (Mead, 1935). Among the cannibalistic Mundugummor, both men and women were ruthless, aggressive, and very masculine by North American standards. In contrast, both sexes among the agricultural Arapesh seemed traditionally feminine (noncompetitive, nonaggressive, warm, and emotional). And in a third tribe, the Tchambuli, where the men spent most of their time adorning themselves and devising new dances while the women gathered food, there appeared to be a reversal of sex roles. Mead claimed this was striking evidence of the power of culture in shaping important characteristics like masculinity and feminity.

Freeman (1983) argues that this is not so. After six years of research in Samoa (where Mead had done much of her work on culture), Freeman found little evidence of cultural differences as striking as those described by Mead. Her observations and conclusions, he writes, were highly subjective and largely undocumented. Freeman suggests that Mead was so convinced of the importance of culture that her biases blinded her to contradictory evidence.

In the same way as subjects may not be told whether they are members of the experimental or control group (to guard against the possibility of subject bias), so too can experimental observers be kept ignorant of who is an experimental subject and who is not (a **single-blind procedure**). A **double-blind procedure** is when neither subjects nor experimenters know which subjects received which treatment. For example, tests might be scored and interpreted without the investigator knowing whether the testee is part of an experimental group.

SUBJECTS IN PSYCHOLOGY

Many of psychology's most important observations come from controlled investigations of animals and of people.

Animals as Subjects

Animals have been used extensively in investigations where, for practical, ethical, or legal reasons, humans cannot easily be employed. To study what controls feeding, blowflies have had the nerve from their foreguts severed (they subsequently ate until they burst). To investigate the roles of transmitter substances in learning and remembering, worms have been trained and then minced and fed to other worms. Investigations of the effects of mothering on infants have seen infant monkeys raised in isolation, deprived of their mothers. Rats have had brain surgery in studies of obesity and have been used in studies of eating disorders—for example, to investigate the relationship of activity and anorexia. Experiments on genetic transmission have involved the selective breeding of different strains of mice and rats.

In many cases, results of studies such as these can be generalized, at least tentatively, to humans. Still, there is always the possibility that conclusions based on animal research might not apply to people. And ultimately, it is people in whom psychology is most interested.[11]

The Ethics of Animal Research

Note that some animal research is unacceptable on moral and ethical grounds, and that some of the studies mentioned above are objectionable to many. Even though the goal of science is to improve human welfare, this objective does not automatically justify causing pain or even death to an animal. There are some who believe that under *no* circumstances should animals be harmed in the interests of science. And there are others, of course, who insist that the benefits that might ultimately be derived justify animal research under certain circum-

---

[11]Throughout their history, many humans have been at great pains to ascertain that they are fundamentally different from nonhuman animals, and have expended considerable effort and time trying to discover exactly how it is that they are different. Some propose that it is the *soul* (sorry, I can't really define or describe this) that separates the two; others suggest *language* or *consciousness*; still others claim that some Maker made humans according to a self-likeness, and that this accounts for a critical, basic difference. Some psychologists argue that because humans and nonhumans are different, animals make poor subjects in investigations of human behavior; others argue that in some ways they are very similar, and that because of the fact that certain experimental procedures are better performed with animals, it makes sense to use animals in psychological research. My fourth report in this series will place humans exactly where they belong on the cosmic scale. (Kro)

stances. Among the American Psychological Association's principles governing the conduct of member psychologists doing research with animals are guidelines suggesting the following (APA, 1989, p. xxxi):

- Animal care must comply with existing laws and regulations.
- All animal research must be supervised by a psychologist trained in the care of laboratory animals.
- All animal workers must be explicitly trained in animal care.
- Every effort must be made to minimize animal pain and suffering.
- Animals must be subjected to surgery, pain, and discomfort only when this is justified by the potential value of the research.
- If animals need to be killed, this must be done quickly and painlessly.

Humans as Subjects

Human subjects are seldom subjected to pain and suffering as obvious as that among monkeys who develop experimentally induced ulcers, or rabbits exposed to allergenic cosmetics. But there are experimental treatments with humans that are psychologically stressful; some might even have lasting negative consequences. As a result, the APA has developed a set of guidelines governing the conduct of research with human subjects. The most important principle underlying these guidelines is that of *informed consent*: Subjects are to be made aware of the nature and purpose of the research, and are to be given complete freedom *not* to participate. This is especially important where investigators are in a position of power over potential participants, as is the case where the latter are students or residents in homes for the elderly.

In practice, virtually all investigations conducted in North American schools, whether with animals or with humans, are subject to approval by ethical review committees. Their purpose is to ensure that appropriate ethical standards are met. These standards are explicit in the APA's guidelines for member psychologists doing research with human participants:

- The investigator is responsible for evaluating the ethical acceptability of the research.
- Investigators need to determine whether subjects are "at risk" or "at minimal risk."
- Prior to the investigation, all participants should be made fully aware of all aspects of the research that might affect their willingness to participate.
- When an investigation requires that participants be deceived, investigators need to (a) determine whether the potential benefits of the study justify the use of deception, (b) determine whether other nondeceptive approaches might answer the same questions, and (c) provide participants with a sufficient explanation as soon as possible after the deception.
- Participants must be free not to participate.

- Participants must be protected from physical and mental danger or dis-comfort. As the APA (1989) words it, "If risks of such consequences exist, the investigator informs the participant of that fact. Research procedures likely to cause serious or lasting harm to a participant are not used unless the failure to use these procedures might expose the participant to risk of greater harm, or unless the research has great potential benefit and fully informed and voluntary consent is obtained from each participant" (p. xxxi).
- Where there *are* harmful consequences to participants, the investigator is responsible for removing and correcting these consequences.
- Information about participants is confidential unless otherwise agreed in advance.

LEARNING THEORY

Because learning is defined as changes in behavior that result from experience, the psychology of learning is concerned with observations of behavior and behavior change. Not surprisingly, the terms *learning theory* and *behavior theory* are essentially synonymous in psychological literature. **Learning theories** (or be-havior theories) are attempts to systematize and organize the observations, hypotheses, hunches, laws, principles, and guesses that have been made about human behavior.

Learning theories have become increasingly complex as psychologists rec-ognize that earlier positions don't account for all the facts. Early theories, however, are rarely discarded completely; instead, they are often incorporated into later theories. But that story comes later.

Recent Origins of Learning Theory

Among the origins of contemporary psychological theory are early attempts by psychologists to explain behavior on the basis of instincts and emotion. Early psychologists—for example, William James and Edward Bradford Titchener—relied heavily on **introspection** (examining one's own feelings and motives and generalizing from these) as a way of discovering things about human learning and behavior. Ironically, probably the most profound and long-lasting effect of this early work stems from the strong negative reaction against it at the turn of this century, especially in the United States.

The establishment of a psychological laboratory in Leipzig, Germany, by Wilhelm Wundt in 1879 is considered by many as the beginning of psychology as a science. Although Wundt and his followers, both in Europe and in North America, continued to deal with such mentalistic concepts as consciousness, sensation, feeling, imagining, and perceiving, they attempted to use the more objective methods of science to study them.

TABLE 1.2   Major Divisions in Learning Theory

	Symbolic Representation	Variables of Concern	Representative Theorists
Behaviorism	S–R	Stimuli Responses Reinforcement	Pavlov Watson Thorndike Guthrie Skinner Hull
A transition	S–0–R	Stimuli Responses Reinforcement Mediation Purpose Goals	Hebb Tolman Gestaltists

Cognitive theories	0	Perceiving
		Organizing
		Information processing
		Decision making
		Problem solving
		Attention
		Memory
			Bruner
			Piaget
			Other theorists who
			  develop computer
			  models of human
			  learning and behavior

Classifications of Learning Theories

By the early 1900s an orientation toward behavior rather than thought had begun to appear in the United States (it eventually became known as **behaviorism**). This orientation led to learning theories concerned mainly with objective events like stimuli, responses, and rewards. Stimuli (conditions that lead to behavior) and responses (actual behavior), these theorists argued, are the only directly observable aspects of behavior; hence, they are the objective variables that can be employed in developing a science of behavior. Behavioristic theories include those of Pavlov, Watson, and Guthrie (see Chapter 2); Thorndike and Hull (Chapter 3); and Skinner (Chapter 4). Other theorists who shared many of the beliefs of the behaviorists, but whose use of more mentalistic concepts serves as a transition to the second major division of theories, **cognitivism**, include Hebb and Tolman (Chapter 6).

Cognitive psychologists are typically interested in perception, decision making, information processing, and understanding. Gestalt theories are among the first of the cognitive theories (see Chapter 6). Other examples include Bruner and Piaget (Chapter 7). Information processing approaches, evident in computer models of thinking (Chapter 8) as well as in current investigations of memory (Chapter 9) and motivation (Chapter 10), are also unequivocally cognitive (see Table 1.2).

The main importance of the distinction between behavioristic and cognitive approaches is that it permits a simple classification of explanations of human learning and so makes it easier to understand, remember, and apply learning theories. You should be warned, however, that behaviorism and cognitivism exist only as convenient labels for extremely complex theories. Even theories that might appear very different often share common ideas. Few are clear examples of only one theoretical approach.

PREVIEW OF THE TEXT

This section presents short previews of each of the remaining ten chapters of the text. They are offered as hors d'oeuvres; they may whet your appetite, satiate you completely if your appetite is extraordinarily tiny, or make you quite ill. You may choose to go directly to the entrée (there is no dessert).

Chapter 2 (Pavlov, Watson and Guthrie: Early Behaviorism)

There is a story that Watson once had the human urge to impress his friends with his dog's intelligence. So at dinner one night, he knelt with the dog and began to bark the way he thought an intelligent dog might. The dog listened politely and then ate. The next night Watson did the same thing; again, the dog listened attentively and then ate its supper. Watson was trying to teach the dog to bark—not just in an ordinary way, but "intelligently"—for its supper. The procedure, called conditioning, half worked: At the end of two weeks the dog still wouldn't bark, but it absolutely refused to eat until Watson had knelt and barked. Why?

Chapter 3 (Thorndike and Hull: The Effects of Behavior)

Some professors complain that their students often go to sleep when they present their magnificent lectures on Hull. They think that the students are bored, but perhaps most of them are simply suffering from symbol shock.

What does this mean: $_sE_R = {_s}H_R \times D \times V \times K$?

Chapter 4 (Skinner's Position: Operant Conditioning)

A bright psychologist once decided that he would show a rat how to eat. "Pshaw," his grandmother croaked, "rats already know how to eat." But that was not what her grandson meant. He intended to teach this rat how to eat properly, using a tiny spoon, sitting at the table, chewing with its mouth closed. He also expected the rat eventually would learn to wipe its chops delicately on a napkin after an especially mouth-watering chew.

The psychologist tried and almost succeeded. Unfortunately, both the rat and the grandmother died of old age before the learning program was completed. How was the rat trained?

Chapter 5 (Conditioning: Biological Influences)

When he was much younger and living with his grandmother, Lefrançois says he ate a lot of rabbits—dozens every winter.[1] But one night when the stew was too old, the milk rancid, or the rabbit diseased, all who had been at dinner

---

[1] Probably more like hundreds. (GRL)

became violently ill shortly afterward. From then on, says Lefrançois, he does not molest or eat rabbits—or even write about them. Why?

Chapter 6 (Hebb, Tolman, and the Gestalts: From Behaviorism to Cognitivism)

A poverty-stricken graduate student in psychology, driven by hunger for both food and knowledge, accepted a summer job at an isolated fire-lookout tower. They flew him to the tower by helicopter and left him there completely alone. The second morning, his radio broke.

The sixth morning, the helicopter came back with a radio repair technician. But the student was gone. He had scribbled a note: *Can't take it. Going home.* Home was only 300 miles of spruce forest and muskeg away. He was never seen again. Why? (Not why was he never seen again, but why did he leave? He wasn't stupid.)

Chapter 7 (Bruner and Piaget: Two Cognitive Theories)

If I say to you, "Red hair, blue eye, scar," do you simply see a thatch of reddish hair, a single blue-irised eyeball, a length of surgical scar? Or have you already built a face, added a nose and ears, and drawn your scar from cheek to jowl? Could you help going beyond the information given?

Chapter 8 (Neural Networks: The New Connectionism)

Can machines think? How do they think? What do they think? Can they deliberately lie?

Chapter 9 (Learning and Remembering: Models of Memory)

In a carefully guarded psychological laboratory of a large North American university, a small, bespectacled, shabbily dressed undergraduate student sits on a straight-backed kitchen chair. Her name is Miranda. In front of Miranda is a dish filled with curled, grayish pieces of food. She doesn't know what the food is, but when well salted and peppered it's quite palatable. She hasn't been fed for 24 hours and is now busily eating.

Just before being given this meal, Miranda was given a simple problem in advanced calculus, which she failed miserably. After eating four dishes of this food, she is expected to be able to solve the problem. Why? (And do you really believe this one?)

Chapter 10 (Motives: Behavior's Reasons and Causes)

Three radical student leaders are cleverly coerced into volunteering for a psychological investigation. They later discover that they will be required to write an essay strongly advocating a pro-Establishment, nonradical point of view. None of them dares refuse for fear of incurring the wrath of the psychology instructor. For their efforts, one student is paid $50, the second is paid $10, and the third is presented with a crumpled $1 bill. The students are told that their essays are quite good and that the authorities would like to see them published; the money is ostensibly payment for publication rights. The students agree to allow their work to be published. A day later a skilled interviewer uncovers how each of the subjects really feels now about the Establishment. A human grand-mother would almost certainly predict that the student who was paid $50 would be most likely to feel better about the Establishment. But the grand-mother would be wrong. Why?

Chapter 11 (Analysis, Synthesis, and Integration)

There are many different ways of learning, distinct outcomes of the learning process, and varied models of the learner. For example:

SUMMARY

1. Psychology is the science that studies human behavior and thinking. Learning can be defined as relatively permanent changes (actual or potential) in behavior that are caused by experience.
2. Theories are collections of related statements intended to summarize and explain important observations. These statements are seldom laws (absolute, verifiable fact), but more often take the form of principles (statements relating to some general predictability) and beliefs (more personal convictions, which are sometimes accurate and sometimes not; these are the basis of bubba psychology).
3. Learning theories are attempts to systematize and organize what is known about human learning. They are useful not only for explaining

but also for predicting and controlling behavior, and they may also lead to new information.

4. Good theories reflect the facts, are clear and understandable, are useful for predicting as well as explaining, are based on few untested assumptions, and are satisfying and thought provoking.

5. Science refers to collections of related information (chemistry, for example) as well as to an attitude toward the search for knowledge (insisting on objectivity, replicability, consistency) and a collection of methods to ensure objectivity (ask the question; make a hypothesis; collect relevant observations; reach a conclusion).

6. Experiments are science's most powerful tool for determining cause and effect relationships. They can be thought of as ways of testing if-then statements, where the "if" refers to independent variables that can be manipulated to see what the effect will be on dependent variables (the "then").

7. Psychological research should be subjected to critical questions such as these: Does it provide an explanation or does it simply label? Have chance factors been ruled out? Is the sample on which conclusions are based representative? Is there a possibility that the subjects were dishonest or behaved as they did because they knew they were part of an experiment? Might the investigators have been influenced by their own expectations?

8. Although animals are essential for some studies, findings based on animal studies have to be generalized with caution. In addition, there are important ethical guidelines for research with both animals and people.

9. The traditional divisions in theories of learning are based on the primary concerns of different theorists. Behaviorism describes an approach that deals mainly with the observable aspects of human functioning; cognitivism refers to a preoccupation with topics such as perception, information processing, concept formation, awareness, and understanding.

Part 2

MOSTLY BEHAVIORISTIC THEORIES

Chapter 2

Pavlov, Watson, and Guthrie: Early Behaviorism

28

MIND, n.—A mysterious form of matter secreted by the brain. Its chief activity consists in the endeavor to ascertain its own nature, the futility of the attempt being due to the fact that it has nothing but itself to know itself with.

Ambrose Bierce, *The Devil's Dictionary*

PRELIMINARY NOTE TO THE HUMAN READER: CHAPTER 2 OBJECTIVES

"Explain what you're doing and why," said Lefrançois. "For human readers." OK. What I'm doing is a report on theories of human learning for the behavioral division back home—well, actually an update of my cousin Kongor's old report. If I get it right, I get to go to Heel for a week, which doesn't mean anything to you but, take my word for it, it's worth it.

The first chapter of the report defined important terms, concepts, and approaches in theory building. This second chapter traces the early beginnings of behaviorism, which is an explicit concern with actual behavior in contrast with a concern with more mental things (like knowing and thinking). The chapter describes one of the simplest forms of learning: classical conditioning.

After you finish this chapter, you may be overcome by an overwhelming urge to stop perfect strangers on the street and explain to them the following:

- What classical conditioning is
- The meanings of CS, CR, US, UR, generalization, discrimination, transfer, extinction, spontaneous recovery . . .
- How emotions might be learned
- Similarities among Pavlov, Watson, and Guthrie
- Differences among them
- The difference between contiguity and reinforcement
- Thorndike's laws of learning
- Why it is so hard to teach a cow to sit up

If you don't know these things when you finish, leave your grandmother alone. Instead, write to Lefrançois.[1]

SIXTH TIME CUBE, 49TH HEXALOG, POINT 213.5

I've been out of the hunting shack and into the big house for a couple of weeks now. To begin with, it was a little rough. For the first few days, the dog (a stunningly stupid version of that animal) kept driving me against chairs and walls and, on one unhappy occasion, into an antique cabinet—with her schnozz, I might add. The new glass on the antique cabinet is much more durable.

After three or four days of trying alternately to avoid the dog and to reason with her when I couldn't avoid her, it became clear I should try some other tactic. So the next time she stuck her

---

[1]This is just Kro's strange sense of humor, apparently taught to him by his cousin, Kongor, who thought he understood our humor. He didn't. So don't write unless you're sending gifts. Just ask your grandmother. (GRL)

nose too close to my personal one, I hauled off and yelled at her in my loudest voice. It was one-shot learning; she now keeps her nose out of my businesses. [2]

    There are some simple explanations for this change in the dog's behavior. They are the substance of this chapter.

THE BEGINNING OF SCIENTIFIC PSYCHOLOGY

As mentioned in Chapter 1, early psychologists relied heavily on introspection as a tool for investigating human behavior. Using this approach, the psychologist would systematically analyze and interpret his or her own personal thoughts and feelings, trying to arrive at an understanding that could then be generalized to others. American psychologist William James was among the better known of these early "armchair introspectionists." He tried to understand human experience and consciousness as a whole, claiming that it could not meaningfully be chopped up into little bits like stimuli and responses, or understood in terms of sensations or associations. "A river or a stream are the metaphors by which it is most naturally described," he insisted, giving rise to the common expression *stream of consciousness* (James, 1890 (1890/1950, p. 239).

    At the time that James was lecturing and writing in America, a powerful, contradictory movement was well underway in Europe. Represented by the work of people like Wilhelm Wundt (see biography), this movement was strongly influenced by biology and physiology, and attempted to apply a scientific approach to the study of the mind. Its methods were those of **psychophysics** (the measurement of physical stimuli and their effects) rather than simply introspection.

Early Psychophysics

Imagine you are standing in a completely darkened room staring in the general direction of an unlit 100-watt light bulb. The light is controlled by a rheostat that allows a continuous range of settings. As long as the light is off, you won't see the bulb. Even if the light is turned on, you still will see nothing until light intensity has reached a sufficient minimum level.

Absolute Thresholds

Early psychologists like Wundt and Fechner in Europe and Titchener in the United States were very interested in questions like the one implied above: What is the minimum amount of light the human eye can detect? The softest sound that can be heard? The lightest touch that can be felt? What they wanted to do through their psychophysical measurements was to determine exactly the

---

[2]Kro sometimes exaggerates just a little. To tell the truth, he yelled at her far more than once, although "yell" might also be an exaggeration, because he had rather a tiny voice. In the end, I think it was his accidentally hitting the chair and knocking the coat rack over—causing the big painting with the four baboons to come crashing down on the dog—that convinced her to leave him alone. (GRL)

absolute threshold for each sense—that is, the least amount of stimulation required for sensation.

It turns out that this is not possible, because some people are more sensitive than others (have better hearing or better vision, for example). Thus there is no single threshold level of light or sound or pressure. But for each individual, there is a lower limit below which a stimulus will never be detected and an upper limit above which it will always be detected. Between the two, there is a point at which it will be detected 50% of the time. This point is called the absolute threshold, although it is more approximate than absolute.

Just-Noticeable Differences

Psychophysicists measured not only thresholds but also what they called **just noticeable differences** (or JNDs). The difference you feel in the pull on your muscles if you lift a sack containing 1 pound of black beans and another containing 2 pounds is a noticeable difference. Fechner (1860) and his brother-in-law, Weber, were interested in finding out the least amount of change in stimulation that would be noticeable—that is, the just noticeable difference or JND.

If you can tell the difference between 1 and 2 pounds, does that mean that the JND for weight is something less than 1 pound? No. You can tell the difference between 1 and 2 pounds, and perhaps between 6 and 7 pounds, but you can't so easily tell the difference between 10 and 11 pounds, much less between 99 and 100 pounds. In the same way, you can tell the difference between a 25-watt bulb and a 60-watt bulb, a difference of 35 watts. But you can't discriminate between 1000 watts of light and 1100 watts. Even though the difference is almost three times greater in the second case, it is not a noticeable difference.

JNDs, said Weber, are a *constant proportion* of a stimulus. For lifted weights, for example, the constant is about 1/30. This means that a weight lifter who normally lifts 300 pounds would probably not notice an addition of 5 pounds, but would notice a difference of 10 pounds; one who lifts 600 pounds would require an addition of 20 pounds before noticing the difference (Figure 2.1). Fechner labeled this conclusion **Weber's Law**.

Unfortunately for the field of psychophysics, Weber's constants are not very constant. Some people are more sensitive to stimulus changes than are others; furthermore, people's sensitivity can vary from day to day—or even from moment to moment—depending on fatigue and other factors. Nevertheless, Weber's law appears to be true as a general principle (Falmagne, 1985).

WILHELM WUNDT (1832–1920)

Wundt was one of four children born to a Lutheran minister and his wife in Mannheim, Germany; only he and one brother survived childhood. He was reportedly a profoundly introverted boy whose only friend was somewhat older and mentally handicapped. His upbringing was extremely strict; a terrified Wundt often was locked in a dark closet when he had misbehaved.

Wundt's early school career was difficult and not very successful. When he went to university though, Wundt became fascinated by the anatomy and mysteries of the brain, and almost overnight he became a scholar. At the age of 24, Wundt obtained a medical degree and subsequently became an instructor in physiology. He spent 17 years at Heidelberg University on the medical faculty, 1 year in Zurich as a professor of philosophy, and 42 years at Leipzig, where he founded the psychological laboratory that is generally associated with the beginning of psychology as a science. He was apparently a quiet, unassuming man who seldom left his laboratory and his home. He wrote more than 500 books and articles; Boring (1950) estimated that Wundt wrote an average of one published word every 2 minutes, day and night, for 68 years. His major textbook on psychology appeared in three volumes in its first edition: 553, 680, and 796 pages of very complex German.

Ivan P. Pavlov (1849–1936)

Early psychologists like Fechner, Weber, and Titchener were as much physiologists as psychologists. Another physiologist who had a profound influence on the development of psychology throughout the world was the Russian Ivan Pavlov.

Amazingly, the experiment for which Pavlov is most famous was the result of an almost accidental observation. Pavlov had been studying the role of various juices in digestion, one of these being saliva, and he had developed a procedure that allowed him to detect and measure salivation in the dogs he used in his experiments. (In fact, in 1904 he was awarded a Nobel prize in medicine and physiology for his work on digestion.)

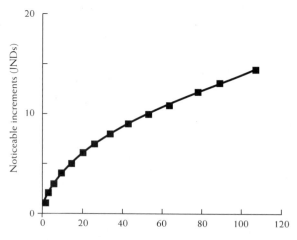

FIGURE 2.1   A graphic portrayal of Weber's Law. Proportionally greater increases in stimulation are barely noticeable as intensity of stimulation increases.

In the course of this work, Pavlov happened to notice that some of the dogs in his laboratory began to salivate before they were fed. He saw, too, that this occurred only in dogs that had been in the laboratory for some time.

IVAN PETROVICH PAVLOV (1849–1936)

Pavlov was born the son of a poor village priest in Russia. His was a mediocre school career, with little indication that he would one day win a Nobel prize. His early education was in a local seminary. From there Pavlov went to the University of St. Petersburg, specializing in animal physiology and in medicine. After he obtained his medical degree, he went to Germany, where he studied physiology and medicine for another 2 years. Pavlov then returned to St. Petersburg and worked as an assistant in a physiology laboratory until he was appointed professor of pharmacology and head of a physiology department at the age of 41. His work continued to deal almost exclusively with physiological topics, specifically with digestive processes. It wasn't until the age of 50 that he began to study classical conditioning; these studies lasted another 30 years. To the end, however, Pavlov insisted that he was a physiologist and not a psychologist. In fact, he viewed psychology with such disdain that he fined any of his laboratory assistants who used psychological rather than physiological terms (R. I. Watson, 1971).

Classical Conditioning

In attempting to arrive at some scientific explanation for this phenomenon, Pavlov developed a series of now-famous experiments in **classical conditioning**. Classical conditioning became the basis for a large number of early learning theories and continues to be an important part of contemporary psychological knowledge. In his experiments, he demonstrated that not only could the sight of food eventually bring about salivation in his dogs, but almost any other distinctive stimulus could have the same effect if paired with the presentation of food often enough. Ever the physiologist, Pavlov thought he had discovered "psychic secretions."

In the Pavlov demonstration, the food is referred to as an **unconditioned stimulus** (US). It is termed a stimulus because it is an environmental event that affects the organism, and it is labeled *unconditioned* because it leads to a response (muscular or glandular reaction) without any learning taking place. The initial salivation to the food is called an **unconditioned response** (UR) because it is associated with an unconditioned stimulus. Thus it is a response that occurs without any learning. The US and UR are an unlearned stimulus-response unit, called a **reflex**.

Pavlov showed repeatedly that if a US (like food) is paired with another stimulus often enough, this other stimulus will eventually lead to the response originally associated only with the US (in this case, salivation). For example, if a buzzer is sounded every time food is presented to the dog, eventually the buzzer—called a **conditioned stimulus** (CS)—will elicit the response of salivation—now a **conditioned response** (CR). Illustrations of this procedure are given in Figures 2.2, 2.3, and 2.4.

Classical conditioning is also referred to as *learning through stimulus substitution* because the conditioned stimulus, after being paired with the unconditioned stimulus frequently enough, can sometimes be substituted for it. The conditioned stimulus often evokes a similar, but weaker, response. This form of conditioning is also referred to as *signal learning* because the conditioned stimulus serves as a signal for the occurrence of the unconditioned stimulus.

Varieties of Conditioned Responses

Most responses that can reliably be elicited by a stimulus can be classically conditioned. For example, the knee-jerk reflex, the eye-blink reflex, and the pupillary reflex can all be conditioned to various stimuli.

In addition, some glandular responses (such as salivation) and other internal reactions can also be conditioned. Salivation is a CR when it occurs in response to a buzzer, a bell, a verbal command, or any other CS that has been paired often enough with an unconditioned stimulus (US) like food. The term **interoceptive conditioning** is used to describe the conditioning of actions involving glands or involuntary muscles.

Illustration 1.   Keller (1969) describes a procedure in which subjects are asked to dip their right hand in a pitcher of ice water. This causes an immediate drop in the temperature of that hand and, interestingly, also causes a more easily measured drop in the temperature of the other hand. If the hand is dipped in the ice water at regular intervals (3 or 4 minutes) and each dip is preceded by the sound of a buzzer, after 20 or so pairings the buzzer alone will cause a measurable drop in hand temperature.

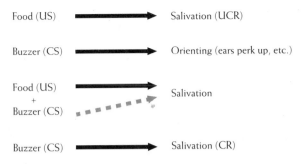

FIGURE 2.2   Classical conditioning. Food elicits salivation in a dog, but a buzzer does not. After successive pairings of food and buzzer, the buzzer begins to elicit salivation.

Illustration 2.   Pavlov's work on conditioning influenced many Russian psychologists, some of whom have conducted experiments involving the conditioning of responses not ordinarily under control of the organism. For example, blood vessel constriction or dilation (brought about by the external application of cold or hot packs) can be conditioned to a bell or a buzzer. Urination can also be classically conditioned. If sufficient air is introduced into a person's bladder, it increases pressure inside the bladder, and urination occurs. If the introduction of air is paired with a bell or buzzer, after a relatively small number of pairings the bell alone will elicit urination. (Why don't they use this for toilet training children?)[3]

Another type of response that can readily be classically conditioned involves what is termed **taste aversion**—a powerful disinclination to eat or drink something. Some taste aversions are hereditary; they prevent animals (and people) from eating bitter-tasting substances, which often taste bitter precisely because they are toxic. (Classical conditioning of taste aversions is discussed in more detail in Chapter 5).

How easily a classically conditioned response is acquired is related to a number of factors, not the least important of which is the distinctiveness of the conditioned stimulus. Buzzers and other tones have been particularly good conditioning stimuli in animal experimentation because they can be highly distinctive stimuli.

Explanations for Stimulus–Response Associations

Basically, conditioning theory offers two different explanations for learning: **contiguity** and **reinforcement**. Contiguity, the simultaneous or nearly simultaneous occurence of events, is the explanation used by theorists like Pavlov, Watson, and Guthrie. They maintained that in order for behavior to change

---

[3]Because, Kro, they are not only human, but humane. (GRL)

FIGURE 2.3   What Pavlov first noticed was that the sight of the handler alone was enough to cause many of his experimental dogs to salivate. Through further experiments, he reconstructed and validated the process that must have produced the effect.

(that is, in order for learning to occur), it is sufficient that two events be paired—sometimes only once; sometimes more often.

Reinforcement is a more complex concept that refers to the *effects* of a stimulus. Thus there is positive reinforcement where an effect (like the satisfaction of hunger, for example) leads to learning. Reinforcement, which is defined in more detail and illustrated in the next chapter, is not an explanation for Pavlovian conditioning.

Variations in Contiguity

Events are contiguous when they occur at the same time and place. But contiguity in classical conditioning does not always mean that the CS starts and ends at exactly the same time as the US. In fact this arrangement, termed **simultaneous pairing**, is not the most effective way of classically conditioning a response.

Far more effective is **delayed pairing**, in which the CS is presented before the unconditioned stimulus and continues during presentation of the unconditioned stimulus. It is termed *delayed* because of the time lag between the presentation of the CS and beginning of the US. In **trace pairing**, the CS starts *and ends* before the US, so that there is a time lapse between the two. In **backward pairing**, the US has already been presented and removed before presentation of the CS.

In the classical Pavlovian demonstration, simultaneous pairing requires that the buzzer be sounded at exactly the same time as food powder is injected in the mouth. Delayed pairing would occur when the buzzer is turned on, food powder is injected into the dog's mouth, and then the buzzer is turned off. Trace conditioning would require that the buzzer be turned on and then off again *before* food powder is injected in the dog's mouth. In backward pairing, food powder is injected first; then, after a brief time lapse, the buzzer sounds.

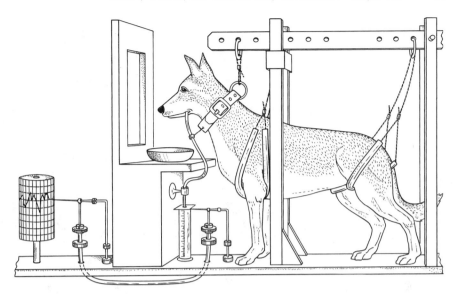

FIGURE 2.4   Pavlov's dogs were placed in a harness like this one. Food powder can be placed either in the dog's mouth or in the dish. Saliva is measured as it drops into a tube in the dog's mouth. The resulting movement of a tiny balancing mechanism in the tube is transmitted to a pen, whose movement in turn is recorded on a revolving drum. In the experiment illustrated here, the US (food) is paired with a CS (light shining in the window).

These four options are shown in Figure 2.5, in order from most to least effective.

Backward Pairing and Biological Predispositions

Backward pairing—where the conditioned stimulus follows the unconditioned stimulus—was long thought to be completely ineffective, and in most circumstances classical conditioning does not ordinarily occur with this arrangement. In a small number of highly specific experiments, however, investigators have succeeded in bringing about backward conditioning. In one experiment representative of these studies, Keith-Lucas and Guttman (1975) classically conditioned an avoidance response in rats by shocking them electrically (US) and subsequently placing a plastic hedgehog toy in their cages (CS). A significant number of rats responded with apparent fear when shown the plastic toy the following day, providing it was placed in their cages within 10 seconds of the electric shock; those that experienced a 40-second delay showed little fear.

The significance of this study and of related studies is not so much that they establish that backward conditioning is possible, but rather that they add to the growing evidence that some types of learning are far easier for certain organisms than are other types. As is shown in Chapter 5, people seem to be *prepared* to learn certain things (language, for example) and *contraprepared* to learn others. Similarly, rats are prepared to learn to fear hedgehogs. The discovery

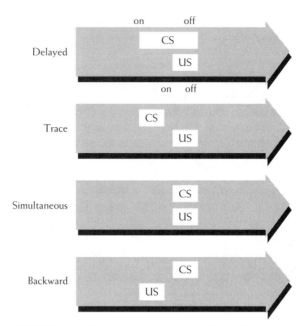

FIGURE 2.5   Impact of variations in CS–US pairings. The pairing sequences are shown here in the order of effectiveness. Conditioning takes place most quickly in the "delayed" sequence, when the conditioned stimulus (for instance, the buzzer) is presented shortly before the unconditioned stimulus (food powder) and continues throughout the time the US is presented.

and elaboration of these *biological constraints* on learning constitute an important and growing area of psychological research and theorizing (see Chapter 5).

Acquisition, Extinction, and Recovery

In the course of more than 20 years of detailed experimentation on classical conditioning, Pavlov and his students discovered a range of phenomena, many of which continue to be investigated even today.

Acquisition

For example, they found that **acquisition**—the formation of the stimulus–response association—requires a number of pairings of CS and US. After only one or two pairings, the CS alone does not ordinarily lead to a CR. But with increasing numbers of pairings, the CR occurs more frequently *and more strongly*. For example, in the salivation experiment, amount of salivation in response to the CS increases until it reaches a peak, after which it levels off. Psychology researchers and students have plotted thousands of **learning curves** illustrating this. One is shown in Figure 2.6.

Learning curves are affected not only by the number of CS-US pairings, but also by the strength of the US. In general, the stronger the US (the bigger

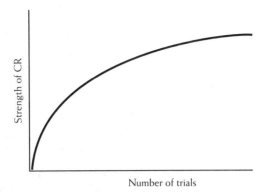

FIGURE 2.6   A hypothetical learning curve. Note that the strength of the conditioned response increases rapidly at first and then levels off as it reaches its asymptote.

the steak, the louder the noise, or the stronger the puff of air), the more quickly the CR will reach its peak.

Extinction and Recovery

Another important Pavlovian finding is that classically conditioned associations are remarkably durable. A dog conditioned to salivate to a tone and then left alone to do nothing but dog things for months will immediately salivate again (although perhaps in a more restrained way) when brought back into the laboratory and presented with the same tone. Similarly, Lefrançois's brother, who had a terrifying experience with a snake and a tricycle as a young boy, would break into a cold sweat if you showed him a snake today, even though he hasn't actually seen a snake for many years.

But classically conditioned responses can be eliminated through a process that Pavlov termed **extinction**. A simple way to extinguish a conditioned response is to present the conditioned stimulus repeatedly *without* the unconditioned stimulus. For example, if the buzzer sounds repeatedly but no food is presented, the dog will eventually stop salivating. Interestingly, however, if the CS (the buzzer) is presented again later, the dog will again salivate, although at lower intensity than when the response was first learned—a phenomenon called **spontaneous recovery**. To extinguish the response completely, it would be necessary to present the CS without the US again, and perhaps to repeat the procedure a number of different times. Eventually there would no longer be evidence of spontaneous recovery. (See Figure 2.7.)

JOHN B. WATSON (1878–1958)

Profoundly influenced by Pavlov's discoveries about classical conditioning, a young rebel set out determined to revolutionize American psychology—and succeeded. His name was John Broadus Watson.

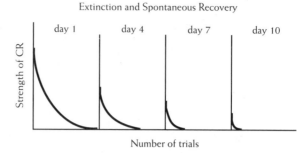

Extinction and Spontaneous Recovery

FIGURE 2.7   A hypothetical representation of spontaneous recovery following extinction. Note how the strength of the CR is less following each extinction period, and how progressively fewer trials are required for extinction.

Behaviorism

Recall that in the early years of this century, psychology continued to be a highly intuitive and subjective discipline based largely on ideas developed by Wundt. Its principal methods of inquiry were introspection, contemplation, and speculation, and its most important questions had to do with consciousness. Watson (1930) was convinced that there had been no significant discoveries since Wundt established his laboratory, and that it had been, in his words, "proved conclusively that the so-called introspective psychology of Germany was founded upon wrong hypotheses" (p. 5). "The subject matter of human psychology," Watson insisted, *"is the behavior of the human being"* (p. 2; italics in original). A science based on this approach would have to be completely objective and concern itself only with actual behavior, not with mentalistic things like thoughts and emotions. The science would be called **behaviorism**.

In 1913 Watson wrote a brief article, now often referred to as the behavioristic manifesto, entitled "Psychology as the Behaviorist Views It." The opening sentence makes his position—and his antagonism to introspection—very clear: "Psychology as the behaviorist views it is a purely objective experimental branch of natural science. Its theoretical goal is the prediction and control of behavior. Introspection forms no essential part of its methods" (Watson, 1913, p. 158).

Watson went on to argue that consciousness is an irrelevant concept because human behavior can be understood in terms of actual behaviors that can readily be observed and studied. Doing so, he claimed, would do away with a much of the contradiction that exists in psychology. "Consciousness," he insisted, "is neither a definite nor a usable concept" (Watson, 1930, p. 2).

The term *behaviorism* has come to mean concern with the observable aspects of behavior. It is an orientation that assumes behavior comprises responses that can be observed and related to other observable events—such as conditions that precede and follow behavior. The ultimate goal of a behavioristic position is to derive laws to explain the relationships existing among antecedent conditions (stimuli), behavior (responses), and consequent conditions (reward, punishment, or neutral events).

JOHN BROADUS WATSON (1878/1958)

The founder of American behaviorism, John Watson was born in Greenville, South Carolina, in 1878. He was apparently a highly aggressive boy, and he was arrested at least twice (once for fighting; another time for firing a gun within city limits). By his own admission, he was not an especially good student, although on one occasion he was the only person who passed a final Greek exam. He later claimed he was able to do so as a result of having spent the previous afternoon cramming and drinking an entire quart of Coca-Cola™ syrup (Murchison, 1936).[4]

Watson took his graduate training at the University of Chicago, working his way through school as a rat caretaker and lecturing at the school after he graduated. Several years later he was offered a full professorship at Johns Hopkins. While there he became interested in doing research on physiological changes during sex, and he promptly enlisted the help of a young graduate student, Rosalie Rayner. As always, Watson kept careful notes and records of all his experiments—which his wife later discovered and used in a suit for divorce. The ensuing front-page scandal led to Watson being fired from Johns Hopkins.

Watson moved to New York, married Miss Rayner, had two more children (he had already fathered two), and went to work for the J. Walter Thompson Company. His first assignment required that he go up and down the Mississippi River asking people what brand of rubber boots they wore; he eventually worked in virtually every department in the company before he became its vice president. During this time he wrote popular psychology articles for magazines such as *Harper's, McCall's, Liberty, Collier's,* and *Cosmopolitan.* With Rosalie Rayner, he also wrote a book on infant and child care in which he advocated precise and controlled approaches to dealing with children. Watson's business and writing activities, for which he was well paid, did little to endear him to his former colleagues, who spent some time and effort criticizing the articles and books. (Rayner also wrote popular articles, including one entitled "I Was the Mother of a Behaviorist's Sons" in 1930).

Watson never returned to academic life. But in 1958, just before he died, the American Psychological Association honored him for his outstanding contributions to psychology, presenting him with a gold medal.

---

[4]I tried to tell Kro the ™ was not really necessary, but he refused to believe me. He fancies himself a bit of a lawyer. "Nobody's gonna sue me for nothing," he said, lapsing into the broken slang he's been practicing with the children and the dog. (GRL)

A Classical Conditioning Explanation of Learning

Watson's (1930) explanation for learning is based directly on Ivan Pavlov's exploration of classical conditioning. Humans are born with a number of reflexes, says Watson; these include not only physical and glandular reactions (like salivating in response to food, or blinking in response to a blast of air) but also a handful of emotional responses (like fear and rage and love). Each of these reflexes can be brought about by a specific stimulus. For example, feelings of love might result from being stroked; fear, from being dropped suddenly from a height. Pavlov's account of classical conditioning makes it clear, insists Watson, that any distinctive stimulus present at the time that a reflexive response is brought about can serve as a CS. If this stimulus is present often enough, it will eventually become associated with the response.

Emotional Learning

According to Watson, emotional behavior, like all other behavior, is simply another example of classical conditioning. He assumed that individual differences are virtually nonexistent to begin with—that is, all people are born with the same emotional reflexes of fear, love, and rage. These reflexive responses occur in response to certain specific stimuli: for example, loud noises and sudden loss of support lead to fear reactions, stroking and fondling elicit love, and confinement in tight clothing evokes rage.

Eventually, however, humans react emotionally to a variety of things that initially have no emotional significance at all.[5] Watson proposed to explain this important phenomenon in terms of classical conditioning. All later emotional reactions, he explained, result from the pairing of initially neutral stimuli with stimuli that are associated with emotional responses. To illustrate and validate this belief, he performed one of his most famous and controversial experiments (with his assistant, Rosalie Rayner: Watson & Rayner, 1920).

Little Albert

The subject of this experiment was "Little Albert," an 11-month-old boy. At the beginning of the experiment, Little Albert showed no fear of a great variety of objects and people. "Everything coming within twelve inches of him was reached for and manipulated," said Watson (1930, p. 159). Among the things he always reached for was a white rat that he had played with for weeks.

But Watson and Rayner quickly established that Albert, like most infants, would react with fear to a loud noise: "A steel bar about one inch in diameter and three feet long, when struck with a carpenter's hammer, produced the most marked kind of reaction" (Watson, 1930, p. 159). And so began the experiment

---

[5]Emotional response is an intriguing phenomenon seldom found among most species throughout any of the explored galaxies. Because it so often contradicts (even defies) reason, natural evolutionary pressures or, as in the case of the Phyrigians, chemical surgery, have pretty well eradicated it. But not here. It makes the human species far more difficult to figure out. (Kro)

with Little Albert at the age of 11 months, 3 days. He was sitting on his mattress, reaching for the white rat, his hand just touching it when—kaboom!—Watson pounded the bar "just behind his [Albert's] head", and poor Albert "jumped violently and fell forward, burying his face in the mattress." But Albert was a staunch little fellow; he didn't cry. In fact, he reached for the rat again—and again, Watson (or Rayner; the point isn't clear from Watson's notes) banged on the steel bar just as Albert's hand touched the rat. This time Albert began to whimper, and, as Watson put it, "on account of his disturbed condition, no further tests were made for one week" (p. 160).

A week later the procedure was repeated, the rat and the loud sound being combined a total of five more times. Now Albert's behavior had changed dramatically. When the rat was presented alone, Albert no longer reached for it. In Watson's (1930) words, "The instant the rat was shown the baby began to cry. Almost instantly he turned sharply to the left, fell over, raised himself on all fours and began to crawl away so rapidly that he was caught with difficulty before he reached the edge of the mattress" (p. 161).

Watson considered this experiment extremely important to his theory. "Surely this is proof of the conditioned origin of a fear response," he argued. "It yields an explanatory principle that will account for the enormous complexity in the emotional behavior of adults" (p. 161).

Transfer

The explanatory principle has two facets. First, emotional responses are conditioned to various stimuli as a result of pairings that occur between conditioned stimuli (like distinctive sounds, smells, sights, or tastes) and unconditioned stimuli (like those that produce fear, love, or anger). Second, emotional responses can spread to stimuli to which they have not been conditioned, but that resemble conditioned stimuli.

Both these principles are clearly illustrated in the Little Albert experiment. First, after only seven separate pairings of the rat with the frightening noise, Albert had become very frightened of the rat. And second, when Little Albert was tested again five days later (at the age of 11 months, 15 days), he was afraid not only of the rat but of a white rabbit, a seal coat, white cotton wool, a white-bearded Santa Claus mask, and Dr. Watson's hair—all objects with which he had previously played.[6]

This phenomenon, which Watson called **transfer** or "spread," is most commonly referred to as **stimulus generalization**. It involves making the same or similar responses when presented with any of a number of related stimuli. An opposite phenomenon, stimulus **discrimination**, involves making different responses to distinctly different stimuli. Watson (1930) illustrates

---

[6]Because this study makes such a good story, says Gilovich (1991), it has been exaggerated and misrepresented by many textbook writers. Some have had little Albert fearing cats, white gloves, his own mother, and a teddy bear. Others have insisted that Watson later cured little Albert of his fear. He didn't, as I explain in another paragraph or so. (Kro)

stimulus discrimination by reference to studies showing that although dogs conditioned to salivate in response to a given tone subsequently salivate generally in response to a wide range of tones, they can nevertheless be conditioned not to respond to a second tone that varies in pitch only slightly from the original conditioned stimulus. This, says Watson, is equally true of conditioned human habits.

Positive Emotions

The Little Albert study indicates that it is possible to condition negative emotional reactions by repeatedly pairing a stimulus ordinarily associated with some negative emotion and another distinctive stimulus. By the same token, it is also possible to condition positive emotional reactions to neutral stimuli. It is highly probable, for example, that if the white rat had been paired with a dish of ice cream or a wet kiss, Little Albert might very soon have come to love white rats with some passion. Similarly, even after Albert had been conditioned to respond with fear to the presence of a white rat, it might still have been possible to condition a positive response to the rat. This procedure, termed *countercondi- tioning*, is illustrated in the next section on Edwin Guthrie.

It seems clear from his original article that Watson had intended to do just that (see Harris, 1979; Prytula, Oster, & Davis, 1977). Unfortunately, Albert was Watson's subject only because he happened to be in a hospital at the time. As luck would have it, he was released from the hospital the day before Watson was to have begun his counterconditioning procedures. That these procedures would probably have been successful was demonstrated four years later when Mary Cover Jones found a small boy, Peter, who had a profound fear of rabbits. She cured him of his fear through a classical conditioning procedure (Jones, 1974).

The Controversy

Although this study is extremely well known and very widely cited as an example of emotional conditioning, it remains controversial for a number of reasons (apart from the fact that it has often been misreported). First, only a single subject was used in the study, and many who have tried to replicate the findings have experienced difficulty (Eysenck, 1982). Second, Watson seems to have been very unclear about exactly what he did with Little Albert. Samelson (1980) found that in one published report, Watson complained that whenever Little Albert was upset, the child would stick his thumb into his mouth—and then calm down. In fact, as long as he was sucking his thumb, he showed no signs of the conditioned fear response, so that when Watson and Rayner were trying to film the experiment, they continually had to pull Little Albert's thumb from his mouth. Samelson raises the interesting possibility that Little Albert could have been crying not because he was afraid of the rat, but because the researchers wouldn't let him suck his thumb! And although Watson does not suggest it, it is conceivable that thumb sucking might also have been a classically conditioned response.

Watson's Environmentalism

A recurrent theme in psychological literature is the controversy over the so-called nature/nurture question. Are humans primarily a product of genetic makeup, or are they molded and shaped mainly by their environment? The chief spokesman for the "nature" position at the turn of this century was Francis Galton (1870), a cousin of Charles Darwin. He believed that genes are largely responsible for the differences that exist among people. Accordingly, he advocated that people should be selected and bred for desirable characteristics like intelligence and strength in much the same way as horses are bred for speed, dogs for appearance and hunting instincts, and turkeys for breast size—a practice termed **eugenics**.

The chief spokesman for the environmental (or "nurture") camp was Watson (1930). He was convinced that there are no individual differences at birth, that what people become is a function of their experiences. "There is no such thing," claimed Watson, "as an inheritance of *capacity, talent, temperament, mental constitution* and *characteristics*" (1930, p. 94; italics in original).

When Watson arrived on the scene, John Locke, the philosopher, had already given scholars his famous **tabula rasa** metaphor that the mind is a blank slate upon which experience writes its message. Watson (1930) accepted the proclamation wholeheartedly. "Give me a dozen healthy infants," he said in what may well be his most widely quoted (and longest) sentence, "well-formed, and my own specified world to bring them up in and I'll guarantee to take any one at random and train him to become any type of specialist I might select—doctor, lawyer, artist, merchant-chief and yes, even beggar-man and thief, regardless of his talents, penchants, tendencies, abilities, vocations, and race of his ancestors" (p. 104).

Interestingly, this sentence seems to have been an elaboration of an earlier statement with essentially the same meaning: "Give me the child and my world to bring it up in and I'll make it crawl or walk; I'll make it climb and use its hands in constructing buildings of stone or wood; I'll make it a thief, a gunman, or a dope fiend. The possibility of shaping in any direction is almost endless" (Watson, 1926, p. 35).

The controversy surrounding this question is far from being completely resolved, although most psychologists readily admit that both heredity and environment are involved in determining most facets of human behavior and personality. As Anastasi (1958) put it, the important question may not be how much environment or heredity contributes, but rather how each exercises its influence.

Higher Learning

All learning, said Watson, is a matter of responses that are selected and sequenced. Even very complex sequences of behavior result from a conditioning process where the most recent behavior is linked with a stimulus through a chain of responses. More complex learning simply requires the conditioning of more stimulus–response sequences, eventually leading to what he called *habits*. Even something as apparently complex as language begins as simple stimulus–response links. Speech, Watson claimed, involves actual movements of the vocal cords and the larynx as well as of the mouth, tongue and lips. These movements are conditioned to occur in the presence of appropriate stimuli. As he put it, words are simply substitutes (through conditioning) for objects and situations, and thinking is nothing more complicated than "subvocal" speech. Watson believed this subvocal speech is accompanied by minute movements of the larynx, which he attempted to measure and describe.

Applying Watson's Psychology

Watson's unwavering conviction that experiences determine all that people do and know leads logically to the belief that all humans are basically equal, that the differences between the eminent and the unknown, the rich and the poor, and the brave and the timid are simply a question of different experiences and opportunities. This inherently egalitarian view of the human condition has proven immensely popular. As Stagner (1988) notes, it fit remarkably well with the zeitgeist—the spirit of the times.[7]

But the theory also lends itself to rigid prescriptions for child-rearing and education, as well as for training and control in the military, in industry, and elsewhere. It asserts that people's behavior can be controlled through the judicious and clever arrangements of stimulus and response events. Don't kiss and cuddle your children, Watson urged; shake their hands, then arrange their environments so that the behaviors you desire will be brought under the control of appropriate stimuli.

Behavior Modification

The deliberate application of theories such as Watson's in efforts to change or control undesirable behavior is labeled **behavior therapy**. One well-known example of the use of classical conditioning in behavior therapy is provided by Mowrer and Mowrer's (1938) technique for curing nocturnal bed-wetting (enuresis) by placing a water-detecting device under the bedsheet. A single drop of moisture is enough to activate the device, causing an alarm to sound and awaken the child, who then goes to the bathroom. Within a relatively short period of time, the child goes to the bathroom as necessary, even when the alarm is no longer connected. Why?

In classical conditioning terms, the alarm is an unconditioned stimulus (US) linked with the UR of waking up, which causes a tightening of the muscles so that urination doesn't occur immediately. After a few pairings, the US (alarm) quickly becomes associated with the sensation of a full bladder (a CS). Through

---

[7]The spirit of what times, you might ask. Looking over human history, it seems to me that although various societies have, from time to time, paid lip service to egalitarian principles, the fact is that most societies don't behave as though they actually believe that all are initially equal (and, by extrapolation, equally valuable). My 23rd report will explore this in more detail. (Kro)

classical conditioning, the CS (sensation of full bladder) eventually substitutes for the US (the alarm), leading to the conditioned responses of waking up and not urinating in bed. (Other behavior management techniques are discussed in Chapter 14.)

A Brief Appraisal of Watson's Theory

As will become clearer when we consider the development of more recent psychological theories, much of what earlier theorists such as Watson and Pavlov believed has either been contradicted, greatly elaborated and qualified, or simply discarded as no longer suited to the spirit of contemporary times. For example, Watson's early theorizing about emotional development has not stood the test of objective inquiry. Despite his attempts to deal only with objective variables, the fact remains that fear, rage, and love are emotional reactions that are difficult to verify empirically in young children. Controlled studies have shown, for example, that babies left completely unclothed in temperature-regulated environments show as much rage as do babies wrapped in cumbersome clothing (Irwin & Weiss, 1934). Similarly, Watson's attempts to explain more complex learning (like language and thinking) are incomplete and unsatisfying. It remains true, however, that many human behaviors are the result of classical conditioning: fear in response to the sound of a dentist's drill, although the *sound* of the drill has never hurt anyone; salivating on seeing food (usually with more restraint than a dog); and countless other responses that result from previous stimulus pairings.

Watson's contribution to the understanding of human behavior is difficult to assess, largely because the behavioristic approach for which he was clearly the strongest spokesman continues to exert a profound influence on contemporary psychological thinking. Among other things, he did much to make the science of psychology more rigorous and more objective; he popularized the notion that environmental experiences are potent forces in shaping behavior patterns; and he elaborated a learning explanation (classical conditioning) that explains at least some simple animal and human behaviors. In addition, he exerted a profound influence on the thinking of other psychologists such as Guthrie, whose theory we will look at next.

EDWIN GUTHRIE (1886–1959)

In retrospect, it is perhaps astounding that virtually all human learning textbooks still discuss someone like Edwin Guthrie. He wrote little (only a handful of books and articles), had almost no students and followers (unlike most other well-known psychologists of that time, such as Pavlov, Watson, and Thorndike), and his theory consisted of only a single law with virtually no original experimental support. That one law of learning, you might suppose, must be pretty big.

Like Watson, Guthrie believed that psychology should deal with what can be seen rather than what has to be inferred. "Only the observable conditions under which learning occurs are of any use for a theory or for an understanding of learning," he insisted (Guthrie, 1935, p. 143). But he didn't share Watson's determination to revolutionize American psychology, overthrowing the mentalism of his predecessors and putting in its stead a completely objective, experimental behaviorism. In fact, Guthrie performed only one experiment, which studied the behavior of cats escaping from puzzle boxes to obtain food (Guthrie & Horton, 1946).

EDWIN R. GUTHRIE (1886–1959)

Edwin Guthrie was born on January 9, 1886, in Lincoln, Nebraska. This was rural country, and it perhaps is not surprising that when he later felt the need to illustrate his theory, many of his examples dealt with horses and dogs.

Guthrie received an arts degree from the University of Nebraska in 1907. Three years later he received a master's degree that included a major in philosophy and a minor in mathematics—and an additional minor, almost as an afterthought, in the fledgling new discipline of psychology. Subsequently he spent three years as a high school teacher. (Many years later, he was to co-author a textbook in educational psychology; Guthrie & Powers, 1950).

Guthrie then went to the University of Pennsylvania, where in 1912 he obtained a Ph.D. in philosophy. Most of the remainder of his 42-year academic career was spent at the University of Washington. His shift to psychology, which occurred in 1919, was largely influenced by the philosopher Edgar Arthur Singer, who believed that many philosophical problems could be reduced to problems of behavior. A contemporary of Watson's (he was only 8 years younger), Guthrie was also profoundly influenced by Pavlov's work on classical conditioning.

The most important of Guthrie's writings is *The Psychology of Learning*, published in 1935 and revised in 1952. He was widely recognized during his academic career, served as dean of graduate studies at the University of Washington, and was honored by the American Psychological Association (of which he was president for a time).

A Law of Learning

And he explained the cat's behavior the same way he explained all learning, using that one, single, all-encompassing law of learning: "*A combination of stimuli which has accompanied a movement will on its recurrence tend to be followed by that movement*" (Guthrie, 1935, p. 26; italics in original).

What the Law Means

"This is a short and simple statement," claimed Guthrie (1935, p. 26). He was only half right: It's short, but only superficially simple. What the law says, in effect, is that when an organism does something on one occasion, it will tend to do exactly the same thing if the occasion repeats itself. Furthermore the full strength of the "bond" between a stimulus and a response is attained on the occasion of the first pairing; it will neither be weakened nor strengthened by practice. In behavioristic terms, if a stimulus leads to a specific response now, it will lead to the same response in the future. Thus learning occurs, and is complete, in a single trial.

But this isn't true, you protest![8] He must have meant something else.

One-Shot Learning

Yes, it is true, said Guthrie: People, and animals, learn in one shot. What they learn is not a connection between two stimuli (as happens in Pavlovian classical conditioning, for example), but a connection between a stimulus and a response. If you do X in situation Y, you will do X again the next time you're in situation Y. To learn X, you don't need to repeat it over and over again, nor does it need to be reinforced. If X has been performed once in response to Y, the link between X and Y is as strong as it will ever be.

So if a woman shouts "Kro!" (as happened last night) and I turn my head in her direction (as I did), does this mean that every time this woman shouts my name, I will turn my head in her direction? No, says Guthrie. Note the wording of the law: *A combination of stimuli which has accompanied a movement will on its recurrence tend to be followed by that movement.* Guthrie (1935) used the word *tend* because, as he put it, "the outcome of any one stimulus or stimulus pattern can not be predicted with certainty because there are other stimulus patterns present" (p. 26). So the answer is that I, Kro, will *tend* to turn again in the woman's direction, because that is the last thing I did when I was previously in this situation. But the answer is also that I might *not* turn in her direction, because the "combination of stimuli" will not be identical the second time. I might be tired; her voice might be more plaintive or more strident; there might be other voices in the background; I might be paying attention to something else; or my head might be in the refrigerator.[9]

Practice

Hence the value of practice and repetition. What practice does is clear, says Guthrie: It provides an opportunity for making the same response in a wide variety of different situations. "An act is learned in the single occurrence," he

---

[8]Kro liked to pretend he knew what you, his readers, would be thinking. And then he'd pretend to be talking to you. But I think he often misread human readers. For example, were any of you actually protesting, "No, that isn't true"? Or were you just waiting for Kro to explain to you why it *might* be true? (GRL)

[9]It certainly often was. (GRL)

insists. "The need for repetition comes from the need for executing the act in a *variety* of circumstances" (Guthrie, 1935, p. 138). The more often an action has been practiced, the wider the range of combination of stimuli to which it has been exposed *and connected.* Hence the more likely it is that it will be repeated in a given situation.

One-Shot Classical Conditioning

Does this mean that Pavlov's dog learned to salivate in response to a buzzer in a single trial? Yes, said Guthrie, even though Pavlov reported that in his earlier work he sometimes needed as many as between 50 and 100 pairings of CS and US before the US reliably elicited salivation. According to Guthrie, the need for a large number of trials was brought about by the fact that the conditions under which the learning was taking place were not perfectly controlled: "Standing in the loose harness the dog can shift his weight from one leg to another, turn his head, prick up his ears, yawn, stretch, in fact alter his whole pattern of proprioceptive stimulation, and a certain amount of his exteroceptive situation" (Guthrie, 1935, p. 98). (**Proprioceptive stimulation** refers to internal sensations such as those associated with movements of muscles; **exteroceptive stimulation** relates to sensations associated with external stimuli and involving the senses of vision, hearing, taste, and smell.) As a result, the learning required dozens of trials simply to ensure that the response would be associated with most of the various combinations of stimuli possible. That Pavlov was later able to condition salivation in dogs in as few as 10 to 20 trials simply reflects the fact that he was eventually better able to control stimulus conditions.

Movement-Produced Stimuli (MPS)

To understand Guthrie's law of learning—which, in fact, implies his entire theory—it is important to understand that a stimulus is not just one sensation, but a combination of a large number of sensations. In Guthrie's words learning involves associating a response to a *combination of stimuli.*

Similarly, for Guthrie a response is not just a single, final act; rather, it is a sequence of actions. To simplify, the sound of a bell leads to a number of alerting responses: turning of the ears, movements of the eyes, perhaps movements of the head and neck, and so on. "Every such motion," says Guthrie (1935), "is a stimulus to many sense organs in muscles, tendons, and joints, as well as the occasion for changing stimuli to eyes, ears, etc." (p. 54). Guthrie labeled these stimuli **movement-produced stimuli** (MPS). Movement-produced stimuli in turn give rise to other responses that can also have an effect on muscles, glands, and tendons, thus giving rise to more stimuli.

Contiguity Through MPS

Thus the sequence between the initial presentation of a stimulus and the occurrence of response is filled with a sequence of responses and the proprioceptive stimulation that results. Each of these responses and their corresponding MPS are in contiguity (that is, they occur at the same time), and so each becomes associated. These learned associations are what guide behavior, claims Guthrie (1935): "One movement starts another, that a third, a fourth, and so on" (p. 54). And the entire sequence is learned because each individual MPS is present at the same time as the response occurs. One of the clearest examples of MPS is found in the learning of athletic skills. These skills often consist of long sequences or chains of responses. Each response in the sequence serves as a signal for the next response.

Habits

Learning, Guthrie insists, occurs in one trial. But this does not mean that a complex behavior can be learned in one trial. What it means is that each individual component of the vast number of stimulus–response associations that make up a complex act requires only a single pairing. A number of trials might be required, however, before all have been associated as they need to be. When they are all linked so that a particular combination of stimuli reliably leads to a particular combination of responses, what we have is a **habit**—a stereotyped, predictable pattern of responding.

But humans are seldom completely predictable (or rational).[10] They don't respond exactly the same way every time they're placed in the same situation.

There are several possible explanations for this, according to Guthrie. One is that if responses to two stimuli are different, it is because the stimuli are not exactly identical. Another is that through one of a number of procedures, an old habit has been replaced by a new one. The old one is not forgotten—it is merely replaced.

Forgetting

Guthrie (1935) tells the story of two young boys whose Friday afternoons were "made dreary" by the pastor's weekly visit, during which they were required to unharness, groom, feed, and water the good man's horse. One day they got the bright idea of retraining the horse. One of them stood behind the animal, shouted "Whoa," and at the same time jabbed it sharply with a pitchfork. It isn't clear, says Guthrie, how many times they did this, nor does the story report exactly what happened later when the pastor drove his horse home and shouted "Whoa!" But apparently the boys were quite happy with the outcome.

The point, explains Guthrie, is not that the horse forgot how to stop; that is hardly likely. Rather, it is that the old habit of stopping in response to the command "Whoa" had been replaced by a different habit.

The best explanation for forgetting, says Guthrie, is not that associations are wiped out with the passage of time, but that time allows for new learning to replace the old. It follows from the theory that whatever response was last

[10]Nor are Koronians. These derogatory asides were less common in Kongor's original report than in this revision. I think they demonstrate a certain emotionality that Kro found difficult to admit. (GRL)

performed in a stimulus situation will tend to be repeated again when that situation next arises.

Reward and Punishment

It is for this reason that reward is sometimes important in learning. According to Guthrie, a reward doesn't do anything to strengthen the link between stimulus and response. But what it does is change the stimulus situation, thus preventing the animal (or person) from learning something different.

Punishment, too, can change a stimulus situation and serve, in Guthrie's words, to "sidetrack" a habit. The important point is that because learning depends on contiguity (that is, on the simultaneity of stimulus and response events) to be effective, punishment has to occur either during the response or very soon afterward. And because punishment works by interrupting the unwanted habit, anything that grabs attention and brings about a different behavior will work. "Picking up a small child and tossing him or swinging him by the heels," writes Guthrie (1935),[11] "is just as effective in overcoming a balky fit as is a sound spanking" (p. 141).

Applications

Guthrie was very interested in making his theory highly practical. As a result, his writing is filled with examples of how learning and remembering can be improved, both with animals and with people.

What this one-shot theory of contiguity-based learning means from a practical point of view, says Guthrie, is that to bring behavior under control, it is necessary to arrange for the behavior to occur in the presence of stimulus conditions that are under control. If you want a dog to come when you call it, he explains, you first have to get him to come to you, either by holding up a bone, running away from him, pulling him toward you, or doing whatever else you suspect might entice the dog to approach. If you yell "Come" at the same time, an association may soon form between the command and the action.

Note that the dog has not learned a new response; he already knew how to run toward you. Here, as in all learning, what changes are associations between the response of running toward a person and a signal. What makes it easy to teach a dog to come, says Guthrie, is that this is something that dogs do, just as they fetch sticks, lie down, roll over, and so on. "We can not teach cows to retrieve a stick because this is one of the things that cows do not do," claims Guthrie (1935, p. 45). Elsewhere, he argues that "it would be a waste of time to try to teach a cow to sit up" (Guthrie & Powers, 1950, p. 128). (It appears that

---

[11]Guthrie doesn't explain where the child should be tossed. But in the Middle Ages, baby tossing was one of the sports by which the gentry amused themselves. It involved throwing infants from one gamesman to another. One of the unlucky babies was King Henry IV's infant brother, who was killed when he fell while being tossed from window to window. (I swear this is true. I read about it in deMause, (1974). (Kro)

Guthrie had never seen a cow sitting up, smoking a cigar, and reading. I have. Honest.)[12]

Breaking Habits

Consistent with his theory, Guthrie maintained that responses are never forgotten; they are merely replaced by more recently learned responses. "Unlearning becomes merely a case of learning something else," he says (Guthrie, 1935, p. 66). Hence the best way of breaking a habit is to find the cues that initiate the habit and to practice another response to these same cues. For example, if you smoke, a wide range of stimulus conditions will have become associated with the action of smoking: finishing a meal, drinking, watching television, meeting a friend who smokes, getting up in the morning, and so on. A general *unconditioning* of all these links is a long process, says Guthrie, because it requires that the smoker attach other responses to the situations associated with the beginning of the smoking sequence.

Guthrie (1952) describes three specific techniques for breaking habits: the fatigue method, the threshold method, and the method of incompatible stimuli. What each of these has in common is that it involves what Guthrie terms *inhibitory conditioning*—that is, the conditioning of a response that inhibits the habit that is to be broken.

The Fatigue Method

The **fatigue technique**, sometimes termed *flooding*, involves presenting the stimulus repeatedly in order to elicit continued repetition of the undesired response. Eventually the organism will become so fatigued that it can no longer perform the response; at that point a different response will be emitted (even if the response is to do nothing). It follows from Guthrie's theory of one-shot learning that this new response, because it is the most recent reaction to the stimulus, will be repeated if the stimulus is presented again. In this way the original undesirable habit has been broken.

The Threshold Method

The **threshold technique** involves presenting the stimulus that forms part of the undesirable S–R unit (habit), but presenting it so faintly that it does not elicit the undesirable response. If it doesn't elicit the undesirable behavior, then it probably elicits another response; again, it may simply be the response of not reacting in an undesirable fashion. The stimulus is then presented with increasing intensity over a succession of trials, but the degree of increase is carefully kept so small that the undesirable response will never be elicited. By the time an intensity is reached that would initially have stimulated the undesirable behavior, a different habit has been formed.

---

[12] I think Kro is just trying to be funny. (GRL)

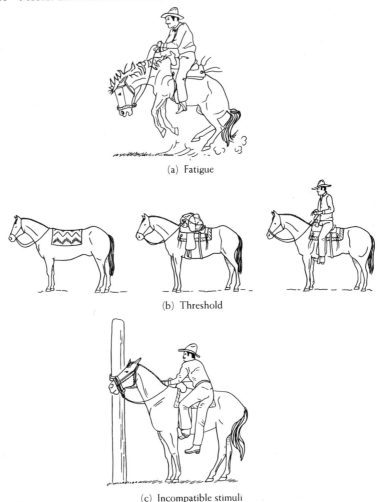

(a) Fatigue

(b) Threshold

(c) Incompatible stimuli

FIGURE 2.8 Guthrie's three ways of breaking habits. In (a), the horse is "broken" in the traditional sense, being allowed to buck until fatigued. In (b), the horse is "gentled" by having progressively heavier weights placed on its back, beginning with a blanket and culminating with a saddle and rider. In (c), the horse is tied down so that it cannot buck when mounted.

The Method of Incompatible Stimuli

The **method of incompatible stimuli** involves presenting the stimulus when the response cannot occur. Because the undesirable reaction is prevented, a different response takes its place by default; eventually, it replaces the old habit entirely.

An Illustration

Each of these techniques can be illustrated in the training of horses, a subject about which the Nebraska-raised Guthrie knew something (see Figure 2.8).

A bucking horse, most people will readily admit, has a bad habit—a bad S–R unit, as the behaviorists would say. The stimulus part of this unit is represented by the various things (like saddles and people) that lead the horse to react in an antisocial manner when they are put onto its back. The response part of the S–R unit is represented by the antisocial activity (the bucking response). According to Guthrie's theory, any attempt to modify a horse's behavior will take the form of one or more of the three techniques just described.

The common rodeo technique of breaking a horse is simply to throw a saddle on its back and ride the living _____ out of it.[13] When it gets sufficiently tired, it will stop responding in an undesirable way, and if the rider is still on its back, the horse may eventually begin to respond by standing, walking, or running. This is Guthrie's fatigue technique.

The threshold method is also commonly used for breaking horses. It breaks as many horses as the rodeo technique, but fewer riders. This method involves "gentling" the horse—beginning by placing a light blanket on its back and increasing the weight (that is, increasing the intensity of the stimulus) over successive trials. Given sufficient time and patience, a horse may be broken in this fashion.

The third technique, that of incompatible stimuli, is probably used less frequently with horses, but it can also be effective. It involves presenting the stimulus (saddle and rider on the horse's back) when the response cannot occur. The incompatible stimulus usually involves tying the horse to a post ("snubbing short") so that it can't buck.

Breaking Habits and Humans

The above heading doesn't refer to the breaking of humans, but to the breaking of human habits (heh, heh).[14]

Each of Guthrie's three techniques can be applied to people. Of course, it is quite unacceptable to "break" a child in the same manner that a horse would be broken. But with due consideration for the *humanity* of children—and without having to hold each of them up by their heels or toss them about—it's possible to remove certain bad habits that might be acquired even in the very best of homes. Consider, for example, a small boy who habitually responds to the sight of his grandfather with very intense fear because the old man once punished him with a short whip. (Of course, this illustration is fictitious.) In the manner of Jones and her subject Peter, one can remove the boy's fear by having him eat something pleasant while the grandfather stands quietly in the distance. Over succeeding trials, grandpa can be invited to move a little closer each time but never close enough to bring about the fear reaction (threshold method). Eventually the fear response will be replaced by a more desirable behavior.

---

[13]Kro had originally filled this space with some very colorful expressions, which he quite loved although he didn't always understand them. For your sake, we had to edit them out of the final earthbound text. Those of you who are old enough and are curious might try writing me and begging for a copy of the original. (GRL)

[14]Heh, heh. (GRL)

Guthrie's threshold technique is highly similar to another approach, popularized by Wolpe (1958), that is sometimes called **counterconditioning** or systematic desensitization. This method has often been successfully employed with patients suffering from severe fears (known as phobias). In its simplest form, the technique requires that the patient list all stimuli associated with the phobia. These are ranked hierarchically beginning with the stimulus associated with the least amount of fear, progressing through other stimuli associated with increasing fear, and culminating with those associated with the most intense fear reaction. Following this first step, the therapist trains the patient in one or more of a variety of relaxation techniques. Therapy (which generally occurs over a number of sessions) then involves having the subject imagine or describe a situation low on the hierarchy of fear-producing stimuli. While this is happening, the patient is continually instructed to relax. The object of the procedure is to have the patient imagine fear-producing stimuli without feeling anxiety. Care is taken to ensure that the stimuli being imagined remain below the threshold for fear—in other words, that they do not lead to the phobic reaction (hence the similarity to Guthrie's threshold method). In the end, if the therapy is successful, the undesirable fear reaction will have been replaced by a response that is essentially incompatible with it: a response of relaxation.

Lefrançois's Uncle Renault

The fatigue method and the method of incompatible stimuli can also be used to correct various behavior and emotional problems, a fact of which Lefrançois's Uncle Renault is still painfully aware. The story, only slightly distorted by time, is that his sweet tooth would have led him unerringly in the direction of juvenile criminality had it not been for his grandmother's cunning and resourcefulness. You see, this Renault guy, as devious as any other fledgling criminal, had become so successful at pilfering doughnuts, pies, cakes, and other assorted delights from his grandmother's kitchen that the poor lady was quite at her wit's end. She had eventually realized that beating little Renault with her poplar cane wasn't likely to teach him anything other than to dislike poplar and to fear her. And cleverly inserting vinegars, mustards, pickles, and other surprises in her pastries had done nothing but make him more cautious; now, like a dog, he smelled everything before he ate it. But eat it he did, almost as fast as the old lady baked. And once more Renault would decline his supper, except perhaps for one or two small cookies or a wedge of pie if there was one left. And if there wasn't? Well, OK, then, a little corn syrup and brown sugar, thank you.

It was about then that the old lady considered the method of incompatible stimuli. "Make a muzzle for him," she told Frank, Renault's grandfather, "and he'll have to leave my baking alone." But the muzzle was never made; they both realized that Renault would learn little from wearing a muzzle other than not to eat with it on.

As a last resort, Renault was exposed to the fatigue technique. The story has it that one June day, when the sun hung forever in the hot sky, Renault's grandmother baked: pies and cakes, creamy tortes and almond cookies, chocolate wafers and sugar doughnuts, lemon meringues and cherry cupcakes. And

Lefrançois's Uncle Renault ate. Sitting on a straight-backed wooden chair, with his grandfather encouraging him, he ate jubilantly at first, then less gladly, and finally quite reluctantly. In the end, he said he was certain he could eat no more—but even then he ate a little more, because he had no choice. "Eat," his grandmother urged. "You never have enough. You're going to sit there and eat everything."

Renault is reported not to have eaten everything. Even now he still turns slightly green at the thought of eating dessert.[15]

A Brief Evaluation

Pavlov, Watson, and Guthrie were concerned mainly with discovering and explaining regularities that underlie relationships among stimuli and responses. Among the important regularities that these theorists discovered were those now described as Pavlovian or classical conditioning.

But were these good theories in terms of the criteria discussed in Chapter 1? Yes and no. First, how well did they reflect the facts? Perhaps not all that well. Although they fit the facts reasonably well *as the facts were known then*, many observations had yet to be made (as is shown in later chapters). In addition, the "facts" explained by these theories are those that the theorists in question thought to be most in need of explanation, an observation that is true of virtually all psychological theories. Accordingly, these early behaviorists did relatively little to explain "higher" mental processes: language, thought, problem solving, perception, and so on.

---

[15]The story used to be entirely true, but Kro has exaggerated it somewhat. Still, it's remarkably close to the honest-to-God truth. (GRL)

With respect to the other criteria, the theories fare much better. They tend to be clear and understandable; they are internally inconsistent; and their insistence on objectivity generally meant that they would not be based on many unverified assumptions. And although the extent to which they explain (and consequently the extent to which they can be employed to predict behavior) is severely limited by the fact that they were typically based on incomplete data, their contributions to the subsequent development of learning theories can hardly be overestimated. In fact, the terms and concepts used today in investigations of classical conditioning are almost entirely terms and concepts first explored and labeled by Pavlov almost a century ago!

It's clear that these early behavioristic positions don't explain all of human learning. In fact, however, doing so was *not* every theorist's goal. Many theorists, such as Pavlov, for example, were concerned mainly with investigating one or two interesting and important phenomena in detail. They believed that other phenomena, many of which might seem more important and more interesting, would eventually be understood—that science needs to progress in increments beginning with simple concepts and progressing toward the more complex.

The explanations of these early behaviorists provide valuable insights into human and animal functioning. They should not be dismissed on the basis of their failure to explain symbolic functioning or so-called higher mental processes. Instead they should be looked at in the light of their contribution to the development of a science that might not yet explain all of human behavior but that explains more behavior more clearly with each succeeding theoretical contribution.

SUMMARY

1. William James used introspection to try to understand human behavior; others, like Wundt and Fechner in Europe and Titchener and Weber in the United States, used objective measurements of physical stimuli and their effects (psychophysics—for example, absolute thresholds and JNDs) to understand behavior.

2. Pavlov, a physiologist, is famous for his elaboration of classical conditioning, a procedure wherein a neutral (conditioned) stimulus (CS) is paired with an unconditioned stimulus (US) linked with an unconditioned response (UR) until it can eventually substitute for it in bringing about a conditioned response (CR)—like salivation in response to a tone, in the case of Pavlov's dog. Classical conditioning explains learning on the basis of contiguity (the simultaneity of the stimuli that become associated).

3. Stimuli need not be perfectly simultaneous in classical conditioning; the conditioning can also be delayed (CS before US but overlapping; this method is the most effective), trace (CS starts and ends before US), or backward (US occurs before the CS; this method is the least effective). Organisms seemed predisposed to learn certain behaviors.

4. Acquisition depends on the number of CS–US pairings, as well as on the strength of the US. CS–US bonds are remarkably durable but can be extinguished by repeatedly presenting the CS without the US. Spontaneous recovery normally occurs after a period of time following extinction; subsequent extinction is faster.

5. Watson originated and preached behaviorism in North American psychology. His position was a carefully objective reaction to an earlier, more mentalistic psychological orientation. He based much of his theory on the work of the Russian physiologist Pavlov.

6. Watson found classical conditioning useful for explaining the learning of emotional responses in people. He felt that reactions of fear, love, hate, and so on can often be traced to experiences where previously neutral stimuli are associated with emotion-producing stimuli. Through generalization, these responses can then be associated with other related stimuli.

7. Watson was a strong believer in the power of the environment in determining people's behavior. Probably the most often-quoted statement attributed to Watson is his claim that he would be able to make anything he wished out of a dozen healthy infants if he were given a free hand in determining their environments.

8. Guthrie's explanation of learning is referred to as a one-shot learning theory based on contiguity. He maintained that whatever response follows a stimulus will be likely to follow that stimulus again when the latter is repeated. In addition, the strength of the bond between the stimulus and the response is thought to be fixed after the first pairing.

9. In Guthrie's system, practice is important because it permits an association to be formed between a behavior and a variety of stimulus complexes. Reinforcement is effective because it changes the situation, preventing the person (organism) from learning another response. Similarly, punishment works because it disrupts the learning sequence, forcing the individual to do—and therefore learn—some other response.

10. The notion that stimuli and responses occur in temporal contiguity was made plausible by Guthrie through his statement that external stimuli give rise to muscular and glandular movements that produce internal (proprioceptive) stimuli. These movement–produced stimuli (MPS) are stimuli for other responses in the chain of events between the presentation of an external stimulus and the occurrence of an ultimate response.

11. Sequences of stimuli and responses form habits. These are never forgotten, but they may be replaced. Guthrie describes three ways of breaking habits: repeated presentation of a stimulus (fatigue method); presenting the stimulus so faintly that a response is not elicited (threshold method); and presenting the stimulus when the response cannot occur (method of incompatible stimuli).

12. It is fairer to evaluate these theories not in terms of their shortcomings but in terms of their sometimes monumental contribution to the development of psychological theory.

Thorndike and Hull: The Effects of Behavior

A new scientific truth does not triumph by convincing its opponents, but rather because its opponents die, and a new generation grows up that is familiar with it.

Max Planck

PRELIMINARY NOTE FOR HUMAN READERS: CHAPTER 3 OBJECTIVES

There's a word in this chapter which, I'm told, may profoundly shock some of you human readers. Ah, isn't that too bad![1]

Well, I make no apology for it whatsoever. After all, this book was written for Korons and is being left here only because of the deal I made with the good doctor in exchange for his help—which he hasn't had time to give me yet, but he promises he will as soon as it gets a little colder and the whitefish stop biting.

The word, by the way, was included in the original other-world version as a piece of humor (on Koros, the absurd *is* comic). I've left it in the earth version because, judging from what I know of the limited powers of the human mind, it seemed to me that some of you might be overcome by some of the symbols in Hull's system. For some of you, the word should be an antidote.

After you finish this chapter, you should be able to describe the following in words so simple and clear your grandmother would be astounded:

- The principal features of Thorndike's connectionism
- Thorndike's laws of effect and readiness, and the five main subsidiary laws
- Changes in Thorndike's thinking after 1930
- The nature of Hull's system
- Relationships among input, intervening, and output variables
- What is meant by a habit-family hierarchy
- What fractional antedating goal responses are
- A bunch of other things, including the awful word

If you do try to explain this chapter to your grandmother, please have the good sense to leave the word out of your explanation.

SIXTH TIME CUBE: 49TH HEXALOG, POINT 217.75

One day, when I was still staying out at Lefrançois's hunting cabin, I watched a pair of horses crossing a pasture. The first, who seemed to be the leader, walked very determinedly about 75 steps in front of the other, as though he had fixed very clearly in his mind where he was going. The other just followed along, not seeming to pay much attention to anything but his leader.

Twice the lead horse stopped as though he had just seen or smelled something, or as though he had been momentarily distracted by some important thought. And both times, the horse

---

[1] One of the few editorial changes we made in Kro's report was the deletion of that awful word—we just drew a line right through the middle of it and substituted a more acceptable expression in its place. You'll find it on page . . . I forget, but I know it's in this chapter somewhere. (GRL)

following him also stopped. But the second horse didn't look around as did the first, or stare pensively into the distance; he simply stood and watched his leader, as though waiting for some signal.

Finally the lead horse reached the top of a rise and started to munch at bunches of grass sticking out through the snow. The other horse, as if following some unwritten rule, also stopped immediately although he was still at the foot of the rise. The snow where the second horse stood was much deeper, completely covering the grass. Still, he raked through the snow with his hoof, and he too began to eat.

And I captured² myself wondering, why are these horses acting this way? What are they thinking?

On earth, what I have written above is sometimes called **anthropomorphism**— giving nonhuman animals or objects characteristics that are solely human. But who is to say that horses don't think? Who is to say what characteristics of emotion and intelligence are solely human? These are simple questions, but they have no simple answers.

At about the time that scientific psychology was being born, Charles Darwin's highly influential *The Origin of Species* . . . (1859–1962) seemed to suggest that humans are just another species of animal—evolved with certain distinctly different characteristics to be sure, but nevertheless basically animal. Did this mean that so-called lower species might possess capacities that had previously been considered beyond the abilities of "dumb" animals.³

Perhaps. Certainly Darwin's writings contained numerous anecdotes illustrating what seemed to be animal intelligence. For example, Darwin described how monkeys who cut themselves with a sharp object never make the same mistake twice. He also noted how monkeys who have been fed sugar lumps wrapped in paper and then are given a wrapped sugar lump that also contains a wasp reason that they must from then on hold the wrapping to their ear to hear whether there might be a wasp inside.

EDWARD L. THORNDIKE (1874–1949)

People are anxious to find intelligence in animals, claimed a psychologist named Edward Thorndike (1898). If a dog gets lost and then happens to find its way home over a long distance, newspapers all run stories about how intelligent dogs are. But there are no stories about the hundreds of other dogs who go out for an evening stroll in the neighborhood, make a wrong turn, and never find their way home again.

Similarly, if a cat stretches upward on the refrigerator, seeming to reach toward the handle with its paw, people immediately assume that the cat has

---

²Like many nonnative speakers of a language, Kro had a lot of trouble with idioms. Most of his more stupid blunders have been cleaned up in editing. Here, he meant "I caught myself . . . " (GRL)
³Or did it mean that humans were just another dumb, brute animal, no more special or noble than a turkey or a baboon? Of course not, shouted the anthropomorphists! (Kro)

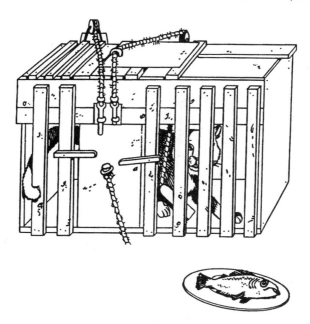

FIGURE 3.1 Thorndike's puzzle box. To get out of
the box, the cat had to pull a string to release one of
the door locks, step on the lever to release the second,
and then flick one of the door latches down. From
E. L. Thorndike (1898). Animal intelligence: An
experimental study of the associative processes in
animals. *Psychological Review Monograph Supplement,* 2(8).

somehow figured out the connection between the handle and the door. Hog-
wash, said Thorndike. Anecdotes make a poor source of evidence for scientific
theories. If psychology is to determine whether animals can actually reason out
complex relationships in their solutions of day-to-day problems, researchers
should carry out controlled experiments to this end.

The Puzzle Box

And so Thorndike devised a number of what he called *puzzle boxes*. The most
typical, shown in Figure 3.1, is designed so that a cat locked into the box can
escape only if it does three things: pull a string to release one lock, step on a
lever to release a second, and flip a latch upright to open the door. To make
sure the cat is interested in getting out of the cage, some tidbit of food—like
a dead fish—is placed not far away, but beyond reach. Most cats have a
number of ready-made solutions for this problem—like trying to squeeze
between the bars, scratching and clawing at the door or at the floor, or
meowing indignantly for help. Of course, the puzzle box is designed so that
none of these works.

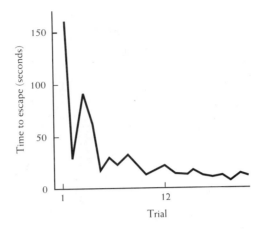

FIGURE 3.2   The behavior of one cat in Thorndike's
puzzle box. The cat took almost 3 minutes to escape
the first time, but almost always less than 1 minute
after the first successful escape. From E. L. Thorndike
(1898). Animal intelligence: An experimental study of
the associative processes in animals. *Psychological Review
Monograph Supplement*, 2(8).

Basically, there are two ways for the cat to solve this problem. One is to
try a dozen different actions, or 100 or 200, until all three required actions
have been performed and—*voilà!*—the door is open. The other is to sit back,
look the situation over, think about possible courses of action, and—bang!—
figure out what needs to be done. The psychologist Köhler (whose theories
are considered in Chapter 7) carried out a similar experiment with chimpanzees and decided that this second solution is essentially what chimpanzees
do. In a typical Köhler (1927) experiment, a caged chimpanzee cannot reach
a bunch of bananas hanging outside the cage until, in a sudden flash of
insight, it occurs to him to use a stick or to pile boxes on top of one another
to reach them.

But Thorndike's cats didn't do that at all; instead, they used the first approach, the trial-and-error approach. As Figure 3.2 shows, it didn't take them
very long to get out of the cage—only about 3 minutes the first time. But after
that, it seldom took them more than 1 minute.

It seems clear, concluded Thorndike, that cats don't learn by developing
some special insight into a situation. Instead, they learn through **trial and
error**. People, he insisted, learn in exactly the same way: "These simple,
semi-mechanical phenomena . . . which animal learning discloses are the
fundamentals of human learning also" (Thorndike, 1913b, p. 16).

Simply put, in a given situation the organism makes a number of responses,
one or more of which leads to a solution (or, in Thorndike's words, "a satisfying
state of affairs"). Subsequently, a connection is formed between response and
situation. This connection is learned, or "stamped in," as Thorndike put it.

Contiguity or Reinforcement

How does this "stamping in" occur? As we saw earlier, in learning theories that are based on the formation of connections or associations (in other words, conditioning theories), one of two different explanations for learning is typically advanced: *contiguity* or *reinforcement*. A contiguity explanation maintains simply that an association is formed between stimuli, or between stimuli and responses, because they are presented simultaneously or in close temporal proximity. The second alternative, reinforcement, maintains that learning occurs because of the consequences of the behavior—more specifically, because the behavior leads to pleasant consequences or the elimination of something unpleasant (or both).

Pavlov, Watson, and Guthrie used contiguity to explain learning. Pavlovian conditioning is based on the notion that the simultaneous presentation of two stimuli leads to the development of some sort of equivalence between them. For example, the bell becomes at least partly equivalent to food when it elicits a response similar to that elicited by the food. Guthrie maintained that a link is formed between a stimulus and a response because they are simultaneous (that is, in contiguity). In order to maintain this position in light of the apparent time lag between the presentation of most stimuli and their responses, he invented the concept of movement-produced stimuli—sequential chains of minute stimuli and responses that occur between an overt stimulus and a response.

Clearly, said Thorndike, this is only part of the story. Surely the cat would not learn to escape from the puzzle box were it not for the consequences of so doing.

Thorndike's Pre-1930s Theory

For Thorndike, learning consists of the formation of bonds between stimuli and responses—bonds that take the form of neural connections. Consequently, the theory is often labeled **connectionism**. Learning, Thorndike explains, involves the *stamping in* of S–R connections; forgetting involves *stamping out* connections.

Thorndike's theory summarizes the effects of classical conditioning's three important variables (recency, frequency, and contiguity) in a single law: the Law of Exercise.

The Law of Exercise

The **Law of Exercise** (Thorndike, 1913a) states that bonds between stimuli and responses are strengthened through being exercised frequently, recently, and "vigorously." As we will see, this law played a very minor role in Thorndike's final system, but it had a tremendous influence on educational theory and practice in the early decades of this century. Although Thorndike did not invent the notion that practice and repetition improve learning (these ideas had long been the basis of classical education), his theory gave the idea scientific credibility. Thorndike rapidly became one of the most respected educational psychologists in North America. It was his belief in the effectiveness of "exercising" S–R connections that did a great deal to encourage the repetitive "drill" approaches to learning that became immensely popular in the 1930s and 1940s.

EDWARD LEE THORNDIKE (1874–1949)

Like Pavlov, Thorndike was the son of a minister. The significance of this fact probably relates to the somewhat greater probability that the children of ministers and pastors would receive a higher education; in fact, three Thorndike brothers (including Edward) later taught at Columbia University. Edward's upbringing is reported to have been strict and to have emphasized hard work and good manners, and Edward Thorndike grew up to be extremely industrious and highly self-controlled (Joncich, 1968).

Thorndike began his academic career studying English at Wesleyan and then went to Harvard, where he switched to psychology. While at Harvard he raised chickens in the basement of William James's house, using them in studies of animal intelligence. Later Thorndike transferred to Columbia, where in 1898 he obtained a Ph.D. in psychology. His thesis on animal intelligence, published that same year (Thorndike was then only 24), is still a classic. It tried to establish through experimentation that animals (specifically cats) learn through a gradual process of trial and error that eventually leads to the "stamping in" of the correct response. Much of his later career in psychology involved generalizing this observation to demonstrate how humans, too, learn through trial and error as a function of reward or punishment.

Thorndike wrote extensively, publishing more than 78 books and at least 400 articles. His writing deals with an extremely wide range of topics in education and psychology (it is said that all of his course outlines eventually became books). He almost single-handedly defined and established educational psychology; he changed the study of child development into an objective science; he established the use of tests and statistical methods in psychology and education; he was instrumental in the psychological testing movement; and he conducted literally hundreds of experiments on learning and transfer using human subjects. During his lifetime he was widely honored not only in North America but also in Europe.

Law of Effect

Whether a connection is stamped in depends in part on how often it is exercised (the Law of Exercise) but far more importantly on its consequences or effects. Hence Thorndike's most important law, the **Law of Effect** (Thorndike, 1913a).

Simply stated, the Law of Effect maintains that responses just prior to a satisfying state of affairs are more likely to be repeated. That is, the satisfying state of affairs increases the strength of the connection between the situation and the behavior that produced the satisfying outcome. The converse also applies, although it is less important in explaining learning: Responses just prior to an annoying state of affairs are more likely not to be repeated. Thus what Thorndike called *satisfiers* and *annoyers* are critical to learning.

Behaviorists would naturally object to the use of such mentalistic terms. Thorndike tried to get around these objections by defining *satisfiers* and *annoyers* objectively. A satisfying state of affairs, he said, is one that the animal (or person) either does nothing to avoid or attempts to maintain. An annoying state of affairs is one that the animal (person) does nothing to preserve or attempts to end.

The significance of the Law of Effect in the development of learning theory can hardly be overestimated. Bitterman (1969) described it as one of Thorndike's two great contributions to psychology. The other is his notion of intelligence, a notion essentially denying that the human being is simply another animal that can reason. Instead, Thorndike maintained that intelligence can be defined solely in terms of greater or lesser ability to form connections. According to Bitterman (1960), this view has been widely and uncritically accepted until recently.

The Law of Effect explains what is termed **instrumental learning**. An organism performs a response and establishes some connection between it and the stimulus preceding it if it is followed by satisfaction. One important aspect of this explanation is the assumption that the connection is formed between the stimulus and the response, rather than between the reward and the response. As is made clear later in this chapter, Hull accepted Thorndike's view and made it one of the central features of his system (Bitterman, 1967).

Law of Readiness

A third major law formed an important part of Thorndike's pre-1930 system: the **Law of Readiness**. It has to do primarily with the learner's motivation (forces that lead to behavior). In effect, this law recognizes that certain behaviors are more likely to be learned (stamped in) than others. When a conduction unit is ready to conduct, said Thorndike, to do so is satisfying and not to do so is annoying. By the same token, when a conduction unit is *not* ready to conduct, being forced to do so is annoying.

Although Thorndike's use of vague expressions like *conduction unit* and *ready to conduct* detract from the objectivity of his system, the law of readiness has been made more concrete (and more useful) in educational practice. Readiness, Thorndike explained, is closely related to the learner's maturation and to previous learning, and it has much to do with whether an activity is satisfying or annoying. Specifically, a pleasant state of affairs results when a learner is ready to learn and is allowed to do so; conversely, being forced to learn when not ready—or prevented from learning when ready—leads to an annoying state of affairs.

Subsidiary Laws

Five additional laws also form part of Thorndike's explanation for learning. These laws are outlined below.

1. Multiple Response

The **law of multiple response** states that in any given situation the organism will respond in a variety of ways if its first response does not lead immediately to a more satisfying state of affairs. In other words, it is through *trial and error* that an individual will attempt to solve problems—an observation well illustrated in the most famous of Thorndike's hundreds of experiments, the cat–puzzle box study described earlier.

2. Set or Attitude

The second law makes the observation that learning is partly a function of attitude or *set* (defined as a predisposition to react in a given way). This law applies not only to satisfiers and annoyers but also to the nature of the responses that will be emitted by a person. There are culturally determined ways of dealing with a wide variety of problems; for example, many cultures find it generally acceptable to react to aggression with aggression. Individuals in these cultures are *set* to respond aggressively. Doing so presumably has the potential of leading to a satisfying state of affairs for the aggressor—and perhaps an annoying state of affairs for those aggressed upon.

3. Prepotency of Elements

Thorndike suggested that it is possible for a learner to react to only the significant (or prepotent) elements in a problem situation and be undistracted by irrelevant aspects of the situation. For example, recognizing that a figure is a square rather than a rectangle requires only that the subject respond to the relationship among the sides of the figure—not to its color, placement, and so on. For this problem, stimuli associated with shape are *prepotent;* others are irrelevant.

4. Response by Analogy

The fourth principle recognizes that a person placed in a novel situation may react with responses he or she would employ for other situations with some identical elements. When Cindy uses a subtraction rule she learned at school to determine that if she buys 40 cents worth of black jelly beans, she'll still have 60 cents left from her dollar, she is responding by analogy. The reason she does so, explains Thorndike, is that she recognizes important similarities between her current situation and a problem-solving situation in school. This allows her to *transfer* what she has learned. This principle, Thorndike's theory of transfer, is sometimes referred to as the *theory of identical elements.*[4]

Thorndike's theory of identical elements was his explanation for how people respond in novel situations—that is, how they transfer or generalize re-

---

[4]Response by analogy was well illustrated by Kro when he chased after the skunk behind the cabin, calling, "Here, kitty! Here, kitty, kitty!" Apparently cats and skunks share enough identical elements, at least in Kro's understanding, to lead readily to transfer. Heh, heh. (GRL)

sponses. When people are faced with a new situation, their "habits do not retire to some convenient distance" (Thorndike, 1913a, p. 28). Instead they recognize aspects of the novel situation as being similar to some more familiar situation, and they emit a response accordingly. And if the response doesn't lead to a satisfying state of affairs, a second is emitted, followed perhaps by a third, a fourth, and so on.

5. Associative Shifting

The last of the five subsidiary principles is closely related to stimulus substitution. *Associative shifting* recognizes that it is possible to shift a response from one stimulus to another. Thorndike illustrated this process by training a cat to stand. Initially the cat stands because the experimenter holds up a piece of fish; gradually the amount of fish is decreased until the cat stands even when no fish is presented.

A clear experimental illustration of associative shifting is provided in a study by Terrace (1963). He trained pigeons to discriminate between red and green by rewarding them with 4 seconds of access to a food hopper when they pecked a key that was backlit with a red light—and, of course, no access to food if they pecked the key when filters were used to make it appear green. Once the pigeons had learned to discriminate readily between red and green, Terrace superimposed a vertical line over the red key and a horizontal line over the green one. The pigeons, having learned the red = satisfying state of affairs link, continued to peck the red key and not the green. Terrace then slowly faded out the color over a series of trials until the keys had nothing but a vertical or a horizontal stripe on them. He found that these pigeons had transferred their responses without error, so that they now pecked vertically striped keys but not those with a horizontal stripe.

In a variation of this procedure, Terrace superimposed stripes on the keys over a number of training trials, but did not gradually fade the colors. Pigeons trained this way later made a number of errors when presented with keys containing only stripes.

Associative shifting may explain the effectiveness of countless advertisements which pair a stimulus associated with positive emotions (or with greed or lust) with what might otherwise be a relatively neutral stimulus—for example, scantily dressed models with new automobiles, macho *hombres* with cigarettes dangling from their lips, and ecstatic couples with fists full of lottery tickets.

Thorndike's Post-1930 Theory

Although many of Thorndike's beliefs about human learning remained unchanged throughout his long career, he is nevertheless one of several theorists who remained active long enough—and open to change long enough—that his system underwent some major modifications. Beginning around 1930, Thorndike admitted he had been wrong about some things.

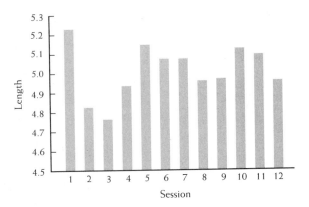

FIGURE 3.3   Median lengths of 3000 separate lines drawn by a single subject with eyes closed, over 12 sessions, when instructed to draw a line 4 inches long. Data from E. L. Thorndike (1931). *Human learning* (p. 9, Table 1). Cambridge: MIT Press.

Repeal of Law of Exercise

For one thing, I was wrong about the Law of Exercise, he confessed. Why? Because he had determined through experimentation with humans (rather than simply with cats or chicks) that mere repetition does not cause learning. In one of these experiments, for example, he had subjects sit at their desks with their eyes closed (Thorndike, 1931); each subject had been given a large pad of paper and a pencil. Their instructions were to draw, with one quick movement, a line intended to be about 4 inches long. They were asked to do this over a number of sessions on successive days until they had each drawn a total of 3000 lines—always with their eyes closed.

Results for one subject are shown in Figure 3.3. The results illustrate two general truths, claims Thorndike (1931): "(1) that of multiple response or variable reaction, and (2) that of the failure of repetition of the situation to cause learning" (p. 10).

In other words, exercise—or repetition—does not affect learning. "The repetition of a situation may change a man as little as the repetition of a message over a wire changes the wire. In and of itself, it may teach him as little as the message teaches the switchboard. . . . The more frequent connections are not selected by their greater frequency" (p. 14).

Half a Law of Effect

What does lead to learning is not repetition, Thorndike insisted, but the *effects* of the action. Specifically, as he had always maintained, actions that lead to satisfying states of affairs tend to be stamped in and maintained. But hadn't he also thought that responses leading to annoying states of affairs tend to be stamped out? I was wrong, Thorndike admitted again, now claiming that annoying outcomes do relatively little to the strength of a connection.

To investigate the law of effect, Thorndike (1931) devised a number of experiments. For example, 9 non-Spanish-speaking subjects were asked to select one from among five possible meanings for 200 different Spanish words. After each correct selection, the experimenter said "Right"; for each incorrect selection, the experimenter said "Wrong." In a second trial, all the words that the subject answered correctly were omitted, and the procedure was repeated—as it was a third and a fourth time. The object was to see whether there would be an increased tendency to select words that were initially followed by the response "Right." Not surprisingly, there was: Subjects were between 50% and 90% more likely to select a word that has twice been followed by the response "Right."

Was there a corresponding reduction in the probability of selecting a response followed by a "Wrong"? The answer is no. In fact, subjects were only between 7% and 23% less likely to select an incorrect response already selected twice (see Figure 3.4). "Other things being equal," said Thorndike (1931), "an announcement of 'Right' strengthens the connection which it follows and belongs to much more than the announcement of 'Wrong' weakens the one which it follows and belongs to" (p. 45).

Learning by Ideas

There were several other important ways in which Thorndike revised his theory after 1930. These changes were typically prompted by a need to take into account observations about human learning that didn't readily fit the original theory. Because these observations tended to reveal that thoughts, or ideas, are important in human learning, his revised theory hinted at cognitive concerns. For example, Thorndike (1931) now spoke of "ideational learning"—a "higher" form of learning that involved analysis, abstraction, and meaningfulness.

> Learning by ideas is, as the name implies, characterized by the frequent presence of ideas as situations or as responses or as both. Whereas the bulk of the learning which dogs and cats and chicks and rats display consists of connections leading from external or perceptual situations straight to bodily acts or to impulsive tendencies closely attached to such acts, the insight learning of man operates with the aid of ideas which are free from narrow confinements. (p. 138)

Although terms such as *ideas, analysis,* and *insight* are not defined very clearly in the system, they are reflected in two additional concepts that Thorndike investigated and incorporated into the system. The first is the **principle of belongingness**, evident in the finding that if two or more elements are seen as belonging together, they are more easily learned. One of Thorndike's (1931) studies illustrating this principle asked subjects to pay attention while the experimenter read out 1304 pairs of words and numbers. Among these were four words that each recurred 24 times, each time being *preceded* by exactly the same number. Afterward, subjects were asked to write which numbers came after specific words (including the four frequently repeated words) as well as which words came after specific numbers (including the four numbers each repeated 24 times).

The subjects' performance was no better than would be expected solely by chance. Why? Because, explains Thorndike, they thought each word "belonged" to the number that followed it, rather than to the number that preceded it.

The second post-1930 Thorndikean concept that is relevant here is labeled **spread of effect**. It relates to Thorndike's discovery that when a response is reinforced, other related responses also seem to be affected. As an illustration, Thorndike (1931) had subjects choose any number between 1 and 10 to go with each word in a series, among which were a number of frequently repeated words. Whenever subjects chose the number the experimenter had previously selected for each often-repeated word, they were told their choice was right. Not surprisingly, "right" numbers were chosen more frequently. More surprising, choices of numbers immediately preceding and following these "right" numbers also increased, although not as dramatically.

Summary of Thorndike's Theory

These revised laws and principles present a relatively clear (although simplified) picture of Thorndike's view of learning. According to this view, learning consists of the formation of physiological bonds or connections between stimuli and responses. The bonds are stamped in because of the satisfying nature of their consequences, influenced as well by the individual's sense of what goes with what—that is, what *belongs*.

Thorndike claimed that humans arrive at appropriate responses largely through trial and error. They may also respond in given ways because of a predetermined set (or attitude) determined by culture or by more immediate aspects of the situation; for example, a hungry person will respond to food in a different way from one who is not hungry. Some responses will be based on behavior learned in other somewhat similar situations (response by analogy), whereas others may result from a conditioning procedure (associative shifting). In many cases, the person will engage in behavior only in response to the most important aspects of a situation (the most prepotent elements).

Thorndike's Contribution

One of Thorndike's most important contributions to the development of learning theory is the emphasis he placed on the consequences of behavior as determiners of what is learned and what is not. In addition, he was largely responsible for the introduction of animal studies as a means of verifying predictions made from theory. A third area in which Thorndike made significant contributions is the application of psychological principles, particularly in teaching. A large number of his writings were devoted specifically to pedagogical problems, sometimes in such specific areas as arithmetic (Thorndike, 1922), Latin (Thorndike, 1923), and the psychology of interest (Thorndike, 1935).

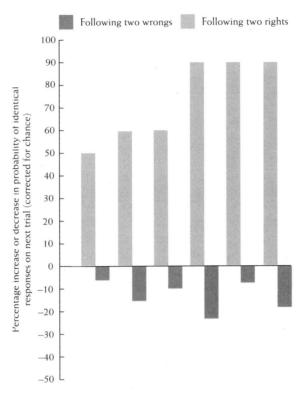

FIGURE 3.4   The influence of two consecutive
"Rights" or "Wrongs" on the next choice of possible
word meanings for an unknown word for nine subjects
in six experiments. Data from E. L. Thorndike (1931).
Human Learning (p. 44). Cambridge: MIT Press.

Thorndike also serves as an impressive example of a theorist strongly com-
mitted to a definite point of view, yet willing to examine other ideas and to make
dramatic changes in his own thinking. Unlike a number of behaviorists whose
commitment to their point of view serves as much to blind as to inform them, he
realized that his brand of connectionism still had a long way to go if it were ever
to explain some profoundly human (and profoundly important) mental activites.
"The connectionist theory of life and learning," he wrote, "is doubtless neither
adequate nor accurate. Its explanations of purposive behavior, abstraction, general notions, and reasoning are only a first and provisional attack on these problems. It has many gaps and defects." (Thorndike, 1931, p. 131).

CLARK L. HULL (1884–1952)

Since Thorndike, many others have tried to fill the gaps and fix the defects.
Among them was Clark L. Hull, probably the most ambitious of the behavior
theorists. The final system he developed is of such complexity and scope that

only a brief glimpse of it can be given here. A complete account of the system is found in Hull's own books (Hull, 1943, 1951, 1952).

Hull's Basic View of Behavior Theory

Science has two essential aspects, Hull (1952) tells us. One is concerned with the actual facts of the discipline; the other tries to make sense of the facts by organizing them into a logical system. In the process of organizing facts and discovering how they are related, the scientist arrives at the basic laws that describe the system's functioning. Once the scientist has done so, it is then possible to deduce all sorts of additional information about the system, to make predictions, to test them, and to expand and elaborate on the system.

That is what Clark L. Hull intended to do in psychology. This energetic, mathematically oriented, and very scientific young man proposed to develop a logical, scientific, and mathematical system that would explain human learning and behavior.

The system Hull devised consists of 17 laws—which Hull (1952) called *postulates* rather than laws because, science being a young discipline, "a certain amount of uncertainty surrounds these basic laws" (p. 1). These 17 postulates define and systematize relationships among a large number of variables assumed to be involved in human behavior. From these postulates, Hull derived 133 specific theorems and numerous corollaries (Hull, 1943). Hence the widely used description of Hull's theory as a **hypothetico-deductive system**.

Although the 17 postulates that are the foundation of Hull's system cannot easily be tested, the theorems and their corollaries can be. Each is precise and mathematical; each gives rise to specific predictions that can be tested experimentally. Results can then be interpreted as either providing support for or refuting not just the theorems or their corollaries, but also the postulates on which the theorems are based.

Hull's system is elaborated in two major books. He had also planned a third book describing the application of the system to behavior in social interactions. Unfortunately, he died at about the time he was finishing the second book; the third was never begun.

CLARK L. HULL (1884–1952)

Hull was born in Akron, New York, on May 24, 1884. He was from a poor family and apparently missed a lot of school as a result of having to work on the family farm. He is reported to have been in poor health throughout much of his childhood, had extremely poor eyesight, and was laid low by poliomyelitis for a lengthy period during his early college years (a disease that left him crippled in one leg). Nevertheless, at the tender age of 17 Hull spent an entire year teaching in a one-room school in Michigan before continuing his education at Alma Academy in Michigan. He had considerable talent for mathematics (as well as philosophy), and his initial aspiration was to become a mining engineer. After reading James's *Principles of Psychology*, though, Hull switched to psychology and went on to the University of Wisconsin, where he obtained a Ph.D. in 1918.

Hull's early interests were highly varied. They included systematic investigations of human and animal aptitudes, thinking machines (robots), hypnosis (to which he devoted a full ten years of study and research), and the effect of tobacco on intellectual functioning. In 1929 he went to Yale, where he became a research professor and generated (with a number of ardent disciples) the monumental system that, in extremely simplified form, makes up the rest of this chapter. Following his first major descriptions of this system in *Principles of Behavior* (1943), he rapidly became the most frequently cited psychologist in the United States. A final revision of this book was published just after his death in 1952.

General Nature of the System

Hull's explicitly behavioristic system is marked by all of the behaviorist's concerns for objectivity, precision, and rigor. Thus, although he began by inventing postulates, he derived specific, testable hypotheses from them, then attempted to verify the hypotheses in laboratory situations. As is clear from an examination of the system, this was an enormous task; consequently, Hull was only partially successful.

True to the behavioristic approach, Hull looked at human behavior in terms of stimuli and responses. However, he dealt with them in considerably more detail than had most of his contemporaries. For Hull, stimuli consist of all the conditions that affect the organism but that might or might not lead to behavior; he referred to these antecedent conditions as **input variables**. Similarly, he described responses as **output variables**. A number of his postulates are devoted to explaining the nature of input and output variables as well as the relationships that exist between the two. A third set of behavior variables that forms a central part of Hull's system is referred to as **intervening variables**.

Important aspects of input and ouput variables can be observed and measured. In contrast, intervening variables are purely hypothetical; they are inferred from input and output. Intervening variables are the scientist's best guesses about what might be happening between the presentation of a stimulus and the occurrence of a response.

Hull's interest in intervening variables is a significant departure from the preoccupations of the early behaviorists such as Watson and Guthrie, who actively shunned speculation, trying to keep the study of behavior as objective as possible. For this reason, Hull sometimes described himself as a *neobehaviorist* rather than simply as a behaviorist.

Hull was greatly impressed by Pavlov's work on reflexive behavior and classical conditioning. This Pavlovian influence is reflected in part by the fact that the cornerstone of Hull's system is his belief that all behavior consists of S–R connections. The central concept in behavior is that of *habit*, and a habit is an S–R connection, or a collection of such connections termed a **habit-family hierarchy** (habit-family hierarchies are explained later in this chapter).

Another source of profound influence on Hull was the work of Thorndike, particularly relating to the latter's Law of Effect. The influence of reward on learning became the main explanatory notion in Hull's final system.

Summary of Hull's System

It might seem a little backward to begin this discussion with a summary. In this case, however, the summary is as much an outline of the following pages as it is a recapitulation of their content.

The system is choked with symbols and mathematical terms and values. Although the mathematical terms are not essential to this discussion, the symbols simplify the presentation of the theory—although they do impose some strain on memory. Lefrançois claims that on several occasions, he has had to take special precautions to prevent "symbol shock" from occurring in undergraduate classes being exposed to Hull's theory for the first time. These precautions consist largely of indelicate stories (told in a delicate manner so as not to offend) interspersed with good Hullian terminology. Symptoms of symbol shock include lower respiration rate, some lowering of body temperature, a change in EEG pattern from beta to alpha waves, and closed eyelids. On occasion, some sufferers make strange noises through their mouths. These students are probably in more extreme states of shock.

Figure 3.5 is a summary, in symbolic form, of the major variables in Hull's system.[5]

Input Variables

Presenting Hull's system in this highly symbolic form may make it appear more difficult to understand than it really is. Although it is extremely complex in scope and detail, its most fundamental ideas are quite straightforward.

First, to simplify the model in Figure 3.5, interpret it not as a general description of human behavior but as representing only one specific behavior for one person at one given time. Understanding how the system can describe one behavior makes it easier to interpret it more generally.

Next, keep in mind that Hull, the precise and logical mathematician, truly believed that human behavior could be predicted if psychologists had the right information and the right equations. Hence his main goal was to develop a system that would allow him to do just that—that is, to predict a person's behavior, given knowledge about the stimulus. Input variables represent the

---

[5]I tried to convince Kro that he shouldn't cover most of this stuff in Hull's system, that the maze of variables, the technical frills, the symbols complete with subscripts and superscripts might make some of his human readers ill. But he was adamant. "This is for Korons," he retorted, "and all of it is important." My advice to you, you fellow human, is that you concentrate only on the main ideas and ignore Figure 3.5 (and the detailed textual explanations of it) completely. (GRL)

information the psychologist needs to predict correctly how a person will respond; the output variables represent the response, or what is predicted. In different terms, the stimulus variables are *independent* variables, and the response variables are *dependent* variables.

In brief, input variables represent a stimulus. But a stimulus is not just a simple sensation (like the sound of a bell) but a complex product of a large number of preceding events. Thus one of the major difficulties in using this system to predict behavior is that the psychologist needs a tremendous amount of knowledge about the subject's past experiences. Figure 3.5 makes it clear that complete knowledge of input requires knowing how many times in the past the S–R bond in question has been reinforced (N). This variable, combined with knowledge about the physical intensity of the stimulus (S), the drive conditions of the organism (C_D), the reward attached to responding (ω), and the amount of work required in responding (W), will theoretically allow prediction of the output variables.

Intervening Variables

Although the input and output variables are the only directly observable and measurable events described in Hull's system, the intervening variables are probably more important for understanding what his theory is really about. These variables have important links with the external variables; they intervene between stimulus events and response events to determine whether a response will occur for a stimulus.

Note that the power of intervening variables in determining responses is completely determined and controlled by input variables. In a sense, the intervening variables are a mathematical description of S–R relationships. That is, each stimulus (input) variable has a specific intervening variable related to it by some mathematical function. Thus characteristics of input variables (like num-

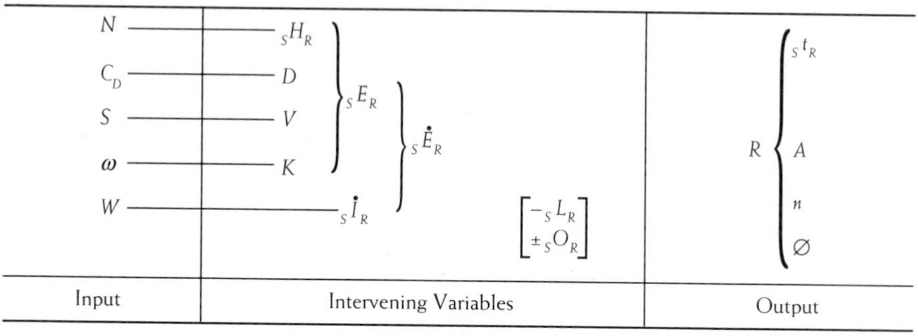

FIGURE 3.5   The Hullian system. Adapted from Hilgard and Bower (1966, p. 164).

Input variables

- N = number of prior reinforcements
- C_D = drive condition
- S = stimulus intensity
- ω = amount of reward (weight)
- W = work involved in responding

Intervening variables

- $_sH_R$ = habit strength
- D = drive
- V = stimulus-intensity dynamism
- K = incentive motivation
- $_s\dot{E}_R$ = reaction potential
- $_s\dot{I}_R$ = aggregate inhibitory potential
- $_s\bar{E}_R$ = net reaction potential
- $_sL_R$ = reaction threshold
- $_sO_R$ = oscillation of reaction potential

Output variables

- R = the occurrence of a response, measured in terms of $_st_R$, A, and n
- $_st_R$ = response latency
- A = response amplitude
- n = number of nonreinforced trials to extinction
- $\varnothing$ = no response (not used as a symbol by Hull)

ber of prior reinforcements) are reflected in the value of intervening variables which, in turn, determine whether a specific response will occur. Keep in mind that Hull's objective was to develop a mathematical system that would make it possible to calculate human behavior given sufficient knowledge about antecedent conditions—a sort of human behavior calculator. Viewed in this way, the intervening variables are much easier to understand. Each of Hull's nine intervening variables is described in turn below.

1. $_sH_R$. The most important intervening variable, **habit strength** ($_sH_R$), is a behavioristic concept defined in terms of the strength of the bond between a specific stimulus and response. For Hull, habit strength was determined largely by the number of previous pairings of a stimulus with a response, provided that reinforcement occurred on every trial. It is here that Thorndike's influence on Hull is most evident. Unlike contiguity theorists, both Thorndike and Hull maintained that the strength of a habit (of an S–R bond) is a function of reinforcement rather than of simple repetition.

Hull introduced specific numerical functions to illustrate the precise relationship between number of reinforced S–R pairings and habit strength (these are of much more academic than practical interest). Though at first glance it might appear that habit strength would be the most influential factor in determining behavior, this assumption is not correct. In fact, habit strength is only one of several variables that affect behavior.

2. *D*.   Because of its connection with reinforcement, **drive** (D) is a central concept in Hull's learning theory. Hull saw learning as the process of responses becoming connected with stimuli when the responses lead to a reduction in drive—or, more precisely, when they lead to the removal or reduction in number or intensity of stimuli associated with drive.

Drive can be primary or secondary (as can reinforcement, because it involves reducing drive). Primary drives are those associated with tissue needs like the need for food or water; secondary drives (for example, the need for high grades or money) are conditioned to primary drives. As an intervening variable, drive corresponds to the input variable *drive condition*, which is defined in terms of number of hours of deprivation. Hull identified two components of drive: the *drive proper* increases as a direct function of the length of deprivation, and the *inanition component* reflects the fact that drive decreases if deprivation (starvation) lasts too long.

Drive has three central functions in Hull's theory: (a) It provides for reinforcement, without which learning would not occur; (b) it activates habit strength—meaning that without drive, behavior will not take place even if there is a strong previously established habit (sH_R); and (c) drive stimuli become attached to specific behaviors through learning. Otherwise, people might engage in totally inappropriate behavior. They might drink when hungry, eat when cold, or cover up when thirsty. Essentially, it is this distinctiveness of drive stimuli that determines whether a response will be reinforcing.

As I note later, research has established that learning can occur, even in animals, in the absence of drive (that is, when drive is defined in terms of deprivation). This observation does not necessarily invalidate Hull's system, although it does point to some of its inadequacies.

3. *V*.   **Stimulus-intensity dynamism** is the label applied to the intervening variable that corresponds to the input variable S, or stimulus intensity. As Pavlov had demonstrated, the physical intensity of a stimulus increases the probability of a response occurring. This effect is manifested in stimulus-intensity dynamism, which interacts in a multiplicative fashion with habit strength and drive to determine the probability of a response.

4. *K*.   The symbol K in Hull's system stands for **incentive motivation**. It is determined by amount of reward (w as an input variable), and was added to Hull's system as a function of some important experiments reported by Crespi

(1942). These experiments made it apparent that drive (D) alone could not account for motivation. In Crespi's experiment, three groups of rats received different amounts of food pellets for running to a goal box. The fact that the rats that received the greatest reward ran faster than those that received less supports Hull's original notion that drive is reduced *more* by greater reward, hence leading to a stronger habit. But Crespi also found that when these three groups of rats were subsequently given the same amount of reward, those that had previously had the least amount now ran fastest, whereas those who had received the greatest amount reduced their speed the most. Accordingly, Hull had to modify his system to take into account the fact that previous reinforcements are also effective in determining behavior. The effects of these previous reinforcements, described by Hull as involving incentive motivation, interact with other intervening variables (including drive) to determine the probability that a response will occur.

5. sE_R.   The four intervening variables described thus far (sH_R, D, V, and K) make up the first and most important term in the equation Hull used to determine the probability that a stimulus would lead to a response, or what he called **reaction potential** (sE_R): $sE_R = sH_R \times D \times V \times K$. Reaction potential, sometimes called *excitatory potential*, is essentially a measure of the potential that a stimulus has for eliciting a specific response. As the formula indicates, this potential will depend on how many times the stimulus has been paired with the response and reinforcement, how intense it is, how great the reward is, and how strong the drive is.

Note that because reaction potential is a multiplicative function of these variables, if the value for any of them is zero, reaction potential will also be zero. In other words, in the absence of drive, it makes no difference how intense the stimulation is, how great the reward is, or how strong the habit is; the response (R) will not occur. Similarly, in the absence of the appropriate stimulus at sufficient intensity, in the absence of reward, or in the absence of a previously learned habit, there will also be no response. Consider the case of a person sitting at a table on which is set a variety of appetizing dishes. If that

Decreased drive after too many hours of deprivation

person has just eaten, not a single dish may be touched, despite the fact that the stimulus, the reward, and the habit are all very strong. In this case, drive would be too low ($D = 0$). By way of further illustration, consider the other possibilities: no food ($K = 0$); the person is blind and cannot smell ($V = 0$); or the person has not learned to eat ($_sH_R = 0$). In none of these cases will the response occur.

Note, too, that because the probability of responding ($_sE_R$) is a multiplicative function of drive, habit strength, and so on, identical changes in one of these variables will have different absolute effects, depending on the values of the other variables. Doubling drive, for example, will make a greater difference if habit strength ($_sH_R$) is already large than if it is small. To put it another way, increasing the motivation of a professional golfer should have more effect than increasing that of a rank amateur.

The significance of the magnitude of reaction potential in this system is that a minimum amount of potential is required before behavior will take place. Increasing reaction potential will be reflected in shorter response latency ($_st_R$), more response amplitude (A), and longer extinction time (n).

~~BULLSHIT~~ PSHAW

The indelicate expression above (delicately crossed out) is not a description of content but simply an antidote to the symbol shock that might by now have overcome the careful reader. (Kro)[6]

6. $_sE_R$. The use of two symbols denoting reaction potential might appear to be somewhat confusing. (Actually, Hull used three symbols for reaction potential, the third one being based on the potential for responding that is carried over—in other words, generalized—from related behaviors.) This second symbol refers to *net* reaction potential, which is the reaction potential that results from summing the generalized potential with the ordinary reaction potential that results from drive, habit strength, stimulus-intensity dynamism, and incentive motivation, and then subtracting inhibitory potential (see below).

7. $_sI_R$. **Aggregate inhibitory potential** (or reactive inhibition, $_sI_R$) results from two input variables: the amount of work involved in responding (W) and any habits of not responding that might have been acquired by the organism. Responses requiring a high expenditure of physical energy are less likely to be engaged in than those that require less work. Also, with continued repetition of a response, inhibitory potential accumulates. Its effect is to lower the net reaction potential until eventually the response no longer occurs. Because inhibitory potential dissipates quickly, though, the response might reoccur again very soon.

---

[6]In the words of one of this book's reviewers, "This is probably not as exciting now as it was in 1972." I agree. I told Kro the same thing. I said, today's students are serious and very sophisticated, and they know things like this aren't amusing. But he insisted. "This isn't amusement," he squeaked in that little voice of his, "it's therapy!" (GRL)

8. ($_s\hat{L}_R$).   The **reaction threshold** ($_s\hat{L}_R$) is the magnitude that net reaction potential must exceed before a response will occur. If $_s\hat{E}_R > {_s\hat{L}_R}$, a response ($R$) occurs; if $_s\hat{E}_R < {_s\hat{L}_R}$, no response (0) occurs).

9. $_sO_R$.   Even given relatively complete information about input variables, predictions are not always accurate. Guthrie's answer for this problem was simply that the stimulus situation might have changed. Hull's answer was that reaction potential is not exactly fixed; instead, it varies around a central value. This variation he labeled **behavioral oscillation** ($_sO_R$).[7]

Output Variables

The response variables of concern to Hull include the time lapse between the presentation of the stimulus and the appearance of the response (**response latency,** $_st_R$), the amplitude of the response in a physical sense (**response amplitude,** A), and the number of unreinforced responses that would occur before extinction (n). Hull postulated that response latency would decrease with increasing reaction potential, whereas both resistance to extinction and amplitude of response would increase.

Two additional symbols standing simply for the occurrence of a response (R) or its nonoccurrence (Ø) have been included in Figure 3.5. The following formula is essentially a summary of the contents of that figure:

$$\text{If } _s\hat{E}_R = (_sH_R \times D \times V \times K) - {_s\hat{I}_R} > {_s\hat{L}_R}, \text{ then } R$$

This expression reads as follows: If net reaction potential—which is the product of habit strength, drive, stimulus-intensity dynamism, and incentive motivation, minus aggregate inhibitory potential—is greater than the threshold, a response will occur.

Note how this is very much the kind of mathematical formula that a logic-based machine charged with predicting human behavior might produce. In fact, Hull was very much interested in robotics, and he actually designed a type of computer to sort and score some of his tests.

Not surprisingly, Hull's main problem turned out to be the near impossibility of arriving at precise mathematical functions for each of the variables in the equation. Nevertheless, the system led to the development of additional concepts, two of the most important of which are habit-family hierarchies and fractional antedating goal reactions. Both represent significant departures from theories that had preceded Hull, and both are relevant for the development of cognitive positions.

---

[7]These last four paragraphs illustrate why I urged Kro to simplify Hull's system. It's an impressive and vastly important system, but not all the symbols are still relevant, and the mathematical relationships are assumed rather than verified. (GRL)

Fractional Antedating Goal Reactions

Recall that the major explanation for learning advanced by Hull is a reinforcement explanation. Specifically, he maintained that reinforcement consists of drive reduction. The ordinary way of reducing a drive is to attain a goal, or to make a *goal reaction*. Goal reactions, as described by Hull, are often consummatory responses, as in the case of food. A **fractional antedating goal response** (r_G) is a conditioned response made by an organism prior to the actual goal reaction. One of Hull's examples is that of a rat who has learned that there is food at the end of a maze. Through conditioning, the rat's goal reaction (eating) has become linked with the food box as well as with various other stimuli also present, such as other sights and smells. Hull suggested that because many of these smells and sights are also present in other parts of the maze, the rat's *antedating* goal responses might eventually occur when it is first put into the maze. Although overt behaviors might be associated with these antedating goal reactions, such as the rat's licking its chops, they are conditioned *internal* responses.

These antedating (Hull sometimes called them "anticipatory") responses are important in that they serve as stimuli that maintain behavior toward a goal. It's as though there are strings of s_G–r_G sequences that precede goal reactions. In this sense they serve the same purpose as Guthrie's movement-produced stimuli (MPS). But unlike MPS, r_G–s_G are linked with reinforcement and therefore become rewarding.

Foresight and Expectancy

Perhaps most significant, Hull's notions of antedating goal response foreshadowed some fundamental cognitive notions. In effect, what Hull attempted to do with r_G–s_G's was explain things like knowing or anticipating without having to

resort to *mentalistic* explanations. It was a clever and distinctive contribution to the development of learning theory.

Even though he was determinedly behavioristic, Hull could hardly avoid the use of nonbehavioristic ideas. In a section of his 1952 book entitled "Terminal Notes: Foresight, Foreknowledge, Expectancy and Purpose," he admits that "since time out of mind, the ordinary man has used the words expect, expectation, expectancy, and expective in a practically intelligent and intelligible manner" (p. 151). Hull goes on to explain that although the fractional antedating goal response is a conditioned mechanism, because it occurs before a response, it "constitutes on the part of the organism a molar foresight or foreknowledge of the not-here and the not-know. It is probably roughly equivalent to what Tolman has called 'cognition' " (p. 151).

What Hull was trying to do with his fractional antedating goal responses was account for intention and expectancy without resorting to subjective definitions and interpretations. In other words, he was trying to objectify purpose. Although the term *purpose* "has a bad metaphysical history," he wrote, "it represents an undoubted aspect of mammalian behavior" (Hull, 1952, p. 151).

The Habit-Family Hierarchy

In the course of acquiring habits (S–R bonds), an individual will learn a number of different responses for the same stimulus; in many cases, each response will lead to the same goal. These alternative responses constitute a *habit family* arranged in hierarchical order. They are referred to as a family because they are assumed to be integrated by common fractional antedating goal reactions, and as a hierarchy because there is a preferential ordering based largely on previous reinforcements. In other words, one alternative will usually be preferred over another because it has been rewarded more often in the past; the reaction potential ($_sE_R$) associated with it will therefore be higher.

Hull's Contribution: A Brief Evaluation

Abstract and apparently remote theoretical systems such as that advanced by Hull (and his student Kenneth Spence) are sometimes met with indifference or skepticism. Yet there are at least two important reasons for studying this theory. One is that understanding the system contributes greatly to an understanding of later theoretical developments. Another is that the system is such an overwhelming example of theory building (or attempted theory building) that it deserves to be studied simply for that reason.

With respect to the criteria that we have been employing to evaluate psychological theories, Hull's formulations present some difficulties. To begin with, we cannot easily assert that they reflect the facts even as they were known at the time, because much of this theorizing is speculative. Hull's system consists largely of what are termed *logical constructs*. These are entities that are inferred; they follow logically from what is observed, but they cannot themselves be observed. Thus reaction potential, aggregate inhibitory potential, behavioral oscillation, incentive motivation, and the raft of other related intervening variables cannot be shown to be facts. This does not mean that they are invalid or that inferred entities have no place in psychological theorizing. Rather, logical constructs, like other theoretical "truths," should be judged in terms of their usefulness.

Are Hull's intervening variables useful? Clearly within the system itself they are immensely useful, providing a compelling logic. That they contribute to explanations of human behavior, that they lead to more accurate predictions than would otherwise be the case, that they are clear and understandable, and that they are based on few unverified assumptions is not nearly so apparent. Ironically, then, in spite of the impressive logic and mathematics that are fundamental to the Hull system, his theory does not fare particularly well with respect to our criteria.

But Hull's system contributed in a number of tangible ways to the advancement of psychological theory. First, the introduction of concepts such as fractional antedating goal reactions foreshadowed more cognitive concerns. Second, Hull has had a profound influence on the design of a wide variety of psychological experiments. This influence has resulted largely from his insistence on precision, rigor, and quantification, as well as his emphasis on logical consistency. This last characteristic of his system most sets Hull apart from other learning theorists.

It remains true, however, that Hull's system has failed where he most wanted it to succeed: Behavior remains largely unpredictable. His failure has discouraged others from attempting the development of such formal and inclusive systems. Instead, smaller systems dealing with a limited number of aspects of learning are typically advanced.

Summary

1. Thorndike's attempts to determine whether animals think—whether they are intelligent in human terms—resulted in his trial-and-error connectionism.

2. Two alternative explanations for the formation of relationships between stimuli (S–S), between responses (R–R), or between stimuli and responses (S–R) are contiguity and reinforcement. The contiguity explanation maintains that the co-occurrence of the events in question is sufficient; the reinforcement position takes into consideration the consequences of behavior. Watson and Guthrie were contiguity theorists; reinforcement is central in Thorndike and Hull's theories.

3. Thorndike described learning as involving the formation of bonds (connections) between neural events corresponding to stimuli and responses. Learning involves stamping in bonds; forgetting involves stamping out bonds.

4. Thorndike's major contribution is his Law of Effect, which specifies that the effect of a response will be instrumental in determining

whether it will be stamped in or out. After 1930, he stressed that pleasure is much more effective in stamping in responses than pain is in stamping them out. Before 1930 he also believed that repetition (the Law of Exercise) was important, but he rejected this notion after 1930.

5. Readiness (the idea that when an organism is ready to learn, to do so is satisfying) was an important part of Thorndike's pre-1930 system; belongingness (the belief that things that are seen as belonging together are learned more readily) became more important after 1930.

6. Five subsidiary laws also form part of Thorndike's system. Most important is the law of multiple response (learning occurs through trial and error). Other laws state that behavior is generalizable (response by analogy), that culture and attitude affect behavior (set or attitude), that people are selective in responding (prepotency of elements), and that stimulus substitution or transfer (associative shifting) occurs.

7. Among Thorndike's most important contributions are his emphasis on the importance of the consequences of behavior (reward and punishment), popularization of the use of animals in psychological research, and a determined attempt to apply psychological principles to real problems, particularly in the area of education.

8. Hull's analysis of behavior is a highly formalized attempt to account for behavior in terms of the precise relationships thought to exist between input, intervening, and output variables. It is a hypothetico-deductive system based on 17 laws (called postulates) from which more than 100 theorems and many corollaries are derived.

9. A summary of the major Hullian variables and the relationships that exist between them is given by the equation $sE_R = sH_R \times D \times V \times K$. It states that reaction potential is the product of habit strength, drive, stimulus-intensity dynamism, and incentive motivation. If reaction potential (the tendency to respond) minus inhibitory potential (a tendency not to respond based on work involved and previous habits of not responding) is greater than a threshold value, a response occurs. Even within this system, however, behavior is not completely predictable because the value of reaction potential varies (that is, oscillates) around a fixed point.

10. Two Hullian concepts that are of special significance in the development of learning theories are those of fractional antedating goal responses and habit-family hierarchies. The former is a behavior that precedes the reaching of a goal but becomes associated with the goal through conditioning and hence acquires reinforcing properties. Habit families are hierarchical arrangements of habits that are related by virtue of the fact that they have common goals.

11. The concept of fractional antedating goal responses represents Hull's behavioristic definition of expectancy or purpose, and it foreshadows important cognitive concerns.

12. In spite of the impressive mathematics and logic of the Hull system, it does not fare well with respect to several criteria of good theories. Not

only is it based on a number of untested assumptions, but it does not always explain clearly or lead easily to useful predictions. Nevertheless, its contribution to the further development of learning theories is vast. In addition, Hull's work profoundly influenced a wide variety of psychological experiments.

Skinner's Position: Operant Conditioning

It is dangerous and foolish to deny the existence of a science of behavior in order to avoid its implications.

B. F. Skinner (1973)

Preliminary Note for Human Readers: Chapter 4 Objectives

I might comment that these little notes at the beginning of each chapter are absent in the Koronian edition of this text; Korons don't need to be told where they're going or why.

You do. So allow me to tell you that this chapter deals with what is undoubtedly the most influential and the best known of all the behaviorist positions, that of Burrhus F. Skinner. Some of you, when you finish this chapter, will undoubtedly have been converted to behaviorism. You'll know this has happened when the dreams—perhaps even the nightmares—that awaken you in the night are no longer about the lotteries you fantasize winning or the dramas of which you are the perpetual hero. They will deal instead with the following:

- Respondents and operants
- The basics of operant learning
- Effects of different schedules of reinforcement
- The nature and uses of punishment
- Possible origins of superstition
- What is meant by terms like fading, generalization, discrimination, aversive control, and rat
- How to unwind your dog . . . or your grandmother

If you try to operationalize the last item, please take into consideration all of the ethical issues involved, and treat your dog with respect.

SIXTH TIME CUBE, 49TH HEXALOG, POINT 221.15

The Lefrançois dog, an animal for which I personally have little use, has a number of habits I find strange. One is that whenever she is about to lie down on the rug at the foot of my bed, she first spins around in a tight circle counterclockwise until she has completed three, sometimes four, rotations. Then she flops down, her bones thumping loudly through the mat, almost as though she might be trying to wake me as I rest from these labors.

"Why," said I to Doctor L. one day, "does she do this, your dog?" But he was busy just then, I think, and probably didn't hear me.

Another thing she does happens when we're all sitting there at the table in the kitchen eating. She comes in from the living room, sniffs a couple of times as if she's trying to decide whether or not she's interested, and then walks out again. Nine times out of ten, she comes back within a couple of minutes with a chewed-up, slobbered-on slipper, which she stuffs vigorously onto Doctor L.'s lap. (She tried mine once, and I bit her ear—not off, not even real hard, but what was I to do?) Next thing she does is park her rump on the floor, lift up her paw, and wrap it over her head, which makes her look rather stupid.

"Why's she do that?" said I. Again, I don't know if he heard me.[1]

Skinner's Theoretical Orientation

In this chapter, there are explanations for both these canine behaviors—and many other things as well. They are found in Skinner's theory.

Was Skinner Antitheoretical?

That Skinner even has a theory may seem strange to some, given that he is widely considered to have been deliberately antitheoretical. In 1950, he wrote an article entitled "Are theories of learning necessary?" (Skinner, 1950). His answer, in one word, was no. In a later article he declared that theories, though they could be amusing to their creators, were of little practical value (Skinner, 1961).

Hordes of Skinner's critics—and supporters as well—concluded that Skinner was against all theories, that he had, as Westby (1966) put it, developed the "Grand Anti-Theory." Skinner disagreed. "Fortunately I had defined my terms," he said of his original article (Skinner, 1969, p. vii). The type of theory he objected to is expressed very clearly in that article: "Any explanation of an observed fact which appeals to events taking place somewhere else."

As an example of the kind of theorizing to which he most strongly objected, Skinner (1969) described an educational film he had recently seen. To illustrate a reflex, this film showed electrical impulses (which looked like flashes of lightning) running up neural pathways, finally appearing on a television screen in the brain. A little man in the brain would then burst into action, pulling a lever that sent return flashes of lightning scurrying down the neural pathways to muscles, which then responded to complete the reflex.

This is a very old explanation for human behavior that dates back to the ancient Greeks, who attributed behavior to a little **homunculus**—a little man inside the big man (or woman, presumably). In Skinner's view, psychological theorizing often takes the form of inventing "little men" in the brain: for example, Freud's notions of the subconscious or cognitive psychology's descriptions of mental maps or other unobserved "fictions" (Skinner's term). These are misleading and wasteful, Skinner claims; they suggest mysterious intellectual activities and do little to advance science. "Behavior is one of those subject matters," says Skinner (1969), "which do not call for hypothetico-deductive methods. Both behavior itself and most of the variables of which it is a function are usually conspicuous" (p. xi).

---

[1] I heard, and I answered immediately—completely and clearly. Kro simply wasn't paying attention just then, possibly because the dog had tried again to place the slipper on his rather indefinite lap. And I'm sure he didn't mean literally that he bit her ear; I think he was trying to use the idiomatic expression "I bit her head off" but screwed it up—as he so often did in such attempts. (GRL)

Skinner's View of Theory and Behavior

To summarize, what Skinner objected to were theories whose explanations can't actually be seen or measured. In fact, his acceptance of the central function of theories could scarcely be more explicit: "A theory is essential to the scientific understanding of behavior as a subject matter" (Skinner, 1969, p. viii). His point is simply that theory should be limited to organizing relationships and events that can be observed.

Two Basic Assumptions

Skinner's theory is based on two fundamental assumptions. First, he believed that human behavior follows certain laws. Second, although psychology has typically looked for the causes of behavior *within* the person, Skinner started (and ended) with the absolute conviction that its causes are *outside* the person, and that these can be observed and studied.

Accordingly, Skinner's theory is the result of a search for the laws that govern behavior. As such, it takes a clearly objective, descriptive form and not a highly inferential, speculative one. Interestingly, it is precisely for this reason that his work remains free from sound, invalidating criticism. The main critics are those who interpret Skinner's system as implying that principles of operant conditioning can eventually be used to explain and control *all* human behavior, and that the principles can then be misapplied. Other critics include those who feel that the Skinnerian view of lawful and unexplainable behavior somehow makes humans less than they are. We will look at these criticisms again toward the end of this chapter.

BURRHUS FREDERIC SKINNER (1904–1990)

B. F. Skinner—he was called Fred; Burrhus was his mother's maiden name—is one of the giants of 20th-century psychology. He was born in Susquehannah, Pennsylvania, in 1904 to a staunchly Presbyterian (and Republican) family. His father was a successful, though largely self-taught lawyer. His mother was an attractive woman who, Skinner claimed, always stood for 20 minutes after every meal to maintain her figure and her posture. Skinner also confessed that he thought she was frigid.

Like many of psychology's pioneers, Skinner did not enter college with the intention of becoming a psychologist, majoring instead in English at Hamilton College in New York. At the end of his undergraduate career, he met Robert Frost, who read some of the things Skinner had written. Frost's suggestion that he might have some talent convinced Skinner he should be a novelist, and so he asked his father to support him for a year while he wrote his first novel. His father reluctantly agreed, and Skinner spent what he was later to describe as "my dark year at Scranton" discovering that he had nothing to say.

Subsequently he undertook graduate studies at Harvard. From the beginning, Skinner was an avowed behaviorist; he found psychology fascinating and already dreamed of "making over the entire field to suit myself" (Skinner, 1979, p. 38). In 1931 he obtained his Ph.D. in psychology and spent the next five years doing research before beginning a career as lecturer, researcher, and writer (at Minnesota, Indiana, and Harvard, in that order). Chief among his early works was *The Behavior of Organisms* (1938), which laid the groundwork for operant conditioning principles. A novel, *Walden Two* (1948), did much to popularize his conception of an ideal society based on scientific principles of human behavior and engineered in such a way that positive rather than aversive techniques of control would predominate. By the late 1950s Skinner had become recognized as the leading proponent of the behavioristic position, a position that he continued to develop and defend throughout his life.

In addition to numerous clearly written scholarly books and articles, Skinner—perhaps ever the frustrated novelist—wrote three autobiographical books totaling more than a thousand pages (Skinner, 1976, 1979, 1983).

Basic Variables in the System

The causes of behavior, Skinner insisted, are outside the organism. The whole point of a science of human behavior, then, is to discover and describe the laws that govern interactions between the organism and the environment. To do so, the psychologist must specify three things: "(1) the occasion upon which a response occurs, (2) the response itself, and (3) the reinforcing consequences" (Skinner, 1969, p. 7).

Skinner's observations deal with two kinds of variables: independent variables (factors that can be directly manipulated experimentally, like reinforcement) and dependent variables (the characteristics of actual behaviors, like rate of responding). Dependent variables are not manipulated by the experimenter but are affected by the independent variables. The goal is to describe the laws that govern relationships between dependent and independent variables. Achieving this goal would make it possible to increase and refine control over dependent variables—in other words, to control behavior. The essential elements of the system, viewed in terms of dependent and independent variables, are summarized in Table 4.1.

Two Types of Learning

In his attempts to explain behavior, Skinner had available the classical conditioning explanation that had already been proposed by Pavlov and elaborated on by people like Watson and Guthrie. But it seemed to him that classical conditioning explained only a very limited variety of human and animal behavior. Specifically, classical conditioning explains the acquisition of behaviors *only* where the initial response can be elicited by a known stimulus. The learning that then occurs results from pairing this stimulus with another over a number of trials.

Though Skinner accepted this model as accurate for explaining some behavior, he declared that many of the responses that people manifest do not result from obvious stimuli. He further maintained that the stimuli, whether

TABLE 4.1   Skinner's System

Independent variables	Dependent variables
Type of reinforcement	Acquisition rate
Schedules of reinforcement	Rate of responding
	Extinction rate

observable or not, are often not important for an accurate and useful explanation of learning.

Respondents and Operants

Responses elicited by a stimulus are labeled **respondents**; responses simply emitted by an organism are labeled **operants**. In respondent behavior the organism reacts *to* the environment, while in operant behavior it acts *on* the environment. In a sense, respondents correspond to involuntary behavior, whereas operants are more voluntary. Skinner would probably not have said this, however, because the terms imply what he would have considered unnecessary speculation. We don't need to ask or wonder whether the organism wants or doesn't want to do something, Skinner insists; we need only note what it does, the circumstances under which it acts, and the consequences of its actions. These three things, taken together, are the *contingencies* of behavior. And the experimental analysis of behavior requires nothing more—or less—than the analysis of these contingencies.

Skinner suggested that classical conditioning only works on respondent behavior. Skinner called this type of learning *Type S* (for stimulus) conditioning. He advanced a different model to explain learning based on operant behavior: the model of operant or instrumental conditioning, also referred to as *Type R* (for response) conditioning. The distinctions between these two forms of learning are detailed in Table 4.2.

Prevalence of Operant Behavior

Skinner (1938) believed that most of the important behaviors in which people engage are operant. Walking to school, writing a letter or a textbook, answering a question, smiling at a stranger, fondling a rat, fishing, shoveling snow, skiing, and reading are all examples of operant behavior. Although there might be some known and observable stimuli that reliably lead to some of these behaviors, the point is that these stimuli are not central in any learning that takes place. What is central are the consequences of the responses.

The Darwinian Influence

Skinner's most fundamental ideas owed a great deal to Charles Darwin as well as to Edward Thorndike. Darwin believed that in nature, all sorts of different traits appear; forces of nature act to select those that contribute to survival— precisely because they *do* contribute to survival. Similarly, in behavior all sorts of responses appear; their consequences act upon these responses, selecting

TABLE 4.2   Classical and Operant Conditioning

Classical (Pavlov)	Operant (Skinner)
Deals with respondents that are elicited as responses to stimuli and appear involuntary Type S (stimuli)	Deals with operants that are emitted as instrumental acts and appear voluntary Type R (reinforcement)

some and eliminating others. Thorndike made this observation the cornerstone of his theory of trial-and-error learning. And Skinner based his theory of operant learning on much the same idea. In a nutshell, operant learning is the survival (and death) of responses. "Both in natural selection and in operant conditioning," Skinner (1973) wrote, "consequences take over a role previously assigned to an antecedent creative mind" (p. 264).

A Pavlov Harness and a Skinner Box

When Pavlov placed a dog in a sling and injected food powder or an acid solution into its mouth, it salivated. That is a clear and unambiguous example of a respondent—of a stimulus reliably eliciting a predictable response.

In his investigations, Skinner used a dramatically different, highly innovative piece of equipment. It has come to be known as a **Skinner box**; he called it an *experimental space*. The most typical of these experimental spaces is a cagelike structure that can be equipped with a lever, a light, a food tray, a food-releasing mechanism, and perhaps an electric grid through the floor (see Figure 4.1).

When a naive rat is placed in this box, it doesn't respond as predictably and automatically as does the dog in the Pavlov harness. Instead it might cower for a while; then it might sniff around the cage, occasionally rearing up on its hind legs to smell the bars, spending a little more time near the food tray as it senses the faint odors of some other rat's long-eaten reward. Eventually the rat might happen to depress the lever, causing a food pellet to drop into the tray. The rat will eat this pellet; in time, it will depress the lever again. After a while, the rat will run straight to the lever whenever it is put into the cage. Its behavior has changed as a result of that behavior's consequences: The rat has been operantly conditioned.

How Operant Responses Change

Stated very simply, the operant conditioning explanation says that when a response—regardless of the conditions that might or might not have led to its emission—is followed by a reinforcer, the result will be an increase in the probability that this response will occur again under similar circumstances. Further, the explanation states that the circumstances surrounding reinforcement may serve as a **discriminative stimulus** (abbreviated S^D) that can come to have control over the

(a) Light   (b) Food tray   (c) Bar or lever
          (d) Electric grid   (e) Rat

FIGURE 4.1   A Skinner box. Skinner called it an "experimental space."

response. Essentially any behavior that is acquired as a result of reinforcement can be interpreted as an illustration of operant conditioning. Figure 4.2 shows one example: a fly fisherman who becomes conditioned to using a certain type of fly because he has been reinforced for using it in the past.

Not S–R Learning

Note that unlike Thorndike's explanation, Skinner's theory of reinforcement does not involve the formation of associations between stimuli and responses. In fact, Skinner took pains to point out that he was not an S–R theorist. By definition, an operant is *never* elicited. Thus, although the rat in the Skinner box might eventually learn to press the lever only when a light is turned on, this particular discriminative stimulus does not *elicit* bar pressing, claims Skinner. It simply allows the rat to discriminate reinforcing situations from those that aren't reinforcing.

The extent of the applicability of this model to human behavior becomes evident through a discussion of the variables involved.

REINFORCEMENT

Skinner's explanation of learning through operant conditioning is based on the notion that the consequences of behavior determine the probability that the behavior will occur again. The concept is very similar to Thorndike's belief that

A. Operant conditioning

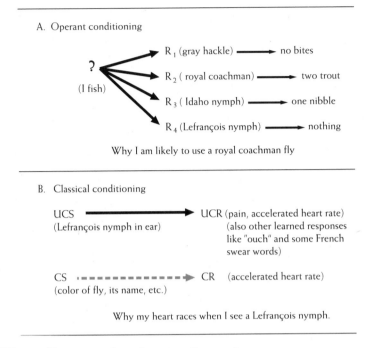

Why I am likely to use a royal coachman fly

B. Classical conditioning

UCS ——————————————▶ UCR (pain, accelerated heart rate)
(Lefrançois nymph in ear)   (also other learned responses
                                    like "ouch" and some French
                                    swear words)

CS ◼ ◼ ◼ ◼ ◼ ◼ ◼ ◼ ◼ ◼ ▶ CR   (accelerated heart rate)
(color of fly, its name, etc.)

Why my heart races when I see a Lefrançois nymph.

FIGURE 4.2   Two types of conditioning, illustrated.

responses that lead to "satisfying states of affairs" are more likely to be learned. Subjective terms such as *satisfying* and *annoying*, however, have no place in a theory as clearly and explicitly objective as Skinner's. Accordingly, Skinner defines a reinforcer as *an event that follows a response and that changes the probability of a response's occurring again.* Reinforcement is simply the observed effect of a reinforcer.

This definition makes it unnecessary to speculate about what is pleasant or unpleasant. Whether an event is reinforcing or not depends solely on its effects; its intrinsic nature is irrelevant. Thus the same event might be reinforcing on one occasion, but not on another.

To illustrate, consider Henry, a freckle-faced, lovable little school child of 10. Henry takes a spelling test for which he has studied very hard, using a number of mnemonic devices. For example, to remember how to spell *separate*, he talked himself into remembering that there is "a rat" in the word. He receives a score of 95% on his spelling test. This event serves as a reinforcer; it increases the probability that Henry will again use mnemonics.

Now consider Agnes, a bright little girl who always gets 100% in spelling without using mnemonic tricks. But this time she does use one; in fact, she uses the same mnemonic device as Henry. Unlike Henry, though, she becomes confused on the test and thinks there is "erat" in *separate*. She also receives a grade of 95%. This event is not a reinforcer for Agnes, however, and will probably have the opposite effect on her behavior.

Types of Reinforcement

Skinner distinguishes between two types of reinforcement: positive and negative. **Positive reinforcement** involves a positive consequence of a behavior—that is, it occurs when the consequences of the behavior, when *added to* a situation immediately after a response, increase the probability of the response's occurring again in similar circumstances. In common speech, this type of reinforcement is similar to *reward*.

Negative reinforcement involves a behavior that results in the elimination or prevention of a negative outcome. It occurs when the probability of a response's occurring increases as a function of something being *taken away from* a situation. In everyday speech, negative reinforcement is similar to *relief*.

Note that the effect of both positive and negative reinforcement is to *increase* the probability of a response's occurring. Note, too, that the effect of the event—not the nature of the stimulus itself—determines whether or not it is reinforcing.

Punishment

Like reinforcement, **punishment** is also defined in terms of its effects. In this case, however, the effect is not a strengthening of the behavior but rather a suppression of it.

In the same way as there are two types of reinforcers—positive (reward) and negative (relief)—there are two types of punishment, each the converse of a type of reinforcer. One is the kind of punishment that occurs when a pleasant stimulus is removed (what might be termed a *penalty*); the other, where an unpleasant event follows a behavior, is what is more commonly thought of as punishment.

Punishment Versus Negative Reinforcement

Punishment and negative reinforcement are often confused, but they are really quite different. Negative reinforcement is an event that *increases* the probability of a behavior; punishment does not. Consequently, negative reinforcement typically involves the termination of an event that might be considered aversive; punishment involves introducing an aversive event or terminating a pleasant one.

Any lingering confusion can easily be clarified by reference to Table 4.3, which shows the four possibilities that result when either pleasant or aversive events follow behavior or terminate following behavior. In everyday speech, these four possibilities represent reward (positive reinforcement), relief (negative reinforcement), penalty (one kind of punishment), or castigation (another kind of punishment). Each of these four possibilities is illustrated below with a rat and then with a person.

TABLE 4.3   Reinforcement and Punishment

	Pleasant event	Noxious event
Added to a situation after a response	Positive reinforcement (reward) [Sam is given a dollar for behaving well]	Punishment I (castigation) [Sam has his ears pulled for misbehaving]
Taken away from a situation after a response	Punishment II (penalty) [Sam has his dollar taken away for misbehaving]	Negative reinforcement (relief) [Sam's ears are released when he behaves well again]

Illustrations of Reinforcement and Punishment

The rat illustrations relate to the behavior of a typical rat in a Skinner box; the people illustrations refer to the behavior of Bill, a typical toddler on this planet.

Positive Reinforcement (Reward)

If the food mechanism releases a pellet of food into the tray when the rat depresses the lever, the effect may be an increase in the probability that bar-pressing behavior will occur again. In this case, the food is a positive reinforcer; its effect is positive reinforcement. It leads to an increase in the preceding behavior.

If toddler Bill offers to kiss his mother one morning, and she praises him for this touching filial gesture, there may be an increase in the probability of this kind of behavior in the future. Mama's praise is a positive reinforcer.

Negative Reinforcement (Relief)

If the current is on continuously in the grid but is turned off every time the rat presses the lever, there will again be an increase in the probability of bar-pressing behavior. In this case, termination of the electric current is a negative reinforcer; its effect is negative reinforcement. It, too, leads to an increase in the behavior that precedes it.

If toddler Bill is later isolated in his room while having a temper tantrum or crying fit (because his mother insists that no, he can't sit on the cat like on a horse), allowing him to come out when he stops crying illustrates negative reinforcement. This event may increase the probability that he will stop crying when again in this situation.

Punishment I (Castigation)

If the rat, which must stand on the electric grid when it depresses the bar, is given a mild shock every time it does so, it will probably attempt to avoid the bar in the future. The shock in this case is one type of punishment, and it may lead to avoidance (or escape learning). It does *not* lead to an increase in the rat's bar-pressing behavior.

Note, however, that although the electric shock in this case serves as punishment for bar pressing, it is also an example of negative reinforcement *with respect to avoidance learning.* That is, if the removal of the shock leads to an *increase* in avoidance behavior, it serves as negative reinforcement for that behavior. If, at the same time, it leads to a *decrease* in bar pressing, it serves as punishment for *that* behavior.

If toddler Bill kicks his sister in the posterior, and she turns around and whacks him on the side of the head, he may be less likely to kick her again in similar circumstances or places. The sister's whack is a castigation kind of punishment with respect to Bill's kicking.

Punishment II (Penalty)

Once the rat has been trained, if the experimenter *removes* the food pellet unless the rat gets to it within a specified period of time after pressing the lever, the rat may soon stop dawdling and licking its chops on the way to the food tray. In this illustration, removal of the food pellet is an example of punishment involving a penalty. The responses being punished are those that delay the rat.[2]

If toddler Bill has his jelly beans taken away at lunchtime because he licked them, rubbed them on the wall, ground them into the floor, and then hurled them at his sister, this is an example of a penalty punishment. It might decrease the probability of some of his jelly bean behaviors.

Sources of Reinforcement

In addition to distinguishing between positive and negative reinforcement, Skinner describes reinforcers that are primary, secondary, and/or generalized. **Primary reinforcers** include events that are reinforcing without any learning having taken place. Examples of primary reinforcers are stimuli such as food, water, and sex, each of which satisfies basic, unlearned needs (primary needs).

Secondary reinforcers include events that are not reinforcing to begin with but become reinforcing as a result of being paired with a primary reinforcer. The light in the Skinner box is sometimes used as a secondary reinforcer. Over a succession of trials, it is turned on every time the animal is fed (given a primary reinforcer). Eventually the animal will respond simply to have the light go on. At this point, the light has acquired secondary reinforcing properties.

A **generalized reinforcer** is a secondary reinforcer that has been paired with a number of different primary reinforcers; as a result, it can reinforce any of a wide variety of behaviors. For humans, generalized reinforcers include things like money, prestige, power, fame, strength, intelligence, and a host of other culturally prized attributes. Manifestations of these attributes constitute generalized reinforcers that are extremely powerful in determining human behavior.

---

[2]This, Kro admitted, is a hypothetical illustration. He could find no evidence in the literature that anyone had actually conducted this experiment. And he claimed he had no time to do it himself. (GRL)

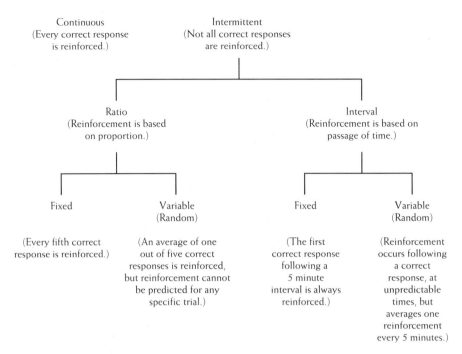

FIGURE 4.3   Schedules of reinforcement.

SCHEDULES OF REINFORCEMENT

To develop a science of behavior, Skinner insisted, the psychologist needs to observe what the organism does, under what circumstances, and to what effect. In the studies that proved most useful for developing his views of operant conditioning, rats depressed levers, or pigeons pecked at disks. These are easily observed behaviors that Skinner could quantify in terms of how rapidly they were acquired (acquisition rate), how many responses were emitted over a given period of time (rate of responding), and how long it would take for the responses to stop if reinforcement were discontinued (extinction rate). Recall that these represent *dependent* variables; they are not under the investigator's control.

Probably the most easily manipulated and most effective *independent* variable in operant conditioning is the way rewards are administered. In a carefully controlled laboratory situation, experimenters can determine precisely what reinforcements will be used and how and when they will be used. In other words, experimenters are in complete control of **schedules of reinforcement**.

Continuous or Intermittent Reinforcement

Basically, the experimenter has two choices: **continuous reinforcement**, in which case every desired response is reinforced, or **intermittent** (or partial) **reinforcement**, where reinforcement occurs only some of the time (see Figure 4.3). If reinforcement is continuous, there are no further choices to make; every correct response is rewarded in the same way. (It is entirely possible, however, to use a combination of continuous and intermittent reinforcement schedules. This type of arrangement is sometimes referred to as a *combined schedule*.)

Interval or Ratio Schedules

If experimenters use an intermittent schedule of reinforcement, they can make one of two further choices. The intermittent schedule can be based on a proportion of responses (termed a **ratio schedule**) or on the passage of time (called an **interval schedule**). For example, a ratio schedule might reinforce one out of five desired responses; an interval schedule might provide reinforcement once every 5 minutes.

Fixed or Random Ratio and Interval Schedules

An experimenter using either of these intermittent schedules (ratio or interval) would further have to decide whether the reinforcement would be administered in a fixed or in a random (variable) way. A **fixed schedule** is one in which the experimenter predetermines the exact time or the precise response that will be followed by a reinforcing event. For example, in the case of a fixed-ratio schedule, reinforcement might occur after every fifth correct response. Fixed-interval reinforcement might occur at the very beginning of each 5-minute interval, but only immediately after a correct response.

Random schedules provide reinforcing events at unpredictable times. A random ratio schedule of reinforcement based on a proportion of one reinforcement to five responses might involve reinforcing the first 4 trials, not reinforcing the next 16, reinforcing numbers 21 and 22, not reinforcing the next 8 trials, and so on. After 100 trials, 20 reinforcers would have been administered.

Superstitious Schedules

A special kind of fixed-interval schedule is one where reinforcement occurs at fixed time intervals *without the requirement that there be a correct response*. It follows from the law of operant conditioning that any behavior just prior to reinforcement is strengthened. Whether the behavior is related to the reinforcement in a causal manner is not always important; it seems that for both humans and other animals, temporal contiguity alone is enough to establish a relationship between reinforcement and behavior.

Numerous examples of superstitious behavior in animals are cited in the literature. In fact, it appears that in most conditioning sequences there are behaviors that accidentally precede reinforcement and temporarily become part of the animal's repertoire. For example, a rat that has just learned to depress a lever may do so with its head always to the right or with its left leg always dangling. Both actions are examples of superstitious behavior.

Skinner (1951) left six pigeons on a superstitious schedule overnight; they received reinforcement at fixed intervals no matter what they were doing. By morning, one bird regularly turned clockwise just before each reinforcement, another always pointed its head toward one corner, and several had developed unnatural swaying motions.

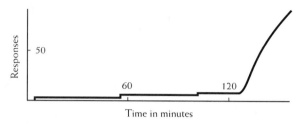

FIGURE 4.4   A cumulative recording showing the responses of a naive rat on a continuous schedule of reinforcement. Passage of time is shown on the X axis; total number of responses on the Y axis. Note how, after four reinforcements, this rat's rate of responding increased dramatically. From *The Behavior of Organisms: An Experimental Analysis,* p. 67, by B.F. Skinner. Copyright © 1938 by Appleton Century-Crofts. Reprinted by permission of Prentice-Hall, Inc.

There is no better place to observe superstitious behavior associated with thinking than in an examination room crowded with human students at the end of a semester. Some people scratch their heads; others frown; some move their lips, hands, legs, or feet; some chew their hair, and others engage in a variety of behaviors not causally related to clear thinking.

Effects of Different Schedules

The importance of schedules of reinforcement has to do with their possible effects on responding.

Cumulative Records

Responses like pressing a bar or pecking at a key are easily observed and measured. Skinner used a simple but ingenious way of recording such responses by having a pen trace a line on a continually moving drum of paper. Every response (bar press or key peck) causes the pen to jump up one step, thus providing a **cumulative recording** of the number of responses on the Y (or upright) axis. The rate of responding, which is the number of responses emitted during a fixed period of time, is indicated on the X (or horizontal) axis because of the movement of the drum; the faster the animal responds, the steeper will be the line on this recording. A line that stays parallel to the X axis indicates that no response occurred during the time period marked.

Figure 4.4, for example, shows a cumulative recording produced by Skinner (1938) of the bar-pressing responses of an initially untrained rat. In the training session, all lever-pressing responses were reinforced. Note how the first three reinforcements (responses, and hence reinforcements, are indicated by the first three upward steps in the recording) seemed to have little effect; the rat took almost 120 minutes to press the lever three times. But immediately after the fourth reinforcement, the rate of responding zoomed upward so that almost 100 responses were emitted within the next 30 minutes. When conditioning bar pressing in rats, it isn't uncommon to reach close to a maximum rate of responding in 30 minutes or less.

Effects of Schedules on Acquisition

In training rats to press levers or pigeons to peck disks, Skinner typically deprived the animal of food for 24 or more hours (sometimes reducing its weight to 80% of normal) in order to increase the effectiveness of the reinforcer. Initial training usually begins with "magazine training" during which the animal is trained to eat from the food tray and, consequently, is exposed to the noise made by the food mechanism as it releases food pellets. After magazine training, all correct responses—and sometimes even responses that merely approximate the desired behavior—are reinforced.

Initial learning is usually more rapid if every correct response is reinforced (a continuous schedule). In contrast, changes in responding appear to be haphazard and slow if any of the intermittent schedules of reinforcement are utilized.

Effects on Extinction

One measure of learning relates to number of responses in a given period of time; another is the rate of extinction after the withdrawal of reinforcement.

Interestingly, although a continuous schedule of reinforcement results in a faster rate of learning than does an intermittent schedule, it also leads to more rapid extinction after withdrawal. Further, the fixed schedules of reinforcement, although they have shorter acquisition times associated with them than variable schedules, also lead to more rapid extinction than the variable schedules. Hence the best training combination for an animal is a continuous schedule initially, followed by a variable-ratio schedule. (The ratio may also be varied over training sessions, with a decreasing ratio of reinforced to nonreinforced trials usually leading to even longer extinction periods.)

Figure 4.5 shows a typical extinction curve. Note how rate of responding (indicated by the steepness of the curve) remains unchanged for the first few minutes after reinforcement stops, but then rapidly flattens out (showing that few or no responses are occurring).

Spontaneous Recovery

Recall that a classically conditioned response (like salivation in response to a tone) can be extinguished by presenting the CS (tone) repeatedly without the US (food). Remember, too, that if the CS is presented again after the passage of some time, the CR (salivation) might occur again—a phenomenon Pavlov labeled *spontaneous recovery*.

Spontaneous recovery also occurs in operant learning, as is illustrated in Figure 4.6. "If the rat is replaced in the apparatus at a later time," wrote Skinner (1938), "a small extinction curve will be obtained" (p. 78). In the case shown in Figure 4.6, for example, the first curve shows initial extinction of bar pressing in a rat over a 1-hour period without reinforcement; the adjoining curve shows

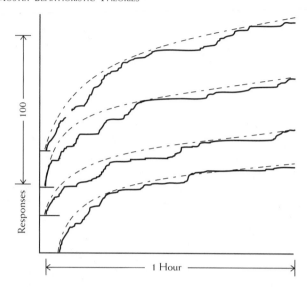

Responses

100

|← —————————— 1 Hour ——————————→|

FIGURE 4.5   A cumulative recording showing four typical extinction curves. Note how rate of responding is high immediately after reinforcement stops, and then occurs in sporadic outbursts until, less than an hour later, few responses still occur. From *The Behavior of Organisms: An Experimental Analysis,* p. 75, by B. F. Skinner. Copyright © 1938 by Appleton Century-Crofts. Reprinted by permission of Prentice-Hall, Inc.

recovery of the same rat's bar-pressing response when placed back in the cage 48 hours later.

Extinction and Forgetting

In Skinner's system, the terms *extinction* and *forgetting* are not identical. Extinction occurs when an animal or person who has been reinforced for engaging in a behavior ceases to be reinforced; the outcome is a relatively rapid cessation of the responses in question. Forgetting, in contrast, is a much slower process that also results in the cessation of a response, but not as a function of withdrawal of reinforcement. According to Skinner, forgetting occurs simply with the passage of time when there is no repetition of the behavior during this time.[3]

These concepts can be illustrated by reference to a pigeon who has been conditioned to peck at a colored disk. If food is used as the reinforcer for this response and this reinforcement is suddenly withdrawn completely, the pigeon will in all likelihood continue to peck at the disk sporadically for some time. In a relatively short time, however, it will cease pecking entirely, at which point extinction will have occurred.

[3]See Chapter 9 for a more detailed discussion of remembering and forgetting. (Kro)

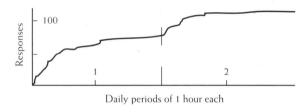

Daily periods of 1 hour each

FIGURE 4.6   A cumulative recording showing initial extinction over a 1-hour period (left half of the graph), and spontaneous recovery of the rat's bar-pressing responses over a second 1-hour period when placed back into the Skinner box 48 hours later. Note how much more rapidly extinction occurs during the second period. From *The Behavior of Organisms: An Experimental Analysis*, p. 69, by B. F. Skinner. Copyright © 1938 by Appleton Century-Crofts. Reprinted by permission of Prentice-Hall, Inc.

As noted above, a behavior that has been extinguished through withdrawal of reinforcement often reappears (that is, spontaneously recovers) without any further conditioning when the animal is again placed in the same situation. The extinction period following spontaneous recovery is almost invariably much shorter than the first. But assume that the pigeon that has been conditioned to peck at a disk is taken out of the cage and not allowed to return to it for a very long period of time. If it does not peck at the disk when it is reintroduced into the cage, one can say that forgetting has occurred. Skinner reported the case of at least one pigeon that had still not forgotten the disk-pecking response after six years. He also reported one instance of a pigeon that emitted 10,000 pecks prior to extinction.

Effects on Rate of Responding

A third measure of learning is the rate of responding, which is a dependent variable that is remarkably sensitive to schedules of reinforcement. It appears that, in general, an animal behaves as would be expected if it is valid to assume that the animal develops expectations and has some time sense. For example, under variable schedules of reinforcement, when the animal is less likely to develop an expectation of receiving a reward at a given time, the rate of responding will be uniformly high and relatively unvarying. If the variable schedule is a ratio schedule rather than an interval one, the rate of responding will be higher. Under a fixed-interval schedule of reinforcement, the rate of responding drops dramatically immediately after reinforcement and often ceases altogether. Just prior to the next reinforcement, however, the animal again responds at a high rate (see Figure 4.7).

Skinner, of course, would not normally use mentalistic concepts such as *expectation* or *goal* or *purpose* to explain why people or animals do things. When he does use such terms, which he does freely when discussing the implications of his science of behavior, he defines them in terms of the organism's reinforce-

ment history. "What gives an action its purpose?" he asks. "The answers to such questions," he then responds, "are eventually to be found in past instances in which similar behavior has been effective" (1969, p. 105).

Scientists need not speculate about goals or expectations; they need only note that this organism has been reinforced this way or that, eventually discovering that there is a relationship between characteristics of the reinforcement and subsequent responding. But to explain this relationship, it's useful to use words like *expectation*.

Schedules of Reinforcement in Everyday Life

Powerful reinforcing events for humans, says Lefrançois, are money, praise, satisfaction, and food.[4] Two of these stimuli, money and food, appear to be on fixed-interval schedules. For a large number of people, money arrives regularly in the form of a paycheck, and food is taken routinely in the form of meals. For both of these rather important reinforcers, however, often there are no immediate, simple operants that predictably result in their presentation. The operants involved in acquiring money have become so complex and so remote from the actual source of reinforcement that it has become difficult to see the relationship between the two. The confusion is further compounded by the fact that the reinforcers themselves are inextricably bound together. That is, money allows one to buy food and—in some cases—praise, satisfaction, and other reinforcers as well.

So the relationship between behavior and reinforcement is not always simple or obvious. But this doesn't invalidate the notion that many human behaviors are affected by reinforcers and their scheduling. Indeed, in many cases, the person whose behavior is affected remains completely unaware of the relationship between behavior and its consequences. There are countless examples of how behavior is controlled and modified by reinforcements.

Illustration 1

A fisherman has fished in the same stream for 22 years. Every time he goes fishing he catches at least four fish (continuous reinforcement). Now, at the beginning of this pollution-conscious decade, he suddenly stops catching fish

---

[4] I didn't say these things in precisely this order. And I also included other extremely powerful reinforcers, like sex, that Kro didn't really understand and so completely ignored. Too bad. (GRL)

(withdrawal of reinforcement). After four fruitless trips to the stream, he stops going altogether (rapid extinction following continuous reinforcement).

Illustration 2

Another man has also fished in the same stream for 22 years. Sometimes he catches fish, and sometimes he doesn't. On occasion he doesn't catch a single fish for an entire season, but he's caught as many as 18 trout in one day (intermittent reinforcement). Now he, too, stops catching fish (withdrawal of reinforcement). At the end of the decade, he might still be going to the same stream (slow extinction following intermittent reinforcement).

Illustration 3

A young child is given her first rattle, not knowing that a cruel but clever psychologist has yanked out its innards. The child holds the rattle up, looks at it, shakes it, bites it, strikes her knee with it, drops it, and forgets it. (The unreinforced response of shaking the rattle is not strengthened.)

Illustration 4

The same infant is given a rattle that has been carefully kept from all psychologists. She looks at it, shakes it, looks at it again, and then proceeds to shake it vigorously for some time (the sound of the rattle serves as a reinforcer and strengthens the operant that precedes it).

Shaping

Why is it so easy to train a rat to press a bar, or a pigeon to peck a disk? Simply because these are among the things that rats and pigeons do. They are operants that almost invariably appear within just a short period of time in the experimental spaces that Skinner and his followers have provided for these animals. Similarly, it would be very easy to train the Lefrançois dog to turn in tight little circles because that is one of the things this dog does.

"We can not teach cows to retrieve a stick because this is one of the things that cows do not do," claims Guthrie (1935, p. 45). The same is thought to be true of horses. Yet at the National Finals Rodeo to which Lefrançois dragged me last week, there was a guy with a horse that not only fetched things the man would throw—much like a dog might—but that also sat down when he was

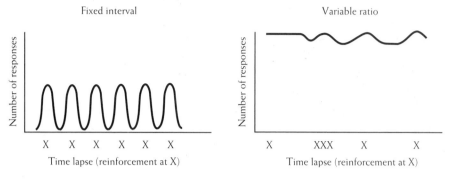

FIGURE 4.7   Idealized representation of the effects of two schedules of reinforcement on rate of responding.

invited to do so. This horse's behavior had been shaped using operant conditioning techniques.

Shaping is the technique used to train animals to perform acts that are not ordinarily in their repertoire. It isn't required for behaviors like pressing a bar in a Skinner box, because bar pressing is one of the behaviors the rat emits in the course of exploring the environment. But if the experimenter wanted to train a rat to go to corner A of the cage, pick up a marble in that corner, carry it to corner B, drop it there, return to the center of the cage, lie down, roll over, get up, return to corner B, pick up the marble again, and carry it to corner C, the rat would probably die of old age before it emitted the operant.

Nevertheless it is possible, through shaping, to teach a rat to engage in behaviors that are very impressive, if not as complex as the behavior described above. An experimenter using the technique of shaping reinforces every behavior that takes the animal closer to the final response, instead of waiting for the final desired response to be emitted. For this reason, shaping is sometimes referred to as the *method of successive approximations*, or as a method involving the *differential reinforcement of successive approximations* (Skinner, 1951).

Most animal trainers employ techniques that amount to shaping procedures. Thus parrots are trained to walk on tightropes, parachute, play tunes, and ride bicycles; porpoises to jump incredible heights with military precision in predetermined order; bears to play guitars, dance, roll somersaults, and clap hands; chickens to play ball; and horses to sit down.

One important requirement for the successful use of shaping procedures is that the environment be controlled. For example, the Skinner box is constructed so that the rat can't perform very many responses other than those the experimenter wants to reinforce. Similarly, a professional animal trainer would not attempt to condition a dog when the dog is chasing a rabbit but would first confine the dog and get its attention. In other words, the environment is arranged to facilitate the appearance of the desired response.

Chaining

An important phenomenon in operant learning is **chaining**, the linking of sequences of responses. Even a behavior as apparently simple as pressing a

bar in a Skinner box involves sequences of different responses. "Most of the reflexes of the intact organism are parts of chains," said Skinner (1938, p. 52),[5] going on to describe how chains integrate all behavior. For example, he explained, a rat in a Skinner box makes all sorts of responses. Some of those made in the vicinity of the food tray become learned as a result of being associated with discriminative stimuli (S^D), such as the sound of the food mechanism, that have become secondary reinforcers. Initially, the discriminative stimuli that become secondary reinforcers are those directly associated with reinforcement (like the sound of the food mechanism). Over time, though, those discriminative stimuli that are further removed (like the smell of the lever) can also become secondary reinforcers. Thus a chain of responses can be woven together by a sequence of discriminative stimuli, each of which is a secondary reinforcer associated with—in this case—food as a primary reinforcer.

"Such movements become fully conditioned," Skinner (1938) wrote, "and are made with considerable frequency by a hungry rat" (p. 53). Each movement, in sequence, changes the situation and hence the discriminative stimuli, giving rise to the next response. Vastly simplified, the chain involved in bar pressing might be something like this: the sight of the inside of the cage serves as an S^D associated with the response of turning toward the bar; the sight of the bar is an S^D for approaching the bar; proximity to the bar is an S^D for pressing it; the sounds and muscular sensations associated with pressing it are discriminative stimuli for turning toward the food tray; the sight of the food pellet is a stimulus for responses associated with eating.

---

[5]Profoundly influenced by Pavlov, the then-current giant in psychology, Skinner (1938) continued to use the term *reflex* in his first major work, although he was not speaking about simple reflexes of the type investigated by Pavlov. In his later writing, he largely abandoned the term in favor of *operant*, or simply *response* or *behavior*. (Kro)

Chains in Shaping

When a behavior is shaped, chains are established. What the professional animal trainer tries to do is link a series of discriminative stimuli and responses long enough to astound you and perhaps even your grandmother (although she's seen a lot more than you have). This way, in the final performance the trainer doesn't have to hold a steak above the dog's head, yell "Somersault," and move his or her hand quickly backward when the dog leaps for the steak, forcing the animal to describe a crude semicircle in the air. (Your grandmother wouldn't be impressed.)

Holding the steak over the dog's head and "forcing" the somersault is the first step in the chain, because all chaining works backward from a primary reinforcer. Over a period of training sessions, a clever trainer arranges for the conditioning of chains by *differentially reinforcing* certain responses leading to the final and complete sequence of responses. In the end, the dog will bound onto the stage, race through an obstacle course, rescue a drowning baby, spell its name with wooden letters, and finally do a most amazing somersault. And neither you nor your grandmother will ever see the steak.

Shaping and People

Many more human behaviors are probably acquired through shaping than people are aware of. For example, in the course of learning any task involving muscular coordination, a large number of inappropriate or ineffective responses are abandoned, whereas appropriate (and consequently reinforced) responses become more firmly established and linked in chains.

The verbal behavior of people is also susceptible to the effects of reinforcement (Skinner, 1957), a phenomenon that Greenspoon (1955) illustrated experimentally through a technique referred to as *verbal conditioning*. In this study, the experimenter simply interviewed subjects and asked them to say words. The subjects, who had no idea what words were required, began to speak. Each time they said a plural noun, the experimenter reinforced them by saying "Mmhm." Over the course of the training session the incidence of plural nouns increased significantly.

Although this type of experimental procedure may at first glance appear to be somewhat remote from the realities of everyday life, on closer examination it becomes evident that people engage in many behaviors that are examples of the effects of verbal conditioning. For example, a high-pressure door-to-door salesperson often gets customers to commit themselves by employing a verbal conditioning technique. First the salesperson suggests that the customers are intelligent, and then he or she reinforces all declarations of intelligence made spontaneously by the customers. Eventually they will have admitted either that they are so intelligent that they can't pass up such a good deal or that, being so intelligent, they are sufficiently concerned for their children to purchase an encyclopedia.

Since I've been on this planet, I've discovered that verbal fluency (sometimes called verbosity) can sometimes be turned on or off by a skillful listener who reinforces certain responses or withdraws reinforcement through subtle facial expressions and gestures. A rather striking, although sometimes boring, illustration of the power of reinforcement in conversation can easily be provided by almost anyone. The procedure involves simply making the decision that your next conversation will be with someone who will talk only about herself. It is quite likely that by making only a minimum number of comments but by expressing great interest in certain personal expressions, you can easily direct the conversation.[6]

An Illustration

Lefrançois reports trying to demonstrate for a class the power of reinforcement in shaping the verbal behavior of subjects by replicating the Greenspoon experiment with a few variations. A student in a large undergraduate psychology class volunteered to be a subject, and he was asked to leave the room for a few minutes. The Greenspoon experiment was then explained to the other students, and they were instructed to reinforce all plural nouns the subject might emit by paying attention, nodding occasionally (but not too obviously), and smiling from time to time. They were asked to appear less interested when the subject said words that were not plural nouns. The subject was brought back in, seated in front of the class, and asked simply to say anything he wanted. One member of the class surreptitiously recorded the number of plural nouns emitted during each 2-minute interval of the session.

The experiment didn't work as planned for several reasons. For one thing, it appeared that not all members of the class immediately recognized plural nouns. In addition, being a psychology student, the subject was somewhat suspicious and apprehensive. In the end, frequency of plural nouns didn't increase over a 20-minute period. However, what happened was nevertheless a clear illustration of verbal conditioning. It appeared (and it was verified through an interview afterward) that the subject had, on the previous Saturday night, gone to a country dance, drunk himself silly,[7] and then challenged some of the local citizens to display their pugilistic skills for him. As a result he had spent the rest of that night in the local jail.

As this brave subject sat in front of his fellow students the following Monday morning, looking at them through bleary eyes, it was inevitable that he should, in the process of free association, say such sequences of words as "Saturday night, drunk, fight, yippee, . . . police, jail . . . " The mood of the class was such that each of these words occasioned titters and suppressed laughter. And the subject repeated some of them again, when he was uncertain what to say next. In the end the class laughed openly every time he said a Saturday-

---

[6]As I make clear in Chapter 4 of my anthropological report, this planet's human species is in some ways the most self-centered of all the various human species. Paradoxically, many nevertheless display depths of caring and compassion that our own Koronian dictionaries have yet to define. (Kro)

[7]"In these prudish days," writes one reviewer, "the author should try to find another example." That's what I, too, told Kro. But he refused. "If the guy drunk himself silly," he retorted, not really understanding what he was saying, "then that's what he did." (GRL)

night–related word, and these words increased dramatically in frequency as the session progressed. The subject's behavior was being shaped by the reaction of his audience.

Fading, Generalization, and Discrimination

Shaping is one technique employed in training animals to perform complex behaviors. Another is **fading**, a process that involves both generalization and discrimination. Recall that generalization involves making similar responses in different situations; discrimination involves making different responses in similar but discriminably different situations. Fading is best explained through illustration.

Illustration 1: Pigeons Reading

For example, Reese (1966) describes a fading procedure whereby a pigeon is taught to "read" the words *peck* and *turn*. If the pigeon pecks when it sees *peck* and turns when it sees *turn*, says Reese, it will have satisfied the typical conditions for our saying it can read.

This type of training presents some special problems. Although it is relatively simple to train a pigeon either to peck or to turn using a shaping procedure, the bird will then immediately generalize the learned response to the other word. If the pigeon is taught to peck in response to the word *peck*, it will also peck in response to the word *turn*. But if the two stimuli are made highly different so that the pigeon can easily discriminate between the two, it can be taught to respond appropriately to each stimulus through shaping. For example, the word *turn* might be printed in large black letters and the word *peck* in small red letters (pigeons have excellent color vision). After the pigeon has learned to peck and to turn as instructed, the differences between the stimuli are slowly faded out over a number of sessions: the large black letters become smaller, and the small red letters become both darker and larger, until finally each word is black and the letters are of uniform size. The pigeon can now *discriminate* stimuli that would have been very difficult to distinguish without the training.

Illustration 2: Quail Loving

"Copulatory behavior," Domjan, Huber-McDonald, and Holloway (1992) inform us, "rarely occurs in responses to an arbitrary inanimate object" (p. 350). But such behavior can be conditioned through fading. These investigators arranged for male Japanese quail to copulate with live female quail while being exposed to a terry-cloth-covered dummy, prepared by a taxidermist, that had a head and neck made of real female skin and feathers. Over 15 to 20 conditioning trials, the "birdness" of the dummy was gradually faded out as it was progressively covered with terry cloth. In the end, many of the male quail tried to copulate with the cloth-covered lump.

Relevance to Human Learning

Generalization and discrimination are of considerable importance in human learning. Generalization involves engaging in previously learned behaviors in response to new situations that resemble those in which the behaviors were first learned. One example is that of the pigeon turning in response to the word *peck* before it has learned to discriminate between *turn* and *peck*. Another is the perhaps even more impressive finding that pigeons can learn with relative ease to discriminate between spherical and nonspherical stimuli and will, after fewer than 150 trials of training, generalize the "concept" spherical to hundreds of other stimulus objects (Delius, 1992).

Generalization

Examples of generalization in human behavior are numerous. Any 5-minute segment of behavior in the life of a normal person is likely to be filled with instances of old behaviors being generalized to new situations. New cars are driven in ways similar to those used in driving old ones; someone who hits a stranger accidentally may apologize; when faced with the problem of adding 27 kangaroos and 28 zebras, a farmer reasons that the sum is the same as that of 27 pigs and 28 horses; people assume that objects fall from mountaintops as they do from treetops; strangers shake hands when introduced; and on and on. All of these behaviors are examples of responses to new situations that are based on previous learning. It is precisely because not all, or even most, situations to which a person must react in a lifetime can be covered in schools or in other learning situations that generalization is of such crucial importance. Hence teaching for generalization (which is really teaching for transfer) is one of the main functions of schools.

Discrimination

As we saw, discrimination is complementary to generalization in that it involves a subject making distinctions between similar situations in order to respond appropriately to each. The pigeon's learning to respond to the two highly similar situations involved in the presentation of the words *peck* and *turn* is an example of discrimination.

Discrimination learning is probably as important for human behavior as is generalization, particularly in learning socially appropriate behavior. Children must learn to discriminate at relatively early ages which responses are appropriate to which situations. For example, it is permissible to kiss one's parents, but not strangers; sisters should not be punched, but neighborhood bullies can be; it is sinful to make noises in quiet churches but permissible to make the same noises in quiet houses; and so on. Thus socially appropriate behavior is very much a function of having learned to discriminate between similar situations calling for different types of behavior.

The processes of discrimination and generalization are illustrated in Figure 4.8. In the first case, the appropriate response is to eat any of the five vegetables; in other words, a generalization of the eating response is appropriate. In

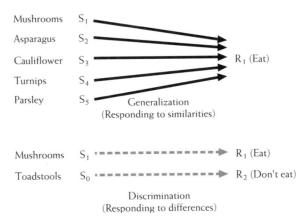

FIGURE 4.8   Discrimination and generalization.

the second case, it is necessary to discriminate between two stimuli. Generalization here is inappropriate.

THE SCIENCE APPLIED TO HUMANS

Although it was initially developed largely through the study of rat and pigeon behavior in highly controlled environments, Skinner's explanation of operant conditioning is as much a science of humans as of other organisms. Skinner saw no important discontinuity between how humans and nonhumans respond to the contingencies of their behaviors. And he considered criticisms that accused the system of neglecting higher mental processes like thinking to be unfair and inaccurate. "A science of behavior does not, as is so often asserted, ignore awareness," he declared. "On the contrary, it goes far beyond mentalistic psychologies in analyzing self-descriptive behavior" (Skinner, 1969, p. 245).

For Skinner (1969), concepts such as awareness and purpose depend on verbal rules that result from analyzing the relationship between behavior and its contingencies: "An advanced verbal community generates a high level of such awareness" (p. 245). But this doesn't mean that people are always aware of the relationships between behavior and consequences. In fact, it is possible to control people through the clever manipulation of rewards and punishments—and societies do just that, claimed Skinner.

Positive Control

As Skinner (1971) notes repeatedly, however, societies make extensive use of *aversive* control when positive control would be far more humane and probably more effective as well. He writes, for example, that the world's major social institutions operate to a large extent through aversive control. These methods are sorely evident in schools, where reprimands, detention, low grades, and threats of punishment are often a more salient fact of a student's daily life than are praise, the granting of favors, the promise of high marks, or the possibility of other important reinforcement.

Positive Control in Schools

It is possible to draw an analogy between a classroom and a Skinner box. In this analogy, teachers are like experimenters; they administer rewards and punishments. Students, in contrast, are analogous to Skinnerian rats; their responses are shaped by their various scheduled consequences.

As experimenters, teachers can profit from knowing that reinforcement is effective in bringing about changes in behavior, that schedules of reinforcement can be varied to good advantage, that punishment is not very effective for learning, and that some reinforcers are more powerful than others. They can profit from greater knowledge about sources of reinforcement. For example, Bijou and Sturges (1959) describe five categories of reinforcers: consumables (such as candy); manipulatables (like toys); visual and auditory stimuli (for example, a bell signal that means "good work"); social stimuli (like praise); and **tokens** (such as disks that can be exchanged for other reinforcers). To this list can be added the **Premack Principle** (Premack, 1965), which states that behavior that occurs frequently and naturally—and that must therefore be reinforcing—can be used to reinforce less frequent behavior. For example, children who read a great deal but dislike arithmetic might be allowed to read if they do an arithmetic assignment.

Each of these classes of reinforcers can be employed effectively by a teacher. Indeed, there are numerous illustrations of their use in psychological literature, particularly in investigations of behavior modification. Briefly, this label describes the systematic application of principles of learning. These principles are typically behavioristic; indeed, most are based directly on operant conditioning. Behavior modification is employed extensively in schools, hospitals, and other institutions and is described and illustrated later in this chapter.

Aversive Control

There are two types of aversive (or negative) control described by Skinner: punishment and negative reinforcement. Recall that these are fundamentally different from each other: Whereas negative reinforcement increases the probability that a response will occur again, punishment usually has the opposite effect.

Against Punishment

Few topics in child-rearing and education have received more attention than punishment. It's interesting that much of this attention results from the prevalence of punishment rather than from its effectiveness. Since Thorndike's (1932) work, it has generally been accepted that punishment is much less effective in eliminating undesirable responses than reinforcement is in bringing about desirable ones.

From a learning theory point of view, a number of practical and theoretical objections to the use of punishment can be raised. First, the likelihood that punishment will lead to appropriate behavior is often remote. Essentially, punishment serves to draw attention to undesirable behavior but does little to indicate what the desirable behavior should be.

Second, instead of eliminating behavior, punishment usually only suppresses it; what is affected is the rate of responding. The advantage that nonreinforcement has over punishment is that, theoretically, it leads to the extinction of the unreinforced behavior.

Third, punishment can lead to emotional states that will probably not be associated with love, happiness, or any other pleasant feeling. Through contiguity, these negative emotional states may become associated with the punisher rather than with the undesirable behavior.

A fourth, more general objection to punishment is that it often does not work. Sears, Maccoby, and Lewin (1957) cite evidence to show that mothers who punish children for toilet accidents are more likely to have children who wet their beds, and those who punish aggression are more likely to have children who are aggressive.

For Punishment

Psychology's most passionate objections to the use of punishment apply primarily to physical punishment. The same objections are not nearly as pertinent with respect to several other forms of punishment, some of which are quite common in schools and homes. These include time-out procedures, response cost, and reprimands.

A **time-out** procedure is one in which children are removed from a situation where they might expect reinforcement and placed in another situation where they are less likely to be reinforced. Children who are removed from a classroom in response to some misbehavior are being punished not by the administration of an unpleasant stimulus (unless, of course, they are sent to the principal's office or given detention) but rather by being removed from what is assumed to be a reinforcing environment. Similarly, when children who have received tangible reinforcers for good behavior later have some of these reinforcers taken away for misbehaviors, they are being exposed to **response-cost** punishment.

Other common punishments include the use of **reprimands**, most of which are verbal, but a number of which might be nonverbal (a negative shake of the head or frown, for example). A series of studies in classroom situations (O'Leary & Becker, 1968; O'Leary, Kaufman, Kass, & Drabman, 1974) found that the most effective verbal reprimands are those described as "soft." Soft reprimands are those given in such a way that only the child involved can hear them. In classes in which teachers employed loud reprimands, there was a significantly higher incidence of disruptive behavior. In this connection, it is also worth noting that praise—a highly effective reinforcer in the classroom—is far more effective if it is "loud." In brief, in most cases reprimands should be soft, and reinforcement should be more public.

The case for the use of punishment is based on a number of observations. First, although reinforcement, imitation, and reasoning might all be highly effective in bringing about and maintaining desirable behavior, there are numerous instances when they do not appear to be sufficient. As Ausubel (1957) notes, it is not always possible for a child to determine what is undesirable by generalizing in reverse from what has been identified as desirable. Nor, of course, is the child always going to be immediately convinced through gentle persuasion of the undesirability of certain behaviors. If Johnny persists in throwing the cat in the bathtub even after being told that the poor thing cannot swim, punishment might be in order. And although psychologists have long noted that punishment does not appear to be very effective in eliminating undesirable behaviors, there is considerable evidence that it might be very effective in at least suppressing these behaviors (see, for example, Parke, 1974). In fact, the argument that punishment does not lead to the extinction of the behavior in question is really irrelevant. If Johnny now stops throwing the unfortunate cat in the bathtub, his grandmother will surely not believe that he has forgotten how to do so—but she might justifiably hope that he would refrain from doing so in the future.

Like reinforcement, punishment appears to be most effective when it immediately follows behavior. However, this observation is far more valid for other animals than it is for humans, presumably because of the human ability to symbolize. This allows for associations between behavior and its consequences even when these are separated by significant expanses of time.

In addition, punishment appears to be most effective when administered by a warm and loving parent (or other adult). And there is no evidence that the affection that exists between parent and child is damaged or reduced as a result of the judicious use of punishment (G. C. Walters & Grusec, 1977).

Negative Reinforcement

One final distinction needs to be emphasized again. It involves the difference between negative and positive reinforcement, both of which lead to an increase in the probability of a response occurring, but each of which is likely to have different effects. As Lefrançois (1983)[8] notes, a rat can be trained to jump a stool by being fed every time it does so (positive reinforcement). It can also be trained to jump onto the same stool by being given an electric shock when it does *not* do so. In the end it may jump onto the stool with equal haste no matter how it has been trained, but there is little doubt that the positively reinforced rat will display considerably more enthusiasm for jumping than will its aversively trained colleague. There is a fundamental difference between learning an *approach response* (as is generally the case with positive reinforcement) and *escape* or *avoidance learning* (which often results from negative reinforcement). And much like the rat that has learned to jump onto a stool to escape an electric

---

[8]Although I offered often, Kro refused to read any of my writing. "Why should I?" he asked. "I'll write my own stuff better." Obviously, he lied. (GRL)

shock, students who are attentive and studious because of aversive control (negative reinforcement or punishment) cannot be expected to like school as much as those who are attentive and studious because of positive reinforcement. Perhaps the same is true of those who go to church to avoid hellfire and damnation.[9]

It is worth noting that the environment constantly provides people with a variety of aversive stimuli that appear to be extremely effective in shaping behavior. Stoves that are hot, insects that bite, mushrooms that poison—all of these quickly lead to important learning. If they didn't, the human species probably would not have survived this many generations. Although it is important to recognize the importance of emphasizing positive rather than aversive control, aversive control should not be dismissed too glibly.

IMITATION AND OPERANT CONDITIONING

Skinner's model of operant conditioning describes learning as an increase in the probability of occurrence of an operant (emitted response) as a function of reinforcement. One class of operants that is especially important in human behavior, claims Albert Bandura (1977), is **imitation**, also termed **observational learning**.[10] In fact, argues Bandura, important aspects of **social learning** (that is, learning of socially appropriate behavior) cannot easily be explained using simple learning principles without also considering imitation.

Imitation is a type of emitted behavior that occurs as a function of observing a **model**. Imitative behaviors are extremely common. Not only are they evident in similarities in the ways in which people dress, eat, walk, and talk, but differences among cultures are also testimony to the prevalence and the power of imitation.

Imitation ranks high among the alternative explanations for complex social learning because it provides a good explanation for complex learning. Skills like learning to drive a car can't easily be acquired solely through contiguity or trial and error but require the presentation of models (usually other drivers, as well as verbal or written instructions). Similarly, children would probably never learn to speak if they had to do so through trial and error, without benefit of the models that are presented by other speaking humans. Also, it seems clear that

---

[9]The reason I am paraphrasing Lefrançois here is not because his stuff is better than mine. It's simply because I am not yet entirely familiar with things like hellfire and damnation. Also, I find his use of such remarkably nonbehavioristic images as that of rats jumping on stools "enthusiastically" at least amusing, if not entirely meaningful. (Kro)

[10]This section presents only a small part of some of Bandura's earlier theorizing—specifically, the part that is most closely related to Skinner's work and is immediately relevant in the application of learning principles. Bandura's theory is an exceptionally good example of a theoretical position that has not remained static but has changed with new discoveries and new emphases. Thus in Chapter 10 we will look at some highly cognitive aspects of his later theorizing, and in Chapter 11 we will see again how his theoretical ideas span most of the learning theory chronology covered in this text. (Kro)

people learn what is acceptable and unacceptable in matters of speech, dress, and behavior largely by observing the models presented by others.

Reinforcement in Imitation

Like all operants, explain Bandura and Walters (1963), imitative behaviors are subject to the effects of reinforcements and punishments. These authors list four separate sources of reinforcement in observational learning—three involving reinforcement for the observer, and one involving the behavior of the model.

First, an imitator is often reinforced directly by the model whose behavior is being copied. Proud parents are quick to praise their children for behaviors that resemble those of Daddy or Mommy. Even grandmothers are occasionally heard saying, "Look at little Norbert standing there with his finger in his nose, just like his daddy."

A second source of reinforcement has to do with the actual consequences of the imitated behavior. If the activity is socially acceptable or leads to the obtaining of reward, it is reinforced by its own consequences. A child who learns to say "milk" as a result of hearing her mother say the word 40 times a day for 18 months not only incurs the praise of that proud parent but may actually *get* milk as a result of saying the word.

Third, the observer in a modeling situation often appears to be influenced by what Bandura (1969) calls **vicarious reinforcement**. This is a type of second-hand reinforcement in which the imitator is not actually reinforced. It's as though the observer assumes that if the model does this or that, then this or that must be reinforcing. Therefore, in the imitator's unconscious logic, a similar sort of reinforcement is expected for the imitator.

The fourth source of reinforcement for imitative behavior, which affects the model rather than the observer, is based on the supposition that simply being imitated may be reinforcing. Thus entertainers who display bizarre dress fashions or hairstyles and are subsequently imitated by their fans may be more likely to persist with their unusual tastes.

Models and Their Effects

Although there is a tendency to think of models as people whose behavior is copied by others, a model is any pattern for behaving that can be imitated. In advanced technological societies, **symbolic models** such as those presented by television, books, verbal directions, and the like, are extremely important. In fact, explains Bandura, one of the problems with older theories of learning is that "most of them were cast long before this tremendous technological revolution in communications. . . . These theories do not encompass the tremendous power of the symbolic environment" (Evans, 1989, p. 6).

Through observational learning, children (and adults) learn three different classes of responses, which Bandura and Walters (1963) describe as the *three effects of imitation*. These are described below.

The Modeling Effect

When observers learn through imitation something that is new for them, they are said to model. Hence, the **modeling effect** involves the acquisition of novel responses. When grandmothers eagerly describe how their grandchildren acquire undesirable habits from the neighbor's undisciplined ruffians—habits that are clearly novel, because the grandchildren never did such things previously—they are describing the modeling effect.

The classical experimental illustrations of the modeling effect are Bandura and Walters's (1963) often-replicated experiments on aggression in young children. In these experiments, participants are exposed to filmed, actual, or cartoon models of other children or of adults engaging in novel aggressive behavior with a large, inflated, plastic "Bobo" clown. Occasionally the model is verbally aggressive; at other times he or she strikes the clown (with fist, foot, or mallet), sits on it, scratches it, or otherwise attacks it. Subjects are later exposed to the same clown, and their reactions are noted. Frequently these reactions take the form of precisely imitative aggressive responses. When the responses are clearly new for the child, *modeling* is assumed to have occurred.[11]

Inhibitory and Disinhibitory Effects

The second effect of imitation doesn't involve novel responses; it deals instead with the suppression or disinhibition of previously learned *deviant* behavior. Inhibition and disinhibition usually occur as a result of seeing a model punished or rewarded for engaging in deviant behavior. For example, a group of thieves may stop stealing after a member of the group is apprehended and punished (the **inhibitory effect**). Conversely, the same group may have begun stealing as a result of seeing a member become wealthy through stealing (the **disinhibitory effect**). The disinhibitory effect involves engaging in a previously inhibited deviant behavior as a result of observing a model. The inhibitory effect involves refraining from a deviant behavior.

A striking illustration of the power of models in disinhibiting deviant behavior is found in the classic punishment studies (Walters & Llewellyn, 1963; Walters, Llewellyn, & Acker, 1962). In these studies, subjects were asked to volunteer for what was ostensibly an experiment in memory and were then shown one of two short sequences of film: a violent episode from *Rebel Without a Cause*, or an excerpt from a film showing adolescents engaged in art work. Afterward, subjects were asked to help the experimenter with another study designed to investigate the effects of punishment on problem-solving behavior.

---

[11]Another example of modeling of which Bandura is fond involves the film *The Doomsday Flight*, in which an altitude-sensitive bomb is used in an attempt to extort money from an airline. Bandura wrote to the Federal Aviation Administration to find out about extortion attempts before and after airings of this film. As he expected, these attempts went up dramatically, often on the day following an airing. What is perhaps most striking is that many of these attempted extortions involved very precise modeling, including the use of allegedly altitude-sensitive bombs designed to explode at an altitude below 5000 feet. One would-be extortionist out of Montreal on a London-bound flight was foiled when the airline decided to land in Denver (altitude 5300 feet) instead. But in Alaska, an extortionist received $25,000; in Australia, another succeeded in getting $560,000 from Qantas Airlines! (Evans, 1989). (Kro)

Now another male student, who posed as a subject but who was in reality a confederate of the experimenter, sat at a panel working out problems and signaling his answers by pressing a switch. Whenever he answered correctly, a green light would flash on a second panel; when he was incorrect, a red light would go on. This second panel also contained 15 toggle switches labeled 15 volts, 30 volts, 45 volts, and so on. The switches appeared to be connected to the electrodes fastened to the imposter subject's wrists. Instructions were given to the actual subject (after he had been administered a mild shock in order to ensure that he realized what he was doing) to administer punishment in the form of an electric shock every time an error was made.

Results of this study indicated that exposure to films with violent content significantly increased the intensity of shocks subjects were willing to give (the confederates weren't actually given shocks, because one electrode was always disconnected). This and related studies have often been cited as evidence of the potentially harmful effects of televised violence—about which final conclusions are still tentative, although it now seems likely that television violence does contribute to aggressive behavior (see Lefrançois, 1995).

The Eliciting Effect

A third manifestation of the influence of models on human behavior, the **eliciting effect**, involves eliciting responses that, instead of matching the model's behavior precisely, are simply related to it. In a sense, it's as though the model's behavior serves to encourage similar behavior in the observer. For example, a brother's being praised for winning athletic competitions might encourage another brother to try to excel academically. Similarly, the tastes and the fashions of television and movie heroes might influence the behavior of their admirers. Thus, bizarre dress and behavior among members of a rock band might facilitate even more bizarre actions among fans. The eliciting effect, explains Bandura, "is the social facilitation function. . . . The whole fashion and taste industry relies on that modeling functioning" (Evans, 1989, p. 5).

Behavior Management

One of the goals of the fashion and taste industry is to mold and change people's tastes and, ultimately, their behavior. Similarly, one of the goals of the business of teaching is to bring about learning (which, by definition, involves a change in behavior), and one of the goals of psychotherapy is to change people's emotional and behavioral responses.

All of these can involve what is termed **behavior management**, which is the deliberate and systematic application of learning principles in an attempt to modify behavior. The application of Pavlovian principles is often labeled **behavior therapy**; the systematic use of operant learning principles is more often termed **behavior modification**.

Positive Reinforcement and Punishment

As we saw earlier in this chapter, positive reinforcement and punishment can be highly effective for modifying behavior, and both are well known and widespread in everyday life. Parents praise children to toilet-train them, employers give bonuses for hard work, and teachers smile at diligent students. Each of these is an example of reinforcement. Parents may also withhold praise or scold when children fail to reach the bathroom in time, employers may withhold pay for tardiness, and teachers might express disapproval toward lazy students: Each of these is an example of punishment.

The systematic use of rewards, and occasionally of punishment as well (often in the form of response-cost or time-out procedures, described earlier), is a common aspect of many behavior modification programs. For example, these might be used to control misbehavior in a classroom, to encourage verbal interaction for children who are shy, or to bring about better study habits. Sometimes the exact relationship between specific behaviors and rewards (or punishments) is spelled out in a written document (labeled a *contingency contract*). Often reinforcers consist of tokens that are later exchanged for more meaningful reinforcement (see Kazdin, 1989).

Counterconditioning

One way of modifying responses that have been conditioned to certain stimluli is to condition different, *incompatible* responses to the same stimuli—a process called **counterconditioning**. Counterconditioning has been extensively studied with animals. For example, Bouton and Peck (1992) associated a stimulus with food (conditioning) and then associated the same stimulus with shock (counterconditioning). Under these conditions, the animal first learns an appropriate food-related response to the stimulus (eating), but then quickly learns a shock-related response (like jerking its head). Interestingly, however, counterconditioning does not destroy the original association. Bouton and Peck report that after a 28-day lapse, the original response had recovered spontaneously.

Counterconditioning is sometimes used in **psychotherapy** and is well illustrated by *systematic desensitization* (Wolpe, 1958), a method used primarily in the treatment of anxieties and phobias (fears). Highly simplified, systematic desensitization involves three steps. First, the patient describes all of the situations that bring about the unwanted behavior, listing these in hierarchical order from least to most likely to produce the behavior. Next, the therapist teaches the patient a response that is incompatible with the unwanted response—almost invariably a relaxation response, because relaxing is incompatible with fear or anxiety. The final step is to present the mildest stimulus *while the patient is relaxing* and to continue presenting stimuli in hierarchical order until the patient begins to feel uncomfortable; at that point the therapist stops, and relaxation is again practiced. The object of the procedure is eventually to present the strongest stimulus without eliciting the unwanted reaction. (This procedure is evidently a sophisticated version of Guthrie's *threshold* technique, described in Chapter 2, or of your grandmother's "don't throw him in the water; let him get used to it slowly, damn it" approach.)[12]

Extinction

Just as Skinner's rats could be made to stop pressing a lever by disconnecting the food mechanism, so can humans often be made to stop engaging in some unwanted form of behavior by removing their source of reinforcement. This technique can be used whenever a behavior is maintained by positive reinforcement that is under the control of the experimenter or therapist. For example, there are attention-seeking behaviors in young children that can be extinguished simply by not paying attention to them. Walker and Shea (1991) describe a situation where a student, John, continually disrupted his class by making weird noises that made everybody laugh. Each time the teacher drew attention to the behavior by reprimanding John, the class would laugh again (and John would laugh hardest). In the end, the class was instructed to ignore John; all students who did would be rewarded with free time. John continued to make noises for a few days, but no one paid any attention. A week later, the behavior appeared to have been extinguished.

Imitation

Each of the three effects of imitation described by Bandura can be used systematically both to promote desirable behavior and to eliminate deviant behaviors. For example, children might be taught something new by being shown what to do (modeling effect); they might be discouraged from doing something by witnessing someone else being punished for the behavior (inhibitory effect); or they might be encouraged to engage in a certain class of behaviors after being exposed to a relevant model (eliciting effect).

Skinner's Position in Retrospect

Skinner stands out in the history of psychological thinking as one of its great spokesmen and popularizers. Although behaviorism was originated and defined by Watson and many other theorists have contributed significantly to its development, it is Skinner's name that is most often associated with behavioristic psychology.

---

[12]This rather long name for a simple behavioral technique was apparently due to Lefrançois's grandmother having said just exactly that when either his Uncle Renault or the cat, I'm not sure which, was thrown off the pier and into the lake in a scientifically motivated attempt to prove that dumb animals instinctively know how to swim. They don't, was the conclusion. (Kro)

Contributions

Probably Skinner's greatest contribution to the understanding of human behavior is his description of the effects of reinforcement on responding. In addition, he has extrapolated these findings not only to individuals but also to social groups (see, for example, Skinner, 1953). Many theorists have incorporated large portions of his system into their own positions.

One of the tangible applications of Skinner's work has taken the form of *programmed instruction*, a teaching technique premised specifically on principles of operant conditioning. Essentially, a program consists of a series of related statements (frames) that require students to emit responses (operants); it provides reinforcement by telling them that they have answered correctly. A second very important application of Skinnerian principles, as we saw, is behavior modification.

Evaluation as a Theory

With respect to the criteria for good theories described in Chapter 1, Skinner's system fares relatively well. It is a well-defined, highly researched system that reflects the facts, especially as they relate to the relationships between reinforcing events and the characteristics of responding. It is a clear and understandable system that explains some aspects of behavior remarkably well, and that allows predictions that can be verified. It isn't based on many unverified assumptions, and it has led to a tremendous amount of research and advancement in the understanding of behavior.

Critics insist, however, that Skinner's operant conditioning does not explain symbolic processes and says little about other topics that are of interest to contemporary cognitive theorists (decision making, problem solving, perception, and so on). Others are dissatisfied with his attempts to explain language in terms of reinforcement theory. Still others, as we will see in the next chapter, think he neglected the role of biology in learning.

Philosophical Objections

If most important human behaviors are operant, the importance of Skinner's observations can hardly be overestimated. There is controversy, however, about the extent to which behavior is controlled by reinforcement contingencies. Many—most notably *humanistic* psychologists—consider Skinner's view an assault on human freedom and dignity. If we are controlled by the environment (that is, by the reinforcements and punishments of the environment), the argument goes, then we cannot be free. Thus, on the surface, a Skinnerian position seems totally incompatible with a concern for human worth and individuality.

"When I question the supposed freedom of autonomous man," Skinner (1973) retorted, "I am not debating the issue of free will. I am simply describing the slow demise of a prescientific explanatory device" (p. 261). "Autonomous man," Skinner (1971) explained elsewhere, "is a device used to explain what we cannot explain in any other way. He has been constructed of our ignorance, and as our understanding increases, the very stuff of which he is composed vanishes" (p. 200). Humans are controlled by their environments, Skinner insists, but it is an environment that humans have themselves built and which, to some extent, they continue to control. A science of human behavior, the development of which was always Skinner's goal, brings the possibility of applying science for the benefit of all mankind.

In his controversial and sometimes violently attacked novel, *Walden Two*, Skinner (1948) described how his science of behavior might be applied in a community of about 1000 people. These people lead what Skinner termed "the good life": working only a few hours a day, enjoying the highest standards of education, health, and recreation, intelligent and happy. "Some readers may take the book as written tongue in cheek," he wrote, "but it was actually a quite serious proposal" (Skinner, 1969, p. 29).

Skinner's ultimate defense against his critics was that many were objecting not to the theory but to their interpretation of its implications. In short, they don't like what humanity seems to be. But as Skinner (1971) noted, "No theory changes what it is a theory about; man remains what he has always been" (p. 215).

SUMMARY

1. Although sometimes interpreted as antitheoretical, Skinner objected not to theories (he considered them essential) but to the kinds of theories that appeal to speculative, mentalistic inventions to explain observed events. Skinner believed human behavior to be lawful, and to have external rather than internal causes.

2. Skinner observed and described the relationship between independent variables (reinforcement types and schedules) and dependent variables (rate of acquisition, rate of responding, and extinction rate). He identified two major types of learning: that involving stimulus-elicited responses (respondents; Type S or classical conditioning), and that involving emitted instrumental acts (operants; Type R or operant conditioning).

3. Operant conditioning involves a change in the probability of a response as a function of events that immediately follow it. Events that increase the probability of a response are termed reinforcers. Aspects of the situation accompanying reinforcement become discriminative stimuli (S^D) that serve as secondary reinforcers.

4. Reinforcers can be positive (effective through their presentation) or negative (effective through their removal). Punishment involves removing a pleasant stimulus or presenting an unpleasant stimulus (following behavior) and does not increase the probability of a response occurring.

5. Primary reinforcers satisfy basic needs (such as food), secondary reinforcers become reinforcing through association with a primary rein-

forcer (for example, a light in a Skinner box). Generalized reinforcers are stimuli that have been paired with a variety of primary reinforcers and are consequently reinforcing for a variety of behaviors.

6. Reinforcement schedules can be continuous (every correct response is reinforced) or intermittent (or partial). Intermittent schedules can be based on proportion of responses (ratio) or on time lapse (interval). Both ratio and interval schedules can be either fixed (unvarying) or random (variable). Superstitious schedules are fixed-interval schedules where reinforcement occurs at fixed times no matter what the organism is doing.

7. Continuous schedules lead to rapid acquisition and rapid extinction. Intermittent schedules lead to longer associated extinction times but are less efficient for early training. Rate of responding typically corresponds to the expectations of reward an animal or person is likely to develop during training.

8. Extinction (a rapid process, sometimes followed by spontaneous recovery) is the elimination of a behavior through the withdrawal of reinforcement. Forgetting (a slower process) is the elimination of behavior through the passage of time.

9. Shaping, a technique used to bring about novel behavior in animals, involves reinforcing responses that move in the desired direction until the final response has been conditioned. Chaining is the linking of sequences of responses by virtue of discriminative stimuli that are all linked to the same primary reinforcer. Verbal conditioning involves reinforcing certain verbal behaviors, often through nonverbal signs of approval.

10. Fading brings about discrimination learning by exaggerating differences in early training and then phasing them out. Generalization involves transferring one response to other stimuli; discrimination involves making different responses for highly similar stimuli.

11. Social control through the use of positive reinforcement is common and effective. Control through more aversive means (such as negative reinforcement and punishment) is also effective and prevalent. Objections to punishment are based on the observations that (a) it does not tell the offender what to do but merely what not to do; (b) it is often ineffective, suppressing behavior but not eliminating it; and (c) it may have some undesirable emotional side effects. Some forms of punishment (like reprimands, time-out, and response-cost methods) are not subject to the same criticisms.

12. Imitation is an important type of operant. Models are not only people but also symbolic patterns for behavior, such as are provided by books, instructions, religions, television, and so on. Imitation can be reinforced directly by the model, or vicariously.

13. Observational learning can be manifested in the modeling effect (novel, precisely imitative responses), the inhibitory or disinhibitory

effects (the suppression or appearance of deviant behavior), and the eliciting effect (social facilitation of related responses).

14. Techniques for modifying behavior include positive reinforcement, extinction, counterconditioning, and modeling. Another important practical application of Skinnerian principles is programmed instruction.

15. Skinner's system explains and predicts certain behaviors remarkably well, is internally consistent and clear, and reflects some facts well. It has passionate critics, however, many of whom object to its search for all explanations outside the person and the resulting denial of freedom and autonomy.

Chapter 5

Conditioning: Contiguity, Information, and Biology

The Brain—is wider than the Sky—
For—put them side by side—
The one the other will contain
With ease—and You—beside

　　—Emily Dickenson

Preliminary Note for Human Readers: Chapter 5 Objectives

The first four chapters of this text have described the development of two basic types of conditioning: classical and operant conditioning. Theorists associated with each of these—for example, Pavlov, Watson, Guthrie, Thorndike, and Skinner—typically assumed (a) that they provided broad descriptions of learning, generally applicable in all similar situations; and (b) that contiguity and reinforcement were basic explanatory principles also applicable in all situations.

These views are not entirely correct, as I explain in Chapter 5. After you finish this chapter you will, with startling ease and elegance, be able to write long dissertations explaining the following:

- The Rescorla-Wagner view of Pavlovian conditioning
- The significance of phenomena such as blocking, instinctive drift, and autoshaping
- The meaning of biological constraints and preparedness
- Why some long-lived butterflies are flying cyanide factories

You will also know why Lefrançois no longer eats stewed rabbits. I asked his grandmother.

SIXTH TIME CUBE, 49TH HEXALOG, POINT 224.00

He won't eat 'em," the old lady answered my question about Lefrançois and rabbits, "'cause he doesn't like 'em." The answer is admirably brief and to the point, but it's hardly the kind of answer to satisfy a behavioral scientist.

"Why doesn't he like them?"

"The last time he ate rabbit," she croaked,[1] " was that November when he was staying with me to go to high school." And then she went on to explain how her grandson had snared some rabbits and she had cooked them up like she always did, first sautéed with garlic and butter, then fricasseed briefly, roasted, and eventually stewed . . . well, the details are of little academic interest.

"He ate buckets of it like he always did," claimed the old lady. "Great platefuls. Maybe three second helpings." ("Help me here," says I. "How could a person have three second helpings? Wouldn't one of them be a third helping, and another a fourth?" The old lady ignores my question.)

"Then he barfed," she added, refusing to mince words. "And he never ate rabbit again."

---

[1]My grandmother never *croaked*, as Kro put it; even in very old age, she had a round and robust voice. Kro had a tendency to exaggerate by using language that was more colorful than exact. (GRL)

TASTE AVERSION

In psychological terms, what Lefrançois had acquired is a **taste aversion**: a marked dislike for a particular food. Taste aversions are sometimes very important in biological terms. If poisons have distinctive tastes, and if they don't immediately kill the organism that eats them but simply make them sick, then developing a strong aversion to those tastes might prevent a later poisoning. What is important biologically is that the taste aversion be powerful, and that it develop immediately—preferably after a single exposure to the poison.

How the Heliconius Survives

Most adult butterflies live about ten days. One exception is the Heliconius, a brightly colored butterfly that survives several months.[2] Remarkably, the Heliconius doesn't flit about unpredictably, as do most butterflies, thus providing a difficult target for birds and other predators. Instead, it flies a slow, deliberate pattern. Yet the Heliconius flies among butterfly-eating birds at will, without danger.

Why? Simply because the Heliconius is a "flying cyanide capsule" (Murawski, 1993, pp. 133–134). You see, the Heliconius is immune to a poisonous vine—the passion vine—that even leaf-eating caterpillars avoid. And the Heliconius not only gorges itself on the passion vine but synthesizes its poisons, thus becoming toxic itself. And so birds avoid these brilliant, slow-flying butterflies.

Do they avoid Heliconius butterflies as a result of a built-in aversion? No, says Murawski. In fact, naive birds attack (and generally consume) just about anything. But once they have eaten one poisonous Heliconius, they don't eat a second.

They learn this taste aversion, as did Lefrançois with his grandmother's rabbit stew, in a single trial. Not only does it prevent them from getting sick or even dying, but it also saves the lives of countless slow-flying Heliconiuses.

Problems for a Classical Conditioning Explanation

At first glance, classical conditioning might appear to be a good explanation for taste aversion learning. Neutral stimuli (CS) like the sight and taste of a butterfly (or the sight and taste of a rabbit) are paired with a powerful unconditioned stimulus (US) like the poisons in the butterfly (or whatever was in the rabbit stew) and become associated with the same illness-related responses (CR).

But there are several characteristics of acquired taste aversions that make a simple classical conditioning explanation less than perfect. First, a traditional

---

[2] Another exception is the Monarch butterfly, who survives for months and migrates enormous distances (say, from Canada to California). The Monarch survives for much the same reasons as does the Heliconius. (Kro)

view of classical conditioning maintains that conditioning results from the *repeated* pairing of stimulus or response events; yet taste aversion learning often occurs in a single trial.

Second, classical conditioning is thought to depend on contiguity—that is, on the near simultaneity of events. In taste aversion learning, though, the unconditioned response (the violent illness) sometimes occurs many minutes, or even hours, after the CS.

Third, classical conditioning principles maintain that *any* neutral stimulus can be associated with any US if paired with it often enough; but in taste aversion learning, certain associations are never learned.

These characteristics of taste aversion learning are well illustrated in controlled experiments.

Taste Aversions in One Trial

Birds don't need to eat bushels of Heliconius butterflies before learning to avoid them; a single experience is sufficient. Similarly, rats exposed to a single dose of radiation so that they become ill after eating will subsequently avoid the food they ate prior to getting sick. This effect has been found as long as 32 days after a single pairing of food and radiation (Garcia & Koelling, 1966).

Backward Conditioning

As noted in Chapter 2, backward classical conditioning has always proven difficult. Yet taste aversion in rats can be learned following a single trial, and it can be extremely powerful even when there is a significant delay between the conditioning stimulus (the taste of food, in this case) and the unconditioned stimulus (radiation)—and even if the effects of the US (illness) don't occur for some time.

In humans, too, taste aversions are powerful and quickly learned. And they are learned not just by children but by adults. Bernstein and Webster (1980) gave adult patients who were receiving chemotherapeutic drugs (which cause nausea) one of two distinctly flavored ice creams. Subsequent testing revealed that these adults had developed strong aversions to flavors they had tasted prior to chemotherapy. This happened even though these adults *knew* that the cause of their illness was the drug and not the ice cream.

Selectivity in Responsiveness to CS

If a rat is injected with a solution of lithium chloride (which makes rats quite ill) while it is drinking saccharin-flavored water, it will later avoid foods that taste of saccharin (although it doesn't become ill until about an hour after the injection). This observation appears reasonable in light of what is known about contiguity and classical conditioning. But if a rat is made ill *and* exposed to flashing lights or a distinct noise while drinking saccharin-flavored water, it will develop no aversion to the lights or the sound, but only to the taste (Garcia & Koelling, 1966).

The same point is made even more dramatically in studies of cross-species aversion learning. Wilcoxon, Dragoin, and Kral (1971) produced aversions in

rats and in quail by feeding them blue-colored, flavored water and later inject-
ing them with an illness-inducing drug. Both the rats and the quail developed
marked aversions, but the nature of these aversions was significantly different.
The rats developed an aversion to liquids with the specific flavor in question
regardless of their color; the quail developed an aversion to blue-colored liquids
regardless of their flavor.

One explanation for these findings is simply that quail have excellent color
vision and probably rely to a considerable extent on visual cues to sort what is
edible from what is not. In contrast, rats—like most other mammals—depend
primarily on olfactory (smell) rather than visual cues. It therefore makes biological sense that rats should make use of smell cues in learning about foods that
should be avoided, and it makes biological sense for quail to use visual cues in the
same kind of learning (Garcia, Ervin, & Koelling, 1965; Rozin & Kalat, 1971).

Blocking

It appears, then, that not just any stimulus can be classically conditioned. For
example, quail acquire a powerful aversion associated with color, but rats do
not. Thus classical conditioning's reliance on contiguity as an explanatory principle is not always appropriate; there is more involved in classical conditioning
than the simple co-occurrence of events. Another phenomenon that presents
problems for a simple contiguity explanation of classical conditioning is known
as **blocking**.

In the first well-known demonstration of blocking, Kamin (1969) paired
two stimuli (a noise and a light) with an electric shock administered to the feet
of rats. The procedure was to turn both the light and the noise on for 3
minutes, then follow them immediately with the electric shock. Classical conditioning theory would predict that after enough pairings with the electrical
shock, either the light or the noise would bring about reactions similar to those
associated with the electric shock. The prediction was correct: Rats responded
to the noise alone, or the light alone, with fear—which is an unconditioned
response to electric shock.

Now Kamin threw a twist into the proceedings. First, he conditioned a
second group of rats using only the noise (we'll call them the B group). As
before, he followed 3 minutes of the noise with an electric foot shock. Then,
after B-group rats had been conditioned to the noise alone, he conditioned
them in exactly the same way as he had the A group—pairing both the noise
and the light again for 3-minute periods, then following each pairing with an
electric shock. (The procedure is shown in Figure 5.1.)

Now B-group rats were exposed to the light alone. Recall that when the A-
group rats were exposed to the light alone they stopped bar pressing, indicating
high fear. Classical conditioning theory would predict exactly the same outcome for B-group rats, because the light had been paired with the noise equally
often for both groups. Amazingly, however, B-group rats continued to press the
bar at about the same rate, seemingly unaffected by the light.

	Pretraining	Conditioning	Testing	Response
A Group (control)	None	Noise + Light → Shock	Light	Freezing (high fear)
B Group (blocking)	Noise → Shock	Noise + Light → Shock	Light	Bar Pressing (no fear)

FIGURE 5.1   A representation of Kamin's study of *blocking* in classical conditioning. For A-group rats, exposed to both noise and light followed by a shock, exposure to the light alone leads to a marked suppression of ongoing bar-pressing behavior. But B-group rats, who had previously learned that noise means shock, failed to learn that light might also mean shock.

An Intuitive Explanation

Why? Well, said Kamin (1968), the most likely explanation is this: Whenever something important happens to an animal, it immediately searches its memory to see what events could have been used to predict the occurrence. When a red-tailed hawk swoops down on a chicken but narrowly misses, the chicken searches its memory banks for immediately preceding events. And maybe it remembers a swift shadow darkening its path, or the whistling of wing feathers braking. And forever after, the chicken races away from shadows and whistling noises.

So when the rat receives a mild foot shock, it stops and scans its memory to see what was *different* and *unexpected* immediately before this event. Because the A-group rat notes that light and noise always precede the shock, it freezes when it later sees the light.

But the B-group rat has had different experiences. First it learned that a noise always precedes a foot shock, and so when it again hears this noise, it cowers and stops pressing the bar. Later it is exposed to both the light and the noise, followed by the shock. But it learns nothing new because the shock is already predicted by the noise; the light provides no new information about the occurrence of the CS. There is no discrepancy between what the subjects expect (the shock) and what occurs (the shock). So, when the B-group rat is later exposed to just the light, it keeps right on pressing the bar. In a sense, having learned that noise means a shock is coming *blocks* the rat from learning that light might mean the same thing.

The Rescorla-Wagner Model

Kamin's pioneering experiments in blocking suggested the need for different explanations of what happens—and why—in classical conditioning. And among the most widely accepted of the resulting explanations is that now known as the **Rescorla-Wagner model**.

What the model says, in effect, is that when an animal is classically conditioned, it learns what goes with what. Contiguity is not as important as the information a stimulus provides with respect to the probability of other events. Thus what is learned is a connection or an expectation. Pavlov's dog learns that a buzzer or the sight of a handler means it can expect to be fed; a rat learns that a light or a sound means a shock is about to occur. In Rescorla and Holland's (1976) words, "Pavlovian conditioning should be viewed as the learning about relations among events" (p. 184).

Second-Order Conditioning

In classical conditioning, the organism typically learns about an association between a normally significant event (like the presentation of food; the US) and one that has less or different importance (like a tone; the CS). As Pavlov pointed out, though, the relations that are learned in classical conditioning are not limited to those that might exist between between US and CS but include what is termed **second-order conditioning**. In second-order conditioning, another stimulus becomes a significant event in place of the US. For example, Rescorla (1980) describes how a Pavlovian dog learns a connection between a metronome and food. Later the metronome is paired with a second stimulus, a black square. And although the black square is itself never paired with food, in time it too elicits salivation.

As Pavlov (and Watson) interpreted it, second-order conditioning expands the applicability of classical conditioning tremendously, explaining how associations build upon each other to construct a repertoire of responses. For Rescorla, second-order conditioning is even more important as a way of understanding how associations are formed. In general, says Rescorla (1988), "conditioning [is] the learning that results from exposure to relations among events in the environment. Such learning is a primary means by which the organism represents the structure of its world" (p. 152).

Not Contiguity But Information

It is clear, according to Rescorla, that continuity is not sufficient to explain classical conditioning. If it were, Kamin's B-group rats would have learned the same thing about the light as did the A-group rats. In fact, contiguity isn't even necessary for classical conditioning—as is clear in taste aversion studies where the aversive stimulus may be presented *after* the conditioning stimulus (for example, in the form of an injection or radiation).

One useful way of looking at classical conditioning is to say that organisms "adjust their Pavlovian associations only when they are 'surprised,'" claims Rescorla (1988, p. 153). That is because organisms experience surprise only when expectations are not met (in other words, when there is new information). The B-group rat who has learned an association between noise and shock does not modify that association when noise *and* light are paired with shock. Thanks to the noise signal, the shock is not a surprise; it doesn't violate expectations. Hence there is no new information in the light, and no new associations result. Thus, says Rescorla (1988), it is nonsense "that a signal simply acquires the ability to evoke the response to the US" (p. 157), as is suggested by simple interpretations of Pavlovian conditioning.

BIOLOGICAL INFLUENCES IN CONDITIONING

A simple interpretation of classical conditioning holds that *contiguity* and repeated pairings are the keys to learning. As we saw, these are inadequate explanations for such phenomena as taste aversion learning and blocking, both of which are better explained in terms of the organism's recognition of associations and development of expectations.

A simple interpretation of operant conditioning holds that reinforcement is the key to learning. But this interpretation, too, is inadequate to explain a number of phenomena.

Autoshaping

If a pigeon receives reinforcement at intervals regardless of what it is doing at the time, the end result might be what Skinner has described as superstitious behavior. That is, the pigeon may learn some "accidental" behavior such as twisting or swaying.

If a response key or disk is illuminated for a few seconds just before the appearance of food, however, the pigeon will quickly learn to peck at the key or disk. That this behavior occurs and is learned in spite of the fact that the pigeon's pecking bears no causal relationship to the appearance of food has led to the use of the term **autoshaping** to describe the learning involved. The strength of an autoshaped response is dramatically illustrated in an experiment by Williams and Williams (1969). Pigeons were initially taught to peck at a light in the manner described above, but response consequences were then altered so that pecking would prevent reinforcement from occurring. In spite of this, the pigeons continued to peck at the light.

The problem that autoshaping poses for a traditional conditioning explanation is that it deals with behaviors that appear to be learned although they are not associated with reinforcement—in fact, that sometimes persist even when they are associated with withdrawal of reinforcement. The point, however, is not that reinforcement exercises little control over operant responses; it is that pecking among pigeons is not a very good operant behavior for experimental purposes. A good experimental operant is one of several equally probable responses emitted by the organism for no particular reason; the response can then be brought under the control of its consequences. Pecking, in contrast, is a highly probable food-related response in pigeons. That a pigeon should continue to peck at a lighted disk even when doing so means that it will not be reinforced says more about the pigeon's evolutionary history than about the inadequacies of operant conditioning.

Instinctive Drift

Autoshaping deals with responses that are highly probable in the animals concerned. So does **instinctive drift**.

In the early 1950s two of Skinner's students, encouraged by the remarkable success that experimenters had enjoyed in shaping the behavior of animals, decided to commercialize this process. These students—a husband and wife by the name of Breland—proposed to train a number of animals to perform stunts sufficiently amusing that audiences might pay to see them. Through the "differential reinforcement of successive approximations" (that is, through shaping), they taught a raccoon to pick up a coin and deposit it in a tin box; a chicken to pull a rubber loop, thereby releasing a capsule that then slid down a chute to where it could be pecked out of the cage; and a pig to pick up large wooden "nickels" and deposit them in a piggy bank. Operant conditioning procedures worked exquisitely; all the animals learned their required behaviors.

But not for long. In the trainers' words (Breland & Breland, 1951, 1961), each animal eventually began to "misbehave." The pig took longer and longer to bring its wooden nickel to the bank and deposit it, although it clearly knew that reinforcement was contingent on doing so.[3] Instead it spent increasingly long periods of time tossing the coins in the air, pushing them around with its nose, rooting around in the dirt with them, and otherwise behaving as might any other uneducated pig on the trail of the elusive truffle. The Brelands tried to remedy the situation by increasing the pig's food deprivation. But that only made matters worse, so that in the end the pig was taking so long to deposit the wooden nickels that it was in imminent danger of starvation.

The raccoon fared no better; it too began to take longer and longer in bringing the coins to the metal box. It often refused to let go of the coins, instead dipping them in the box, bringing them out again, and rubbing them between its paws. And the chicken, not to be left out, became so engrossed in pecking at the capsule that it seemed to quite forget everything else it had learned.

Researchers have now uncovered a large number of situations in which animals initially learn a behavior quickly and well but eventually begin to resort to other behaviors, the nature of which is highly revealing. It is surely no accident that the pig rooted, the raccoon "washed" its coin, or the chicken pecked. These are, after all, what pigs, raccoons, and chickens do with respect to food. "It seems obvious," claimed Breland and Breland (1961), "that these animals are trapped by strongly instinctive behaviors, and clearly we have here a demonstration of the prepotency of such behavior patterns over those which have been conditioned" (p. 69).

In general terms, instinctive drift results when there is competition between a biologically based behavior and a learned response. It appears that with repeated exposure to a situation characterized by this kind of competition, organisms tend to revert to the behavior that has a biological, evolutionary basis. This, the Brelands are careful to point out, does not invalidate general learning principles—but it does emphasize that biology is important. Not all behaviors

---

[3]Well, maybe it didn't actually "clearly know" anything of the sort. After all, this was a behavioristic pig, not a humanistic or a cognitive pig. All we can say for certain, as behaviorists, is that the pig's desired responses had been reinforced often enough that the experimenters could justifiably expect it would continue to deposit wooden nickels in piggy banks. What it actually thought of the entire process is a matter for speculation, not science. (Kro)

can be conditioned and maintained through the careful arrangement of response consequences.[4]

BIOLOGICAL CONSTRAINTS AND PREPAREDNESS

Autoshaping, instinctive drift, and the learning of taste aversions are striking examples of what are called **biological constraints** (Hinde & Stevenson-Hinde, 1973; Seligman, 1975; Seligman & Hager, 1972). In its simplest sense, a biological constraint can be defined as an inborn predisposition that makes certain kinds of learning highly probable and easy and other kinds improbable and very difficult. The most obvious general principle of a biological constraint is that it will favor behaviors that have survival value and discourage those detrimental to survival. For example, that rats (or humans) should learn an aversion to a poisonous taste clearly has survival value. But that they should learn an aversion to a sound or a light when they have been physically poisoned has no such value.

In Seligman and Hager's (1972) terms, organisms are *prepared* for certain kinds of learning and *contraprepared* for others. A rat faced with danger is prepared to flee, fight, freeze, or perhaps become frantic; teaching it to do any of these through the use of noxious stimulation (an electric shock, for example) is a simple matter. But teaching it to engage in a behavior that is opposed to any of these is very difficult. Thus, teaching a rat to depress a lever in order to escape an electric shock is very difficult (Bolles, 1970). Similarly, a pigeon can easily be taught to peck at a key to obtain food, but not in order to escape an

---

[4]I understand this phenomenon more clearly since last fall. That was when instinctive drift led my prize hunting hound to chew up a brace of fine mallards, in spite of the fact that she would previously turn up her nose in utter disdain at the very thought of raw meat. Indeed, lately she will only nibble politely when presented with any meat dish—unless, of course, it has been cooked in an expensive burgundy or a very dry chablis. (GRL)

electric shock. In contrast, the pigeon easily learns to flap its wings to avoid a shock, but not to obtain food.

Biological constraints are clearly involved in the reversion of pigs to rooting and chickens to pecking in the instinctive-drift experiments. Similarly, there are biological constraints at play in autoshaped behaviors. For example, pigeons show a marked preference for pecking at keys that are on the floor rather than on a wall—probably because they feed primarily on the ground (Burns & Malone, 1992). Also, biological influences on learning are dramatically evident in single-trial taste-aversion learning.

It is less obvious that human learning is strongly influenced by biological factors, although it's clear that people are "prepared" to acquire strong taste aversions very easily. Some also argue that humans are biologically prepared to acquire language (Chomsky, 1972), perhaps in much the same way as goslings are programmed to acquire a "following" response if given appropriate stimulation at the right time in their development.

Sociobiology

That humans are also biologically predisposed to engage in certain social behaviors rather than others is the single most important assumption of the discipline that labels itself **sociobiology**. One of its principal spokesmen, Edward O. Wilson (1975), defines sociobiology as "the systematic study of the biological basis of all social behavior" (p. 4).

Sociobiology is based directly on evolutionary theory and draws illustrations liberally from **ethology** (the study of the behavior of nonhuman animals). Sociobiologists believe that certain powerful biological tendencies have survived evolutionary processes. Underlying these tendencies is the single most important law of evolution—namely, that processes of natural selection favor the survival of the fittest. Hence the "fittest" social behaviors (that is, those that have contributed to survival) should be evident as powerful biological predispositions in human behavior.

Note that fitness in an evolutionary sense refers not to the likelihood that a specific individual of a species will survive, but to the likelihood that genetic material itself will survive. Trivers (1971, 1974), Wilson (1976), and other sociobiologists emphasize that the quest for survival is far more meaningful at the group level than at the level of the individual. What is important, says Wilson (1975), is "the maximum average survival and fertility of the group as a whole" (p. 107).

The life of a single individual of a group is important in an evolutionary sense only to the extent that it increases the probability that the genetic material characteristic of the group will survive and reproduce. Thus it is that a honeybee will sting intruders to protect its hive even though doing so means that the bee itself will die (Sakagami & Akahira, 1960). In much the same way, some species of termites explode themselves when danger threatens; the explosion serves as a warning to other termites, which can now save themselves

(Wilson, 1975). These instances of selflessness (or **altruism**) had long presented a puzzle for those who interpreted the law of survival of the fittest as meaning that every single individual does its utmost to survive, come hell or high water (or other catastrophes).

Altruism

Generalizing from observations such as these, sociobiologists have argued that altruism among humans is a biologically based characteristic ordained by years of successful evolution (see, for example, Hamilton, 1970, 1971, 1972). In its purest form, an altruistic act is one that presents some sacrifice to the doer but that results in a net genetic advantage to the species. A blackbird that noisily signals the approach of a hawk may well be detected and eaten, but in the grand scheme of things that is a small price to pay for the eventual survival of all the other blackbirds.

Carrying the argument to its extreme, sociobiology predicts that the extent to which an individual will be willing to undergo personal sacrifice will not only be a function of the net genetic advantage that results for the species but will also be directly related to the degree of genetic relatedness between the doer of the good deed and those who benefit most directly.

Thus you might hesitate to save a total stranger if the probability of losing your life in the process were high; the net genetic advantage in such a situation would be virtually zero. By the same token, you should scarcely hesitate to sacrifice your life to save many others, because the net genetic advantage then is high. It also follows that a father will undergo considerably more risk and sacrifice to save his son than to save a stranger, because he has a great deal more in common genetically with his son.

Criticisms of Sociobiology

In much the same manner, sociobiology suggests that a range of human social behaviors—including aggression, sexual mores, maternal emotion, and so on—may have biological bases. Not surprisingly, this view has met with a great deal of resistance (for example, Eckland, 1977, Wade, 1976). Sociologists in particular have reacted very negatively to the notion that much of human social behavior is genetically ordained. And a number of others have been taken somewhat aback at what is sometimes interpreted as excessive generalization from a handful of evidence, a great deal of which relates more directly to nonhuman animals than to humans. In fact, sociobiology is largely an animal science; its application to humans is mainly speculative.[5]

---

[5]To counter this criticism, some theorists propose that sociobiology needs to look not only at biological but also at cultural evolution (Boyd & Richerson, 1985). This "dual-inheritance" view holds that cultural traits evolve in much the same way as biological traits, and that to understand human behavior it is important to look at the interaction between the two. (Kro)

Although sociobiology has not had a very profound impact on theories of human learning and behavior, it has served to underline the importance of biological factors in learning—factors that traditional psychology has sometimes overlooked. Phenomena such as taste aversion learning, instinctive drift, and autoshaping, however, also point to the necessity of taking biology into consideration when trying to explain and understanding behavior.

TRADITIONAL CONDITIONING THEORIES REEXAMINED

Early behaviorists were highly optimistic that their theories would be widely applicable. They had little doubt that if they could take a response as arbitrary as bar pressing in a rat and bring it under the precise control of specific environmental conditions, it would also be possible to take virtually any operant of which an organism is capable and bring it under precise stimulus control. Similarly, even as it was clearly possible to condition salivation in dogs, eye blinking in adults, and sucking in infants, it should be possible to condition virtually any other reflexive behavior to any distinctive stimulus.

Not so. As we saw, there are numerous examples of behaviors that are very difficult to condition—and of others that are remarkably easy. These behaviors, evident in studies of autoshaping or instinctive drift, emphasize that learning theorists need to take biological factors into consideration. But they don't invalidate conditioning explanations for behavior.

A Review of Basic Conditioning Explanations

The theories described in the early part of this text are of two general kinds: those that deal with behaviors resulting directly from stimulation (respondents), and those dealing with behaviors that are simply emitted by the organism (operants). Traditional behavioristic theories offer two different sets of explanations relating to respondent and to operant learning: classical conditioning and the Law of Effect, respectively (Herrnstein, 1977).

In their simplest and most basic form, the laws of classical conditioning assert that when a neutral stimulus is accompanied or slightly preceded by an effective stimulus sufficiently often, the neutral stimulus will eventually acquire some of the properties formerly associated only with the effective stimulus. Thus a dog eventually comes to salivate in response to a tone (previously neutral stimulus) after the tone has been paired a number of times with food (effective stimulus).

The Law of Effect, also in its simplest form, maintains that a behavior that is followed by a reinforcing state of affairs will tend to be repeated; one that is not followed by reinforcement will tend to be eliminated from the organism's repertoire. Furthermore, the aspects of the situations in which behaviors have been reinforced (or not reinforced) come to exercise a degree of control over the occurrence or nonoccurrence of the behavior. Thus a dog that is reinforced for rolling over whenever its master says "Roll over" may eventually discriminate between the commands "Roll over" and "Fetch my slippers." At this point these verbal commands will have acquired stimulus control over the behaviors in question.

Some Exceptions

As we saw, there are situations where classical conditioning does not require repeated pairings of CS and US (for example, in the case of one-shot taste-aversion learning). Also there are situations where classical conditioning does not occur even after many pairings (as in the blocking studies).

We saw, too, that there are behaviors that are easily learned when reinforced (for example, a pigeon learning to peck to obtain food); and others that are learned with extreme difficulty (a pigeon flapping its wings for food). Also, even after certain behaviors have apparently been well learned through operant conditioning, organisms sometimes revert to other, more instinctual behaviors that interfere with the learned behavior.

Some Qualifiers

These observations don't invalidate conditioning explanations, but they lead to two important qualifications:

- They point out that classical conditioning is not just a low-level, mechanical process whereby one stimulus (the US) passes its control to another (the CS) as a result of repeated pairings. Rather, as Rescorla (1988) notes, it is a process by which organisms learn what goes with what.
- They emphasize that it is essential to take evolutionary factors into account in explaining and understanding behavior (Domjan & Galef, 1983).

Biofeedback: An Application

In addition to their usefulness in the development of theories of human learning and behavior, conditioning theories have a number of practical applications. One is the use of chemical aversion therapy for alcoholism, in which patients are given drugs that interact with alcohol so that they become ill if they drink. Another is **biofeedback**, a procedure by which individuals are given information about their biological functioning. Still another is behavior management, described in Chapter 4.

Operant Conditioning and Autonomic Responses

Early investigations of classical and operant conditioning led quickly to the observation that the types of behavior being explained by each were fundamentally different. Most theorists assumed that such autonomic (involuntary) behaviors as salivation or eye blinking could not be brought under stimulus control through operant conditioning, although they responded very well to classical conditioning procedures. Also, it seemed that operants became more or less probable solely as a function of reinforcement contingencies and not as a function of contiguity.

These assumptions were incorrect. Salivation *can* be conditioned using operant procedures, and so can heart rate, blood pressure, kidney functioning, and a host of other involuntary autonomic functions. Neal Miller (1969) was among the first to demonstrate some of these phenomena when he conditioned increases or decreases of heart rate in rats in response to a combination of a light and a tone. In this experiment rats were administered curare (a skeletal muscle paralyzer) in order to ensure that what was being learned by the rats was actual control of autonomic functioning, rather than some combination of muscular movements that affects heart rate. Although subsequent attempts to replicate this and related experiments were not always successful, there is considerable evidence that any number of autonomic responses can be brought under stimulus control through operant rather than classical conditioning (Dworkin & Miller, 1977; Miller & Dworkin, 1974).

How Biofeedback Works

One of the important applications of this finding has taken the form of *biofeedback*, which refers to information an organism receives about its own functioning. Although people are ordinarily unaware of most aspects of their physiological functions (heart and respiration rates, blood pressure, electrical activity in the brain), there are monitoring devices that can simply and accurately provide information about them. The use of these devices to control autonomic functioning defines biofeedback.

In some common early biofeedback experiments, for instance, subjects were connected to a device that records brain waves (popularly called an alpha recorder) and that produces a distinctive stimulus whenever the subject produces the right type or frequency of waves (for example, Knowlis & Kamiya, 1970). Subjects were simply instructed to try to activate the tone as often as possible. Experimental results suggested that participants could often learn very quickly to control aspects of brain wave functioning. Using an operant conditioning explanation, investigators argued that the tone (or light or other distinctive stimulus) serves as a reinforcer, and the behaviors involved in controlling the autonomic response are operants.

Practical applications of biofeedback include attempts to alleviate migraine headaches, to reduce blood pressure and heart rate, to reduce stress, and even to treat learning disabilities (for example, Lubar, 1991; Stoyva, Kamiya, Barber, Miller, & Shapiro, 1979). N. E. Miller (1978) cautions, however, that early biofeedback experiments have not always been replicated. In some cases it seems that the results of biofeedback may occur without the subject learning to control autonomic functions (Hardt & Kamiya, 1976). For example, certain alpha recorders can be made to respond to changes in eye movement; in these cases, it is perhaps more likely that subjects learned to control eye movement rather than brain activity. In the same way, changes in heart rate can be brought about by skeletal contractions of the lower chest and of the diaphragm, or sometimes by controlling pressure in the thoracic cavity (Anand & Chhina,

1961). Similarly, changes in blood pressure can sometimes be brought about through a combination of muscular movements or through changes in breathing (Levenson, 1976). These observations do not invalidate the practical applications of biofeedback, although they should make researchers and practicioners somewhat more cautious about interpreting the results of these applications.

Contiguity versus Reinforcement

Early distinctions between classical (or Pavlovian) and operant conditioning seemed useful. Among other things, these distinctions claimed that Pavlovian conditioning worked only on autonomic responses and that operant conditioning worked only on operants. However, biofeedback research, as well as research on the conditioning of autonomic responses in rats, leads to the conclusion that classical and operant conditioning are not highly distinct in terms of the classes of behaviors for which each is appropriate. In brief, it has now been demonstrated that autonomic responses can be brought under stimulus control through operant conditioning.

Similarly, operant learning involves classical conditioning procedures as well, suggest Staddon and Simmelhag (1971). Thus, in a Skinnerian bar-pressing procedure, the reinforcer is an unconditioned stimulus that serves to ensure that a specific behavior occurs, and learning occurs because of the temporal relation between reinforcement and bar pressing. In Rescorla and Wagner's (1972) terms, the rat develops an expectation that one leads to the other.[6]

The distinction between contiguity and reinforcement made sense historically (for example, it was fundamental to the distinction between the explanations advanced by Guthrie and Thorndike). But it is no longer as useful. Psychologists have now established that conditioning occurs to the extent that reinforcement (or the US in classical conditioning) is contiguous with the response (or the CS in classical conditioning). Thus both contiguity *and* reinforcement are important in learning.

SUMMARY

1. Taste-aversion learning can be induced in a single trial involving delayed backward conditioning, a phenomenon that has obvious importance as a biological survival mechanism. It is well illustrated by the fact that those who have suffered the malaise of food poisoning frequently find themselves even months later unable to eat the dish that has poisoned them.

[6]But the behaviorist would not speculate that the rat "figures out" this relationship. To do so would presuppose that it knows something about the mechanical functioning of levers and food dispensing mechanisms—or something about the minds of psychological investigators. The rat's "figuring" is limited to a tendency to make associations among things that co-occur, or that always follow one another. (Kro)

2. Taste-aversion learning is not well explained by a traditional view of classical conditioning because (a) it may occur in a single trial, (b) it often involves an effect that occurs long after the conditioning stimulus, and (c) it occurs more readily for certain stimuli than others.

3. Blocking is a phenomenon in which the establishment of a simple conditioned reaction is prevented by previous learning. Kamin explains blocking in terms of the animal's expectations. The occurrence of the unexpected prior to a significant event leads to the development of an association between the event and the unexpected. Rescorla and Wagner suggest that what is learned in classical conditioning is an expectation; hence what is important is the *information* a stimulus provides. Stimuli that present no new information do not lead to learning, in spite of repeated pairings with other events.

4. Second-order conditioning refers to the process by which various nonsignificant stimuli assume some of the functions of an unconditioned stimulus as a result of being paired with it.

5. Many organisms appear to be predisposed to performing certain behaviors and will often learn these behaviors even in situations where they interfere with reinforcement. This phenomenon, known as autoshaping, is illustrated by a pigeon that learns to peck at a key even though pecking at the key has nothing to do with the delivery of a reward.

6. Animals that are taught complex behaviors will sometimes revert to a more instinctual behavior even if doing so means that they will no longer be reinforced. This phenomenon is termed *instinctive drift*.

7. Biological constraints are genetic predispositions that make certain kinds of learning difficult (what Seligman describes as contrapreparedness) and others highly probable and easy (preparedness). Biological predispositions are evident in instinctive drift, autoshaping, and taste-aversion learning.

8. Sociobiology is defined as the systematic study of the biological basis of social behavior. It is premised on the assumption that there are genetic explanations (such as altruism) for much animal and human social behavior. These explanations are based heavily on evolutionary theory.

9. Conditioning theory describes two kinds of behavior (respondent and operant) and two sets of laws for explaining them (classical and operant conditioning). Exceptions to these laws are found in taste-aversion learning, autoshaping, blocking, and instinctive drift. The exceptions underline the importance of taking biological factors into consideration.

10. Biofeedback defines information that organisms receive about their biological functioning. Biofeedback research attempts to modify people's physiological functioning by providing them with information about it. Biofeedback techniques are sometimes employed in therapy, particularly for relieving stress, headaches, and a variety of other complaints.

11. Early conditioning theorists assumed that if an arbitrary response such as bar pressing could be conditioned easily, virtually any other response could also be conditioned. They assumed as well that involuntary responses could not be conditioned through operant means. They were not entirely correct.

A TRANSITION

Chapter 6

Hebb, Tolman, and the Gestaltists: From Behaviorism to Cognitivism

Logically, a scientific theory should never be believed. It is best regarded as a sophisticated statement of ignorance, a way of formulating possible ideas so that they can be tested, rather than an attempted statement of final truth.

—Hebb, *A Textbook of Psychology* (1966, p. 9)

PRELIMINARY NOTE FOR HUMAN READERS: CHAPTER 6 OBJECTIVES

On your planet, new ideas seldom appear completely out of the blue, as they so often do on Koros. If we look carefully at the history of human ideas, we see that long before the appearance of an apparently new idea, there are almost invariably hints that it is coming. Sometimes we find that the idea has appeared fully formed decades or even centuries earlier. Such precocious ideas are often ridiculed loudly and doomed to a premature death—an idea before its time, your philosophers say. But they are wrong, because ideas are never truly before their time; it is people who are behind their own time and therefore cannot recognize the ideas' importance.

Chapter 6 looks at ideas that in many important ways are hints of ideas yet to come, as well as reflections of ideas already spoken and written. Thus Hebb's behaviorism reflects the ideas of conditioning theory, but in it there are many hints of the *connectionism* and *neural networks* that underlie computer models of human thought processes developed decades later (see chapter 8). Similarly, the ideas of Tolman and the Gestaltists hint at growing concern with cognitive topics like perception, problem solving, and decision making.

When you have read this chapter eight times, you will—I promise—be able (and willing) to mumble your way through astoundingly long discourses on the following:

- Hebbian cell assemblies and phase sequences
- Arousal theory
- Tolman's purposive behaviorism
- The basic laws of Gestalt psychology

You will also know something, but not a whole heck of a lot, about saber-toothed tigers.

SIXTH TIME CUBE, 49TH HEXALOG, POINT 226.25
I, Kro 59, searched the literature at length for saber-toothed tigers and could find little beyond inconsistent and savage[1] speculation. I did read, however, that when a woman comes face-to-face with her first saber-toothed tiger (as, the author assured me, most women eventually will), she will turn immediately and run as though the very devil were after her. But when the same woman comes to a stream with the intention of crossing it and finds that the stone she had laid there for that purpose is gone, she will stop; perhaps she will sit on the bank with her chin in her hands. Later she may decide to get another stone to replace the first.

---

[1] I think he meant "wild." But maybe not. (GRL)

In addition to the obvious lack of similarity between a person running from a saber-toothed tiger and one sitting on a riverbank, there is an important distinction between these two behaviors. The first behavior can be interpreted in terms of the now familiar S–R model: The tiger serves as the stimulus; running is the immediate response.

The second behavior presents a different situation, although there is a sense in which the missing stone is the stimulus and the act of leaving to get a replacement is a response. The problem with this stimulus–response interpretation is that there might be a delay of minutes or even hours between the presentation of the stimulus and the response. Because of this delay, the S–R model is less than adequate.

An important question is this: What occurs during the lapse of time between a stimulus and a response?

HIGHER MENTAL PROCESSES: HEBB'S THEORY

It's likely, says Hebb, that something related to the stimulus and response must be occurring at least part of the time because the eventual behavior (response) reflects the situation (stimulus). One phrase that labels what goes on between the stimulus and response is **higher mental processes**—in layperson's terms, thinking or thought processes. A label, however, is not an explanation or a description.

Hebb (1958) describes higher mental processes as "processes which, themselves independent of immediate sensory input, collaborate with that input to determine which of the various possible responses will be made, and when" (p. 101). In other words, higher mental processes are activities that mediate responses; they are mediating processes. What this means is that they are processes that *link* stimuli and responses, sometimes over long periods of time. From the actor's point of view, these processes are experienced as "thinking."

Although Hebb wanted to explain higher mental processes, he is clearly a behaviorist. "The evidence which psychology can be sure of consists of what man or animal *does*," he claims. "The evidence does not include sensations, thoughts, and feelings" (Hebb, 1966, p. 4). But, he hastens to point out, psychology "is essentially concerned with such processes; they are known by inference, not directly" (p. 4). Or, again, "Everything you know about another person's thoughts or feelings is inferred from behavior. Knowledge of behavior is factual. Knowledge of mental processes is theoretical, or inferential" (p. 4).

There is here a profoundly important departure from early behaviorism. With its insistence that the science of behavior be based solely on observations of objective events like stimuli and responses, early behaviorism seemed to deny the existence of mental processes. But behaviorism never really denied that these processes occur, Hebb informs us. What people like Watson emphatically rejected was the *scientific* value of concepts such as consciousness, imagination, and thinking (as well as the scientific value of an approach such as introspection).[2]

---

[2] I find it astounding that consciousness—which seems to me to be as important to the experience of being human as our own self-awareness is to being Koronian—has occupied such an uncertain and controversial role in the development of human psychology. At first it was the very center of the science; later it was sometimes ignored or even denied. Earth psychologists are still not at all certain what they should make of it. (Kro)

Hebb was now suggesting that inferences about such processes might be useful if they are based on actual observations, and if the psychologist keeps clearly in mind the distinction between fact (observation) and inference (theory). "Theory is always open to argument," claims Hebb (1966), "but useful argument is possible only when there is some agreement concerning the facts" (p. 4).

Recall that Hull, too, had suggested that human behavior can be understood in terms of hypothetical (that is, inferred) variables that mediate between stimulus and response. One of the big differences between Hebb's and Hull's **mediational constructs** is that Hull's inferences are unrelated to the structure or functioning of the nervous system. In contrast, Hebb's variables are *physiological;* they are based on neurological fact and speculation.

A Neurological Basis

Hebb points out that psychology deals with the behavior of biological organisms; accordingly, it has to be concerned with humans as products of evolution, as well as with the functioning of glands, muscles, and other organs. Perhaps most centrally, it needs to take into account the functioning of the nervous system—and especially the brain.

Although other behaviorists, such as Skinner, accepted the existence and the importance of human physiological systems, and especially of the central nervous system, they deliberately avoided speculation about what these systems do. Such speculations, claimed Skinner (1938), are fictions; they deal with a *conceptual* rather than a *central* nervous system.

Hebb, in contrast, deliberately chose to speculate about what he labeled "the conceptual nervous system." What he proposed, in a nutshell, was that the mental processes that intervene between stimulus and response can be understood and described in terms of neurological events. This belief forms a cornerstone of his theory—which he described as *pseudobehavioristic* because it is concerned primarily with explaining thought processes and perception, topics not often considered within behavioristic positions (Hebb, 1960).

To understand Hebb's system, it's useful to look at some of the main features of the human nervous system.

DONALD OLDING HEBB (1904–1985)

Hebb was born in the small Canadian town of Chester, Nova Scotia, on July 22, 1904. It was in this region that he spent his childhood, eventually going to Dalhousie University in Nova Scotia. He was reportedly not an outstanding student as an undergraduate; his grade-point average was just barely enough for him to be granted a B.A. in 1925. From Dalhousie he went to McGill University, where he was admitted as a part-time graduate student in part because the chair of the department was a friend of his mother's. He later attended the University of Chicago, where he obtained an M.A., and Harvard University, where at the age of 32 he was granted a Ph.D.

Following his Ph.D., Hebb held appointments at Harvard, at the Montreal Neurological Institute, and at Queen's University in Kingston, Ontario. Other positions included a stint as editor of the *Bulletin of the Canadian Psychological Association;* a research position with the Yerkes Primate Laboratory; the presidencies of both the Canadian Psychological Association and the American Psychological Association; and a professorship in psychology at McGill University in Montreal.

Hebb's many honors include the Warren Medal (presented by the Society of Experimental Psychologists), which was also won by Hull; a distinguished scientific contribution award, also won by Piaget; and a large number of honorary degrees. His publications include many important papers and two major books: *The Organization of Behavior,* published in 1949, and *A Textbook of Psychology,* the third edition of which was published in 1972.

The Central Nervous System

The human **nervous system** consists of billions of cells called neurons (approximately 12.5 billion). Most of these are located in the brain (some 10 billion) and in the spinal cord, which together make up the central nervous system (CNS).[3] The remainder are found throughout the body in the form of complex neural pathways and branches.

A **neuron** is a specialized cell whose function is to transmit impulses in the form of electrical and chemical changes. Neurons form the link between receptors (for example, sense organs) and effectors (muscle systems) and thereby assure that the responses made by an organism will be related to the stimulation it receives. Bundles of neurons form **nerves** to compose the nervous system.

Neurons

Like all cells, neurons consist of a **cell body**. Several arms extend from this cell body. One of these is the **axon;** the others are **dendrites**. (See Figure 6.1.)

The axon is a conductor of neural impulses. In most cases, transmission occurs in only one direction: from the cell body outward along the axon (Glees, 1988). Axons may be microscopically short, but some extend all the way from the brain through the spinal cord, a distance of about a meter (about 40 inches) in an adult.

Near their ends, axons branch out and terminate in a number of little bulbs called **terminal boutons** (or sometimes *synaptic knobs*). These are not connected

---

[3]Estimates of the number of neurons vary widely. Wang and Freeman (1987) say there are "over one billion individual neurons" in the nervous system (p.3); Beaumont (1988) says there are "10 thousand million neurons in the brain" (p. 19), which is 10 billion. N. Cook (1986) is less definite: "Estimates range," he writes, "from 1 to 100 billion neurons" (p. 1). Why don't they just count the dang things? (Kro)

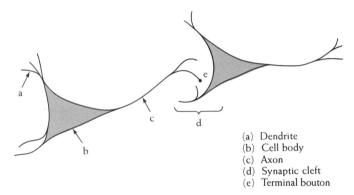

(a) Dendrite
(b) Cell body
(c) Axon
(d) Synaptic cleft
(e) Terminal bouton

FIGURE 6.1   Idealized representation of two neurons.

directly to other neurons, but simply end close to them. The gap between the terminal bouton and an adjacent neuron is a **synaptic cleft**.

Dendrites are hairlike extensions on a neuron's cell body. Whereas neurons have only one axon, they may have a few or many dendrites. The function of dendrites is to receive impulses and transmit them to the cell body (Glees, 1988).

Neural Transmission

Transmission of impulses within and between neurons involves both electrical and chemical activity. Think of each neuron as a little battery, capable of generating an electrical impulse. Electricity is the flow of negatively charged particles (called electrons) toward a positively charged pole; electrical impulses in the neuron operate in exactly the same way. As a result of a series of chemical changes brought about by stimulation, the *electrical potential* of the cell changes causing a flow of charged particles (termed *ions*). This flow is an electrical impulse (called an **action potential**), in contrast to the cell's initial *resting potential*. Within approximately 2 milliseconds of the initial stimulation, the neuron again regains its resting potential. But for a brief period of time, termed a **refractory period**, it is essentially *discharged* and so no longer has the potential to generate an electrical impulse.

From the learning theorist's point of view, what is most important in all of this is that the effect of stimulation is to activate neural cells, which can then activate one another in sequence, and which can ultimately lead to the transmission of impulses that cause glands to secrete or muscles to contract. The basic question is this: What changes occur in neurons or in neural transmission when the organism learns?

Possible Physiological Changes Underlying Learning

So far, this account of the structure and functioning of the nervous system is current (although vastly simplified) fact. It is also known as fact that the transmission of neural impulses underlies sensation and behavior, and that it also underlies higher mental processes (that is, thinking). But the answer to the question of what neurological changes occur as a result of learning is not yet simple fact.

New and More Connections

Two different sorts of answers are typically given, both of which might be correct. One suggests that learning leads to changes in the density or number of connections among neurons; these changes are most likely evident in a proliferation of the number of dendrites or axons, leading to the formation of new synapses. Evidence that this might sometimes be the case is found in studies indicating that rats raised in enriched environments (and who have therefore presumably learned more) have significantly heavier brains than do rats raised in more impoverished environments (Rosenzweig, 1984).

Changes in Existing Connections

The second possibility is that learning might involve changes within existing synapses rather than the formation of new ones. Research with the *Aplysia* snail provides some evidence of this. The *Aplysia* is an especially valuable organism for this kind of research because its nervous system is relatively simple and well mapped. Also, this snail responds predictably by retracting its gills when its siphon (spout) is touched. It quickly *habituates* to repeated touches, however, and stops responding (it *learns* something). Examination of the snail's neurons before and after habituation indicates not that new synapses are formed (or lost), but that the axons of the sensory neurons become less responsive to stimulation (Kandel, 1985). Thus, at least in this organism, a chemical change in the cell itself accounts for changes in behavior.

Hebb's Neurophysiological Assumptions

Although it isn't clear whether chemical or physiological changes in neurons (or both) are involved in learning, both of these possibilities are compatible with Hebb's most basic neurophysiological assumption. Repeated transmission of impulses between two cells, Hebb assumes, leads to permanent facilitation of transmission between these cells. Permanent facilitation is, in effect, learning.

A second assumption central to Hebb's theory is that neural cells may be reactivated repeatedly as a result of their own activity. Stimulation of cell A might cause cell B to fire. This in turn might fire cell C, and cell C might then reactivate Cell A—which again activates B, then C, then A again . . . and again . . . and again (see Figure 6.2). The resulting circular pattern of firing is called a **cell assembly.**

The activation of a number of related cell assemblies can also result in the formation of another hypothetical structure, the **phase sequence** (see Figure 6.3). These units—the cell assembly, and the phase sequence—play important roles in Hebb's proposal for a theory of learning. Each cell assembly corresponds to what Hebb refers to as "relatively simple sensory input." Hence the recognition of even very simple objects will involve the activation of a large number of such cell assemblies or phase sequences.

It is important to keep in mind that these are hypothetical constructs, inventions designed to organize what is known and to lead to new insights.

FIGURE 6.2   Cell assembly. Cell assemblies consist of activity in a large number of related neurons. They correspond to relatively simple input.

Although behavioral and anatomical evidence would suggest that entities like cell assemblies and phase sequences probably exist, there remains the possibility that this theory is inaccurate.

Reactivity and Plasticity

In Hebb's theory, as in most other accounts of learning, two properties of the human organism play a central role: reactivity and plasticity. *Reactivity* refers to the capacity of the organism to react to external stimuli; *plasticity* is the property of the organism that allows it to change as a function of repeated stimulation. A simple demonstration can be used to illustrate these two properties. The procedure involves placing a subject 2 or 3 feet in front of the experimenter. The experimenter then, without warning, kicks the subject squarely and soundly in the seat of the pants. The subject's immediate behavior is an example of reactivity; subsequent refusal to repeat the experiment is an example of plasticity.

Within behavioristic positions, reactivity is interpreted as involving the emission of responses, whereas plasticity is manifested when behavior is modified. The interpretation of these events in Hebbian theory takes the form of an attempt to account for behavior in terms of neurological events. For Hebb, plasticity and reactivity are properties of the CNS that account for behavior, rather than being properties of behavior.

Mediating Processes

Hebb's primary concern was to explain higher mental processes, or thought. His explanation offers a basic hypothesis and makes four principal assumptions related to his view of the physiology of the nervous system.

Basic Hypothesis

The hypothesis, already described, is that mediation (or thinking) consists of "activity in a group of neurons, arranged as a set of closed pathways which will be referred to as a *cell assembly*, or of a series of such activities, which will be referred to as a *phase sequence*" (Hebb, 1958, p. 103).

How are cell assemblies formed?

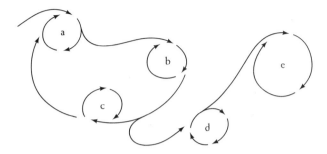

FIGURE 6.3   Schematic representation of a phase sequence: *a, b, c, d,* and *e* can be
thought of as cell assemblies. A phase sequence is equivalent to a concept or a
percept and may consist of activity in a large number of related neurons (Figure 6.2).

Assumption 1

A cell assembly (or mediating process) is established as the result of the repeated firing of cells. It arises as a function of the repetition of a particular kind
of sensory event. In other words, the repeated presentation of a specific stimulus will tend to reactivate the same assemblies each time, serving to facilitate
transmission of impulses across the synaptic spaces between the neurons involved. Hence repetition has a facilitating effect on further neural activity.
Behavioral evidence of this effect is provided by the fact that it is considerably
easier to multiply two numbers if they have been multiplied many times previously. Or, more simply, it is easier to recognize a simple object if it has been
presented frequently than if it has only been seen once. This property of neural
transmission defines in part what is meant by *plasticity* of the nervous system.

Assumption 2

If two cell assemblies are repeatedly active at the same time, an association
between the two will tend to form. In other words, if cell assembly A is always
(or often) active when B is active, the two will tend to become associated
neurologically. That is, the firing of cell assembly A may lead to firing in B and
vice versa. The result will be the formation of phase sequences.

   This assumption serves as an explanation for conditioning through contiguity. If cell assembly A corresponds to one specific sensory event and B does also,
and if A and B represent the components of thought (mediation), then the
establishment of a relationship between A and B means that presentation of the
event associated with A may *remind* a person of the event associated with B.
Intuitively, this makes sense. If you always see George with a cigar in his
mouth, then it's likely that anything that reminds you of George will also bring
the cigar to mind. The smell of wood smoke evokes thoughts of fire; lilacs go
with spring; fish mean water or restaurants; the letter *q* in a word means *u* is
next; and motherhood is a good thing.

   Not only does this assumption explain learning by contiguity, but it also
explains the perception of objects when incomplete sensory data are available.
The lines in Figure 6.4 are almost always perceived as a triangle, although they
really are not. (This phenomenon, referred to as *closure* in Gestalt psychology, is

discussed later in this chapter). For the sake of simplicity, the cell assemblies associated with triangularity can be said to include units representing each of the corners A, B, and C of the triangle, as well as each of the sides. Because these features of triangles have been present in contiguity many times, associations have been formed among the cell assemblies that represent them. It is now sufficient to present only limited sensory input (that is, the three sides of a triangle, but no corners) to evoke activity in the entire sequence of assemblies corresponding to "triangle."

Assumption 3

An assembly that is active at the same time as an efferent pathway (a neural pathway leading outward from the CNS) will tend to form an association with it. This assumption, like assumption 2, allows Hebb to explain the formation of associations between events that are in temporal contiguity. Activity in an efferent pathway may result in some sort of motor activity. Hence the associations that are explained by this assumption involve behavioral events and mediation—in other words, thought and behavior. Again there is ample evidence that such associations are very much a part of human learning. Particular sights, sounds, or smells, for example, become associated with a specific motor activity, so that engaging in the activity recalls the sensory impression. The reverse is also true; activity in assemblies that have often been active during some motor response would tend to elicit the same response. This interpretation is a simple, neurologically based explanation for Pavlovian conditioning. The assemblies relating to the sounding of a buzzer are always present at the time of salivation and are eventually sufficient to elicit salivation.

Assumption 4

Each assembly corresponds to relatively simple sensory input. This property of the cell assembly makes it necessary to involve large groups of such assemblies in explaining the perception of even relatively simple physical objects.

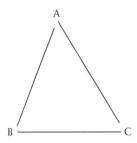

FIGURE 6.4 Perception with incomplete data.

Summary of Hebb's Views

The purpose of these four assumptions is to permit Hebb to describe what learning and thinking are.

Essentially, the term *thinking* is equivalent to *mediation*. Mediation consists of activity in assemblies of neurons, and the nature of the mediation (or of the thought) is determined by the specific assemblies involved. Hebb contends that it is clearly the activated area of the cortex, not the nature of the neural activity itself, that determines the subjective experience of the organism. For example, it is possible to stimulate the optic nerve electrically or by using pressure. In either case, the effect is the same: The subject sees light (Hebb, 1966, p. 267). In contrast, the activation of specific receptors will always affect the same area of the cortex (and presumably the same cell assemblies). Hence it is possible to "feel" the same reaction for the same stimulation on different occasions. If this were not true, of course, human awareness as it is now known would not exist.

The acquisition of learned mediating processes results from the repetition of the same sensory event leading to the formation of associated assemblies. Thus learning consists of the "permanent facilitation" of conduction among neural units. Essentially, a phase sequence is a neurological unit where the transmission of impulses has become so easy that the activation of one part of the sequence is sufficient to activate the entire organization.

Hebb's neurologically based explanation for learning accounts for the formation of stimulus and response associations in terms of connections that are formed between their corresponding neurological counterparts (active cell assemblies or phase sequences). Assumptions 2 and 3 deal with this type of learning. Higher processes involved in learning (insightful problem solving, for example) are assumed to involve the combination of phase sequences (sometimes through chance) in higher-order organizational units—supraordinate phase sequences. Again, these sequences are hypothetical constructs and not necessarily "real."

Hebb also discusses two additional phenomena that are important in human functioning: set and attention, and motivation. We will look at each briefly.

Set and Attention

When a starter at a race tells the contestants that she will fire her pistol a few seconds after saying "On your mark," she is attempting to establish **set**. If she succeeds, the contestants will sprint forward when the pistol sounds. (It would be interesting to see what the effect on the starter would be if all contestants had agreed beforehand to relax when the pistol was fired.)

A superficial behavioristic interpretation of this situation might be that the sound of the pistol is the stimulus that elicits the response of running. But consider what might have happened if the starter had said, "I'm going to fire this pistol to see if my blanks are any good. Just relax." If she then fires the pistol and no one runs, it becomes obvious that the pistol alone is not the stimulus that leads to the running response; the initial instructions are also important. In other words, the set given to the contestants together with the stimulus influence the behavior.

Consider, further, what would happen if a celebrity strolled along the track just prior to the sounding of the gun. Would the contestants' perspiration change? Would their blood pressure and heart rate go up? Would their temperature jump? Probably not. But if these same contestants had already finished the race and were lounging around recuperating when the celebrity walked by, the phase sequences activated might be quite different.

These two examples are illustrations of the effect of **attention** on behavior. Set refers to selectivity among responses; attention refers to selectivity among input. Hebb assumed that both set and attention are largely a function of the preactivation of specific cell assemblies. When racers are told to get ready to run, they are set to respond by running when they hear a bang. When they are attending to the imminent sound, they are less likely to attend to other distracting stimuli.

Set and attention are especially important for teachers. Set is involved in choosing appropriate responses; attention is essential for learning; and each is obviously affected by the other. In addition, both attention and set are closely related to arousal, a concept that is central to Hebb's theory of motivation.

Motivation

For Hebb learning and motivation are different only in that they relate to different questions. Learning refers to actual changes in behavior—to the *what* of behavior; motivation refers to the reasons for behavior—to the *why* of behavior.

Two Functions of Stimuli

Stimuli have two important functions, claimed Hebb (1972): the **cue function** and the **arousal function.**[4] The cue function is the message function; it tells the organism how to feel, think, or react. The arousal function is defined by the general activating, or arousing, effect of stimuli.

In Hebb's terms, the cue function involves the activation of the specific cell assemblies corresponding to the stimulation. In contrast, the arousal function involves the activation—or, more precisely, *preactivation*—of a larger number of

---

[4]Hull made exactly the same distinction, referring to the *cue* and *drive* components of stimuli—a testimony to the appeal of the idea. (Kro)

cell assemblies. This preactivation is brought about through the reticular formation, a structure that forms part of the brain stem and through which most neural pathways branch on their way from sensory systems to the brain. Arousal (preactivation of cell assemblies) is essential for the cue to have its effect, claims Hebb. At extremely low levels of arousal, for example, the individual is asleep and stimulation might have no discernible effect.

Arousal

Hebb's theory of motivation is a *single-drive* theory. The drive is defined in terms of generalized arousal, with arousal referring to the degree of alertness, or vigilance, of an organism. Arousal level is a function of the nature of the stimulation being reacted to, and it varies from very low (sleep or drowsiness) to very high (anxiety or panic).

Hebb makes two important assumptions about the relationship between arousal level and behavior: First, there is an optimal level of arousal, above and below which behavior will not be maximally effective; and second, people behave so as to maintain arousal at or near the optimal level. This implies that there is a need for maintaining a moderate level of arousal. This assumed need is the reason arousal theories are referred to as *drive* theories. (There is more detail about arousal theories and motivation in Chapter 12).

The Need for Stimulation

The question of whether there is a need for arousal has been indirectly examined through an investigation of the effects of prolonged reductions in arousal. The original experiments in a sequence of related investigations in this area were conducted at McGill University under Hebb's direction (Bexton, Heron, & Scott, 1954). They have since been replicated a number of times (Zubek, 1969.)

The original experiment, referred to as a sensory-deprivation or perceptual-isolation[5] study, involved a group of male college students who had volunteered for an experiment in which they would be paid $20 a day for doing absolutely nothing (Heron, 1957). In fact, not only were they not asked to do anything, but they were not *allowed* to do anything. Instead they lay on cots, getting up only to use the toilet or to eat, and sitting up only to eat their meals. Each cot was isolated in a soundproof cubicle, and subjects wore translucent visors that did not allow them to see but permitted diffuse light to enter. Over their ears they wore U-shaped foam pillows designed to prevent hearing. As a further precaution against the perception of sounds, air-conditioning equipment hummed ceaselessly and monotonously. In addition, participants wore cotton gloves and had cardboard cuffs that extended over their fingertips to discourage tactile sensation.

---

[5]Zubek (1969) distinguished between sensory and perceptual deprivation. The former is assumed to involve conditions of darkness or silence, whereas the latter indicates an unvarying stimulus field, such as in the Hebb experiments. (Kro)

In short, the experimenters tried to make sure that participants would experience a minimum of sensory stimulation as long as they remained in isolation. Interestingly, none of the subjects lasted more than 2 days. In some later experiments where conditions of deprivation were more severe (for example, complete darkness, no sound, body immersed in water to simulate weightlessness), subjects often didn't last more than a few hours (see, for example, Barnard, Wolfe, & Graveline, 1962; Lilly, 1972).

Effects of Sensory Isolation

Because the chief source of arousal is sensation, perceptual deprivation should result in a lowering of arousal. This assumption has been confirmed through measures of electrical activity in the brain (EEG recordings) before, during, and after isolation (Heron, 1957; Zubek & Wilgosh, 1963). After prolonged isolation, the brain activity of subjects who are awake is often similar to that normally associated with sleep.

Other effects of sensory deprivation include impairment in perceptual and cognitive functioning that is evident in performance on simple numerical or visual tasks (Heron, 1957). In addition, subjects often become irritable, easily amused or annoyed, and almost childish in their reaction to limited contact with experimenters. For example, they often attempt desperately to engage the experimenter in conversation, acting in much the same way a child does when trying to gain the attention of a preoccupied parent.

Among the most striking findings of sensory-deprivation studies is that subjects sometimes report experiencing illusions of various kinds—in some cases hallucinations—after prolonged isolation. These are relatively infrequent and are markedly affected by the subject's preisolation attitudes (that is, set; Zubek, 1969).

These studies of sensory deprivation tend to add further support to arousal-based explanations of human behavior. There seems to be little question that behavior is more nearly optimal under conditions of moderate arousal. In addition, it seems that people try to maintain arousal at that level. For example, subjects in isolation often talk to themselves, whistle, recite poetry, or (as noted above) attempt to draw the experimenters into conversation. Such behavior led Schultz (1965) to hypothesize that the need for arousal is really a need for stimulation.

Hebb: Review and Evaluation

Hebb's theorizing represents a significant departure from the more traditional S–R theories that we have considered earlier. Most notably, it is concerned mainly with internal neurological events, few of which are nearly as objective as the stimuli and responses that interested Watson and Skinner. And his goal was less to explain the formation of relationships between stimuli and responses than to account for higher mental processes. In this sense, Hebb's ideas serve as a transition between behavioristic and more cognitive theories.

As we noted, much of Hebb's theorizing is based on speculation about the nature of neurological events that mediate between stimuli and responses. He claims that this speculation is not really a theory but instead a proposal for one; nevertheless, his ideas represent a coherent and systematic attempt to explain important observations and can be evaluated as a theory.

Hebb made at least three important contributions to the development of learning theory: First, he brought a consideration of physiological mechanisms back into the study of learning and behavior (much as had Pavlov many decades earlier). Some of the implications of his ideas are now apparent in neural network models (described in Chapter 8).

Second, Hebb's work on arousal theory gives him an important position as a motivational theorist and sets the stage for a considerable amount of research on the relationship between motivation and performance.

Third, his work on sensory deprivation had an important influence on research in learning. Among other things, it called attention to a whole new class of motivational systems relating to things like curiosity, novelty, and exploration.

Viewed in terms of the criteria we have been employing, Hebb's theory can be described as reflecting some facts rather well. Thus it is highly compatible with what is known about neurological functioning. But it also goes some distance beyond what is known. Psychologists don't really know whether neurological functioning is organized in ways similar to Hebb's description of cell assemblies and phase sequences, or whether an entirely different description might be more accurate and more useful. As we see in Chapter 8, neural network models, although they owe much to Hebb's concepts, present a somewhat different view.

In defense of the system, it bears repeating that the logical constructs represented by inventions such as cell assemblies have an important explanatory function. Like all theories, Hebb's hypothesis should not be judged in terms of its "truthfulness" but in terms of the extent that predictions based on it agree with actual observations and the extent to which it provides a clear and useful explanation of observations. Indeed, no psychological theory need be blessed with "truthfulness." Science would not recognize it in any case. What science insists on is objectivity, replicability, consistency, and usefulness—and usefulness is sometimes better judged by history than by science.

FROM BEHAVIORISM TO COGNITIVISM

"Isms" are a little like religions on your planet. Even when dealing with ostensibly scientific systems of ideas, faith and emotion often seem to have as much to do with people's responses as does science—or good sense. That's the way it has been with behaviorism and cognitivism.

Amsel (1989) uses a parliamentary metaphor to describe historical confrontations between behaviorism and cognitivism. "I like to point out," says he, "that the S–R psychologists, who at one time formed the government, are now in the loyal opposition, the cognitivists being the new government" (p. 1). But the change in government from the first behaviorists (who shunned all mentalistic concepts) to current cognitive psychologists (who have largely abandoned the stimuli and responses of the first behaviorists) didn't happen overnight.[6] It happened slowly. And it happened partly as a result of the influence of people like Donald Hebb and Edward Tolman.

For his part, Hebb was a neobehaviorist—a *behaviorist* in that he retained a commitment to the need to preserve the objective, scientific nature of psychological investigation, but *neo* in that he sensed the need to include inferences about profoundly important mental processes like thinking and imagining. And for his part, Edward Chase Tolman—another neobehaviorist—deliberately gave behaviorism a different twist; he gave it a *purpose*.

EDWARD CHACE TOLMAN (1886–1959)

Tolman was born into a Quaker family in Newton, Massachusetts, on April 14, 1886 (also the year of Guthrie's birth). He attended the Massachusetts Institute of Technology, from which he received a B.S. in electrochemistry in 1911. From there he went to Harvard, where he obtained his M.A. in 1912 and his Ph.D. in 1915, both in psychology.

Tolman began his teaching at Northwestern University. He was released 3 years later, ostensibly for lack of teaching competence but more likely because of his Quaker-based pacifist convictions at a time of war. From Northwestern he went to the University of California at Berkeley, where he spent most of the remainder of his academic career. For a few years, however, Tolman was compelled to leave Berkeley as well—this time after refusing to take a controversial loyalty oath spawned by the McCarthy purges. As a result, in 1950 he accepted teaching positions at the University of Chicago and at Harvard. As a member of the American Civil Liberties Union, Tolman was instrumental in bringing about the granting of certain elements of academic freedom. One of the results of this effort was that he returned to Berkeley in 1953.

Tolman (who, like Skinner, Hebb, and Guthrie, served as president of the American Psychological Association) was often accused of not being as serious and single-minded as he might have been with respect to the development of his theories. In fact, his writings are filled with whimsy and anecdotes. And perhaps his tongue was at least partly in his cheek when he dedicated one of his most important books to *Mus norvegicus albinus* (the white Norway mouse, although he probably meant the white Norway rat; Sahakian, 1981; Woodworth & Sheehan, 1964).

---

[6]Nor, to extend the metaphor, has psychology's parliamentary system been strictly a two-party system. In the government, there have always been other *-isms* (like humanisms), *-ologys* (like sociobiology), and *-yses* (like psychoanalysis)—some with very loud voices; others very quiet. And sometimes, I think, there have been revolutions outside the established system of government—grass-roots revolts by peasants with machine guns and new theories. (Kro)

Mechanistic Behaviorism

The behaviorism described in the early chapters of this book is sometimes referred to as a **mechanistic behaviorism**. By this is meant that it emphasized and tried to understand the predictable aspects of human behavior—in other words, its *machine-like* qualities. Early mechanistic theories shared a number of characteristics. First, and perhaps most obviously, these early behavioristic positions came about largely as a reaction to the more mentalistic approaches that had previously characterized psychology. In contrast to these approaches, behaviorism sought to be impeccably objective. Accordingly, its most devoted theorists concentrated almost entirely on aspects of behavior that could readily be observed and measured. The science of behavior thus became a question of discovering reliable relationships among stimuli and responses. And when theorists such as Hebb and Hull began to break away from this orientation by including intervening (mediating) variables in their systems, they were always careful to link them as directly as possible to observable events.

A second characteristic of some early behavioristic theories—especially those of Watson's and Guthrie's—is that they tried to explain behavior by analyzing it at a *molecular* level. These theorists were more interested in specific responses and in sequences of individual responses than in more global and perhaps less easily managed behaviors. This approach is termed *reductionism*. Reductionism was not characteristic of Skinner's theory, nor of the more neo-behavioristic theories such as Hull's or Hebb's, which are more *molar* approaches.

A third characteristic of early behaviorism is that it made few assumptions about the objectives or purposes of behavior except insofar as these could be related directly to specific needs or drives. A strict behavioristic interpretation of a behavior does not raise any questions concerning the intentions of the actor; nor does it make any allowances for *wanting* or *willing*. It simply looks for relationships between response consequences and behavior, or it searches for an understanding of the ways in which contiguity of stimuli, responses, and response consequences are important in determining behavior.[7]

Tolman's Challenge

A strong negative reaction to traditional behaviorism took the form of cognitivism, a movement that had various identifiable roots. One was German Gestalt psychology, which is discussed in the later pages of this chapter. The other was Tolman's challenging of behaviorism's eviction of purpose and con-

---

[7]This reminds me that behavioral scientists on Koros used to make exactly the same mistake when investigating behaviors of primitive other-planet species—always trying to be impeccably objective and determinedly mechanistic, absolutely refusing to consider the possibility that something like "will" or "intention" or "purpose" might occasionally drive behavior. But, unlike human behavioral scientists, it was not a mistake we ever made when studying our own behavior. Astounding, isn't it, that a species could so easily *will* itself to ignore something like *will!* (Kro)

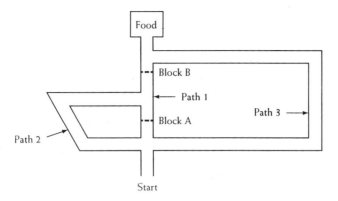

FIGURE 6.5   In the Tolman and Honzik (1930) blocked-path study, rats who had learned this maze almost invariably selected path 3 when path 1 was blocked at B. It seemed they somehow knew that the barrier at B also blocked the much shorter path 2.

sciousness from psychology. The challenge took the form of his theory of *purposive behaviorism*.

TOLMAN'S PURPOSIVE BEHAVIORISM

All behavior has a purpose, insisted Tolman (1967); all actions, whether they be that of rat or woman or man, are directed toward some goal by *cognitions*. Behavior is never simply the result of mindless S–R connections. But ever a behaviorist, Tolman (1932) insisted that "mental processes are to be identified in terms of the behaviors to which they lead" (p. 2).

Do Rats Have Purpose?

What evidence is there that a rat, for example, directs its behavior as if it had certain purposes? Why should you believe that the direction of the rat's behavior is not just a manifestation of learned S–R connections—that it is actually a result of cognitions?

A Blocked-Path Study

The evidence, claimed Tolman, is convincing. Take, for example, the *blocked-path* study (Tolman & Honzik, 1930). In this study, a rat is released into a maze with several different routes to the goal and is allowed to run freely until it has learned the maze. The next step is to place barriers in some of the paths and then observe the rat's reaction. Figure 6.5 shows an approximate representation of the original Tolman and Honzik maze. The paths vary in length from the shortest, most direct route (path 1) to the longest (path 3).

As expected, once they have learned the maze, hungry rats almost invariably select path 1 when given a choice, and path 2 when given a choice between

2 and 3 only. Also as might be expected, when path 1 is blocked at point A in the figure, rats usually (about 93% of the time) select path 2.

The situation becomes more interesting when path 1 is blocked at point B. S–R theory might still predict that the rat would select path 2, because the entrance to it is not blocked and it is second in overall preference. How can a rat be expected to figure out that the block on path 1 at B also serves as a barrier for path 2, and that there is now only one path to the goal?

But figure it out it does. Now the rat consistently selects path 3 rather than path 2 (14 out of the 15 rats involved in the original experiment selected path 3). Should psychology assume that these rats *know* the same thing you and I do—that they have, in fact, developed some sort of cognitive grasp of the maze?

Yes, said Tolman, psychology should assume just that. Experiments such as these illustrate that learning involves the development of **cognitive maps**. A cognitive map is an internal representation of relationships between goals and behaviors as well as knowledge of the environment where the goals are to be found. What happens is that the organism develops a series of expectations with respect to behavior. These expectations are part of what Tolman labels *sign–significate* relationships. A sign is simply a stimulus; a significate is the expectation of reward that results from learning.

An Expectations Study

Even nonhuman animals behave as though they had expectations. Tinklepaugh (1928), one of Tolman's students, placed a banana under a cup in full view of a monkey; then, when the monkey wasn't watching, a piece of lettuce was substituted for the banana. The monkey was allowed to turn the cup over, and it did so very eagerly. It then became very agitated, searching here and there and

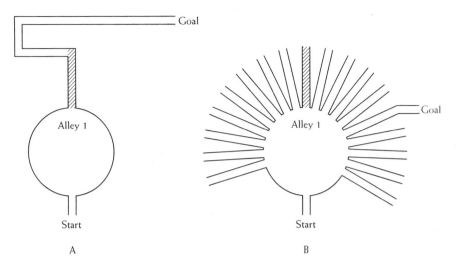

FIGURE 6.6   Place or direction learning in rats. In the Tolman, Ritchie, and Kalish (1946) study, rats learned a simple maze with an indirect path to the goal. In the second part of the experiment, the position of the goal and of the starting area remained the same, but the original path was blocked and 18 new paths were available.

snarling at Tinklepaugh. The monkey's behavior seems to indicate clearly that it had expected to find the banana under the cup. Its agitation and continued search would be difficult to explain using simple conditioning theory.

A Place Learning Study

In a classic experiment, Tolman, Ritchie, and Kalish (1946) trained rats to run across an open, circular area and into a alley that, after three right-angle turns (left, right, and right), eventually led to a goal box (with a food tray; see maze A in Figure 6.6). In the next part of the experiment, the alley leading to the goal box was blocked, and 18 new alleys were made available to the rats (maze B). Which alley would the rats be most likely to choose?

One of the alleys closest to the original, behaviorists would suggest, because these are most similar (generalization). Not so. In fact, far more rats chose alleys that went in the general direction of the original goal box. It appears that what these rats learned was not a series of connected responses, duly reinforced and stamped in, but a *place*. In Tolman's terms, they developed a cognitive map of the area, together with related expectancies. And it was these expectancies, tied to the cognitive map, that directed the rats' behavior.

A second experiment, reported by Macfarlane (1930), makes much the same point in a dramatic way. It again involved rats that were taught to find a goal box in a maze, but these animals had to *swim* through the maze. A plausible behaviorist interpretation of this phenomenon would maintain that the specific responses involved in swimming are chained together, reinforced, and eventually learned as a complete sequence. This same interpretation would also predict that if the maze were drained so that the swimming response was completely useless, the rats would have to learn the maze all over again. In fact, however, when the maze was drained, rats ran to the goal box without hesitation and with no more errors than they had been making while swimming. Again, the evidence strongly suggests that there is more to learning mazes than the simple acquisition of stimulus–response or response–reward connections—a point that is made again in a final illustrative experiment.

A Latent Learning Experiment

In Chapter 1, there is a brief description of a study by Buxton (1940) in which rats were allowed to spend several nights in large mazes without being fed in the maze. Some behavioristic grandfathers would surely predict that these rats would learn very little as a result of their exposure to the mazes. They might be more than a little amazed to find that at least half the rats learned the correct path from the start to the goal box without reinforcement. Buxton determined this by feeding the rat briefly in the goal box and then placing it immediately in the start box; half the rats ran to the goal box without a single error. It appears that rats are capable of developing cognitive maps even in the absence of a food reward. This learning, because it is delayed, is sometimes called **latent**. Latent learning, as we saw in Chapter 1, illustrates an important distinction between *performance* and *learning*: Clearly, what you learn is not always apparent in your behavior.

Four Summary Principles

Several principles are basic for understanding Tolman's system.

Behavior Is Purposive

First, and most important, Tolman believed that all behavior is purposive. By this, he meant that all behavior is guided by cognitions, or expectancies, that are themselves related to goals. In its simplest sense, a cognition is what develops following experience with stimuli and rewards. Note that a cognition is an abstraction—a theoretical invention. Tolman, a behaviorist, believed that cognitions should only be inferred from behavior, not through introspection.

Emphasis on Molar Aspects of Behavior

A second important principle of Tolman's system is his emphasis on the *molar* rather than the *molecular* aspects of behavior. Tolman didn't reduce behavior to its smallest units (the reductionism of Watson's or Guthrie's behaviorism) but dealt instead with large units of behavior that are unified in the sense that they are governed by a single purpose. It is this purpose or search for goals that directs behavior, not the reward itself. Put another way, the connections that explain behavior in Tolman's system involve links not between reinforcement and responses or between stimuli and responses, but between stimuli and expectancies. And the expectancies themselves develop as a function of exposure to situations in which reinforcement is possible.

Reinforcement Establishes and Confirms Expectancies

A third fundamental principle in this system relates to the role of reinforcement in learning. As noted above, the connections that explain behavior in Tolman's system involve links not between reinforcement and responses or between stimuli and responses, but between stimuli and expectancies. Because expectancies develop in situations in which reinforcement is possible, the role of the reinforcement is primarily one of confirming expectancies. The more often an expectancy is confirmed, the more likely it is that the stimuli (signs) associated with it will become linked with the relevant significate (expectancy).

Organisms Learn Cognitions

A final principle in Tolman's system concerns what is learned, and it is therefore implicit in the preceding three principles. In effect, what is learned is not a specific behavior in response to a stimulus or reward but a cognition—an item of knowledge concerning physical space and the possibilities of reward therein. More specifically, what is learned is a sign–significate relationship: knowledge of a link between stimuli and expectancies of acquiring a goal.

Tolman's Link with the Gestaltists

Tolman's principal contribution to the development of psychological theory lies not so much in advances in knowledge and prediction made possible by his work as in the fact that it represents a transition from a strict behavioristic interpretation to a more cognitive approach. It would be far from accurate, however, to convey the impression that psychology went from the mentalistic concepts of the early introspectionists to the interpretations of behaviorists like Watson and Guthrie, then finally to a more enlightened cognitivism. In fact, cognitivism is approximately as old as behaviorism. **Gestalt** psychology, one of the earliest forms of cognitive theory, developed at about the same time as early behaviorism. It is nevertheless true, as we noted at the outset, that North American psychology went from a period when Watsonian and Thorndikian behaviorism were supreme, both in theory and in practice, to a later period when interest turned increasingly to cognitive topics (although behaviorism continued to flourish).

In some important ways, Tolman's thinking reflects something of both schools. This should not be surprising given that although one of his first courses in psychology used Watson's brand-new and thoroughly behavioristic book, before he had finished his graduate work at Harvard Tolman had traveled to Germany and met with leading Gestaltists like Köhler and his associates (Tolman, 1952). Some ten years later (around 1923), he returned to Germany to study with the Gestalt psychologists.

Basic Beliefs of Gestalt Psychology

At the time that World War I broke out, a young German psychologist by the name of Wolfgang Köhler found himself marooned on the island of Tenerife off the coast of Africa, unable to return to his home because of the war. On Tenerife there was a research station for studying apes, and Köhler studied them during the four years that he spent on the island. He reported his studies in a book entitled *The Mentality of Apes* (1925).

There are bright apes and stupid apes, Köhler concluded. Stupid apes seem to learn by association and repetition, practicing the same behaviors over and over again. In contrast, said Köhler, bright apes learn very much like people do, displaying a sometimes astounding capacity for higher mental process.

Köhler used two kinds of studies to study the problem-solving behavior of apes in cages; each led to identical observations. In both types of studies, an ape had to invent or discover a solution for the problem of obtaining a bunch of bananas beyond reach outside its cage. In the studies of "stick" problems, the ape had to use a long stick to reach the bunch of bananas; in some cases it was necessary to join several sticks together so that they would be long enough. In the "box" problems, the ape had to move a box underneath the bananas or pile boxes one on top of the other to reach the reward.

Insight versus Trial and Error

Intelligent apes don't learn by trial and error, claimed Köhler; they don't go about the cage lunging at the bananas repeatedly, climbing the bars, and doing other well-practiced ape things. Even when they do try various approaches, these don't ordinarily solve the problem. Instead, the solution most often comes when the ape is sitting or lying down, perhaps contemplating the problem (how do you know what apes think about, or if they think?) but not actively trying to solve it. Suddenly—bingo!—the ape gets up, tosses the boxes on top of one another or joins the stick fragments, and reaches the bananas. The Gestalt term for the process involved in this kind of solution is **insight**.

Insight is the cornerstone of Gestalt psychology. Essentially, it means *the perception of relationships among elements of a problem situation*. But, cautions Köhler (1929), just because the term *insight* is used to describe what might be considered an extraordinary accomplishment in an ape, we should not misinterpret it to mean "some special and supranatural faculty producing admirable and otherwise inexplicable results. As I used and intended the term, nothing of that sort should be implied in it" (p. 371). As Köhler used it, the term applies to understanding and solving very common, everyday problems and facts.

"I am not sure that even after years of trial and error," Köhler (1929) writes, "a child would *learn* to organize [a sensory field]" (p. 177). And organizing what is perceived, he claims, is far more important than the specific properties of what is perceived. Why? Because it is only through an understanding of their *organization*, through an understanding of their structure, that people know things. .

Take, for example, something as simple as a melody. You know that a melody is made up of individual notes. But you cannot understand the melody—you would know nothing of it—were you to hear the notes in completely random arrangement. Similarly, the meaning of a geometric figure derives not from each of its elements (number of sides, dimensions of its parts, angles of corners), but from their relationships to each other.

The Whole Is Greater Than the Sum of Its Parts

That the whole is greater than the sum of its parts is the cliché most closely associated with Gestalt psychology. Thus the melody, not its component pieces, is the whole, the organization, the *gestalt*—as is the trapezoid, the triangle, and the square. Their meaning comes not from summing their parts willy-nilly, but from the ability of humans (and apes) to perceive their organization. And, in the shell of a small nut, to perceive organization or structure is to achieve *insight*.

Not surprisingly, one way of summarizing Gestalt psychology is to describe it in terms of laws of perception. These laws were developed and elaborated largely by the three men considered to be the founders of the Gestalt movement: Wertheimer (1959), Koffka (1922, 1925, 1935), and Köhler (1927, 1959). Of these three, Wertheimer was the acknowledged leader, but Koffka and Köhler were most responsible for popularizing the movement through their writings.

KURT KOFFKA (1886–1941)
WOLFGANG KÖHLER (1887–1967)
MAX WERTHEIMER (1880–1943)

The ideas and theories of Koffka, Köhler, and Wertheimer are almost inseparable, as are their lives. All were graduates of the University of Berlin (they became known as the "Berlin group"), all had training in philosophy and psychology, and all eventually emigrated to the United States courtesy of Hitler's persecution of the Jews (Koffka and Wertheimer were Jewish). And not only did they work together, sharing their convictions and united in their attacks against both introspectionism and behaviorism, but they were also friends. It is no accident that Köhler's 1929 book, *Gestalt Psychology*, is dedicated to Max Wertheimer, and that Koffka's 1935 book, *Principles of Gestalt Psychology*, bears the inscription, "To Wolfgang Köhler and Max Wertheimer in gratitude for their friendship and inspiration."

Wertheimer, half a dozen years older than Köhler and Koffka, was born in Prague on April 15, 1880. His initial studies were in the field of law in Prague. Later he went to Berlin, where he studied philosophy and psychology and obtained his Ph.D. in 1904. His many interests included writing poetry and composing symphonies.

Acknowledged as the intellectual leader of Gestalt psychology, Wertheimer did far less to popularize the movement than did Köhler and Koffka. He wrote little but designed a number of important experiments, elaborating Gestalt principles in his lectures and recruiting Koffka and Köhler to work with him. It is reported that the idea for one of his most important experiments occurred to him during a vacation at the very beginning of his career. Riding on a train, he began to puzzle over the fact that lights that flash sequentially give the illusion of movement. Wertheimer's subsequent investigations of this "phi phenomenon" involved both Köhler and Koffka as his assistants and led eventually to the elaboration of Gestalt psychology. In 1933 Wertheimer emigrated to the United States, where he remained until his death in 1943.

Köhler was born in Reval, Estonia, on January 21, 1887. He obtained his Ph.D. from the University of Berlin in 1909 and subsequently, along with Koffka, worked with Wertheimer at Frankfurt. During World War I he spent 4 years on Tenerife studying the behavior of apes (and of chickens, too). The results of his investigations were published in an important book entitled *The Mentality of Apes* (1925).

From Tenerife, Köhler went back to Berlin, where he remained until 1935. He published extensively during this time, becoming one of the most important spokesmen for the Gestalt movement. Conflict with the Nazi regime forced him to leave Germany permanently in 1935. He went to the United States, where he had already spent considerable time lecturing and where he stayed until his death in 1967. Köhler continued to write important books in the United States, engaging in fierce battles with behaviorists such as Hull and even publically debating against Watson. He was awarded the Distinguished Scientific Contribution Award by the American Psychological Association and (like Skinner, Guthrie, Tolman, and Hebb) served as president of that association.

Koffka was born in Berlin on March 18, 1886, went to the university there, and obtained his Ph.D. in psychology in 1909. He had earlier studied science and philosophy in Edinburgh. From Berlin he went to Frankfurt, where he and Köhler worked with Wertheimer. There he began the extensive writings that later became very influential in popularizing Gestalt psychology. He was the most prolific writer of the Berlin group, publishing a large number of important and sometimes difficult books.

Like Köhler and Wertheimer, Koffka spent some time lecturing in the United States before moving there permanently in 1927. There he lectured at Smith College and continued to write until his death in 1941 (Boring, 1950; Sahakian, 1981; Schultz, 1969; Woodworth & Sheehan, 1964).

Gestalt Laws of Perception

The first and most basic argument advanced by Gestaltists against procedures that emphasize the analysis of behavior is that behavior cannot be understood in terms of its parts—that the whole really is greater than the sum of its parts.

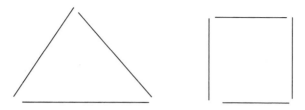

FIGURE 6.7 Closure.

This is not to deny that the whole is composed of parts, nor that the parts can be discovered through analysis.

That the perception of wholes (that is, of gestalts) is different from the perception of parts is evident in countless daily events. As noted above, when listening to music, the overall perception is not of isolated notes but rather of bars or passages. If this were not so, the order of notes and the intervals of time during which they are held, as well as the lapses between them, would not be so important. Similarly, it's clear that physical objects derive their identity not only from the parts that compose them but more from the manner in which these parts are combined. An object as simple as an apple is no longer simply an apple after it has been attacked by a blender; nor is a house still a house when all of its timbers, nails, and other parts have been taken apart and sorted.

Prägnanz: Good Form

The first concern of the Gestaltists, then, was to discover the laws governing the perception of wholes. These laws, first described by Koffka (1935), are summarized briefly here. The laws are primarily perceptual and are discussed here as such. Note, however, that Gestalt psychologists see no discontinuity between perception and thinking, and therefore they consider these laws to be applicable to both.

There is one overriding principle: **prägnanz** (meaning "good form"), which states that there is a tendency for whatever is perceived to take the best form possible. The exact nature of that form for all perceptual experience is governed by four additional principles, which are described below.

Principle of Closure

Closure is the act of completing a pattern or gestalt. It is clearly illustrated in the observation that when you look at an incomplete figure (such as in Figure 6.7), you tend to perceive a completed design. The same phenomenon is readily apparent in perception of a melody with missing notes, or of incomplete words like p–ych–l–gy.

Although the term *closure* was originally employed only with perceptual problems, it now used by psychologists in a variety of situations, retaining much of its original meaning but also acquiring some broader significance. For example, it is not uncommon to speak of achieving closure when referring to solving a problem, understanding a concept, or simply completing a task.

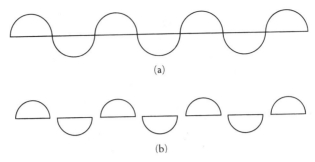

(a)

(b)

FIGURE 6.8 Continuity. The lines in (a) tend to be perceived as a straight line running through a curved one, not as a set of semicircles as in (b).

Principle of Continuity

Perceptual phenomena tend to be perceived as continuous. For example, a line that is started as a curved line (see Figure 6.8) tends to be perceived as having **continuity**—that is, as continuing in a curving fashion.

Principle of Similarity

The principle of **similarity** holds that objects that are similar tend to be perceived as related. For example, a person who hears two melodies at the same time recognizes each as a separate melody rather than hearing both as one. In Figure 6.9, there appear to be four rows of identical letters rather than ten columns of different letters.

a a a a a a a a a a
g g g g g g g g g g
c c c c c c c c c c
x x x x x x x x x x

FIGURE 6.9 Similarity.

Principle of Proximity

Objects or perceptual elements tend to be grouped in terms of their **proximity**. Figure 6.10(a), for example, shows four sets of curved lines, whereas Figure 6.10(b) is perceived as three faces.

Gestalt Views of Learning and Memory

These four principles, along with several others, were developed by Wertheimer and later applied by Koffka to thinking as well as to perception. Because the Gestaltists were not concerned with such molecular aspects of learning and behavior as stimuli and responses, their explanations of learning and memory are considerably more global and nonspecific than those of the behaviorists.

In general, the Gestaltist view is that learning results in the formation of memory traces. The exact nature of these traces is left unspecified, but a number of their characteristics are detailed. The most important characteristic is

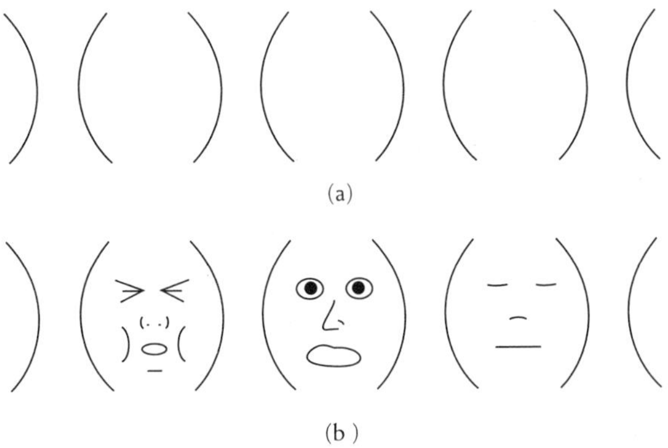

FIGURE 6.10 Proximity.

that learned material, like any perceptual information, tends to achieve the best structure possible (*prägnanz*) in terms of the laws of perceptual organization just discussed. Hence what is remembered is not always what was learned or perceived, but it is often a better gestalt than the original. Wulf (1938) described three organizational tendencies of memory, which he labeled **leveling, sharpening,** and **normalizing.**

Leveling

Leveling is a tendency toward symmetry or toward a toning down of the peculiarities of a perceptual pattern. Figure 6.11 presents a hypothetical illustration of leveling. Koffka assumed that the process of leveling is also applicable to cognitive material. For example, when recalling the feeling of traveling in a train, a person may remember a generalized impression of forward motion and of countryside sweeping by without also remembering the sensation of swaying from side to side.

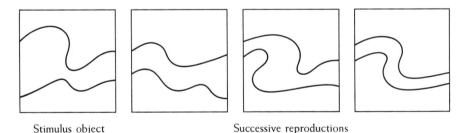

Stimulus object   Successive reproductions

FIGURE 6.11 Leveling.

Sharpening

Sharpening is the act of emphasizing the distinctiveness of a pattern. It appears to be one of the characteristics of human memory that the qualities which most clearly give an object identity tend to be exaggerated in the reproduction of

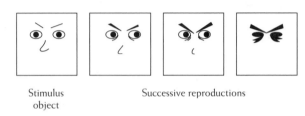

Stimulus   Successive reproductions
object

FIGURE 6.12   Sharpening.

that object. For example, Figure 6.12 shows how successive recollections of a face with distinctive eyebrows tend to exaggerate the eyebrows.

Normalizing

Normalizing occurs when the reproduced object is modified to conform with previous memories. This modification usually tends toward making the remembered object more like what it appears to be. A hypothetical illustration of normalizing is presented in Figure 6.13 in which successive reproductions of the same stimulus object over a period of time become progressively more like something familiar (and hence something "normal").

Beyond Perception: The Psychological Field

The world as it might be seen and described by physics is one thing, Koffka pointed out; the world as it is perceived by the individual is quite another matter. And this, the world of "direct experience," is far more important for understanding the individual's behavior.

The Lake of Constance

To illustrate, Koffka (1935, p. 28) tells the story of a man on horseback who struggles through a fierce blizzard across an open plain, finally arriving at an inn. "Gawd, which way did you come?" asks the innkeeper. The man, half frozen, points out the direction. "Do you know," asks the innkeeper in amazement, "that you have ridden across the Lake of Constance?" And the man, stunned, drops dead at the innkeeper's feet.

There is only one behavior here, that of riding across a frozen lake through a winter blizzard. The physical environment is fixed and clear. But, Koffka points out, the psychologist knows that the man's behavior would have been very different had he *known* about the lake. If the thought frightened him so much after the fact that it killed him, then he surely would not have crossed the lake if he had been aware of it beforehand.

The Behavioral Field

From the man's point of view, his behavior took place in a quite different environment—in what Koffka calls the **behavioral field** (or the psychological field). The behavioral field is the actor's personal view of what is real. In this man's behavioral field there was a windswept plain; as he later discovered, though, in the real physical world there was a frozen lake.

 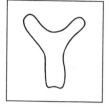  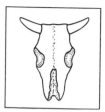

Stimulus object   Successive reproductions

FIGURE 6.13 Normalizing.

A person's behavior is always affected by both the behavioral field and the physical environment, claims Koffka. And although the physical environment clearly affects the psychological field, the two are not the same. Koffka describes as another example the behavior of two apes confronted by the "boxes" problem in separate cages. One, the bright ape, eventually stacks the boxes one on top of the other, climbs up, and retrieves the bananas. The other, the stupid one, ends up sitting on one of the boxes, staring sadly at the unreachable bananas. Both these apes are in exactly the same physical field. But in the psychological field of the bright guy, there are stacking boxes that reach way up; in the psychological field of the other, there is only a stool and some unreachable bananas.

Appearance versus Reality

The Gestalt laws of perception point out that what people see is not necessarily what is really out there. When you saw a complete triangle in Figure 6.7 earlier, you were not perceiving the physical field accurately. But that there is a triangle in Figure 6.7 becomes an actual part of your psychological reality. Thus does Gestalt psychology emphasize the difference between physical reality and what seems to be real.

The Gestaltists believed that to understand behavior, it's necessary to know something of the individual's perception of reality (that is, of the person's psychological field). This is because people respond to appearance (what they think is real) rather than to reality. The task of psychology, claimed Koffka (1935), is "the study of behaviour in its causal connection with the psychophysical field" (p. 67). In many ways, this is a far more complex task than the behaviorists had set themselves—namely, that of understanding responses to *real* stimuli in the actual physical environment. At the same time, because the psychological field includes people's individual perceptions of other people (as well as of things, animals, and all else that might be relevant) it is an approach that lends itself more easily to understanding social behavior.

GESTALT PSYCHOLOGY VERSUS CONTEMPORARY COGNITIVISM

Gestalt psychology is considered to be the forerunner of contemporary cognitive psychology mainly for two reasons: first, because of its concern with perception, awareness, problem solving, and insight; and second, because it rejected behaviorism, considering it overly mechanistic, incomplete, and unsuitable for explaining higher mental processes.

In several important ways, however, Gestalt psychology and contemporary cognitivism represent different interests and different approaches. Contemporary cognitive psychology deals with subjects such as problem solving, decision making, information processing, and understanding (the theories of Bruner and Piaget, discussed in the next chapter, are examples). Cognitive theorists conduct research on a wide range of topics, primarily using *human* subjects—topics such as understanding prose, memory for words, paraphrasing, language learning, and reading. In contrast, Gestalt psychology made extensive use of animal (as well as human) experimentation and dealt mainly with problems of human perception.

A Review and Evaluation of Gestalt Psychology

Gestalt psychology was an important reaction against the introspectionism that had preceded it, as well as against the behaviorism with which it was current. "I find myself therefore with a profound aversion and guard against the behaviorist, or any other one-sided and impractical purism in science," wrote Köhler (1929, p. 34). He argued that the behaviorists' insistence on dealing only with objective reality forced them to reject the validity and importance of what he called "direct experience": "There cannot be the slightest doubt for me that, as a child, I had 'direct experience'. . . . There were experiences which belonged to me personally and privately" (p. 20).

But, and this is central, the direct experience of which the Gestaltists speak is not the personal experience of the introspectionists, who sought to understand others' behaviors by looking inward at their own. Instead it is the sort of direct experience that allows a person to perceive a chair as a chair, to recognize and know a song—in short, to construct a picture of the physical world. Hence Gestalt psychology deals largely with the laws of perception, but it makes an important distinction between what is real (the physical field) and the individual's perception (the psychological field). Both are important for understanding behavior.

Gestalt theorists spent much time and effort—probably too much—criticizing contemporary behaviorists (such as Hull and Watson) and denouncing the efforts of introspectionists (such as William James). In the end, however, their theories don't fare especially well with respect to the criteria listed in Chapter 1. "The theoretical ideas of the Gestaltists were notoriously vague," write Holyoak and Spellman (1993, p. 268). As a result, these ideas don't reflect the facts very well, they are not especially clear, and they don't explain very much. "In the view of most contemporary observers," says Gardner (1987), the theoretical program of Gestalt psychology was not well founded . . . there are too many exceptions or indeterminate cases" (p. 114). As a result, current cognitive explanations of human behavior are quite different from those of Gestalt psychology.

In spite of their shortcomings, some of the concepts of Gestalt psychology have found useful applications in counseling and therapy. For example, Gestalt-like notions of the psychological field play an important role in humanistic theories of counseling such as that of Carl Rogers (he uses the expressions *phenomenological* and *phenomenal field* instead). Rogerian therapy is premised on the notion that to understand a person's behavior, it is essential to look at it from that person's personal view; change in behavior results when the person's views of reality change.

Perhaps even more important, it is theories such as these that were at least partly responsible for subsequent developments in both cognitive and behavioristic theory. In a real sense, Gestalt psychology served as a basis for contemporary cognitive theory, even as Tolman provided a transition from early behaviorism to contemporary cognitivism. Both presented new metaphors for clarifying and explaining human behavior.

Changing Metaphors in Psychology

A metaphor is a comparison. Metaphors abound in literature and especially in poetry, where their purpose is to evoke images (sometimes impossible ones) that are more startling, clearer, and more moving than the reality they represent. Thus in Pablo Neruda's (1972) poem "Little America," the woman the poet loves is not just a woman. She is a country, with "boughs and lands, fruits and water, the springtime that I love . . . the waters of the sea or the rivers and the red thickness of the bush where thirst and hunger lie in wait" (p. 110).[7] And in Neruda's "Letter on the Road," love is not simply a feeling; it is seeds and earth and water and fire, so that "perhaps a day will come when a man and a woman, like us, will touch this love and it will still have the strength to burn the hands that touch it" (Neruda, 1972, p. 148).[8]

In psychology, as in poetry, metaphors abound. But their purpose is psychology is less to move or startle than to inform and clarify. In fact, in the psychology of cognition, claims Bruner (1990), "it is apparent that there have been *nothing but* metaphors" (p. 230). Perhaps the most common of all current metaphors for human cognition is the computer, from which psychology draws notions of humans as information-processing units. Psychologists create cognitive models that speak of processing, storing, retrieving, input, output, and on and on.

But the metaphor was not always entirely welcome in psychology, or in science. For years, physical scientists were convinced that the end result of their many investigations would be a complete, accurate, and absolutely *literal* de-

---

[7]The original is as follows: *"ramas y tierras, fruitas y agua, / la primavera que amo, / la luna del desierto, el pecho / de la paloma salvaje, / la suavidad de las piedras gastadas / por las aguas del mar o de los rios / y la espesura roja / del matorral en donde / la sed y el hambre acechan."* (Kro)
[8]The original: *"Tal vez llegará un día / en que un hombre / y una mujer, iguales / a nosotros, / tocarán este amor y aún tendrá fuerza / para quemar las manos que lo toquen."* (Kro)

scription of the physical world and how it functions. In 1910 there seemed to be little reason to suspect that science might someday discover something about the world that could only be described in terms of black holes, quarks, antimatter, and other metaphorical concepts. Indeed, even in the 1990s many scientists still do not suspect that there might be something not quite literal about their knowledge.

Metaphors in Behaviorism

And so it was in psychology. During the first half of this century, a period dominated largely by behaviorism, psychologists searched valiantly for reliable facts, laws, and principles that might provide a literal description of human learning and behavior. The emphasis, especially for behaviorists like Skinner and Watson, was on keeping theorizing as close to the data as possible. And even neobehaviorists like Hull and Hebb, who allowed themselves to invent new metaphors in the form of hypothetical somethings that mediate between stimuli and response, nevertheless tried to define things operationally (that is, in terms of actual actions or operations). This was the legacy of "logical positivism"—a philosophy of science premised on the fundamental assumption that things are real and exact and that they can therefore be described and measured literally and accurately.

But as Smith (1990) points out, the behaviorists also found themselves using metaphors to explain and clarify. Hull, for example, used machine models of human functioning, describing his theory as the "robot approach." "So far as the thinking processes go," wrote Hull in one of his unpublished diaries, "a machine could be built which would do every essential thing that the body does" (quoted in Hays, 1962, p. 820).

Tolman, too, began to glimpse new metaphors in the imagination of the white Norway rat, for it seemed to Tolman that even the rat learns more than just S–R connections. Rather, it develops representations of the world—cognitive maps of what is out there, and notions that somehow connect what is out there with alternative behaviors. Tolman called these notions "expectancies," and his view of human learning explored the metaphor of cognitive maps and hypotheses. Thus Tolman's expectancies are representations of the world. But they are not the literal representations that a logical positivist might seek; they are metaphors.

Even Skinner used metaphors, claims Smith (1990), in spite of the fact that he was probably the most determinedly positivistic of the behaviorists and consequently held the "aim of eliminating metaphorical discourse from science" (p. 255). His principal metaphor is a Darwinian, evolutionary one. In the same way as species survive or die out as a function of natural pressures interacting with "fitness," so too are responses selected by their consequences. Behaviors survive or are eliminated as a function of how they are reinforced, ignored, or punished.

Metaphors in Cognitivism

As noted above, cognitive psychology is a psychology of metaphors. To explain human functioning, cognitive psychology uses metaphors of mental structures, describing things that don't actually exist to represent things that can't be described literally. All theoretical cognitive concepts—operations, short-term and long-term memory, neural networks—are metaphors. And most descriptions of how humans function (that is, of how cognitive structures are developed and used) rely on metaphors, especially computer metaphors. We will look at these in succeeding chapters.

SUMMARY

1. Hebb's model is based largely on neurological and physiological knowledge and hypotheses. Its aim is to explain higher mental processes—the processes that mediate between stimulus and response.

2. The human nervous system is made up of cells called neurons, which consist of a cell body, receiving extensions called dendrites, and an elongated part called an axon. Transmission among neurons is from axon ends across the synaptic cleft, which is the separation between the axon end and the dendrites of an adjacent cell.

3. Hebb describes higher mental processes (that is, thinking) in terms of activity in neural assemblies. He reasons that this activity must take the form of neurons arranged in such a way that they can keep reactivating one another in patterns he calls cell assemblies; arrangements of related cell assemblies are called *phase sequences*. Mediation (thinking) is defined in terms of activity in cell assemblies or phase sequences.

4. Important assumptions underlying Hebb's theory include the following: that cell assemblies result from the repeated presentation of similar stimulus patterns and therefore the repeated activation of the same neurons; that, if two assemblies are often active at the same time, they will tend to form associations with each other (thus explaining conditioning); that motor activity will become associated with the assemblies that are often active with it; and that each cell assembly corresponds to relatively simple sensory data.

5. Set and attention are central processes in learning and perception. Set refers to selectivity among responses; attention refers to selectivity among input.

6. Hebb's theory of motivation centers on the assumption that there is an optimum level of arousal for maximally effective behavior and that people will behave so as to maintain that level. Hence stimuli have both cue (message) and arousal functions. Studies of sensory deprivation support the belief that humans need a variety of sensory stimulation.

7. Mechanistic behaviorism seeks to be impeccably objective, analyzes behavior at a molecular level, and makes no assumptions about any intentions the actor might have. Tolman challenged these tenets, claiming that all behavior is purposeful and that explanations for it need to take into consideration the organism's expectations.

8. Among Tolman's most important beliefs are the following: all behavior is purposive; behavior should be analyzed at the molar rather than the molecular level; learning involves developing expectancies as a function of exposure to situations in which reinforcement is possible (sign–significate relationships); and expectancies can be described as cognitions, or cognitive maps.

9. Gestalt psychology can be viewed as an introduction to cognitivism. Cognitive approaches to learning are characterized by a preoccupation with topics such as understanding, information processing, decision making, and problem solving.

10. The primary beliefs of the Gestaltists can be summarized in two statements: (a) the whole is greater than the sum of its parts; and (b) people solve problems through insight. The first gives voice to the belief that the analysis of a subject (or object) into its parts is not likely to lead to knowledge of that subject. The second is a rejection of the role of trial and error in solving problems.

11. Wertheimer, Köhler, and Koffka were the founders of the Gestalt school. As a system, it has been identified largely in relation to its studies of perception and its formulation of such laws of perceptual organization as *prägnanz*, closure, similarity, continuity, and proximity. The application of these laws to learning has not received wide acceptance.

12. Gestalt studies of memory have led to the observation that structural changes in information over time involve the processes of leveling (making symmetrical), sharpening (heightening distinctiveness), and normalizing (rendering more like the object should appear).

13. Gestalt theorists make an important distinction between reality (the physical field) and the individual's perceptions (the behavioral or psychological field). Both need to be considered to understand behavior.

14. Gestalt psychology is considered a forerunner of contemporary cognitive psychology because of its concern with cognitive topics such as perception, and because of its rejection of behaviorism.

15. Psychology, especially cognitive psychology, makes extensive use of metaphors, although early behaviorists (reflecting a logical positivism) sought to be more literal than metaphorical. Various machine metaphors have long been popular and are evident in Hull's "robotic approach" and, more recently, in the human-as-computing-machine metaphor.

Part 4

MOSTLY COGNITIVE THEORIES

Bruner and Piaget: Two Cognitive Theories

My brain! That's my second favorite organ.

—Woody Allen, *Sleeper*

Preliminary Note for Human Readers: Chapter 7 Objectives

"If the theory of reinforcement related to the acquisition of knowledge," Bruner (1985) writes, "God would not have had to expel poor Adam and Eve from the garden for eating of the tree of knowledge. He would have arranged, Huck Finn style, for them to have developed a very bad stomachache from the consumption of green apples" (p. 7). As you learned in Chapter 5, if you were paying attention, a bad enough stomachache (or, better yet, a malaise of the kind Lefrançois is reported to have suffered when he ate his grandmother's stewed rabbit) would presumably have led to one-shot taste-aversion learning. Neither Adam nor Eve would have ever had a taste for apples—or knowledge—again.

"Instead," Bruner continues, "He knew that knowledge, once attained, is irreversible" (p. 7). So humans have a taste for knowledge, a hunger for information. More than that, claims Bruner, they're forever going *beyond the information given*.

Even if you don't go beyond the information given in this chapter, you will be astounded to discover that once you have finished digesting its contents, you will be able to (while standing or sitting) answer remarkably complex questions relating to what Bruner meant by the following:

- Concept formation
- Categories and coding systems
- Strategies
- Going beyond the information given

You will also know what Piaget meant by the following:

- Adaptation, assimilation, and accommodation
- Play, imitation, and intelligence
- Sensorimotor, preoperational, concrete, and formal developmental stages

Even better, you will also have stunning new insights into what pigeons know about people.

SIXTH TIME CUBE, 49TH HEXALOG, POINT 230.00

What is a person to a pigeon? you ask. What does a pigeon think of people when it swoops above their houses or flies above their fields and forests? Of what does it dream, hunched in a city tree or huddled on the edge of a roof as people scurry about beneath its perch? In the pigeon's thoughts, is a person just another big, earthbound thing, indistinguishable from horses, cows, goats, and trucks? Does the pigeon have a concept of "peopleness"? Is the pigeon capable of any thoughts of this kind?

It's no easy matter for people to ask pigeons such things. But Herrnstein, Loveland, and Cable (1976) did pose the question. And, even more astounding, the pigeons answered.

What Herrnstein and his associates did was present pigeons with series of slides, some of which contained one or more people doing a variety of things, dressed in different ways (or even nude), and sometimes partly obscured by other objects like trees. The researchers arranged for pigeons to be reinforced only when they pecked in the presence of a slide containing a person. Sure enough, the pigeons learned to do this. They seemed to have what Herrnstein and his associates call "natural concepts" that include complex and indeterminate notions like what a person is. And they were able to identify slides representing this concept even when the "peopleness" of people was disguised in different activities, different contexts, and different clothing.

COGNITIVE PSYCHOLOGY

That pigeons learn concepts may not be all that important for the study of human learning and behavior.[1] But that humans do is, and consequently it is one of the central topics of cognitive psychology.

Differences between Cognitivism and Behaviorism

Cognitive psychology is distinguished from behaviorism not only by the fact that it is more clearly metaphorical, as we saw in Chapter 6, but also by its principal areas of interest, the nature of its research, and the scope of its theory building.

First, cognitive psychology's principal topics deal with higher mental functions, rather than with the stimuli and responses of behaviorism. The most important of these higher mental functions have to do with perception (how physical energies are translated into meaningful experiences), concept formation, memory, language, thinking, problem solving, and decision making.

Second, the shift to cognitivism also saw a shift from an emphasis on animal research to a renewed emphasis on human research. Topics like language learning, reading, strategies in concept attainment, and the growth of logic cannot easily be investigated with rats and pigeons.

Third, cognitive theories tend to be less ambitious in scope than earlier behavioristic theories. There have been few attempts to build systematic and inclusive cognitive theories that would explain all of human learning and behavior. As will become clear in later chapters, the emphasis in the last several

---

[1] But it's probably pretty dang important to pigeons. (GRL)

decades has been on intensive research in specific areas, rather than on the construction of general systems.

Cognitive Topics

The dominant metaphor in cognitive psychology, note Massaro and Cowan (1993), is an **information-processing (IP)** metaphor—which is essentially a computer-based metaphor. Information processing refers to how information (input) is modified or changed. The emphasis is on perceptual and conceptual processes that allow the perceiver to perceive, determine how the actor acts, and underlie thinking, remembering, solving problems, and so on.

The single most important common characteristic of the topics of cognitive psychology is that they presuppose mental representation and, of course, information processing. Accordingly, theory building in the recent development of cognitive psychology has taken the form of metaphors relating to the nature of mental representation and to the processes involved in constructing and using these representations.

Among the important contributions to the development of contemporary cognitive psychology are those made by Jerome Bruner and Jean Piaget, which are discussed in the remainder of this chapter. Subsequent chapters deal with specific areas where current research is primarily cognitive: artificial intelligence, memory, and motivation.

BRUNER'S THEORY: AN OVERVIEW

In a classic article, Bruner (1964) compares the development of a child to the evolution of the human race.

The Evolution of the Brain

In the beginning humans were far from the fastest, the fiercest, or the strongest of the predators on this planet. There is little doubt that the fabled saber-toothed tiger, *Tyrannosaurus rex,* or some other awesome beast would have been highly successful in controlling human population had it not been for one simple fact: The human proved, in the end, to be more intelligent than all who preyed on human flesh. So intelligent was this creature that it eventually took the course of evolution into its own hands. It used its brains.

"Brains are wonderful things," Johanson and Shreeve (1989) tell us. "There is no better solution to one's environment—no claw so sharp, no wing so light that it can begin to bestow the same adaptive benefits as a heavy ball of gray matter" (p. 262).

Advantages of Having Brains

At the very dawn of civilization, human brains allowed access to food sources that would be overlooked by humankind's finned, feathered, or clawed competitors, many of whom had better noses, keener eyesight, swifter movement, and stronger beaks and jaws. Brains are what permitted people to make the connection between sharp sticks and digging beneath the ground for roots and tubers, or between heavy rocks and stunned prey (or predators). Eventually brains led to stone and wooden tools, agricultural and hunting implements, the wheel, the rocket, the computer . . . and whatever may come next.[2]

Maladaptive Brains

Brains, says Cowley (1989), were shaped by the same forces that molded other organs, forces manifested in behaviors that maximize chances of surviving and reproducing. These are forces whose effects take shape over vast stretches of time. Not surprisingly, then, some behaviors that were once highly adaptive persist even though they are now counteradaptive—witness humanity's peculiar and frightening penchant to destroy its environment and to shorten its lives through resting too much and eating too much of the wrong things. Most of human evolutionary history was spent in Pleistocene environments, Cowley (1989) points out. There snakes and other wild creatures posed far greater threats than water and air pollution, and the likelihood of ingesting too much fat, salt, or sugar was laughably scarce. Also, a well-rested and well-fed animal can more easily survive a cold spell or escape from a predator. It's as though the Pleistocene dragons of Sagan's (1977) Eden still whisper in humans' ears when they stand before their refrigerators: "Eat while you can. There may be none tomorrow—if there is a tomorrow."

Evolution of Representation: Bruner's View

Still, if you are human, you *know* there will be food tomorrow, and you know the saber-toothed tiger is not likely to invade your bedroom this night. You can anticipate with startling clarity; you can plan for times that have not yet come, but whose coming can be measured to the very second. Not only can you anticipate the future, but you can remember the past. And more than all this, you are conscious of your awareness; you can reflect on your own reflections.

Put very simply, you have a *mind* that is made possible by your nervous system and your brain. The mind, says Alexander (1989), presents the most striking gap between humans and all other animals—and the most difficult to understand.

Three Series of Inventions

The evolution of the mind, Bruner notes, is evident through three waves of remarkable inventions, each of which served three different functions. First, humans succeeded in developing devices that could amplify their motor capaci-

---

[2]Astoundingly, what may come next, given this species' addiction to entertainment, are the as-yet-uninvented sensatrons. Thus far, human television translates only visual and auditory information, both without real fidelity, the visual flatter than a Piscean rodent under a motor-trawdle. Sadly, little effort is directed toward inventing better social systems. (Kro)

ties: simple machines (levers, pulleys, inclined planes, perhaps even the legendary wheel) and combinations of machines to make weapons (knives, arrows, spears, and hatchets). By amplifying their motor capacities, humans became stronger and less vulnerable.

Centuries later—quite recently in human history—a second group of inventions appeared and again dramatically altered the pattern of human evolution. These inventions amplified sensory rather than motor capacities. They include the telescope, radio, television, and all the other instruments that expand humans' ability to see, hear, feel, and sense things they could not otherwise sense.

The final group of human inventions includes those that amplify what Bruner terms *ratiocinative* (intellectual) capacities. These are human symbol systems and theories; they include computer languages and systems. Humanity is only at the threshold of this last major development and cannot yet easily determine what the impact of these inventions will be.

Three Types of Representation

How does the development of the child compare to this glimpse of evolution? Bruner suggests that the representational systems that children use as they develop closely parallel the history of human inventions. Thus, at the earliest ages, children represent objects in terms of their own immediate sensation of them. In Bruner's words, things get "represented in the muscles." This representation, termed **enactive**, corresponds to the period in human evolution when the emphasis was on the amplification of motor capacities.

Early in development, children progress from a strictly motoric (or enactive) representation to what Bruner calls **iconic** representation. An icon is an image; accordingly, iconic representation involves the use of mental images that stand for certain objects or events. This type of representation corresponds to the period during which human inventions were directed at amplifying sensory capacities.

The most advanced form of representation available to the child is **symbolic** representation, which parallels the development of inventions that amplify intellectual capacities. The fundamental difference between a symbol and an icon is that the icon bears a literal resemblance to its referent, whereas the symbol does not. A symbol is completely arbitrary: The number 2 does not look like a collection of two objects any more than the word *turkey* looks like that much-maligned bird. Yet humans have absolutely no difficulty in understanding what is meant by either of these or, indeed, by most of the thousands of other symbols in this text.

Although enactive, iconic, and symbolic representation develop sequentially, they do not replace one another. Adults continue to represent both enactively and iconically as well as symbolically. Thus, if you are human, you "know" how to ride a bicycle, stroke a cue ball, or execute a golf shot not primarily in symbols or in images but in your body; in contrast, you recognize faces not in activity or even in symbols but in images.

JEROME SEYMOUR BRUNER (1915–   )

Jerome Bruner was born the youngest of four children in a Jewish family in an affluent New York suburb. At the age of 2, he underwent the first of a pair of surgical procedures to correct his early blindness (caused by cataracts), a process about which he retained no memories. He describes his parents as "remote grownups"; the center of his family—the "we" of his childhood—comprised himself, his older sister, a half brother, and two cousins.

When Bruner was 12, his father died. Thereafter his mother moved every year (to Florida; to California; to "the country"), and the effect on young Jerome was, in his words, "too sudden a transformation" (Bruner, 1983, p. 5). He describes shifting schools constantly but never quite shifting his allegiances before moving again, as though caught up in an endless adolescence. "My formal secondary schooling was appalling," he writes (Bruner, 1983, p.17), lamenting that he never stayed in one school long enough to develop any good relationships with teachers, although his marks were acceptable.

Bruner describes himself as shy and ill at ease as an adolescent, and he thought himself ugly. At the age of 16, he and some friends got hold of a motorized racing hull that they smoothed and polished, and with whose engine they tinkered and played until they had become experts. In 1932, they won the Round Manhattan race. (Heady stuff.)

At 17, Bruner entered Duke University in Durham, North Carolina. He obtained a B.A. from Duke in 1937, and 4 years later he received his Ph.D. from Harvard. He has since been a professor at Harvard as well as at Princeton, Cambridge, and Oxford. He was one of the founders, as well as a director, of the Center for Cognitive Research at Harvard.

Bruner's research has been highly eclectic and highly influential, not only in psychology but also in education. He has also been a prolific writer, with more than 10 books and many dozens of articles to his name. In 1972, at the age of 57, Bruner was named Watts Professor of Experimental Psychology at Oxford University— whereupon he and his wife, with a few friends helping as crew, sailed across the Atlantic in his sailboat.

In 1983, still very active at age 68, he concludes his autobiographical essays with the note: "I suppose my life has been a good one . . . psychology has certainly helped it to be so, psychology as a way of inquiry rather than as a basis of wisdom" (Bruner, 1983, p. 293.) And still very active in 1990, he gives readers yet another glimpse of his vision, decrying the new cognitivism for abandoning "meaning" as its theme and embracing too unquestioningly the metaphor of the computer (Bruner, 1990c).

Representation and Cognitive Theory

In summary, adults have at least three distinct modes for representing not only the effects of sensory experiences but also thoughts. The importance of representation—and especially of symbolic representation—can hardly be overestimated. A symbolic representational system, most importantly language, is absolutely essential to systematic reasoning, says Newell (1990). In addition, such a system is essential for sharing knowledge among people. Ultimately, representation is fundamental in determining human culture and in shaping the experience of living a human life. Representational systems, claims Bruner (1990b), are "a very special kind of communal tool kit whose tools, once used, make the user a reflection of the community" (p. 11).

A Theory of Categorization

How people build up and use representations is one of the principal concerns of Bruner's theory. And the metaphor he invents as a basis for this theory is one of **categorization**. All human cognitive activity involves categories, Bruner informs us. Hence, to understand Bruner's theory, it is important to know what a **category** is, how it is formed, and of what value it is?

What Is a Category?

If a man sees a head with long blond hair and an attractive face smiling at him over a sea of foam in a pink bathtub, does he simply see a head with long blond hair and a smiling face over a sea of foam in a pink bathtub? (The question is surely of more than passing academic interest.)[3]

In a literal sense, yes, that is all he sees. But in another sense, he also sees much more. He sees that this must be a woman, who probably has two arms, two legs, toenails, and other things. Yet he can't perceive these things, so what he does, in Bruner's (1957a) words, is "go beyond the information given." First, he decides that this is a woman; second, he makes inferences about this woman on the basis of what is known about *all* women. According to Bruner, inferences are made possible through using categories—in this case, the category *woman.* The category *woman* is a **concept** in the sense that it is a representation of related things; it is also a **percept** in the sense that it is a physical thing apprehended through the senses. Percepts and concepts are roughly equivalent in Bruner's system.

Categories can be compared to the cell assemblies and phase sequences of Hebb's theory. Because they are essentially classifications of objects in terms of properties that are redundant for that type of object, categories are based on associations developed largely through frequency or redundancy. For example, if

---

[3]The observations that follow would have been just as appropriate had it been a woman looking at a head with curly black hair and a beard smiling at her over a sea of suds in a blue bathtub. It wasn't. I know. (Kro)

the first people to arrive from Mars all have warts, eventually warts will become a criterial attribute for the category *Martian*. In Hebbian terms, the cell assemblies activated by warts will become associated with others activated by Martians.[4]

Categories as Rules

"To categorize," writes Bruner, "is to render discriminably different things equivalent, to group the objects and events and people around us into classes, and to respond to them in terms of their class membership rather than in terms of their uniqueness" (Bruner, Goodnow, & Austin, 1956, p. 1). Hence one way of looking at the term *category* is to define it as though it were a rule (or a collection of rules) *for classifying things as being equal*. This is a very logical definition because concepts and percepts—which are achieved through categorizing—are collections of things that are in some way equivalent. For example, the concept (or category) *book* can be thought of as a rule that allows an individual to recognize an object as a book. In fact, this category is a collection of rules that specify that to be a book, an object must have pages, have a cover, contain writing, and have a title (among other things).

Attributes

Categories, as rules, say something about the characteristics that objects must possess before they can be classified in a given way. Characteristics of objects are **attributes**. Bruner (1966) defines attributes are "some discriminable feature of an object or event which is susceptible of distinguishable variation from event to event" (p. 26). Attributes are therefore properties of objects that are not possessed by all objects. They are further distinguished by whether they play a role in the act of categorizing. Attributes that define an object are called **criterial attributes**; those that do not are called *irrelevant*. Having female sexual organs is probably a criterial attribute for the category *woman*; a particular color of hair is irrelevant.

Rules for Categorizing

As rules, categories specify four things about the objects being reacted to. They are described and illustrated here in terms of the category *car*. First, as we just saw, a category is defined in terms of criterial attributes. For the category *car*, these might include the presence of a motor, running gear, and some standard control devices.

Second, a category not only specifies the attributes that are criterial but also indicates the manner in which they are to be combined. If, for example, all parts of a car were disassembled and placed in plastic garbage bags, it is unlikely that anyone would treat the result as though it were a car. As the Gestalt psychologists insisted, the whole is greater than the sum of its parts; the rule for the category *car* says that the parts must be assembled in a prescribed fashion.

---

[4]Two decades ago, all *would* have had warts. But by the time they decide to come to this planet (they're terrible procrastinators—but who wouldn't be if they lived as long as Martians do), it's likely that most will have undergone their recently developed *new-face* surgery. (Some wag on Koros has dubbed it Comic surgery, but in reality, its *Cosmic*. Here, it would simply be *cosmetic*.) (Kro)

Third, a category assigns weight to various properties. A car might continue to be classified as a car even if it had no bumpers and no windows, and perhaps even if it had no wheels. But if it had no motor and no body, it might be categorized as something else because these properties are more criterial for membership in the category.

Fourth, a category sets acceptance limits on attributes. Attributes often vary from event to event; color, for example, can vary tremendously. A rule specifying that a car has four wheels might set the limits of variation at zero. Thus anything with three wheels or less, or five wheels or more, would not be a car.

A Summary of Categorization

In summary, people interact with the environment in terms of categories, or classification systems that allow them to treat different events or objects as though they were equivalent. Incoming information is therefore organized in terms of preexisting categories, or it causes the formation of new ones. In either case, the end product of the processing will be a decision about the identity of the stimulus input, as well as a number of implicit inferences about the object or event associated with the input. Bruner suggests that *all* interaction with the world must involve classifying input in relation to categories that already exist. Completely novel experiences are "doomed to be a gem serene, locked in the silence of private experience" (Bruner, 1957b, p. 125). In short, people probably cannot perceive totally new stimulus input; if they can, they cannot communicate it.

Decision Making

Not only is all information processed through an act of categorization, but all decisions also involve classifying. In fact, in Bruner's system, decision making is simply another aspect of information processing that involves categorization.

First, to identify an object is to make a decision about whether it belongs in a given category. Second, once an object is placed in a category and therefore identified, there is inherent in the category a decision about how the object should be reacted to. For example, the almost unconscious recognition that a traffic light is red is the result of interpreting the input in question as though it were an example of events belonging to the category *red light.* Implicit in this act of categorizing is the decision not to walk across the street.

A second aspect of decision making involves the selection of strategies for attaining concepts. These are discussed in a later section of this chapter.

Coding Systems

Categories allow the classification, and hence the recognition, of sensory input. But going beyond the immediate sense data involves more than simply making inferences on the basis of the category into which the input has been classified. More importantly, it involves making inferences on the basis of related catego-

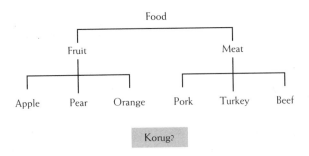

FIGURE 7.1   A coding system.

ries. For example, the inference that a new object (let's call it a "korug") is edible might be made not simply because the korug is pearlike and pears are edible, but also because the korug is orangelike and oranges are edible. In fact, the korug is identified and predictions are made about it on the basis of a wide variety of related categories. These related categories are referred to as a **coding system** (see Figure 7.1).

Coding systems can be thought of as hierarchical arrangements of related categories, such that the topmost category in the system is more generic (that is, general) than all the categories below it. In other words, as one moves up from the specific instances that define related categories, each subsequent concept (or category) is more abstract—freer of specifics, in Bruner's terms. To remember a specific, it is usually sufficient to recall the coding system of which it is a member. The details of the specific instance can then be recreated. And the transfer value of coding systems results from the fact that a generic code is really a way of relating objects and making inferences about them. There is obviously a significant amount of transfer involved in the decision that appropriate behavior toward a korug involves eating it.

Concept Attainment

Bruner's experimental work in the formation of concepts presents a significant contribution to this important area of cognitive psychology. Among other things, his is the first systematic attempt to examine the belief that people form concepts by generating and testing hypotheses about the attributes of the concepts in question. And the fact that he applied a controlled, experimental approach to this difficult cognitive problem did a great deal to make cognitivism more acceptable to psychologists reared in an experimental—and usually behavioristic—tradition.[5]

---

[5]Bruner's work on concept learning had a tremendous influence on psychology in the 1950s. It came at a time when American psychology was largely behavioristic. Prior to Bruner's work, mentalistic notions such as *concepts* had never seemed particularly amenable to objective experimental investigation and verification. But Bruner demonstrated that solid empirical investigations are possible even in the area of human *thinking*. (Kro)

Forming and Attaining Concepts

For Bruner, *concept attainment* involves discovering the attributes that may be useful in distinguishing between members and nonmembers of a class. *Concept formation*, a slightly different process, involves learning that specific different classes exist. For example, when Jack learns that there are edible as well as inedible mushrooms, he may be said to have *formed* the concept of edible versus nonedible mushrooms. But that Jack have formed this concept does not mean that he can now go out into the forest and bring back only edible mushrooms. When he has learned precisely what the differences between edible and inedible mushrooms are, he will have *attained* the concept (and I, Kro, will gladly eat whatever he brings back). Bruner suggests that the process of forming concepts is predominant in humans until around the age of 15, after which there is a prevalence of concept attainment.

Types of Concepts

Bruner distinguishes among three kinds of concepts in terms of the criterial attributes that define them. *Conjunctive* concepts are defined by the joint presence of two or more attribute values. For example, a pen is an object that can be held in the hand and that can be used to write. Both of these conditions must be met if the object is to be a pen; therefore, the concept *pen* is conjunctive.

A disjunctive concept, in contrast, is defined either by the joint presence of two or more attributes or by the presence of any one of the relevant attributes. For example, a human with a serious mental disorder may have delusions of grandeur, an intense fear of persecution, and a mania for stealing, or he or she may simply have the delusions, or the phobia, or the mania. This is a disjunctive concept.

The third variety of concept is referred to as *relational*. It is defined by a specified relationship between attribute values. A rectangle, for example, not only has four sides, but two sides must also be equal in length and longer than the other two, which must also be equal in length. *Rectangle* is thus a relational concept.

Values	Number of Figures	Number of Borders	Shape	Color
	1	1	■	red
	2	2	▲	blue
	3	3	●	yellow

FIGURE 7.2   An experiment on concept attainment strategies. The chart lists the four attributes and three values that, in all possible combinations, made up the 81-card deck used in the experiment. Two sample cards are also shown.

Strategies for Concept Attainment

People form concepts, says Bruner, to simplify the environment and to know how to react to it. Furthermore, to reduce cognitive strain, as well as to ensure that concepts are attained quickly and accurately, they adopt certain strategies. These strategies take the form of regularities, or patterns, in the sequence of decisions that are made in determining whether objects belong to given classes.

To investigate these strategies, Bruner and his associates (1956) developed a series of cards, each of which could be used as an example of either a conjunctive, disjunctive, or relational concept. The 81 cards developed for this purpose included all the possible variations of four attributes, each with three values (see Figure 7.2). For the experiments, disjunctive or conjunctive concepts were explained and illustrated, depending on the specific study. A card with two borders and three red circles, for example, could be an example of several conjunctive concepts—like *red circle*, in which case all other cards also having at least one red circle would be examples of the same concept. If the concept *red circles* were disjunctive, any card that had either red figures on it or circles of any color would illustrate the same concept because disjunction indicates an *either-or* element.

The experimental procedure was to have the subject try to discover (that is, attain) the concept the experimenter had in mind. To make the problem simpler the experimenter told the subject how many values were included in the concept (usually two) and whether the concept was conjunctive or disjunctive.

Following various studies using these cards, Bruner discovered several systematic strategies that subjects used. One group of strategies for the attainment of conjunctive concepts is discussed here as illustration. These are called *selection* strategies because the subject was first presented with all 81 cards, shown one example of the concept, and then allowed to select the card to be tested next. After each test, the experimenter told the subject that the card selected was or was not an example of the concept. The object of the "game" was twofold: to arrive at the correct concept, and to do it in the least number of trials possible. Bruner identified four selection strategies for the attainment of conjunctive concepts.

Simultaneous Scanning.   The first strategy involves generating all possible tenable hypotheses on the basis of the first example (positive instance) of the concept and using each successive selection to eliminate all untenable hypotheses. For example, if the experimenter presents the subject with a card with two borders and three red circles on it, it would give rise to 15 tenable hypotheses (these are all two-valued conjunctive concepts): two borders and three figures, three circles, three red figures, red circles, two borders and red figures, two borders and circles, and so on. Unfortunately, the human mind cannot ordinarily consider so many hypotheses simultaneously. The strategy is theoretically possible but virtually nonexistent in practice.

Successive Scanning. This second strategy imposes much less cognitive strain, because it is simply a trial-and-error approach. It involves making a hypothesis ("Um . . . maybe the concept is red circles") and choosing a card to test the hypothesis directly. If the original guess is not confirmed ("Dang, I was wrong!"), a second hypothesis is made ("Maybe it's red squares"). By chance, the concept may sometimes be arrived at very quickly with this procedure; it may also never be attained.

Conservative Focusing.   For several reasons, this third strategy is the best. It imposes relatively little strain on memory or on inferential capacity, and it also assures that the concept will be attained.

A subject using conservative focusing begins by accepting the first positive instance as the complete hypothesis. For example, suppose the concept is red circles (RO), and the first card has two borders and three red circles (2B3RO). The subject hypothesizes that the concept is 2B3RO. The person then selects a second card, which varies from the original in only one value: for example, two borders and two red circles. The experimenter confirms that this card is still an example of the concept. It follows that the changed attribute, number of figures, is irrelevant. The remaining hypothesis is 2BRO. The next selection changes one more value—the color; the card chosen has two borders and three green circles. Because the instance is now negative, color clearly was relevant. The subject now knows that red is part of the concept. If the next choice eliminates number of borders or confirms shape (which it will if only one value is changed), the subject will have attained the concept (see Figure 7.3).

Focus Gambling.   A slight variation of conservative focusing involves varying more than one value at a time—in other words, gambling. If two values are changed and the card remains positive, progress is accelerated. If, however, the instance becomes negative, the subject learns little, because either or both of the changed values could be criterial.

Strategies in Real Life

The results of Bruner's work on concept attainment are difficult to generalize to nonexperimental situations. People are not often presented with systematic examples from which to select experiences. Nor is there usually an authority immediately available to say, "Yes, this is an example of true love," or "No, that

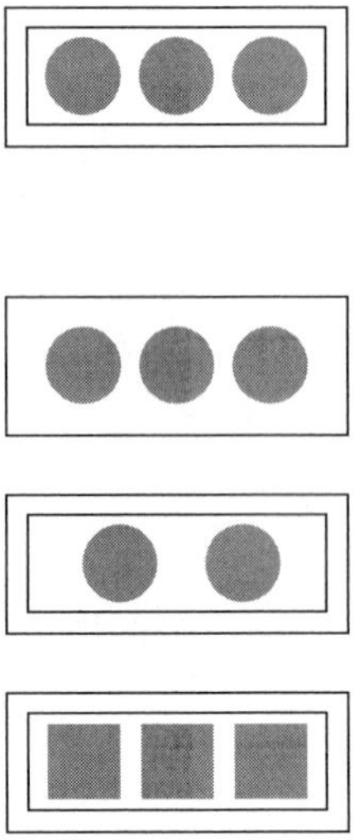

1. Card is presented as an example of the concept:

2. Temporary hypothesis is formed—the concept is two
   borders and three red circles:

   (2B3RO)

3. Card is chosen that changes one value: (1B3RO)

4. Choice is positive: number of borders is irrelevant—   (2B2BO)
   hypothesis becomes 3RO. Second card is chosen that
   changes one of the remaining values:

5. Number was not relevant, since card is still an example   (2B3RS)
   of the concept. Next choice changes one of the remaining
   values—shape of figures:

6. Choice is negative. Therefore, shape was relevant.
   Concept is:

   red circles

FIGURE 7.3   Decision sequence in attaining the concept *red circle* by using a conservative focusing strategy.

is not an example of true love." (And indeed, discovering what true love is appears to be a concept-attainment task of considerable importance.)[6]

A second difficulty is that Bruner employed adult subjects in his experiments, but simpler versions of the problems presented to children have not always led to the identification of the same strategies (Olson, 1963). A third problem is that even adult subjects in Bruner's experiments often used no identifiable strategies. Difficult approaches (such as successive scanning) were never employed by any subject and therefore remain ideal rather than actual strategies.

Despite these problems, some of this work may be related to various aspects of human behavior. For example, the acquisition of inductive and deductive reasoning processes in children may involve the learning of strategies similar to those investigated by Bruner, particularly because the teaching process in schools often involves presenting related examples and information about class memberships. Although teachers and curriculum materials are sel-

---

[6]I studied human love in considerable detail, it being so fundamental to human existence. And my first conclusions were that there was no such thing as *true* love—that it was simply a human expression for an unattainable wish, a longing. "You're wrong," said Lefrançois. "True love *does* exist. It's as real as Koronian goose bumps!" (He has seen mine). He explained that true love is a blend of passion, commitment, and intimacy, and he promised to allow me to experience the first of these three, the passion part, before I leave. I will write of it—and of love—in Report 38. (Kro)*

*My aunt Lucy undertook to provide Kro with the necessary education and experience. I'm not certain that any of it worked; they've been remarkably close-mouthed about the whole thing. But Kro has promised to sonarduct Report 38 back to Earth some time in the coming year. (GRL)

dom as systematic and rigorous as experimental procedures, they can occasionally be patterned after these procedures.

OTHER RESEARCH ON CONCEPT FORMATION

Bruner's description of categories and of the processes involved in categorizing continues to play an important role in cognitive research. "A category," write Mervis and Rosch (1981), "exists whenever two or more distinguishable objects or events are treated equivalently" (p. 89)—a definition essentially identical to that first advanced by Bruner a quarter of a century earlier. "And categorization," Mervis and Rosch continue, "may be considered one of the most basic functions of living creatures" (p. 89). What does more recent research tell us about categorization?

Developmental Trends in Concept Learning

Contrary to what you might expect, children don't begin by learning the most specific concept and progressing from there to the most general. Instead, they typically begin by learning concepts of intermediate generality and then learn those that are more specific. Later they develop more supraordinate categories (coding systems, in Bruner's terms). For example, a child doesn't begin by learning the concept *German shepherd*, a highly specific category, but instead learns the concept *dog*. Eventually concepts such as *poodle, German shepherd*, and others at a similar level of specificity will be learned. Later, the child will be ready to understand the related generic concept *mammal*.

Category Boundaries

Items or events that are included in the same category are not all equivalent, even though they may be reacted to as though they were. For example, although a large range of stimulus input will be interpreted as being blue (that is, as belonging to the category corresponding to blueness), some of that input will be interpreted as being more blue and some as less blue. Similarly, some colors will be more green, others more black, some lighter, and some darker; yet under appropriate circumstances, all will be reacted to as though they were blue.

In the same way, those individuals who fit into your categories for *thin* or *fat* are not all equally thin or fat. So category boundaries are not always well defined, and the definitions that exist may be somewhat arbitrary. Not only might Lefrançois and his grandmother not agree perfectly with respect to the attributes that are criteria for membership in their *fat* and *thin* categories, but, when pressed, each would be forced to recognize that their own personal categories for these qualities have somewhat fuzzy boundaries.

Abstraction

At a superficial level, it might seem that perceiving physical objects requires no more than some knowledge of their physical properties and the availability of an appropriate category—that is, perception simply involves matching sensations with appropriate categories. Thus, to recognize someone as belonging to the category *thin* or *fat*, it should suffice to do no more than sense thinness or fatness (probably through vision, or maybe through palpation as well). In fact, however, "fatness" and "thinness" cannot be sensed directly; they are abstractions. Thus, even at the most elementary level of perceptual recognition, abstraction is often involved.

Two Models of Abstraction

In fact, abstraction is involved in virtually all models of categorization (Holyoak & Spellman, 1993). The main question these models try to answer is this: How do people abstract the central characteristics of a class of objects or events as a result of exposure to examples of that class?

One answer is that people develop a generalized notion of the most typical or representative features of a concept. This abstraction is in effect a **prototype**, a sort of generalized model (Rosch, 1977). Thus, after seeing thousands of different trees, Jane has developed a highly abstract notion of "treeness." If she could represent this abstract notion accurately, she might find that it doesn't resemble any one specific tree or kind of tree, but that instead it embodies all that is essential in trees. Whenever she sees some new treelike thing, she simply compares it to her prototypical tree.

Another possibility is that in the course of learning about trees, Jane has stored in memory a number of good examples of trees. **Exemplar models** (Medin & Florian, 1992) argue that concepts are represented by memories of specific examples that have actually been experienced, rather than an abstraction of some ideal prototype. According to this model, a person determines whether a new treelike thing is a tree by comparing it to the examples that define the concept.

One important difference between these two models is that the prototype model assumes a higher level of abstraction. A prototypical category for birdness, for example, is an abstraction of the characteristics of many examples of birds. In contrast, an exemplar category for *bird* is defined by examples of real birds.

Rosch (1973) argues that the prototype model is better than the exemplar model because for many concepts it is difficult to find good examples that resemble each other closely. For example, an automobile is a good example of a vehicle, and so is a passenger truck or a van. But a bus is less so, a train even less, and a child's wagon even less than that. In classifying each of these as vehicles, argues Rosch, it is likely that the person relies on an abstract, or prototypical, notion of what vehicles are.

Considerable research has been conducted to evaluate these two approaches. In addition, various other models with a host of new labels have been proposed (see, for example, E. E. Smith, Lopez & Osherson, 1992). The last word may yet be some time in coming. Thus far, the research seems to indicate that both highly abstract prototypes and more specific examples are involved in concept learning (Holyoak & Spellman, 1993). As we see in the next chapter, rapidly growing computer-based neural network models present yet another metaphor for understanding how humans learn concepts.

EVALUATION OF BRUNER'S POSITION

Evaluating a cognitive position such as Bruner's presents an interesting difficulty. Whereas some behavioristic positions attempt to describe a state of affairs in a relatively exact and literal manner and can therefore sometimes be judged in terms of how accurate the description appears to be, cognitive theories such as Bruner's are less literal and more abstract. Accordingly, the theory cannot be judged in the same manner as can behavioristic positions. What is being judged is not a description, but a metaphor; it is not an account of things or events that are assumed to actually exist but an abstraction that merely represents (that is, symbolizes).

Still, Bruner's metaphor does not do great violence to what people intuitively suspect about human functioning. More than that, it appears to be relatively clear and understandable, as well as internally consistent. Both of these attributes are important criteria of a scientific theory.

Perhaps the most important question that needs to be asked of any psychological theory concerns its usefulness in predicting and explaining. And although cognitive theories such as Bruner's are not very useful for explaining specific behaviors of the kind most easily explained by behavioristic positions, they are of some value in explaining higher mental processes such as decision making and the use of cognitive strategies.

One of the major contributions of Bruner's writing and theorizing has to do with his role in the so-called cognitive revolution—the revolution by which the cognitive party replaced the behavioristic party in what Amsel (1989) describes as psychology's parliamentary system.[7] "We were not out to "reform" behaviorism," says Bruner (1990b), "but to replace it" (p. 3).

What was this revolution? "It was," claims Bruner (1990), "an all-out effort to establish meaning as the central concept of psychology—not stimuli and responses, not overtly observable behavior, not biological drives and their transformation, but meaning" (p. 2). But the revolution was only partly successful, Bruner laments, because the emphasis changed from "constructing meaning" to "processing information." And the dominant metaphor became that of the computer, which unfortunately led to the requirement that new models and theories be "computable."

The proper study of man, says Bruner (1990b) in his book of that title, is man (and presumably, women and children too). "There is no one explanation of man," he explains, adding that no explanation of the human condition can make

---

[7]Perhaps he was wrong. Perhaps it wasn't a parliamentary system after all, but a dictatorship—a benevolent dictatorship. Otherwise, why the need for a revolution? (Kro)

sense "without being interpreted in the light of the symbolic world that constitutes human culture" (p. 138).

A Note on Educational Implications

Bruner (1966, 1973, 1990c) has been especially concerned with pointing out some of the educational implications of his work. His emphasis on the formation of coding systems, together with his belief that abstract coding systems facilitate transfer, improve retention, and increase problem-solving ability and motivation, has led him to advocate a discovery-oriented approach in schools. This emphasis on **discovery learning** is premised in part on his belief that the formation of generic coding systems requires the discovery of relationships. Accordingly, Bruner advocates the use of techniques by which children are encouraged to discover facts and relationships for themselves.

For this purpose Bruner stresses that some form of *spiral* curriculum is probably the best. A spiral curriculum is one that redevelops the same topics at succeeding age or grade levels as well as at different levels of difficulty. For example, in early grades learners are exposed to the simplest concepts in a particular area; at succeeding grade levels they are reexposed to the same area but at progressively more advanced conceptual levels.

Renewed interest in discovery approaches to education are evident in the *constructivist* approach to teaching advocated by writers like Brown, Collins, and Duguid (1989). Agreeing with Bruner, this approach argues that students need to build knowledge for themselves—that, in Bruner's (1986) words, they need to "make meaning." Similarly, the *conceptual change* movement in education is discovery oriented (Farnham-Diggory, 1990). A curriculum directed toward conceptual change presents problems and puzzles, challenges old ideas, and leads to the continual construction and reorganization of knowledge.

Not all educators or theorists are as enthusiastic as Bruner about the use of discovery methods in schools (see, for example, Ausubel, 1977; Ausubel & Robinson, 1969). A relatively mild controversy pitting discovery teaching against more didactic approaches (sometimes called **reception learning**) has been going on in educational circles for a number of decades, and research that has attempted to examine the relative merits of these two approaches is equivocal (see Lefrançois, 1994). This fact, though, need not be of any great concern. Teachers do not need to use only one of these methods; they can use both.

JEAN PIAGET: A DEVELOPMENTAL-COGNITIVE POSITION

Another cognitive theorist whose research and theories have had a profound influence on psychology and education is Jean Piaget. Piaget's system is cognitive in that its primary concern is mental representation; it is also *developmental* in that it looks at the processes by which children gain a progressively more advanced understanding of their environment and of themselves. In brief, Piagetian theory is an account of human cognitive development. His work covers an enormous range of topics: for example, language (1926); reality

(1929); morality (1932); causality (1930); time (1946); intelligence (1950); play, dreams, and imitation (1951); and consciousness (1976), to name but a few. The theory is scattered in dozens of books and hundreds of articles, many of which were coauthored by Piaget's long-time assistant, Barbel Inhelder.

A Different Approach: The *Méthode Clinique*

Much of the data on which Piaget based his theories was derived from a special technique he developed for studying children: the **méthode clinique**. The *méthode clinique* is a semistructured interview technique in which subjects' answers to questions often determine what the next question will be. It is quite unlike the more conventional approach, in which predetermined questions are asked in a predetermined order.

One of the advantages of the *méthode clinique* lies in the considerable flexibility it permits. Piaget's argument is that when investigators do not know what all the answers might be, they are hardly in a position to decide beforehand how the questions should be phrased or even what questions should be asked.

One possible disadvantage of this flexible, approach is that the data-gathering process may be difficult to replicate. Interestingly, however, more standarized approaches have tended to corroborate most of Piaget's findings—though it is unlikely that structured methods could have uncovered the findings in the first place. The "father/experimenter" role of the *méthode clinique* adopted by Piaget has led to observations that are often surprising, and to be surprised in psychology is a rare and pleasing thing.

JEAN PIAGET (1896–1980)

Jean Piaget was born in Neuchatel, Switzerland, in 1896. Although he didn't begin his formal work until some time later, there are indications that he was a precocious child. At the age of 10 he published his first "scholarly" paper: a one-page note on a partly albino sparrow he had found. This early writing was an intimation of the wealth of published material he was to produce later.

Piaget's first interests were primarily in biology, a field in which he obtained his Ph.D. at the age of 22. By the time he was 30 he had already published two dozen papers, most of them dealing with mollusks and related topics. After receiving his doctorate, Piaget spent a year wandering through Europe, uncertain about what to do next. During this year he worked in a psychoanalytic clinic (Bleuler's), in a psychological laboratory (that of Wreschner and Lipps), and eventually in Binet's laboratory, then under the direction of Simon.

One of Piaget's duties while in the Binet laboratory was to administer Burt's reasoning tests to young children in order to standardize the items. This period probably marks the beginning of his lifelong interest in the thought processes of children. It was at about this time, too, that Piaget's first child was born. This event enabled him to make the detailed observations of breast feeding (more specifically, of sucking behavior) that are incorporated in the origins of his theory, and that ultimately led to his voluminous writings. The bulk of Piaget's work is found in *Archives de Psychologie* (of which he was coeditor), much of it untranslated.

When Piaget died in 1980, he was still publishing and doing research at an amazing pace. In fact, a book he finished shortly before his death introduces important changes and advances in his thinking (Piaget et al., 1980). In Piaget's own words, "At the end of one's career, it is better to be prepared to change one's perspective than to be condemned to repeat oneself indefinitely" (quoted in Inhelder, 1982, p. 411).

Theoretical Orientation

Consistent with his early training in biology, Piaget borrowed two of the zoologist's big questions: (a) Which properties of organisms allow them to survive, and (b) how can species be classified? These he rephrased and directed at the development of children: What characteristics of children enable them to adapt to their environment? And what is the simplest, most accurate, and most useful way of classifying or ordering child development?

Assimilation and Accommodation Permit Adaptation

The newborn infant, Piaget notes, is in many ways a stunningly helpless organism, unaware that the world is real, ignorant of causes and effects, with no storehouse of ideas with which to reason nor any capacity for intentional behaviors—only a few simple reflexes.

But infants are much more than this. In the language of the computer metaphor, they are also remarkable little sensing machines that seem naturally predisposed to acquiring and processing a tremendous amount of information. They continually seek out and respond to stimulation, notes Flavell (1985). As a result, all the infant's simple reflexes—the sucking, the reaching and the grasping—become more complex, more coordinated, and more purposeful. The process by which this occurs is **adaptation**. And to answer the first of the questions of biology as simply as possible, **assimilation** and **accommodation** are the processes that make adaptation possible.

Assimilation involves responding to situations in terms of activities or knowledge that have already been learned or that are present at birth. To use Piaget's example, an infant is born with the capability to suck—with a sucking **schema**, in Piaget's terms (pluralized as *schemata*; sometimes used interchangeably with *scheme*). The sucking schema allows the infant to assimilate a nipple to the behavior of sucking. Similarly, a child who has learned the rules of addition can assimilate a problem such as 1 + 1; that is, he or she can respond appropriately in terms of previous learning.

Often, however, the child's understanding of the world is inadequate. The newborn's sucking schema works for ordinary nipples, but it isn't very effective for fingers or pacifiers. Similarly, preschoolers' understanding of number allows them to keep track of toes and fingers, but it doesn't impress kindergarten teachers. If there is to be any developmental progress, changes are required in information and behavior. These changes define accommodation.

In summary, assimilation involves reacting on the basis of previous learning and understanding; accommodation involves a change in understanding. And the interplay of assimilation and accommodation leads to adaptation.

Equilibration

All activity, claims Piaget, involves both assimilation and accommodation. The child cannot react to an entirely new situation without using some old learning and some old behaviors (hence assimilating). At the same time, even reacting to the same situation for the 1000th time nevertheless implies some change, however subtle (hence some accommodation). Flavell (1985) notes that these activities are simply the two sides of the same cognitive coin.

It is important, explains Piaget, that there be a balance between assimilation and accommodation—an *equilibrium*. Hence he uses the term **equilibration** to signify the processes or tendencies that lead to this balance. If there is too much assimilation, there is no new learning; if there is too much accommodation (that is, change), behavior becomes chaotic.

Piaget called assimilation and accommodation *functional invariants* because they are functions, or ways of behaving, that don't change throughout development. These functional invariants are clearly illustrated in two important activities of early childhood: play, which involves mainly assimilation, and imitation, which is mostly accommodation.

Play

When children play, Piaget explains, they continually assimilate objects to predetermined activities, ignoring attributes that don't really fit the activity. For example, when children sit astride a chair and say "Giddyup," they're not paying particular attention to those attributes of the chair that don't resemble a horse.

This type of play behavior involves little change, and thus little accommodation—which is not to deny its importance in the course of development. Indeed Piaget does quite the opposite, emphasizing repeatedly that although young children engage in activities (such as playing "horse") simply for the sake of the activity, the effect is to stabilize the schema (the activity), to make it more readily available, and consequently to set the stage for further learning.

Stages of Play

In the course of their development, children progress through a series of stages in the playing of games—and, remarkably, a quite different set of stages with regard to their *understanding* of the rules by which they play (Piaget, 1932; see Table 7.1):

At the earliest stage, before age 3, children have no idea that rules exist and play according to none. By age 5, however, they have developed the belief that rules are eternal and unchangeable, but they change them constantly as they play. During the next half-dozen or so years, they come to realize that rules are

TABLE 7.1   Piaget's Description of Rules as They Are Understood and Practiced
by Children

Stage	Approximate age	Degree of understanding	Adherence to rules
Stage 1	Before 3	No understanding of rules	Do not play according to rules
Stage 2	3 to 5	Believe rules come from God (or some other high authority) and cannot be changed	Break and change rules constantly
Stage 3	5 to 11 or 12	Understand that rules are social and that they can be changed	Do not change rules; adhere to them rigidly
Stage 4	After 11 or 12	Complete understanding	Change rules by mutual consent

made by people and can be changed. Ironically, however, they are now completely rigid in their adherence to rules: They never change them! Finally, by about age 11 or 12, they arrive at a complete understanding of rules. Both in behavior and thought, they accept rules as completely modifiable.[8]

Imitation

Whereas play involves a preponderance of assimilation, imitation is primarily accommodation. This is so because when they are imitating, children constantly modify their behavior in accordance with the demands imposed on them by their desire to *be* something or to be *like* someone else. Piaget argues that through the imitation of activity, children's repertoires of behaviors expand and gradually begin to be internalized. **Internalization** is, in Piaget's terminology, equivalent to the formation of concepts. It is the process by which activities and events in the real world become represented mentally; the term implies that the actual activity or experience precedes mental representation of it. Internalization is the basis of cognitive learning.

Many of the young infant's imitative behaviors occur only in the presence of the model being imitated. For example, even very young infants can imitate

---

[8]This striking inconsistency between behavior and thought might seem excusable given that these are children. Unlike newly-made Korons, human children come with relatively little prewiring; as a result, they have an awful lot to learn and they make mistakes. Astoundingly, however, there are countless examples of similar behavior-belief contradictions among human adults. Among other things, this phenomenon fuels an enormous gambling industry. For example, in spite of the fact that reasonably intelligent humans know that the probability of correctly selecting 6 out of 49 numbers is about 1 in 13 million, they continue to give away their credits. "They're buying a dream," said Lefrançois. I don't understand. (Kro)*

*I don't think Kro ever did understand about human dreams and fantasies. (GRL)

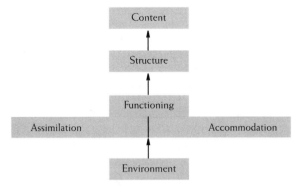

FIGURE 7.4   Intelligence-in-action is viewed as the interaction of an individual with the environment through the "functioning" processes. This interaction results in cognitive structures, which in turn account for the content of behavior.

simple behaviors like blinking, winking, and opening the mouth (Meltzoff & Moore, 1989), but the imitation does not continue when the model is no longer present. Piaget explains this in terms of the infant's failure to realize that objects continue to exist independently—that they aren't there only when the infant is actually sensing them. The world of the infant, claims Piaget, is a world of the here and now; it does not include an understand of the permanence of objects (termed the **object concept**).

At about age 1, an important change occurs when young Ralph puts on his father's jacket, takes his toy shovel, sits on his imaginary car, and pretends he is going to work. Piaget explains that **deferred imitation**, the ability to imitate things and people not immediately present, is evidence that the infant has internalized a representation of that which is being imitated. It is evidence, as well, that the infant has begun to realize that things continue to exist on their own even when out of sensory range—evidence, in other words, of the object concept.

Intelligence

Piaget's concept of intelligence differs markedly from the traditional approach, which is concerned with its measurement. Instead of describing intelligence as a relatively fixed (if somewhat nebulous) quality or quantity, Piaget describes it as *mobile;* intelligence, he argues, exists *in action.* Intelligence is the property of activity that is reflected in maximally adaptive behavior, and it can therefore be understood in terms of the entire process of adapting.

To review briefly, adaptation is the process of interacting with the environment by assimilating aspects of it to cognitive structure and by modifying (or accommodating) aspects of cognitive structure to it. Both activities occur in response to environmental demands; also, both are guided by cognitive structure and result in changes in that structure. Obviously, however, this entire process can only be inferred from behavior (called *content* by Piaget). The substance of Piaget's concept of intelligence is summarized in Figure 7.4.

Cognitive Structure

Although this view of intelligence may be useful for understanding some of the processes involved in intelligent behavior, it is not immediately useful for measuring it. But there is one aspect of the model that has implications for developing tests of intelligence: the part defined by the term **structure**.

Piaget's description of structure is essentially a description of the characteristics of children at different ages. It is his answer for the second of the questions he borrowed from biology: What is the simplest, most accurate, and most useful way of classifying or ordering child development? Hence Piaget's description of changes in structure is a description of the stages of human cognitive development. This is the aspect of his system that has received the most attention.

A Stage Theory

Piaget believed that development progresses through a series of qualitatively different stages, each characterized by the development of new abilities—or, more precisely, each consisting of a more advanced level of adaptation. He describes four major stages, and several substages, through which children progress in their development:

- Sensorimotor (birth to 2 years)
- Preoperational (2 to 7 years)
    Preconceptual (2 to 4 years)
    Intuitive (4 to 7 years)
- Concrete operations (7 to 11 or 12 years)
- Formal operations (11 or 12 to 14 or 15 years)

Each stage can be described in terms of the major identifying characteristics of children at that stage and in terms of the learning that occurs before transition to the next stage.

Sensorimotor Development: Birth to 2 Years

The single most striking characteristic of child behavior in the first 2 years of life results in part from the absence of language and internal representation. As we saw, the child's world, because it cannot be represented mentally, is a world of the here and now. In a very literal sense, it is a world where objects exist only when the child actually senses and does things with them—hence the label **sensorimotor intelligence**. At this stage, when objects are not being sensed, they cease to exist; infants have not yet acquired the object concept (a realization of the permanence of objects).

The Object Concept

Piaget investigated the development of the object concept by presenting young children with an attractive object and then removing it after they had become engrossed in it. In the earliest stages of development they show no signs of missing the object—proof, claims Piaget, that out of sight is literally out of mind. In later stages, however, children will look for objects they have seen being hidden; at around age 1, they will search for objects they *remember* from some previous time.

Exercising Reflexes

During the sensorimotor stage, children perfect and elaborate the small repertoire of reflexive schemata with which they are born. At birth, infants are capable of simple reflexive acts: sucking, reaching, grasping, looking, and so on. Much of the first month of life is spent exercising these reflexes (and sleeping). This first month represents the first of six substages of the sensorimotor period described by Piaget, each of which is identified in terms of the nature of its reflexive activity. For example, the second substage (1 to 4 months) sees the appearance of acquired adaptations that are called *primary circular reactions*. These activities are centered on the child's body (hence the term *primary*) and are circular in that the behavior elicits its own repetition. Thumb sucking is a primary circular reaction in the sense that the activity of sucking produces sensations that lead the child to repeat the activity. Later sensorimotor substages witness the coordination of separate activities, the evolution of language, and so on.

Achievements by Age 2

Piaget's stages are not defined or labeled in terms of the characteristics a child acquires that lead to transition into the next stage, but rather in terms of the characteristics that prevail throughout most of the stage. Thus the sensorimotor stage is so labeled because throughout most of that stage children react to the world in a sensorimotor fashion. Each stage, however, is a preparation for the next; the achievements of each are therefore of critical importance in explaining the transition to the succeeding stage.

Among the most striking and important achievements of the sensorimotor period is the development of the ability to symbolize and to communicate. This is significant because language accelerates thinking and makes possible the transition to a more cognitive interpretation of the world. A second achievement, already noted, is the development of the object concept, the discovery that the world continues to exist even when it is not being seen, felt, heard, smelled, or tasted.

The culmination of sensorimotor learning is marked by a third accomplishment: the child's increasing ability to coordinate separate activities. Adults take the ability to coordinate complex activities very much for granted, but it is no small or unimportant achievement for the child. In the absence of cooperation between such simple activities as looking and reaching, the child could never obtain the object looked at and desired. Even for so uncomplicated a behavior as picking up a pen, not only must vision direct the arm, but the hand, the arm, the shoulder, the torso and perhaps even the head must also be pressed into service.

A final sensorimotor achievement is the recognition of cause-and-effect relationships. At birth, infants don't know that if they reach toward an object,

they can grasp it and bring it closer to themselves, they must learn this. And it is precisely this kind of learning that allows them to develop intentionality, for until children know what the effects of their activities will be, they cannot clearly intend these effects.

Preoperational Thinking: 2 to 7 Years

The next stage in the evolution of a child is a marked improvement over the first in terms of the child's increased understanding of the world—but relative to an adult, it exhibits serious shortcomings. The stage is ordinarily divided into two substages, which are described below.

Preconceptual Thinking: 2 to 4 Years

The **preconceptual** stage is characterized primarily by the child's inability to understand all the properties of classes. Piaget, whose early work typically was based on observations of his own children, illustrates this by reference to his son's reaction to a snail they saw as they were walking one morning. "*Papa,*" said the boy, "*regardez l'escargot.*" Which they did. But later, when they came across a second snail, the boy said again, "*Papa, regardez l'escargot. C'est encore l'escargot!*"[9]

The preconceptual child has acquired the ability to represent objects internally (that is, mentally) and to identify them on the basis of their membership

---

[9]The first conversation means, says Lefrançois, "Pops, look at the snail." The second one, in response to a different snail, means, "Pops, look at the snail. It's the snail again." Not so smart, these human kids, what? (Kro)

in classes, but now reacts to all similar objects as though they were identical. For a while, all men are "Daddy," all women are "Mommy," animals are all "doggie," and the world is simple. If Samuel sees a teddy bear like his at a friend's place, he knows that it's his teddy bear—and the tricycle at the store is also clearly his. Children understand something about classes, because they can identify objects. Their understanding is incomplete, though, because they cannot yet distinguish between apparently identical members of the same class (hence the term *preconceptual*). This mode of thinking occasionally has its advantages for parents: Santa Claus continues to be the one and only individual of his type, even though he may be seen in ten places on one day.

Another feature of the child's thinking during this stage is that it is **transductive** as opposed to inductive or deductive. Inductive thinking proceeds from specifics to a generalization, whereas deductive reasoning begins with the generalization and ends with specifics. In contrast, transductive reasoning involves making inferences from one specific to another. For example, the child who reasoned, "My dog has hair, and that thing there has hair; therefore that thing is a dog," was engaging in transductive reasoning. The thing might well have been a dog, in which case transductive reasoning would have resulted in a correct conclusion. But the thing was a skunk.[10]

Intuitive Thinking: 4 to 7 Years. By the time children reach the age of 4, they have achieved a more complete understanding of concepts and have largely stopped reasoning transductively. Their thinking has become somewhat more logical, although it is governed more by perception than by logic. In fact, the role played by perception in the intuitive stage is probably the most striking

---

[10]If truth be told, the "child" was Kro himself. He had never seen a skunk, and his cousin, Kongor, had not thought it important enough to warn him. There are many skunks here—of both kinds. (GRL)

(a)   (b)

FIGURE 7.5   Material for a simple conservation of
liquid experiment. In (b), one of the containers from
(a) has been poured into a taller, thinner container.
The nonconserving child will assume there is more
liquid in this new container because it's "taller"—or less
because it's "thinner."

characteristic of this period. This role is particularly evident in the now-famous
conservation tasks.

Inability to Conserve.   A typical conservation problem goes like this: Children are shown two identical beakers filled to the same level with water (as in
part [a] of Figure 7.5). The experimenter then pours the contents of one of the
beakers into a tall thin tube (as in part (b) of Figure 7.5). Subjects who had
previously said the amounts in each beaker were equal are now asked whether
there is as much, more, or less water in the new container. At the intuitive
stage, they will almost invariably say that there is more, because the water level
is much higher in the tube. They are mislead by appearance.

Egocentrism.   Intuitive-stage children cannot easily accept the point of view
of others; their thinking is marked by **egocentrism**. In an experiment to illustrate this, an experimenter holds in each hand one end of a wire on which a boy
doll and a girl doll are strung side by side. The child is shown the dolls, which
are then hidden behind a screen, the hands remaining in plain view. The child
is asked which doll will come out first if they are moved out on the left. The
child's answer is noted, the dolls are returned to their original position, and the
question is repeated. Again the dolls are coming out on the left; obviously the
same doll is coming out first. The procedure is repeated a number of times.

Reasonably intelligent children generally answer correctly at first. After a
while, however, they change their minds and predict that the other doll will
come out. If asked why they think so, they are unlikely to admit that they
distrust psychological investigators, because they probably haven't learned to
distrust them yet. Instead they may say something like, "It's not fair. It's her turn
to come out next." It is this solution of a simple logical problem by reference to
how things *should* be from the child's own point of view that illustrates the role
of egocentrism in intuitive thinking.

Classification Problems.   Although children at this stage can identify objects
on the basis of class membership, they don't yet completely understand how

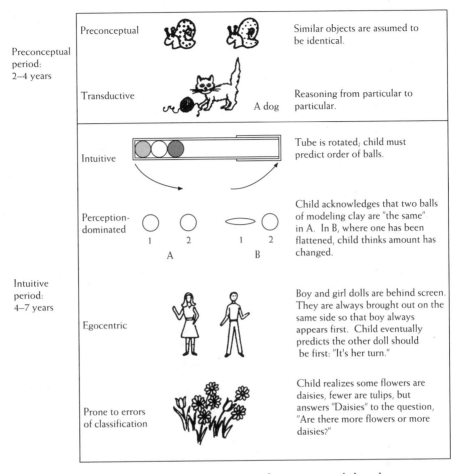

FIGURE 7.6   Some characteristics of preoperational thought.

classes can be nested within larger classes. A 4-year-old child who is shown a handful of seven candies, two of which are chocolates and five of which are gums, immediately recognizes that they are all candies and, if asked, will probably say so. If the experimenter says, however, "Tell me, are there more gums than candies, or less, or the same number?" the child will almost invariably say that there are more gums than candies! When a class is broken down into subclasses and children are asked to reason about the subclass (gum) and the larger class (candy), they cannot do so. For them, the original division destroyed the parent class. (See Figure 7.6 for a summary of the characteristics of preoperational thinking.)

Operations

The preconceptual and intuitive stages are substages of the lengthy *preoperational period,* which is so called because prior to the age of 7, the child does not reason with operations. As the labels for the next two stages indicate, after the age of 7 (or thereabouts), the average child achieves operational thinking. The term **operation** is therefore central in Piaget's system.

An operation can be defined as an internalized activity (in other words, a thought) that is subject to certain rules of logic, the most important of which is reversibility. A thought is reversible when it can be unthought. This is a somewhat inelegant and crude definition of a usually sophisticated and nebulous concept, but it is not incorrect (although it may still be nebulous). In order not to confound the issue further, the definitions given are not elaborated at this point. Some examples of operations and of operational thinking are instead provided in the sections dealing with the last two of Piaget's stages.

A BREAK

Dear Human Reader: This is an aside, which you can ignore if you're as determined and studious as I hope you are. But Lefrançois says the human brain is a little mushy compared with the Koron brain, and he should know.[11] He says you suffer easily from symbol shock and jargon stroke, and so he insists I use this little bit he threw into one of his books when things got too tough in the middle of Piaget (Lefrançois, in press). So here it is.

Stop! It would probably be wise for the reader who is not already familiar with Piaget to stop at this point. If you have available an electroencephalograph machine, a cardiograph, a thermometer, and a pupilometer, as well as any other graph or meter, these should be connected and read at once. Alpha waves, together with decelerated heart rate, abnormal temperature, and reduced pupil size are symptoms of imminent **jargon shock**. This condition in an advanced stage can be highly detrimental to concentration and learning. Several hours of sleep usually brings about a significant amelioration of the condition.

If you don't have any of this sophisticated electronic gadgetry readily available, you can substitute a hand mirror. Hold the mirror up to your face and look at your eyes. If they are closed, you are probably in the terminal stage of jargon shock.

Concrete Operations: 7 to 11 or 12 Years

At about age 7 or so, children make an important transition from preoperations to operations—that is, from a prelogical, egocentric, perception dominated kind of thinking to a more rule-regulated thinking. Perhaps nowhere is this more evident than in the acquisition of the concept of conservation.

---

[11]I'm sure Kro didn't mean what you think he meant here. You have to understand that he had absolutely no sense of humor. (GRL)

The Conservations

Conservation, as we saw, is the realization that certain quantitative attributes of objects don't change unless something is added or taken away. In the previously described water-into-a-different-container experiment (Figure 7.5), children have acquired conservation when they realize that pouring water from one container to another does not change its amount.

There are many types of conservation, each relating to a specific quantitative attribute of an object and each acquired in highly similar order by most children. For example, conservation of substance is typically achieved by the age of 7 or 8, whereas conservation of area is not learned until 9 or 10, and conservation of volume doesn't appear until about 11 or 12 (see Figure 7.7).

The importance of conservation in Piaget's theory is that it illustrates the use of one or more of the rules of logic that now govern thinking—rules such as **reversibility, identity,** and **compensation.** What has happened is that in the course of interacting with things and events—that is, in the course of what Piaget (1972) refers to as "constructing knowledge" (which is the same as what Bruner, 1986, or Kuhn, 1984, call "meaning meaning")—the child discovers that there is a logic that governs actions and relationships.

A thought (internal action) is reversible when the child realizes that the action could be reversed, and that certain logical consequences follow from doing so. For example, with respect to the problem of conservation of liquids described earlier, a child might reason, "If the water were poured out of the tall tube and back into its original container, it would still have as much water as before, so it mustn't have changed." That, in a nutshell, is reversibility.

Alternatively, the child might reason that nothing has been added to or taken away from either container and that there must then still be the same amount in each. This is an example of the rule of identity, which states that for every operation (action) there is another operation that leaves it unchanged. Obviously, adding or taking away nothing produces no change.

A third alternative might be this: "The tube is taller, but it is also thinner, so it balances out." Piaget and Inhelder (1941) refer to this reasoning as compensation (or combinativity), a property defined in terms of the logical consequences of combining more than one operation or, in this case, more than one dimension.

The human reader can clarify these notions further by carrying out some conservation tasks with real children, as shown in Figure 7.7. It might be amusing to perform them in front of a grandmother, *after* having explained the procedure to her and *after* she has predicted what the child's response will be. It's best to use a 4- or 5-year-old to ensure that the grandmother will be wrong.[12] Note that the ages indicated in parentheses in Figure 7.7 are only approximations.

Can Conservation Be Taught?

Just as your grandmother has almost succeeded in overcoming her exasperation and is about to issue a pearl of ancient wisdom that will serve to explain and

---

[12]"I have nothing against grandmothers," said Kro when I asked him. "I swear it. Human readers can use a grandfather if they're sensitive about this." (GRL)

1. **Conservation of number (age 6 or 7)**
Two rows of counters are placed in one-to-one correspondence between the experimenter (E) and the subject (S):

One of the rows is then elongated or contracted:

S is asked which row has more counters or whether they still have the same number.

2. **Conservation of length (age 6 or 7)**
E places two sticks before the subject. The ends are aligned.

S is asked if they are the same length. One stick is then moved to the right:

The question is repeated.

3. **Conservation of substance or mass (age 7 or 8)**
Two modeling clay balls are presented to S. She is asked if they have the same amount of modeling clay in them. If S says no, she is asked to make them equal. (It is not at all uncommon for a young child simply to squeeze a ball in order to make it have less modeling clay.) One ball is then deformed.

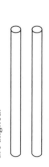

or

or

S is asked whether they contain the same amount.

4. **Conservation of area (age 9 or 10)**
S is given a large piece of cardboard, identical to one that E has. Both represent playgrounds. Small wooden blocks represent buildings. S is asked to put a building on his playground every time E does so. After nine buildings have been scattered throughout both playgrounds, E moves his together in a corner.

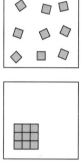

S is asked whether there is as much space (area) in his playground as in E's.

5. **Conservation of liquid quantity (age 6 or 7)**
S is presented with two identical containers filled to the same level with water.

One of the containers is then poured into a tall, thin tube, and the other is poured into a flat dish.

S is asked whether the amount of water in each remains equal.

6. **Conservation of volume (age 11 or 12)**
S is presented with a calibrated container filled with water

and two identical balls of modeling clay. One is squished and placed into the container; the other is lengthened.

S is asked to predict the level to which the water in the container will rise if the longer piece of clay replaces the squished piece.

FIGURE 7.7 Experimental procedures for conservation of six physical attributes, with approximate ages of attainment.

denigrate the results of science, turn to her, dear human reader, and issue this challenge: "Grandma, I challenge you! I challenge you! I say, Grandma, I challenge you!" (Sometimes you have to repeat things several times with grandmothers.)[13] There is certainly no point in explaining the challenge until your grandmother has understood you well enough to repress her pearl of wisdom, at least momentarily, and to say "What?" (or, in Canada, "Eh?"). At that point, continue by saying, "I'll bet you, Grandma dear, that you can't teach little Norbert to answer correctly when I squish this modeling clay into a pie."

Grandma will probably fail, as did many investigators (for example, Smedslund, 1961; Kuhn, 1972). True, a number of psychologists have been successful in accelerating the appearance of concepts of conservation in *some* children (never all), but only after extensive, systematic, and theoretically based training (for example, Lefrançois, 1968; Siegler & Liebert, 1972). None of these psychologists has clearly shown that such acceleration studies have a generally beneficial effect on other aspects of child functioning.

Grandma will fail. Again!

Classes

With the appearance of the logical properties of thinking that define operations, children also acquire new skills in dealing with classes, numbers, and series. Piaget assumed that these abilities are highly dependent on interacting with and manipulating real objects. For example, as a result of combining ob-

---

[13]And for human readers who thought I was being unfair to grandmothers, you have to repeat even more often with grandfathers. They're more likely than grandmothers to lose their hearing and their hair—not to mention their lives. (Kro)

FIGURE 7.8   A test of a child's understanding of seriation. The elements of the series are presented in random order and the child is asked to arrange them in sequence of height. The top row was arranged by a 3½-year-old; the bottom, by an 8-year-old.

jects, separating them, or arranging them into groups, children learn about class membership and develop the ability to reason about nested classes. The candy problem cited earlier (whether there are more jelly beans or more candies) would present so slight a problem for concrete-operations children that they might well laugh in scorn if the question were put to them.

Seriating

Also as a result of experiences with real objects, children acquire the ability to order them in series and to set up correspondences between more than one series. Piaget investigated the understanding of seriation by presenting children with various objects that can easily be ranked in one dimension—for example, dolls and canes. Before concrete operations, children rank objects by comparing two of them at once, but they seldom make the necessary inference that if A is greater than B and B is greater than C, then A must also be greater than C. Preoperational children are not embarrassed about putting C before B if they have just been comparing A and C. The concrete-operations child seldom makes an error of this kind (see Figure 7.8).

Number

The ability to deal with numbers is a logical result of classifying and seriating, because a complete understanding of number requires some comprehension of its cardinal properties (the fact that numbers represent classes of different magnitude: one thing, two things, three things, and so on) as well as knowledge of their ordinal meaning (their ordered sequence: first, second, third, and so on).

Formal Operations: After 11 or 12 years

Formal operations present some important advances over concrete operations. First, children apply the thought structures of concrete operations directly to real objects or to objects that are easily imagined (hence the label *concrete*). In other words, children don't yet deal with what is merely hypothetical unless it can be tied directly to concrete reality. Adolescents, in contrast, are potentially capable of dealing with the hypothetical or ideal (the nonconcrete).

Combinatorial Analysis

Second, concrete operations children respond very differently from those in formal operations when faced with problems that require systematic analysis of a large number of possibilities. In one representative problem, for example, Inhelder and Piaget (1958) presented children with five test tubes containing different chemicals and showed them that a combination of these chemicals would result in a yellow liquid. Their task was to discover which combination(s) produced the desired result. The experiment is illustrated in Figure 7.9.

Typical 10-year olds begin by combining a couple of tubes, then two more, then another two—sometimes maybe trying three at once—until they either stumble accidently on one of the two correct solutions or give up. Their strategy is to test each combination as a real hypothesis—a reflection of the concrete nature of their thinking.

A bright 14-year old, in contrast, approaches the problem quite differently systematically combining all test tubes by twos, threes, or even fours, resulting in all possible combinations illustrated in Figure 7.9. What the 14-year-old has done is *imagine* all possibilities and then exhaust them—demonstrating the hypothetical and combinatorial nature of formal operations thinking.

Hypothetical Nature of Thought

As we saw above, the last stage in the evolution of thought is marked by the appearance in behavior of **propositional thinking**—that is, thinking that is not restricted to the consideration of the concrete or the potentially real but instead deals in the realm of the hypothetical (a proposition is any statement that can be true or false). Children can now reason from the real to the merely possible, or from the possible to the actual. They can compare hypothetical states of affairs with actual states or vice versa; as a result, they can become profoundly upset at the seeming irresponsibility of a generation of adults that has brought itself to the edge of untold disasters. (See Table 7.2 for a summary of Piaget's stages.)

Relevance of Piaget's Theory to Learning

Piaget's position is primarily a theory of development. Largely because of its emphasis on the genesis (or development) of knowledge (what Piaget termed **genetic epistemology**), however, it is also a theory of learning. As a theory of learning it can be simplified and reduced to the following set of statements:

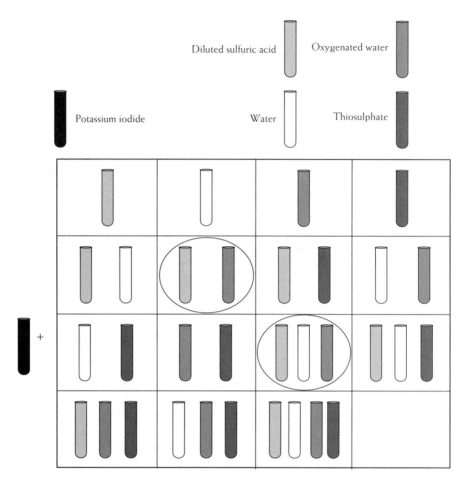

FIGURE 7.9   All possible combinations of the four test tubes to which the fifth can be added. The experiment requires the subject to discover the combination(s) that yields a yellow liquid when potassium iodide is added. The correct solutions are circled.

1. The acquisition of knowledge is a gradual developmental process made possible through the interaction of the child with the environment.
2. The sophistication of children's representation of the world is a function of their stage of development. That stage is defined by the thought structures they then possess.
3. Maturation, active experience, equilibration, and social interaction are the forces that shape learning (Piaget, 1961).

Instructional Implications

The impact of Piaget's theory on school curricula, on instructional procedures, and on measurement practices is profound and significant. Lefrançois (in press) summarizes several educational implications based on Piaget's work. For example, it follows directly from the theory that in early stages, interaction with real objects is crucial to the growth of knowledge and to the development of the

TABLE 7.2   Piaget's Stages of Cognitive Development

Stage	Approximate age	Some major characteristics
Sensorimotor	0–2 years	Motoric intelligence World of the here and now No language, no thought in early stages No notion of objective reality
Preoperational Preconceptual Intuitive	2–7 years 2–4 years 4–7 years	Egocentric thought Reason dominated by perception Intuitive rather than logical solutions Inability to conserve
Concrete operations	7–11 or 12 years	Ability to conserve Logic of classes and relations Understanding of numbers Thinking bound to concrete Development of reversibility in thought
Formal operations	11 or 12–14 or 15 years	Complete generality of thought Propositional thinking Ability to deal with the hypothetical Development of strong idealism

understandings and abilities that underly thinking. Hence *providing activity* is the first of these implications.

A second Piaget-based educational implications relates to *providing optimal difficulty*. Material presented to learners should not be so difficult that it can't be understood (assimilated), nor so easy that it leads to no new learning (no accommodation).

A third important implication has to do with the importance for teachers of *knowing the child's developmental level*—of knowing how the child thinks, and of understanding both the limitations and the potential of child thought.

Related Research

Thousands of studies have investigated and sometimes elaborated on Piaget's work. An overwhelming majority of these studies supports Piaget's general description of the *sequence* of intellectual development, especially at the earliest stages (see, for example, Gelman 1978; Opper, 1977). This sequence appears to hold for children from various countries (Dasen, 1972, 1977; Glick, 1975). In contrast, research provides less sweeping support for Piaget's description of the *ages* at which major intellectual changes occur.

Piaget Underestimated Young Children

Critics point out that Piaget seems to have drastically underestimated the ages at which young children are capable of certain important behaviors. Indications are that verbal difficulties might often have been implicated in Piaget's failure to find certain abilities and understanding during the earlier developmental periods. When the tasks are made simpler, children sometimes respond quite differently.

In the "mountains" problem, for example, children are shown three mountains of unequal height set on top of a table and are allowed to walk around the mountains to become familiar with them. In the testing part of the study subjects are seated on one side of the table, and a doll is placed at some other vantage point around the table. Children are then asked to describe what the display looks like from the doll's point of view. Their initial inability to do so is taken as an example of egocentrism (inability to adopt another's point of view). But when Liben (1975) asked preoperational children to describe what a white card would look like from the experimenter's point of view (as well as from their own) when different colored glasses were being worn by the child or the experimenter (pink glasses on the experimenter, for example, and no glasses on the child), the children were often able to answer correctly.

Baillargeon (1987, 1992) also reports studies which seem to indicate that young infants have some notion of the permanence of objects much before Piaget thought they did. Thus, when 3- and 4-month-old infants saw an object apparently passing through a space that should have been occupied by another solid object, they seemed surprised. Bowers (1989), notes, however, that a 3-month-old infant's fleeting memory of objects does not really contradict Piaget's observation that it will still be some months before that child will deliberately search for a hidden object.

Gelman, Meck, and Merkin (1986) and Aubrey (1993) also point out that preschoolers typically have well-developed understandings of number that Piaget thought more characteristic of older, concrete operations children.

Formal Operations Are Not Highly General

In his earlier writings, Piaget left little doubt that he considered formal operations to be generally characteristic of most older adolescents, as well as of most adults (Inhelder & Piaget, 1958). However, a number of studies provide convincing evidence that this is probably not the case (see, for example, Modgil & Modgil, 1982). Many of these studies have failed to find much evidence of formal operations among adults, let alone adolescents. When Dulit (1972) tested gifted older adolescents for formal operations, he found that approximately half still functioned at the level of concrete operations; approximately one-quarter of average older adolescents and adults operated at a level of formal operations. By the same token, cross-cultural studies have generally been hard-pressed to find much evidence of thinking beyond concrete operations in many cultures (see Gelman, 1978). Ironically, it seems that while Piaget underestimated the abilities of young children, he may have overestimated those of older children and adolescents.

In the light of these findings, Piaget (1972) modified his earlier position by conceding that the formal-operations stage is probably not nearly so general as he had first thought. Available evidence suggests that formal operations are best viewed as cognitive processes that are potential rather than probable. In short, formal operations are probably impossible in middle childhood or earlier; they are possible but far from completely general in adolescence or adulthood.

How Damaging Are These Criticisms?

These criticisms, although more numerous and detailed than indicated here, are probably not very damaging to the basic theory. At most, the various well-substantiated contradictions of Piagetian theory suggest that the ages of attainment are approximate, a point that Piaget always maintained; that children may develop more rapidly in certain areas than Piaget suspected (particularly at the sensorimotor level); and that the final stage in Piaget's description is not generally descriptive, a fact that is not unduly disturbing for Piagetian theorists providing that the preceding stage, concrete operations, remains descriptive of those who have not achieved formal operations. What the criticisms point out most clearly is the child's cognitive development is far more complex than Piaget had thought—perhaps more complicated than psychologists still think.

Evaluation of Piaget's Position

Piaget's critics, of which there are a significant number, have advanced a number of standard complaints. One of the earliest centered on the small number of subjects in his research; the *méthode clinique* does not lend itself easily to large samples. This criticism is not particularly relevant, however, except where more careful studies with larger groups have contradicted Piaget's findings. Other criticisms have to do with the difficulty of understanding the system, with the use of complex and sometimes nebulous terminology, and with the use of a difficult logic whose contribution is not always readily apparent.

An examination of Piaget's system with respect to the criteria described in the first chapter reveals, among other things, that the theory is remarkably consistent, coherent, and comprehensive. As noted above, though, it doesn't reflect all the facts accurately, because it underestimates some abilities and overestimates others.

Is the theory clear and understandable? Yes and no. At one level, that of describing stages, it can be presented simply and clearly. But there is another level, a level of abstract logical systems, that is not very clear—and perhaps not very accurate or useful in any case (Ennis, 1982).

Does the theory explain and predict well? Again, yes and no. It explains some behaviors that were largely undiscovered previously (conservation, for example), and in a general way it predicts the type of cognitive functioning that might be expected of children at various stages of development. The predictions are not always entirely appropriate, however, especially when tied too closely to Piaget's approximate ages.

Finally, how useful and influential is the theory? Very. Piaget's impact in psychology and education has been enormous, even if it has also been controversial. The theory has generated thousands of studies and countless applications in schools. There is little doubt that Piaget is largely responsible for converting a generation of teachers, parents, and child care workers into fascinated observers of children and their development.

SUMMARY

1. Cognitive theories are concerned mainly with explaining higher mental processes (perception, information processing, decision making, and knowing), and they are based more on human than animal research. They typically presuppose some form of mental representation.

2. Bruner compares the development of the child to the evolution of the human race. Thus the child progress from enactive (motoric) representation (corresponding to inventions that amplify motor capacities), to iconic (images) representation (corresponding to inventions that amplify the senses), and finally to symbolic representation (corresponding to inventions that amplify intellectual capacities).

3. Bruner uses the term *categorizing* to describe both perceptual and conceptual activity. A category can be thought of as a rule for classifying things as being equal. As a rule, it specifies the attributes (qualities) that objects must possess before they can be incorporated into a given category.

4. Information processing (and decision making) involves categorization. An object is identified when it is placed in a category, a process that has implicit in it the possibility of "going beyond the information given" (that is, of making predictions about events or objects on the basis of their category membership).

5. Coding systems are arrangements of related categories in hierarchical order. Higher-level categories are said to be more generic in that they subsume more examples and are freer of specifics (that is, are less defined by small details).

6. To form a concept is to arrive at a notion that some things belong together and others do not; to attain a concept is to discover what attributes are criterial for membership in a given category. Concepts can be conjunctive (defined by the joint presence of two or more attribute values), disjunctive (defined by the joint presence of relevant attributes, or by the presence of any of them singly or in other combinations), or relational (defined by a specified relationship between or among attribute values).

7. Bruner's strategies for attaining concepts include simultaneous scanning (generating all hypotheses—impractical and impossible for most subjects), successive scanning (trial and error—uneconomical), conservative focusing (accepting the first instance as the complete hypothesis and varying one attribute value at a time—economical and effective), and focus gambling (riskier than conservative focusing—sometimes a faster payoff, sometimes a slower one).

8. Recent research on categorization is based in large part on Bruner's initial formulations. Among the findings from this research are the following: categories vary in terms of generality, but the most specific category (Holstein cow) is not learned before a more general category (cow);

items and events included in the same category, as well as the values that are employed in determining category membership, are not necessarily equivalent; and abstraction is always involved in categorization.

9. The prototype model of abstraction says people abstract highly general notions of concepts from exposure to various examples of the concept; the exemplar model (which is less abstract) says people remember specific, representative examples of concepts.

10. Bruner is a strong advocate of discovery-oriented teaching methods.

11. Piaget's theory can be viewed as an attempt to answer two biology-related questions: What are the characteristics of children that enable them to adapt to their environment? And what is the simplest, most accurate, and most useful way of classifying or ordering child development?

12. Assimilation involves responding in terms of previous learning; to accommodate is to change behavior in response to environmental demands. Play involves a preponderance of assimilation; imitation, a primacy of accommodation; and intelligent adaptation, equilibrium between the two.

13. The beginning of the sensorimotor stage is characterized by a here-and-now understanding of the world, lack of the object concept, and absence of language. Through interaction with the world, the infant begins to build a representation of reality that includes the development of language, the ability to coordinate activities, the appearance of intentionality, and the recognition of cause-and-effect relationships.

14. Preconceptual thinking is characterized by errors of logic, transductive (from particular to particular) reasoning, intuitive problem solving, egocentrism, reliance on perception, and absence of conservation. It nevertheless sees remarkable advances in language, mathematical understanding, and reasoning.

15. The transition from preoperational to operational thought is marked by the appearance of the ability to conserve (reflecting logical rules of reversibility, compensation, and identity). In addition, children can now deal more adequately with classes, series, and number. Their thinking, however, is tied to what is concrete.

16. Formal operations are defined by the appearance of propositional thinking. The child's thought processes are freed from the immediate and real and are potentially as logical as they will ever be.

17. Among the instructional implications of Piaget's theory are suggestions relating to providing for concrete activity, optimizing the difficulty level of tasks, and trying to understand how children think.

18. Research suggests that sensorimotor children may be more advanced than Piaget suspected, that the sequence he described for cognitive development is generally accurate, and that formal operations may not be generally characteristic of adolescence or adulthood. It is nevertheless a highly influential theory that has stimulated a tremendous amount of research and writing.

Chapter 8

Neural Networks: The New Connectionism

Scientific theories are mountains of sand built grain by grain, and people in the mountain-building business are justifiably wary of anybody who comes their way driving a bulldozer.

—W. F. Allman, *Apprentices of Wonder* (1989, p. 14)

PRELIMINARY NOTE FOR HUMAN READERS: CHAPTER 8 OBJECTIVES

I checked the dictionary, and here's what it said:

black box: 1. A grandmotherly term for a squarish, blackish object. 2. A squarish, blackish object which may or may not contain something.[1]

Which, as is so often the case with cousin Kon's dictionary, didn't tell me a whole whack of a lot. So I read more about earth psychology. Sure enough, I stumbled across *black box* more than once and it all became a lot clearer than mud.

Black box is an expression psychologists have sometimes used to describe the contents of the mind. Interestingly, however, human psychologists haven't yet figured out how to look at theirs. In fact, they haven't quite decided what a mind actually is—although everybody here uses the word at least once a day, sometimes a lot more. "I've a good mind to . . . ," they say. Or "I've changed my mind," or "She's out of her ever-loving mind," or "Mind the kids now," or "Mind the dog," or "Out of sight is out of mind," or . . . well, never mind.[2]

The expression *black box* implies that the contents of the mind are unknown, and perhaps unknowable. So the phrase is often linked with behaviorists like Watson and Skinner, who thought it was a waste of time to speculate about what happens between the presentation of a stimulus and the appearance of a response.

But, as we saw, some behaviorists thought maybe the black box should be opened up. Which, as I've said in so many words, they couldn't quite do. What they did instead was try to guess as intelligently as possible what sorts of things might be going on up there (or down there) in the mind—or in the brain, because most psychologists believe that if the mind is ever discovered, it'll be found in the brain somewhere.

So neobehaviorists like Hull and Tolman and Hebb invented their own versions of what they thought might be in the black box, being very careful all the while to tie their inventions to things they could actually see and maybe measure. At the same time, cognitivists also tried to crack the black box's lid. In fact, some of them—like Bruner and Piaget—became so engrossed in the struc-

---

[1] From *Kongor's Dictionary: A Koronian guide to Earth English* (Hungry Coyote Publishing: Sixth Androneas Time Cube, 48th Hexalog, 654th Point).

[2] The irony is that Kro always interpreted these idiomatic expressions literally when he first encountered them. I remember one day when he'd only been with us a short while and one of the kids said to him, "I've changed my mind." He immediately grabbed her by the head and started to examine it. "How the Dickens did you do that?" he asked. But we always told him the truth. (GRL)

tures and processes they glimpsed inside that, in the end, they ripped the lid right off and filled the box with so much jargon and stuff the lid probably wouldn't go back on at all anymore. And now, far more recently in the history of this whole thing, a new breed of brain/mind explorers, driven by powerful and sometimes intricate computer metaphors, have begun to map regions of the box no one had dreamed of.

The paths on which they have started are the subjects of this chapter. Once you've finished learning the chapter, you will probably want to rent television time so that you might explain to everybody the significance of the following:

- Artificial intelligence and intelligent computers
- Symbolic representation systems
- Parallel distributed processing and connectionism
- Why robots play chess

You will also know more about that lump of tissue inside your skull that you call a brain. But you will not yet know where the paths of this newer connectionism lead because your history, perversely tied to your linear notions of time, will not let you glimpse into the future.

SIXTH TIME CUBE, 49TH HEXALOG, POINT 235.50

As a species, humans seem much better at looking into their past than their future, although how they do so is astonishing. Even at the risk of being inappropriately judgmental, which my mission statement stipulates I must not be, let me say that they do it very badly. It makes no sense, as I explained to Lefrançois, to filter history through the minds of historians who are themselves products of their own history. The resulting biases and misperceptions are staggering. Such historians focus only on what interests them, see precisely what they expect, and report no more than what they understand—which, in turn, they distort through the lenses of their own period in time.

As a result, monumental events are lost to their history, the most fundamental causes of change are masked, and ultimately, they hardly profit from their very own experience. And throughout the galaxy's worlds, profiting from experience has always been an absolutely essential first step in the survival and successful evolution of a species.

The second essential step has been to glimpse into the future—which, as I've said, they can hardly do while they're still tied to their linear notions of time. Besides, for the subject matter of this chapter, glimpsing into the near future would not help very much; it's such a rapidly changing future in this dynamic field of computers, computer metaphors, and computer simulations. In fact, so rapidly does it change that almost everything cousin Kongor wrote in a state-of-the-art chapter entitled "Artificial Intelligence" as recently as 1983 is so far out of date that it isn't even very good history anymore.[3] I've had to throw most of it away.

---

[3]"Same thing'll happen to this chapter," I said to Kro. "It might be out of date before anybody even reads it!" "Well," he shot back, "at least most of the book is historical, and history don't change." (He often used terribly bad grammar and slang in his speech; he tried so hard to fit in. Fortunately, his writing is perfect.) "Besides," he added, "I think this is gonna be timeless too." We'll see. (GRL)

ARTIFICIAL INTELLIGENCE

Much of this older research, very firmly based on a computer metaphor, tried to understand the ways in which brains are like computers, and tried to simulate intelligent behavior using computers. The field came to be known as **Artificial intelligence (AI)**. Those who now work in the field are a varied collection of psychologists, neuro-anatomists, physiologists, linguists, computer specialists, and others. They are united in their efforts to develop programs, procedures, devices, or mechanisms to simulate or duplicate some of the intelligent functions of human mental activity.

Artificial intelligence, according to Bertram Raphael (1976), is a branch of computer science that tries to make computers smarter. Many people think computers are stupid, says Raphael; they think that computers are nothing more than "big fast arithmetic machines" and "obedient intellectual slaves" that can do only what they have been programmed to do. These are myths, claims Raphael. And the first myth—namely, that computers are nothing more than computational machines—is easily dispelled. The functioning of many computers involves countless operations that are noncomputational, including storing in memory, searching memory, making sequences of decisions, activating and turning off equipment, sensing and responding to external conditions, recognizing patterns, and perhaps even (as is shown later in this chapter) learning to read.

The second myth, that of the computer as slave, is more complex. It's true that computers do what they're programmed to do, and in that sense they are slaves to their programs (or, perhaps more precisely, to their programmers). But this doesn't mean that all computers need always be programmed in such a way that their activities will always be completely predictable. There are computers programmed to play chess or checkers that can beat their programmers. Similarly, there are computers that don't operate in linear, sequential fashion; their processing is distributed over a large number of connections simultaneously, leading to what is termed *parallel distributed processing*—a type of processing that makes it possible not only for computers essentially to program (or train) themselves, but also for them to respond in unpredictable and sometimes surprising ways. But this is a story that comes later.

Making Computers Smarter

There are at least two good reasons why people might want to make a smarter computer. One is that such a computer might do some marvelous things for people, freeing them to move on to other even more marvelous things. The other reason, perhaps more important for psychology, is that making such a computer might clarify many questions about human cognitive processes.

Those who deal with artificial intelligence are concerned mainly with the second of these benefits. Their quest is to discover what it is that the study of

computers can do for the study of humans. They use computers in two distinct ways: first, to mimic the functioning of the mind; and second, to generate metaphors of human functioning.

The hope is that the machines and programs that result will reveal information not previously known. Furthermore, attempts to simulate human processes in machines may serve as a fundamentally important test of what psychologists think they know about these processes. Not only is the programmer required to clarify and simplify, but whenever the program fails to simulate as expected, perhaps psychology learns something about what it is like to be human (or what it is like to be a machine).

Can Machines Think? The Turing Test

What sorts of human activities can computers mimic? For example, can they think? This is an old but fundamentally important question with which humans have long struggled. One argument goes like this: If it is true that people can think, and if it is true that a machine can be developed to do everthing that a person can do, then it follows that the machine can think. Logical, what?

Okay, consider this situation, described by Turing (1950) and since dubbed the **Turing test**: Two people—a man (A) and a woman (B)—are placed alone in a room. An interrogator (C) in another room must discover whether A is a man (X) or a woman (Y). At the end of the game, C must say "X is A, and Y is B" or "X is B, and Y is A." To discover who A and B are, C is allowed to ask them questions; A and B type out their responses. The object of the game for A is to impede the interrogator. He may, for example, answer questions as though he were a woman, or he may tell the truth. B, in contrast, attempts to help the interrogator. Obviously, if she attempts to do so by telling the truth ("I'm B, I'm the woman! Believe me!"), A can do exactly the same thing ("Don't believe him; I'm the woman!").

Turing says it will soon be possible to construct a machine that will stump the interrogator at least 70% of the time—which may be even better than what real people can do. By implication, then, the answer to the original question of whether machines can think is yes.

"But," the human reader protests, "the machine wouldn't be thinking. It would just stupidly be churning out responses programmed into it."

Reductio Ad Absurdum

Consider a second "Turing Test" that doesn't even involve a machine (described by Searle, 1980); instead, it involves a human student, Bob. Bob finds himself alone in a room, sitting at a table in front of which is a slot. Through this slot, some Chinese psychologists pass him a slip of paper on which is written a string of Chinese characters—which are all Greek to him. But he has at his disposal a heavy book, and in this book he finds a string of Chinese characters identical to those on the paper, together with instructions to copy out a second string of characters. He does this and passes the paper back through the wall. The Chinese psychologists examine the characters he has written, nod in approbation, and pass him a second piece of paper with a different string of characters on it. Again he responds as his book instructs. After several repetitions, the Chinese psychologists conclude the room—or, more likely, the machine—into which they have been passing these pieces of paper *understands* Chinese. What they've been doing is asking questions about a story, and he's been answering correctly. But he knows, of course, that he understands no Chinese. The Turing test thus is meaningless; it has been reduced to the absurd (*reductio ad absurdum*).

It's a strange thing, notes Searle (1980), that so many psychologists behave as though they believed in the validity of the Turing test. They assume that if a machine simulates intelligent behavior, then the machine must itself *be* intelligent; that if a machine produces correct responses for complex problems, it must *understand* these problems; and presumably that if a slot in a wall returns insightful responses in Chinese script, then something or someone beyond the wall knows not only Chinese but also stories. It's a mistake, notes Searle, that people don't make in other areas where computers are used to simulate complex systems: The meteorologist who tracks the movements and implications of weather systems by simulating them on a computer knows that the computer can't generate hurricanes or hailstorms.

By the same token, a computer that accurately imitates humanlike processes, or that selects responses identical to those a human might select, does not become human because of this. It's clear, as Mellor (1989) points out, that simple machine models are poor metaphors for the richness of human thought. Things like the deliberate manipulation of ideas or the conscious analysis of emotions—as well as the unconscious, "automatic" sorts of things that people learn and do—are not easily contained within a feedback-machine metaphor. That is because, says Mellor (1989), "most mental processes are not computations" (p. 47). In particular, things like pains and other sensations are mental processes that represent nothing, and thus they cannot be represented and computed.

Turing's original proposal established that a machine might be as effective as a pair of humans in a somewhat trivial task. At best, this suggests what psychologists probably knew all along: Something that imitates something else exactly need not exactly imitate. (Or as Lefrançois's grandmother, not always the most creative of linguists, says, there's more than one way to stuff a turkey.)

So, is there more than one way to solve a problem? To remember a poem? To recognize a word? Will studies of artificial intelligence discover a computer way of thinking quite distinct from the human ways? And will humans never know whether a machine can think—until, perhaps, it's too late?

Is it even clear what thinking is? Does the fact that human behavior appear purposive, whereas the behavior of a computing machine does not, prove that humans can think and that the machine can't? Would psychology be more convinced that a machine can think if it could change its "mind"? If it could lie?

Does the Computer Need to Think?

In the final analysis, the fact that the computer may not be able to think—that it is not a mind, and the mind is not a computer—may not be very important. As Gunderson (1964) put it, "In the end the steam drill outlasted John Henry as a digger of railway tunnels, but that didn't prove the machine had muscles; it proved that muscles were not needed for digging railway tunnels" (p. 71).

By the same token, computers don't need to "think," or to feel joy or anger, to do what they do so well. And the fact that they might not be able to think and feel does not imply that computer models are either useless or flatly wrong.

THE COMPUTER AND THE BRAIN

In their characteristically human way, people have assumed all along that a truly smart computer would be quite a lot like a human. It is surely no accident that most of the computers and computerized robots of popular space fiction are given personalities. Not only are these computers superbly "intelligent" in terms of their memory and computational abilities, but they all have a degree of willfulness and of personal idiosyncrasy. Their creators have tried to make them human.[4]

People and Machines: Basis for the Metaphor

In some ways, computers and humans seem highly similar, a fact that has led to the widespread use of computer metaphors in what are sometimes called the cognitive sciences. Similarities that have historically been most important for

---

[4]This is an astonishingly presumptuous intention. As the third of the Universal Great Laws makes clear, human-type life forms *cannot* simply be invented and built, no matter how sophisticated the computing technology available. Real robots are simply machines; they do not have personalities. This, of course, is why the human-invented robots of fiction will always be fictions. (Kro)

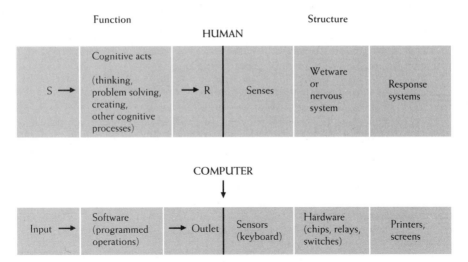

FIGURE 8.1   Analogies between computer and human structures and functions. The basic computer metaphor compares input to stimuli, output to responses, and the cognitive functioning of the nervous system to the computer's software-driven operations.

these computer metaphors have to do with *structure* on the one hand, and with *function* on the other.

Structurally, computers consist of complex arrangements of electronic components: chips, disks, drives, switches, and so on (what is called **hardware**). The human brain consists of complex arrangements of neural material: neurons, various other cells, amino acids, chemical transmitter substances, and so on (termed **wetware**). The basic computer metaphor, shown in Figure 8.1, compares hardware to wetware. Similarly, it equates input and output with stimuli and responses.

Although it is the computer's hardware that permits it to function (even as it is wetware that permits humans to function), it is the computer's instructions or programs (termed **software**) that determine whether and how it will function. With respect to functioning, the basic computer metaphor compares the computer's programmed operations with human cognitive processes. Hence these human cognitive processes are labeled "information processing"; after all, information processing *is* what computers do.

The potential of the comparison between human and computer functioning lies in the possibility that a truly smart computer—one that responds like an intelligent human being—might function as does a human. Put another way, the memory and programs of a smart computer might in some important respects resemble the memories and cognitive processes of the human.

Keep in mind, however, that even a computer that does very humanlike things might nevertheless use very different processes to do them. A machine can milk a cow every bit as rapidly as Lefrançois's grandmother can, but this certainly doesn't prove that the machine has hands (or that the grandmother has suction tubes!). And it might be important, too, that although the machine doesn't sing as it milks, the grandmother sure as the devil does.

How Brains and Computers Are Different

In fact, brains and common computers are different in very important ways. For one thing, brains are very slow; computers are lightning fast. Transmission of impulses in the brain is maybe 100,000 times slower than transmission in a computer. As Churchland and Sejnowski (1992) note, the brain is a product of evolution, not engineering design, and nature is not always the most intelligent designer. Yet a human brain can, in an instant, greet by name a man who has just shaved; understand five languages spoken in dozens of different accents; recognize a drinking container no matter what style of mug, glass, flask, vessel, cup, jug, or flagon it is; write a novel; and on and on.

"What makes a bunch of neurons so smart?" asks Allman (1989, p. 6). He answers his own question by saying that it is a collective phenomenon; it has to do with organization. Or, as Waldrop (1992) argues, what intelligent living things have in common is *organization* and *complexity*. Thus, from a physical point of view, the human nervous system is incredibly more complex than even the largest and most sophisticated of modern computers. As a result, claims Allman (1989), from a psychological point of view the brain's "tangled web displays cognitive powers far exceeding any of the silicon machines we have built to mimic it" (p. 3). For example, the human ability to store information in memory is virtually unlimited; no computer even comes close. Also, the human ability to perceive and to recognize complex, changing patterns cannot be matched by computers.

In contrast, the computer's ability to retrieve flawlessly from memory and to perfom arithmetical computations rapidly and accurately far exceeds that of humans. Computers do complex calculations in elaborate arrays (like spreadsheets) in fractions of seconds. Using the brain to do the same sort of thing, claims Allman (1989), is like using a wrench to pound in a nail: It'll work, but that isn't what it's made for.

So people aren't good at what computers do, says Allman, and computers aren't good at what people do so well. As a result, it would be a mistake to try to compare the brain to a digital computer. That, Allman says, would be a little like trying to understand how airplanes work by studying helium balloons—or like trying to understand how a television works by looking at the wiring diagram in the instruction manual.

The Roots of a New Metaphor

The problem, says Rumelhart (1992), is that cognitive scientists have been basing their metaphor on the wrong kind of computer—specifically, the serial-processing, digital computer. They've been asking how the brain is like a computer—and, in some ways, forcing their interpretation of the brain's workings to their understanding of the functioning of the computer. Instead, they should ask what *kind* of computer the brain might be.

And one possible (in fact, highly probable) answer is that the brain is a computer that doesn't do things one after another with lightning rapidity, arriving at its solutions, its recognition, and its next movement in less time than it takes to say "Bob's your uncle." If the brain actually worked that way, in fact, it would take you a staggering amount of time to blurt out "Bob's your uncle."

Instead, explains Allman (1989), the brain is more like a **parallel distributed processing** (PDP) computer; it does a whole bunch of things at the same time. PDP computers are available even on this planet. But how useful are they for studying human information processing? Is it possible to design and program them so that they perceive the environment as humans do? Can they be made to learn and use language as do humans? Can they be taught to read?

And if a computer can be made to do some (or all) of these things, will its processes be anything like human cognitive processes? Will it then be a "thinking machine?" Will it reveal things about human cognitive processing that are not now known?[5]

Two Computer-Based Models

In effect, there are two different approaches to the computer based study of human cognitive processes, each tagged with a sometimes bewildering array of labels. On the one hand is the **symbolic model** (also associated with the labels *production system* or *declarative knowledge*); on the other is the more recent **connectionist model** (also termed *PDP model*, and associated with the labels *procedural, automatic,* and *implicit;* Holyoak & Spellman, 1993).

Symbolic Models

The basic assumption of symbolic models is that all meaning, and therefore all thought processes, can be represented in terms of symbols such as language. According to this model, all processing of information—and hence all thinking—is interpretable in terms of identifiable rules (Massaro & Cowan, 1993). Simply put, the external world is represented *mentally* in terms of symbols; manipulating these symbols according to certain logical rules is thinking. Therefore, for a computer programer to simulate thinking, it's necessary to

---

[5]PDP computers, as I noted, *are* available on this planet. But even compared to our first generation machines, they are complex and difficult things. Most of the time, what human connectionists do is emulate PDP systems on conventional, serial processing machines such as the one Lefrançois lent me to write this report. In such cases, the PDP system is not actually a different parallel distributed processing machine. Instead, it is simply a set of instructions that makes the machine function like a PDP rather than a serial system. (Kro)

program into the system symbols that correspond to items of information, as well as rules for dealing with these symbols.

A Theory of Human Problem Solving

An early example of a symbolic model is the proposal by Newell, Shaw, and Simon (1958; Newell, 1973; Newell & Simon, 1956, 1972) for a theory of human problem solving. The proposal took the form of a complex program designed to discover proofs for theorems in symbolic logic. The program, called Logic Theorist or LT, was based on *Principia Mathematica* (Whitehead & Russell, 1925). It consisted of storing the axioms of *Principia Mathematica* in the computer, together with all the processes necessary for discovering proofs. The first 52 theorems of the text were then presented to LT; it succeeded in proving 38 of the theorems, almost half of them in less than 1 minute. It even proved a theorem not previously proven.

Newell, Shaw, and Simon (1957, 1958) suggest that the behavior of Logic Theorist was like that of a human in several ways. It solved some problems, though not all; it did better if the information was presented systematically; it performed better with instructions that provided direction; it used processes suggestive of "insight" rather than blind trial and error; it used concepts in solving problems, to the extent that axioms can be considered to be concepts; and it organized itself to do these things, using past discoveries to guide future endeavors. However, LT actually didn't reveal anything new or very important about human problem solving; it did was what it had been programmed to do. And so it tended to reflect only what was then known or suspected about cognitive processing.

Soar

Newell (1989, 1990) has summarized the processes and components of major symbol-based information-processing models within a theory labeled **Soar**. In effect, Soar describes what Earth jargon of the 1980s and 1990s calls the architecture of the human cognitive machine (still very much a machine metaphor). Simon (1990) defines **cognitive architecture** as a "description of the cognitive system at an abstract, usually symbolic, level" (p.13). Thus Soar describes the human cognitive system in terms of ten components. These include aspects similar to the information and processes given the original Logic Theorist, but they also include things that one might not expect to find in a machine model (like "intended rationality").

Soar, claims Newell (1989), "operates as a controller of the human organism, hence is a complete system with perception, cognition, and motor components " (p. 412). Like other symbol-system production models, it is based on the fundamental assumption that all knowledge can be represented by a symbol system, "which means that computation is used to create representations, extract their implications for action, and implement the chosen action" (Newell, 1989, p. 412).

Chess

Symbolic representation systems similar to Logic Theorist have been investigated extensively with respect to problems like those involved in playing chess, and they are perhaps best illustrated in this context.

There is a tendency on this planet to think of computers as mechanical wizards endowed with a type of brute cognitive force that humans do not even remotely approach. In the main, this estimate of the computer, though not entirely incorrect, is highly misleading. Take a straightforward game like chess, for example. The rules of the game are marvelously explicit; each piece can move only in prescribed ways and only on a conventional, easily defined area. The object of the game—to capture the opponent's king—is simple and clear. At any given point there are a limited number of possible moves, a finite number of possible countermoves, and so on.

Surely such a powerful brute as the computer can be programmed to consider and keep in memory all possible moves, countermoves, responses to countermoves, and so on, together with the eventual implications of each of these moves. In other words, a well-programmed computer could at least play to a draw, but more likely beat, any chess master in the world.

Not quite so easily. The total number of moves possible in a chess game approximates 10^{120}—a figure that may not look like much sitting here on this page, but that is absolutely staggering: "There haven't been that many microseconds since the big bang," writes Waldrop (1992, p. 151). Hence there is no conceivable earth-computer that could represent all possible alternatives.

The computer, like people, must rely on heuristics rather than algorithms for situations such as this. An *algorithm* is a problem-solving procedure in which all alternatives are systematically considered; an algorithmic solution for chess problems relies on the computer's brute force. In contrast, a *heuristic* approach to problem solving makes use of various strategies that eliminate and select from among alternatives without having to consider every one separately. A computer programmed to play chess might, for example, make use of heuristics (strategies) designed to protect the king, attack the queen, control the center of the board, and so on.

When artificial intelligence investigators first began to program computers to play chess, none of their computers was large enough or fast enough to make very good use of brute force; hence programmers were compelled to build their programs around the kinds of strategies human chess players might use. Chess masters could lick these early chess-playing computers with one hand.[6]

But now computers are much faster and infinitely larger, and some of them can look ahead and see the implications of millions of different moves within

---

[6]This is another of those strange human English idioms. In fact, chess is one of those games that is normally played with a single hand; using two doesn't help one bit. But to say that something can be done with just one hand means that it requires almost no effort. Peculiar, huhn? (Kro).

seconds or minutes. Modern chess programs, notes Allman (1989), have largely given up trying to imitate human chess-playing strategies. They have reverted instead to using sheer brute force, coupled with a few key strategies. Their strength is not that they "think" better chess than average human players, but instead that they can mechanically compute millions of moves and counter-moves within a few seconds.

So how good a chess player is the best chess-playing computer now? Quite good. Chess masters no longer laugh when they watch good computers play each other, or when they themselves are challenged. They have to play with both hands, and they now risk losing each time they play.

Connectionist Models

Chess masters and computers don't play chess the same way. Human chess players do not—in fact, cannot—rely on brute force. Their computational capabilities don't allow them to foresee the consequences of very many moves and countermoves at one time. But what they can do that the machine doesn't do is recognize patterns on the chess board, based on their previous experiences with similar though probably not identical patterns. And they can select the best move on that basis, in a sense synthesizing the effects of previous experience *without necessarily following explicit rules*. It's as though the human chess players learns from experience, developing implicit, nonverbalized rules. And the logic that characterizes the chess player's behavior is not a formal logic that always leads to one correct solution. Instead it is what is termed a *fuzzy logic*—a logic that is relativistic, takes a variety of factors into account, and has a not entirely predictable probability of being correct.

If all this is true, it suggests that the symbolic model is inadequate or incomplete. Recall that this model is based squarely on the assumption that all information can be represented in symbols (like language), that learning is explicit, and that information processing (thinking) involves the application of identifiable rules.

Two Kinds of Learning

But not all learning is explicit, expressable in symbols, conscious, and subject to definite rules. If Martha throws darts at a dart board long enough, she might eventually reach a point where she will hit the triple- or double-20 spaces almost at will. But she will remain essentially unaware of precisely what it is that she has learned. Her learning will be what is called **implicit learning**. In this case, the learning may be implicit in a complex web of connections between her eye and hand, involving millions of relays among neurons and muscles.

Habitual, well-practiced motor skills are just one example of implicit or unconscious learning. It appears that people also learn all sorts of cognitive things unconsciously. For example, Reber (1989) reports a series of "artificial-grammar" studies in which subjects are shown strings of meaningless letters (like PVKPZ) that have actually been generated following precise pseudo-grammatical rules. In some studies subjects are aware that rules govern the arrangements of the symbols; in others they remain unaware of this fact. Later they are asked whether various new strings follow the same rules (that is, whether or not they are "grammatical"). And although human subjects seldom perform very well on complex tasks of this sort, they respond correctly far more often than would be expected by chance—and, by the same token, far more often than they would if they had not been exposed to examples of the so-called grammar. Strikingly, however, they are seldom able to verbalize the rules by which they arrive at their judgments. That they have learned something is clear from their behavior, but what they have learned is implicit rather than explicit.

Much the same thing happens when children learn language. Within an astoundingly short period of time, they learn to say all sorts of things in ways that are largely correct grammatically. Yet they cannot make explicit their knowledge of the rules that allow them to generate correct language, or to recognize bad or good grammar.

Scientists have assumed that the mind uses rules and symbols to think, notes Allman (1989). But playing chess, learning grammar, recognizing a dog, or mistaking a flying shoveller[7] for a mallard, illustrate a more typically human, prone-to-mistakes, fuzzy-logic kind of thinking. If computer scientists are to investigate and model this kind of thinking, they clearly need something other than the rule-driven, symbol-manipulating, calculating machine that is the serial digital computer.

NEURAL NETWORKS

What they need—and have—is the parallel distributed processing computer. This computer gives rise to the PDP (or connectionist) model of cognitive architecture, whose development was pioneered by McClelland and Rumelhart (1986).

The PDP Model

All parallel distributed processing models, Shadbolt (1988) explains, consist of a set of processing units—but they do not include a central processor. These separate units can be considered to represent words, letters, sounds, elements of visual perception, and so on. They are connected to each other in complex and changing ways, and it is the pattern of connections that determines what the

---

[7] That's a kind of duck, you know. (Kro)

system knows and how it will respond.[8] Learning within such a system involves changing the strength of connections among units.

A Neural Network

The PDP computer serves, in effect, as a model of how the brain might work— a model labeled *connectionism* (or *connectionist*). What this model supposes is that the brain's collection of neurons are like the processing units in a PDP computer. In effect, they form a **neural network**. No central organizer or processor governs their activities. Instead, thousands (or millions) of these units are simultaneously active, activating each other in turn, establishing new connections, and ultimately learning through experience, achieving understanding, and making decisions.

There are three ways in which learning may occur in a neural network, explains Shadbolt (1988): New connections might develop, old connections might be lost, or the probability that one unit will activate another might change. Connectionists have worked extensively on this last possibility.

An Illustration: NETtalk

It is extremely complex to program into a serial-processing computer all the rules it would need to read a letter, or a poem, as a bright 6-year-old might. How a word is pronounced depends on what words come before or after it, what sorts of punctuation marks follow the sentence in which it is found, when it is being said, by whom, intended meanings and emphases of the reader, and on and on. So many exceptions and qualifications have to be built into such rules that even linguists can't agree on them. In fact, it may well be that the 6-year old doesn't learn to read by first learning all the appropriate rules and exceptions and then applying them as required (a symbol production model), but rather that the "rules" are unconsciously made up in the process of learning how to match spoken words to printed symbols (a connectionist model). This is essentially the reasoning that led Sejnowski and Rosenberg (1987) to develop a connectionist program that might learn to read. Their result, NETtalk, is at once a machine and a model. It is a machine made up of processing units, and it is what is called a *neural net model*. Hence its units serve as an analogy for actual neurons in the brain; in the model, they are also referred to as "neurons."

As a machine, NETtalk consists of a "window" that can scan 7 letters at a time. Each of the 7 slots in this window is connected to 29 neurons (input units); hence there are a total of 203 input units. At the output end of the machine are another 26 neurons (output units), each of which is linked with one of the 26 *phonemes* (simple sounds) that make up the English language.

---

[8]Lefrançois said this was too tough, that I should try to summarize, simplify, and illustrate. So I do in just a few paragraphs. All the same, it seems pretty darn clear to me. (Kro)

When one of the output neurons selects a phoneme, it is played through a loudspeaker, thus giving NETtalk its "voice."

Unfortunately, in English there is no direct, one-to-one link between a letter and a sound, or even between combinations of letters and a sound. The *a* in *can* is quite different from the *a* in *cane*. But there is a simple rule to cover that, no? Ah, yes; but how about the *a* in *ah*? Or in *far*? Or the *a's* in *facade*? Or in *aaaargh*?

The guts—or, better said, the brains—of NETtalk consist of 80 "hidden units" that intervene between the 203 input units and the 26 output units. Each of the 203 input neurons is connected to every one of the 80 hidden units, as is each of the 26 output neurons. Thus there are 18,320 connections in this neural network. And each of these 18,320 connections is *weighted*, meaning that some of the connections are strong (the important ones) and some are weak (those that are irrelevant). The highest of weightings (that is, the strongest of connections) might mean that activation of one unit would always lead to activation of the next; conversely, the lowest of weightings would mean that the activation of a unit would never lead to activation of the second.

The essence of the problem for NETtalk is stated simply: Learn to read text. The solution is not so simple: Arrange the weightings among the hidden units in such a way that patterns that are activated by letters lead the machine to select correct phonemes. Sejnowski and Rosenberg (1987) didn't know, of course, what these weightings would be, and so they proposed to let the machine learn them itself by using what is called the **back-propagation** rule. Essentially, a model that uses a back-propagation rule uses information about the correctness or appropriateness of its responses to change itself so that the response might be more correct or more appropriate. In learning to read, for example, a child already knows something about combinations of sounds that are correct (and meaningful); the computer does not.

The solution, Sejnowski and Rosenberg reasoned, might lie in letting the computer know what spoken text should sound like. So they presented NETtalk with 1000 words of text read by a first grader. And they gave it the back-propagation rule, in effect telling the computer to compare its output with the first grader's reading and work back through its hidden units, readjusting weights so as to reduce the difference between what it says and what the kid said.

And the computer did so. Because the initial weights had been set at random, its first pass through the text produced pure garbage. But over and over again the text was fed through NETtalk's input neurons, and over and over again the computer spluttered and babbled strings of phonemes—initially garbled and meaningless, but eventually clearer and more systematic. It was teaching itself to read.

After a day of practice, NETtalk could read not only most of the 1000-word text it had been studying so hard but other texts it had never seen. It had learned rules and exceptions, it had learned to generalize, and it had made some of the same sorts of errors that children make when they first learn to read—for example, pronouncing *have* as if it rhymed with *cave* and *rave*. And in much the same way as the human brain, by the end it needed to use only a small portion of its potential connections.

Implications and Strengths of Connectionist Models

The point of all this is that neural networks respond very much like humans do. They can make inferences *without being given specific rules for so doing*. As Allman (1989) notes, if I see the word *bat* along with the words *ball, diamond,* and *base,* I know something very different about "bat" than if I see the same word along with words like *witch, Halloween,* and *cave*. As Bruner (1957) points out, the inferences of humans are based on experiences that allow them to categorize and relate things. And the neural network computer, given the right series of experiences, might well do exactly the same thing. In a sense, its structure and functioning allows it to reach something that looks like insight. But the conventional computer is quite different; no matter how often it might be presented with bats of various kinds, it would never discover on its own that *bat* in one context is different from *bat* in another—unless it were actually given a rule specifying all the possibilities.

So neural network models—and the parallel distributed processing computers that make them possible—may in the end be far better models of some human cognitive processes than symbol-based models, claims Allman (1989). Among other things, these models suggest that people don't always think all that rationally. They don't systematically consider all the pros and cons, bringing the cold rules of logic to bear, calculating (as might a conventional computer) what the correct response is. They allow for a fuzzier kind of logic, and they emphasize that many aspects of a situation (or of many situations) might be involved in a response or a conclusion.

In addition, neural network models have the advantage of more accurately reflecting the actual physiological structure of the human nervous system, with its maze of neurons and interconnections—although the most complex of neural network machines is ridiculously simple next to the fully functioning human brain.[9] Nevertheless, there is a sort of biological realism to connectionistic models.

Neural network models also present a functional analogy for the notion that experience alters the brain's wiring, as Hebb had theorized so long ago. A neural network that adjusts its own connections is highly compatible, for example, with Hebb's notion that neurons that repeatedly activate each other become increasingly more likely to do so.

---

[9]You oughta' see the Koron brain!" Kro boasted. He had included a representation of it in the original draft of this manuscript for comparison with the human brain. It was totally incomprehensible—"Because it's in four dimensions," he explained, which wasn't an explanation at all. Also, it seemed to diminish the human brain unforgivably. So we had to delete it from this earth-bound edition. (GRL)

Some Cautions and Weaknesses

Because of their close resemblance to the structure and functioning of the human nervous system, it's easy to mistake connectionist models for the real thing—that is, for real, functioning nervous systems. But they aren't; they're just metaphors. As metaphors, they describe and they suggest, but it would be a mistake to confuse a description or suggestion with an explanation. Massaro and Cowan (1993) point out that neural networks with enough hidden units are capable of generating results that are not only unpredictable but have never been observed in the laboratory. Such models, they warn, may not be highly informative.

In addition, in a neural net using a back-propagation model, it may be possible to match *any* input to the desired output if one is given sufficient layers of hidden units and enough time. Thus it might be possible for a neural network to teach itself to "read" a passage of Spanish as if it were really English. If the input does not matter, then the model again teaches psychologists little about the processes involved in learning.

Another problem for self-taught neural network models has been that of *interference*. For example, McCloskey and Cohen (1989) have shown that when neural network models train themselves to recognize pairs of words in what is termed paired-associate learning, and are then given a second set of pairs, the initial learning impedes subsequent learning far more than is the case with human subjects. As Estes (1991) puts it, "Connectionist models are built to learn, but there are reasons to question whether they can be made to learn like human beings" (p. 23).

At the same time, that they learn at all is rather human. And there may be much to be learned by studying some of the ways in which they learn.

A Field in Progress

Much of this book is historical; it deals with theories the meat and gristle of whose principles and assumptions have been well chewed.

This is not true of the subject of this chapter, which is a field in progress. And so the chapter cannot really be concluded, nor can the models and theories presented in it be evaluated. History, as is her habit, will judge.

Summary

1. Artificial intelligence is a branch of computer science that tries to make computers smarter. The attempt generally involves trying to make the computer more humanlike in its "cognitive" functioning.

2. Two myths characterize human reactions to computers: that they are merely computational machines, and that they are nothing more than

slaves to their programmers. New PDP computers can "learn," however, and they sometimes surprise their programmers.

3. The Turing test says that if A can do x, y, and z, and B can do x, y, and z exactly, then B must possess whatever attributes A has that allow it to do x, y, and z. The test reduces easily to the absurd and does not answer the question of whether machines can think. They probably don't need to.

4. The basic computer-as-cognitive-processor metaphor sees parallels between computer hardware (physical components) and the human nervous systems and especially the brain (wetware), as well as between human cognitive functioning and computer programs (software).

5. Brains are much slower than computers and far inferior at doing computations, but they are much better at recognition tasks and at reasoning where insight and "fuzzy logic" are required. They are also enormously more complex in organization and size. Parallel distributed processing (PDP) computers appear to work more like brains, doing many things simultaneously.

6. The symbolic model is based on the serial-processing digital computer, and it assumes that knowledge can be represented symbolically and manipulated with rules. An illustration of the symbolic model is Newell, Shaw, and Simon's Logic Theorist (LT), which is capable of finding proofs for theorems in symbolic logic. Its functioning simulates some aspects of human problem-solving behavior.

7. Newell's Soar, a model of cognitive architecture, also illustrates a symbolic model, as do most of the chess programs. Chess programs are partly heuristic (that is, they make use of strategies and other systematic shortcuts), but they begin to approach the playing level of human chess masters mainly through their use of algorithms (using brute computing force to consider all possible alternatives systematically and exhaustively).

8. Not all human learning is explicit and describable in symbols and rules. Much is implicit or unconscious, including motor skill learning and the learning of abstract relationships through experience. Implicit learning is better modeled on PDP machines than on serial-processing machines.

9. Neural network (or connectionist) models, premised on PDP machines, consist of interconnected units rather than central processors. Patterns and strengths of connections represent knowledge. Sejnowski and Rosenberg's NETtalk is a neural network model developed so that the machine could "teach" itself to read using a back-propagation rule (knowledge of what the output should be) to modify connections so as to eventually match input (written words) to output (spoken words).

10. Connectionist models lead to machines whose functioning is much closer to that of humans. They allow for thinking that isn't completely

logical, that uses intuition and insight. They also reflect human neurological structure well. But they are descriptions rather than explanations, don't always generate plausible results, and don't always function as a human would (for example, they suffer from greater interference effects).

Chapter 9

Learning and Remembering: Models of Memory

The world will little note nor long remember what we say here . . .

—Abraham Lincoln, address at Gettysburg National Cemetery, November 1863

PRELIMINARY NOTE FOR HUMAN READERS: CHAPTER 9 OBJECTIVES

I have to confess that for a minute, I struggled with this chapter. I couldn't quite figure out what your writers meant by the word *memory*, because there is no exact equivalent for that word in either of Koros's two languages. Why? Because we have no memories. Or, more precisely, we don't have its opposite: We never forget. Hence the phenomenon of memory—or, in our case, of *perfect* memory—never suggested itself to us. Strange, huh?

So at first I didn't know what to think when I read G. Johnson's (1992) assertion: "When put on the witness stand, we can swear before God that we will tell the truth, the whole truth, and nothing but the truth. But the best we can really do is read out what is left of our memories, recollections that have been inevitably altered by time" (p. 233).

Now I know what that means, as will you after you have read and studied this chapter—that is, if you remember it. And if your memory serves you as well as mine, you will then be able to weave fascinating tales dealing with the following:

- attention
- sensory, short-term, and long-term memory
- two kinds of long-term memory
- theories of forgetting

You will also have learned a new trick for impressing old people, and you will have gained an important insight into human behavior at cocktail parties (or, for those who prefer, at coffee parties).

SIXTH TIME CUBE, 49TH HEXALOG, POINT 239.23

Lefrançois dragged me to one of these parties last week. Typical human behavior at a cocktail or coffee party is for clusters of people to stand around talking. They start out talking sort of loudly so that they can hear each other above the noise of other people talking, which makes other people talk a little louder so they can hear each other, which then makes others talk even louder, and then they have to talk louder, and in turn they have to talk louder . . . and on and on until the noise is almost deafening, but everybody just goes right on, paying no attention to anything except the conversation they're in the middle of.

Which is what I, too, tried to do at this party, sipping politely on a little bit of a drink, talking about beavers with Doctor L. and a couple of other people, one of whom had the improbable name of Rufus.

"So what'cha got against beaver?" Rufus asked, his face flushed from something or other.

"It's the dang dams they build," I remember Lefrançois saying, or something close to that. "The dang things are about flooding the south quarter—"

Then—sproing!—his neck cranes right around and I can almost see his ears perk up, except human ears can't really perk.

It seemed they might have been talking about him in another group. And sure enough, although he wasn't paying the least attention to them, when somebody made the mistake of saying his name—bango, bongo!—he heard it right away. And he heard enough of the rest of what they said that his wife had to drag him away, because she doesn't like him fighting at parties (or anywhere else, for that matter).[1]

"Don't pay any attention," she said to him. But he couldn't help it.

ATTENTION

Humans are constantly bombarded by thousands of sensory signals. If they always had to pay attention to all of them, they would be absolutely over-whelmed.

William James (1890) defined **attention** as the holding in mind of one among a number of competing objects or "trains of thought" (p. 403). Put another way, to attend to something is to be aware of it. Apparently people attend to only a few things at once; the rest is noise.

The Cocktail Party Phenomenon

But apparently, the "noise" isn't blocked out completely: When Lefrançois heard his name, his attention shifted, and his head whipped right around. Cherry (1953) was among the first to investigate this "cocktail-party problem." In one study he used headphones to feed different messages to each of the subject's ears. Under these conditions, subjects seem to be able to listen to either ear simply by *intending* to do so. But they cannot follow two different messages at the same time.

In a variation of this study, Broadbent (1952) had subjects repeat every-thing they heard in one ear, as they heard it—a process called "shadowing." Even for humans, shadowing is a very simple task. Using this approach, Broad-bent (1952) discovered that subjects don't remember what goes on in their other ear; in fact, when the language was changed from English to German in the unattended ear, the subject remained totally unaware of it. Moray (1959) found that even if the same word were repeated as many as 35 times, the subject was not able to remember having heard it. But if the subject's name was said a single time, that was usually enough to cause a shift in attention. Also, if the investigator interrupted the tape, subjects could recall what had just been said in the unattended ear (although with longer time lapses, the probability of

---

[1] Which I hardly ever do anymore, and which is irrelevant; and which should not have been brought up at this time. (GRL)

The cocktail party phenomenon.

recalling correctly declined dramatically). Apparently, sensory events have some momentary effect even when they're not being attended to.

Attention, Memory, and Learning

As Massaro and Cowan (1993) note, attention, memory, and learning are inextricably linked. It's clear, for example, that learning and memory are virtually inseparable. Learning is a change in behavior that results from experience, memory is the effect of experience, and both are facilitated by attention. Put another way, there will be no evidence of learning without something having happened in memory; by the same token, something happening in memory implies learning. Studying memory is, in effect, another way of studying learning.

Metaphors

As I have noted on a number of occasions, cognitive psychology is a psychology of metaphors. It seeks to understand the grand complexities of human cognitive functioning not so much by uncovering its precise mechanics and exposing its structures and functions but by inventing the most compelling and the most useful of metaphors to describe it. In the end, however, the value of the metaphor will be judged largely in terms of how well it reflects the facts. So it is that the search for the metaphor is premised on the results of scientific investigation. If psychology cannot trust its facts, how then can it trust its metaphors?

It bears repeating that the metaphors of which I speak in these pages are not the moving figures of speech of literature. They are nothing more than models—often simple models. What they say is not "Attention is a damsel with

6	6	8	0
5	4	3	2
1	6	8	4
7	9	3	5
4	2	3	7
3	8	9	1
1	0	0	2
3	4	5	1
2	7	6	8
1	9	2	6
2	9	6	7
5	5	2	0
X	0	1	X

FIGURE 9.1   Luria's subject, S, memorized this table completely within 3 minutes, and could then read off from memory any arrangement of the numbers including the 12 four-digit numbers in the rows, all four-digit diagonals in the array, or the four vertical columns. Also, he was able to convert the entire array to a single 50-digit number and read it off, a feat that required 1.5 minutes. From *The Mind of a Mnemonist: A Little Book About a Vast Memory*, p. 17, by A. R. Luria. Copyright © 1968 by Basic Books. Reprinted by permission of the author.

flowers up her nose," or "Memory is an ancient elephant," or "Motivation is another word for a blue dog." Rather, the metaphors of cognitive psychology are prosaic metaphors. They say only that humans behave *as though* or *as if*, and they describe what it is that humans behave "as if."

MEMORY: BASIC CONCEPTS AND DEFINITIONS

It is sometimes said that there are two kinds of memory, good and bad, and that most ordinary people possess the latter. When referring to "good" memory, people often mention professional entertainers who can faultlessly recall dozens of objects listed by an audience. Or sometimes they refer to the so-called idiot savant, the mentally limited human who possesses a remarkable but highly specific talent—like the guy who could watch a freight train pass by and memorize all the serial numbers on the boxcars.

Another example of extraordinary memory is the well-documented case of a man known to us only as S, described by Luria (1968). S was in most ways an ordinary man who had not been very successful as a musician or as a journalist, but who had an astounding memory. On one occasion, Luria presented S with the array of 50 numbers shown in Figure 9.1. After examining the table for 3 minutes, S reproduced the numbers flawlessly in 40 seconds. When asked to do so, he recited each of the four-digit numbers in the 12 rows as well as the two-digit number in the last row—again without error, and all within 50 sec-

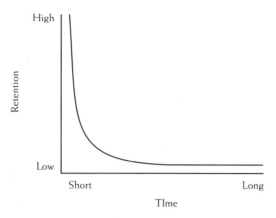

FIGURE 9.2   A memory curve.

onds. And one of the absolutely remarkable things about his memory was not so much that he could memorize these tables so quickly but that he could remember them, without error, at any time in the future. In fact, he recalled perfectly lists of words he had learned as much as 16 years earlier, without having been asked to remember them once in the interim. The only difference was that when asked to remember after several months (or years) had gone by, he needed a few minutes to "revive" the memory. He would usually sit with his eyes closed, Luria (1968) tells us, and he might comment, "Yes, yes . . . This was a series you gave me once when we were in your apartment . . . You were sitting at the table and I in the rocking chair . . . You were wearing a gray suit and you looked at me like this . . . Now, then, I can see you saying." (p. 12).

Most memories are not so phenomenal, as is well illustrated by "memory curves" that have been plotted in connection with experiments on retention since the pioneering work of Ebbinghaus (1885/1964). A hypothetical summary of these curves is presented in Figure 9.2. The most striking thing the curves indicate is that people tend to forget most of what they learn almost immediately after learning it. At the same time, however, some information is retained over long periods of time. These characteristics of human memory are reflected in most current theories of learning and forgetting.

What Is Memory?

In ordinary human speech, the term **memory** refers to the availability of information and implies being able to retrieve previously acquired skills or information. It clearly presupposes learning; that is, memory involves change. The computer metaphor leads naturally to the notion that to remember is to be able to retrieve from storage. Not surprisingly, says Hintzman (1990), one assumption of an intuitive understanding of memory is that if a memory is to influence behavior, it has to be retrievable.

But this is not so. There are numerous examples of what is sometimes termed *unconscious* (or implicit) memory, as Freud argued so convincingly. For example, past learning that cannot be remembered consciously can nevertheless affect later behavior—as happens when someone relearns a long-unused and apparently forgotten language. Similarly, some amnesiacs know all sorts of things, but they cannot remember having learned them.

Remembering and Knowing

Remembering, says Tulving (1989), is not the same thing as knowing. He explains that trees with their growth rings, just like musical recordings and card files, have memory; in a sense, they *know* things. But they remember nothing.

To clarify these concepts, Tulving suggests that psychologists need to pay attention to the two distinct aspects of memory: storage and retrieval. What trees and card files have is storage of certain effects; what humans have is storage *and* retrieval. Being able to retrieve presupposes storage, because things that have not been learned can't be recalled. However, not all that has been stored can be retrieved.

Current memory metaphors speak of three different kinds of storage: sensory, short-term, and long-term. They also speak of at least two different kinds of retrieval from storage: episodic and semantic. These terms are explained and illustrated later in this chapter.

What Is Forgetting?

If the coin of learning has two sides, memory is one side; **forgetting** is the other. Forgetting relates to both storage and retrieval in the same way as memory. Thus forgetting, which implies a loss of memory, might involve either a simple inability to retrieve or an actual change or loss of the physiological effects of experience.

Early Memory Research

It can be said that a person remembers if behavior or responses reflect previous learning, whether or not that person remembers the learning consciously. Most early studies of memory dealt only with conscious retrieval, however, looking at people's ability or inability to reproduce items of information that were presented to them.

Studies of this kind can sometimes lead to results that are unclear if subjects have previous related learning. One way of getting around this problem is to use material that is entirely new for all learners. For example, Ebbinghaus (1885/1964) solved the problem by inventing more than 600 nonsense syllables—completely novel arrangements of letters (for example, *lar, gur, kiv*). For a number of years, he sat faithfully at his desk at periodic intervals, memorizing lists of nonsense syllables and testing his retention of these. The plotted results of these experiments, with Ebbinghaus as the sole subject, provided the first memory curves (see Figure 9.2 above). As noted earlier, these curves indicate that the bulk of what is forgotten is lost very rapidly. At the same time, what is retained for a longer period of time (say, 10 days) is less likely to be forgotten even after a much longer passage of time (for example, 40 days).

TABLE 9.1   Testing Retroactive Interference

	Experimental group (A)	Control group (B)
Time sequence	1. Learn X	1. Learn X
	2. Learn Y	2. Do unrelated things
	3. Recall X	3. Recall X

Note: Lower scores of group A relative to group B indicate the extent to which Y has interfered with X.

TABLE 9.2   Testing Proactive Interference

	Experimental group (A)	Control group (B)
Time sequence	1. Learn X	1. Do unrelated things
	2. Learn Y	2. Learn Y
	3. Recall Y	3. Recall Y

Note: Lower scores of group A compared with group B indicate the extent to which X has interfered with Y.

Subsequent early research on memory continued to make extensive use of nonsense syllables in a variety of experimental situations. Sometimes these syllables were paired with other syllables—or meaningful words were paired with other words—and subjects were required to learn what went with what; this is called *paired-associate* learning. At other times subjects were asked to learn sequences of stimuli (this is called *serial* learning).

In a large number of studies, subjects learned two different sets of material and were then asked to recall one or the other in an attempt to determine whether recall would be interfered with. It often was. When earlier learning interferes with the recollection of subsequently learned material, *proactive interference* is said to have occurred (*proactive* meaning moving ahead in time). When subsequent learning reduces recall of material that had been learned earlier, *retroactive interference* is said to have taken place (see Tables 9.1 and 9.2).

A MODEL OF MEMORY

One of the important contributions of early studies of memory, in addition to their many isolated findings, is in the form of a model of human remembering. This model makes a basic distinction between **short-term memory** and **long-term memory** (Atkinson & Shiffrin, 1968; Waugh & Norman, 1965). In some variations of the basic model, such as the one depicted in Figure 9.3, a third

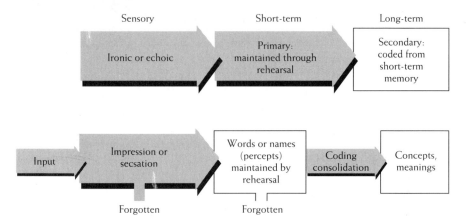

FIGURE 9.3 The three components of memory. The top row depicts three types of memory; the bottom row depicts the content of the memory process. Sensory information first enters sensory memory (iconic or echoic memory). From there it may go into short-term memory (also called primary memory), where it is available as a name or word, for example, as long as it is rehearsed. Some of the material in short-term memory may then be coded for long-term storage, where it might take the form of meanings and concepts. It is important to note that these three components of memory do not refer to three different locations in the brain or other parts of the nervous system, but refer to how we remember—or, more precisely, how we study memory.

component relating to sensation—called **sensory memory**—is included (also called the *sensory register*).

It is important to keep in mind that this model, like most contemporary psychological models, is a metaphor. As such, it probably says as much about the ways in which psychologists choose to investigate and talk about memory as it does about memory itself. In brief, there is not a particular "box" or other structure in human brains that corresponds to short-term memory and another that corresponds to long-term memory. These are not physical structures but abstractions.[2]

Sensory Memory

Sensory memory is a term for the immediate, unconscious effects of stimuli. It is illustrated in the cocktail party experiments, in which subjects recognized their names in conversations to which they were paying no attention. It is

[2]This is another example of how selective humans have been in their attempts to explain what is inside the "black box," and how they have been guided by the metaphor-of-the-day. In the case of memory, for example, for a long time their explanations were guided by a metaphor that saw the human mind as some sort of filing cabinet that slipped items of information into logically ordered files—many of which were later lost. Another metaphor viewed the human mind as a kind of motion picture camera that makes a continuous record of everything it experiences. And a current metaphor pictures human memory as an information processing system whose storage is determined by the nature of the processing it does. (Kro)

evident as well in studies such as that by Sperling (1963) in which he used a tachistoscope (an instrument that flashes stimuli for fractions of a second) to project on a screen three rows of four letters each. Immediately after the presentation, subjects heard one of three distinct tones signaling which of the three rows they were to try to recall. Under these conditions, most subjects could almost always remember all four letters in the indicated row (accuracy of recall was well over 90%). But if subjects were asked to recall all 12 letters, they remembered only an average of 4.5. And the longer the delay was between the presentation of the letters and the request to recall, the less successful were the subjects.

What this experiment illustrates most clearly is that a limited number of stimuli remain accessible for a very brief period of time following presentation, even if they are not attended to. This type of sensory memory is very much like an echo—so much so, in fact, that Neisser (1976) called it *echoic* (for auditory stimuli) or *iconic* (for visual stimuli) memory.

Short-Term Memory

Another way of looking at sensory memory is to say that it precedes attention. When the individual attends to (that is, becomes conscious of) a stimulus, it passes into short-term memory (STM).

Sensory memory refers to a phenomenon that lasts milliseconds; short-term memory is a phenomenon that lasts seconds or a very few minutes at most. Specifically, short-term memory refers to the awareness and recall of items that will no longer be available as soon as the individual stops rehearsing them. STM is what makes it possible for secretary Olga to find a number in a telephone directory and dial it without having to look at the second digit after dialing the first, at the third after dialing the second, and so on. It is also what enables her to forget the number as soon as she has finished dialing—and what then makes it necessary for her to look it up again if she has to redial. Long-term memory (LTM) is what would be involved if Olga decided that she might need to use the number again and attempted to "memorize" it; it would also be involved if the symmetry and poetry of the number so moved her that she found herself remembering it the next day.

A Classical Study

Among the most common early techniques for studying short-term memory was one developed by Peterson and Peterson (1959) in which subjects are presented with a single nonsense syllable and then asked to recall it. Immediate recall is usually close to 100% (errors are usually caused by misperception of the original syllable). But greater delay between the presentation of the word and its recall results in lower recall, the extent of which depends on the subject's intervening activities. Subjects who are not required to do anything and who know they will be asked to recall the syllable usually rehearse the syllable to make sure they can remember it. But if subjects are asked to engage in some unrelated activity (such as counting backwards in time to a metronome) begin-

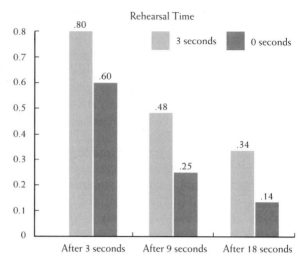

FIGURE 9.4   Proportion of nonsense syllables
recalled correctly in the Peterson and Peterson (1959)
study as a function of rehearsal and time lapse.
Subjects in the zero-time-for-rehearsal group were
asked to start counting backward from a 3-digit
number immediately after they heard the nonsense
syllable. Those in the other group experienced a 3-
second delay before they were given the digit from
which they were to count backward. From "Short-term
Retention of Individual Verbal Items," by L. R.
Peterson and M. J. Peterson. In *Journal of Experimental
Psychology, 58,* 1959, p. 197.

ning immediately after presentation of the nonsense syllable, retention is interfered with. For example, in the Peterson and Peterson (1959) study, subjects
recalled the syllables correctly 80% of the time when given 3 seconds to rehearse them, but only 60% of the time when given no opportunity to rehearse
them. Eighteen seconds after the stimulus had been presented, subjects still
remembered correctly 33% of the time if they had been given an opportunity
to rehearse for 3 seconds; but they were correct only 14% of the time when
given no opportunity to rehearse (see Figure 9.4).

Limited Capacity

Short-term memory refers to the ongoing availability of a small number of
items—an availability that begins to deteriorate within seconds and is usually
completely gone within 20 seconds in the absence of rehearsal. It describes a
phenomenon that makes it possible for readers to "keep in mind" the words that
they are currently reading (or writing) long enough to make sense of the whole,
or a set of directions or plans for dealing with ongoing cognitive processing.
Put another way, short-term memory is what is conscious at any given time. As
Calfee (1981) put it, it is a sort of "scratch pad" for thinking; for this reason,
short-term memory is often called *working memory.*

Following his investigations of short-term memory, G. A. Miller (1956) has concluded that the average adult short-term memory capacity is seven, plus or minus two items. According to him, it is as though there are about seven slots in STM. When these are filled, there is no room for more until one or more of the slots are again emptied—which, given the nature of STM, happens within seconds.

Chunking

But the limited capacity of short-term memory is not a great problem for most people, says Miller (1956), because the items that fill each of these slots don't have to be unitary (a digit or a letter, for example). Instead, they might be composed of a number of other items—a **chunking** of items, so to speak. Thus the short-term memory slots might be filled with seven letters, or with seven words. The seven words represent "chunks" of information that are far more economical (and probably more meaningful) than seven unrelated letters.

In much the same way, long-term memory makes extensive use of chunking. Miller explains the process by making an analogy to a change purse that can only hold seven pieces of money. If there are seven pennies in the purse, it will be full; however, it could have held seven quarters or seven dollars (or seven $1000 bills).

Forgetting in Short-Term Memory

There are several different theories to explain why short-term memory is limited to only a few items, and why forgetting occurs. **Decay theory** holds that memory traces vanish quickly with the passage of time (in the absence of continued rehearsal). **Displacement theory**—essentially the Miller (1956) analogy—suggests that there are a limited number of slots to be filled in short-term memory and that incoming information displaces old information. **Interference theory**, which is highly similar to displacement theory, advances the notion that previous learning (rather than subsequent information) might somehow interfere with short-term memory.

Levels of Processing.   Craik and Lockhart (1972) suggest that loss from short-term memory is simply a matter of inadequate processing. The main difference between short- and long-term memory, they claim, involves the level to which input is processed. In the sensory register, no processing occurs. At the STM level, a "shallow" level of processing occurs, consisting mainly of the recognition of stimuli through perceptual analysis. With deeper processing (involving activities such as analysis, rehearsal, and organization), material is transferred to long-term memory and hence is not lost immediately. Forgetting in short-term memory thus is presumed to result from inadequate processing (Cermak & Craik, 1979).

Which Explanation?   None of these explanations is universally accepted. In fact, most researchers have not been very concerned with forgetting in short-term memory. After all, the function of short-term memory is simply to retain information for only as long as it's useful and then to discard it. If people didn't function this way, it's likely that their long-term memories would be cluttered with all sorts of useless information, and retrieving from it might be far more difficult than it now is.

Loss of material from short-term memory stores becomes a significant problem in those cases when disease, injury, or aging shorten STM to the point that ongoing functioning suffers. That, essentially, is what happens when people forget what they were going to say after they've started to say it. Or what they were going to write next . . .

Long-Term Memory

Prior to the 1950s, most research on memory dealt not with the transitory and unstable recollections of STM but with the more stable and, by definition, longer-lasting remembrances of long-term memory (LTM). In fact, it wasn't until the mid-1950s that psychologists began to recognize the usefulness of distinguishing between LTM and STM.

Two other changes in memory research have been (a) a shift from the use of nonsense syllables and paired associates to the use of meaningful material, and (b) a change in emphasis from the measurement of memory span and the effects of interference to an examination of models for long-term storage and retrieval.

General Characteristics

All that a person can remember that has not just now occurred makes up long-term memory. Thus all that is retained of educational experiences, a complete working knowledge of language, and all stable information about the world is in long-term memory.

Among the important characteristics of long-term memory are the following:

1. Long-term memory is highly stable, unlike short-term memory. Much of what is remembered today or tomorrow, will also be remembered next week. One example of highly stable long-term memories are those having to do with smells. In an intriguing study, Goldman and Seamon (1992) bottled 14 odors, half of them associated with childhood (for example, crayon shavings, Play-Doh, fingerpaints, bubble soap) and the other half partially or entirely associated with adulthood (chocolate, popcorn, soap shavings, cigarette tobacco). Adults correctly identified not only about 90% of recent odors but more than three-quarters of sometimes very distant odors (see Figure 9.5). "Significant memory for odor-name associations remains even over very long recall intervals," Goldman and Seamon (1992) conclude, "much longer than any tested to date" (p. 562).2. Long-term memory is *generative* rather than simply reproductive. Memories are profoundly influenced by preconceived notions and beliefs about what goes with what; these are termed *schemata* or sometimes *scripts* (D. A. Smith & Graesser, 1981). These schemata sometimes lead people to remember things that have never happened—in other words, to generate rather than reproduce. For example, M. K. Johnson, Bransford, and Solomon (1973) showed subjects this passage (p. 203):

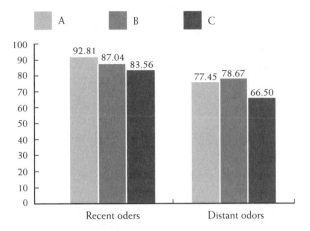

FIGURE 9.5   Accuracy of memory for recent and distant odors. In this study, thirty 17- to 22-year-old students correctly matched odors with names at least two out of three times. Based on Goldman, W. P., & Seamon, J. G. (1992). Very long-term memory for odors: Retention of odor-name associations. *American Journal of Psychology, 105,* 549–563 (Table 1, p. 553). Reprinted by permission of University of Illinois Press.

John was trying to fix the birdhouse. He was pounding the nail when his father came out to watch him and to help him do the work.

Later subjects were shown these two sentences along with a number of others, one of which was the following:

John was using the hammer to fix the birdhouse when his father came out to watch and to help him do the work.

Most subjects were more convinced that they had seen this sentence rather than either of the sentences they had actually seen. Why? Because, say Johnson et al., although the word *hammer* was not mentioned in either of the first two sentences, subjects recalled the idea of the sentences clearly and, based on their knowledge that hammers are what is used to pound nails, they *generated* the word into their recollections.

3. Long-term memory is influenced by understanding. What people remember is often a meaning, a central idea. For example, when Len hears a story and then repeats it, typically what he remembers of it is its general "drift"—its setting and punch line. When he repeats the story, he doesn't remember each of the sentences, pauses, and gestures of the original storyteller. Instead he generates his own, based on his understanding of the story.

The relationship between understanding and long-term memory is illustrated in a Piaget and Inhelder (1956) study in which very young children are asked to draw lines representing the level of water in tilted jars. Although all children have seen fluids in tilted glasses or bottles, that they don't actually remember what this looks like is clear from their reproductions (shown in Figure 9.6). Only after children *understand* that water remains horizontal do they *remember* correctly.

5 years   7 years   9 years

FIGURE 9.6   Children's drawings of water lines.

4. Some things are more easily remembered than others. As noted above, meaningful material is remembered far more easily and for longer periods of time than material that is less meaningful. Also, events that are particularly striking, important, or emotional are often remembered more clearly and for longer periods of time than more mundane happenings (Bower, 1981).

Short-Term and Long-Term Memory Compared

Short-term memory is an active memory, says Wickelgren (1981); it includes that which is "currently being thought of" (p. 46). Hence short-term memory is equivalent to span of attention, and the most important distinction between STM and LTM is not that one lasts for a long time and the other only for seconds, but rather that one is immediately conscious and the other is not.

Other differences between STM and LTM (summarized in Table 9.3) include the fact that as an active, ongoing process, STM is easily disrupted by external or internal events. In contrast, LTM is far more passive and far more resistant to disruption. Also, as we have seen, STM is far more limited in terms of capacity, being essentially synonymous with active attention or immediate consciousness. Finally, retrieval from STM is immediate and automatic—a fact that is hardly surprising, because what is being retrieved is either immediately conscious or not available. Retrieval from LTM may be far more hesitant, may require a search, and may result in a distortion of what was originally learned.

DIFFERENT KINDS OF LONG-TERM MEMORY?

One of the most important insights to emerge from memory research, claim Squire, Knowlton, and Musen (1993), is the gradual realization that long-term memory is not just one thing—that it consists of different components. Different researchers and theorists have proposed various labels as metaphors for these components.

Explicit versus Implicit Memory

For example, as was noted in Chapter 8, there is both explicit and implicit knowledge. When the centipede was asked how it managed to walk so elegantly with its many legs, how it always knew which to move next, it was

TABLE 9.3   Three Levels of Memory

	Sensory	Short-term	Long-term
Alternate Labels	Echoic or iconic	Primary or working	Secondary
Duration	Less than 1 second	Less than 20 seconds	Indefinite
Stability	Fleeting	Easily disrupted	Not easily disrupted
Capacity	Limited	Limited (7 ± 2 items)	Unlimited
General Characteristics	Momentary, unconscious impression	Working memory; immediate consciousness; active, maintained by rehearsal	Knowledge base; associationistic; passive, the result of encoding

From *Psychology for Teaching*, 8/e, p. 127, by G. R. Lefrançois. Copyright © 1994 by Wadsworth, Inc. Reprinted by permission of Brooks/Cole Publishing Company, Pacific Grove, CA 93950.

stunned to realize that it had never really thought about the problem. So it tried hard to think about how it walked, and in the end the poor thing became hopelessly confused and wrapped itself up in a little knot just trying, *consciously*, to walk as it always had.

Human memories relating to how to walk, how to keep upright on a bicycle, how to hit a home run, or how to do a triple lutz in ice skating are implicit. So are the sorts of memories that led Watson's subject, little Albert, to whimper when he saw a rat, or that make Lefrançois's neighbor, Mrs. Shewchuk, turn pale at the sight of a sparrow.

In contrast, memories relating to people's names and addresses, their telephone numbers, and the name of their leader are *explicit*. And so are memories relating to their last birthday or to what they did last Christmas.

"The main distinction," claim Squire, Knowlton, and Musen (1993), "is between conscious memory for facts and events and various forms of nonconscious memory" (p. 457). Conscious or explicit memory is labeled **declarative memory**; nonconscious or implicit memory is **nondeclarative** (sometimes also called *procedural*) **memory**.

Physiological Evidence

The distinction between implicit and explicit memories is especially well illustrated in amnesiacs, some of whom have been extensively studied by psychologists. Many of these amnesiacs have lost huge chunks of declarative (explicit) memory, often forgetting who they are, where they went to school, what they did for a living, who their spouse/children/parents/friends are, and so on. Yet they retain many nondeclarative (implicit) memories relating to motor skills. Interestingly, amnesiacs can be classically conditioned, Hintzman (1990) reports; this finding is evidence of implicit or nondeclarative memory. In such cases, however, they may retain absolutely no memory of the conditioning itself, thus providing evidence of a declarative memory weakness.

Two Kinds of Declarative Memory

Studies of amnesiacs also provide evidence of an important distinction between two kinds of declarative memory. There is, for example, the well-known case of K.C., a 30-year-old man who missed a curve with his motorcycle, suffering severe brain damage and becoming permanently amnesiac (Tulving, Schacter, McLachlan, & Moscovitch, 1988). K.C. is absolutely incapable of bringing to conscious memory anything that he has ever done, seen, or felt in the past. He cannot remember himself ever experiencing or doing anything. "K.C.," writes Tulving (1989), "knows that his family owns a summer cottage, knows where it is located, and can point out the location on a map of Ontario, and he knows that he has spent summers and weekends there. But he does not remember a single occasion when he was at the cottage or a single event that happened there" (p. 363). K.C. remembers all sorts of things that are political, geographical, and musical. In fact, he remembers well enough that his measured intelligence is quite normal, and those talking with him, might not notice anything wrong. But he remembers nothing of the personal episodes of his life.

Semantic and Episodic Memory

There are at least two distinct types of declarative long-term memory, claims Tulving (1972, 1989). On the one hand, there is stable knowledge about the world, abstract knowledge, knowledge that is necessary for understanding and using language, knowledge of principles, laws, and facts, and knowledge of strategies and heuristics. These illustrate **semantic memory**, which K.C. has retained.

On the other hand, there is a body of knowledge consisting of personal memories of events that have happened to the individual. These are not abstract memories (as are rules and principles, for example), but specific memories tied to a time and place. These are autobiographical memories; they always involve the person at a certain time and place. These memories, which K.C.'s amnesia obliterated, are labeled **episodic memory**.

Tulving (1991a) argues that these two types of memories are sufficiently distinct that it is useful to consider them separately. He suggests that there might be some important differences in the way material is stored in each, as well as in how it is remembered and forgotten. For example, episodic memory seems to be far more susceptible to distortion and forgetting than is semantic memory; humans have considerably more difficulty remembering what they ate for breakfast 3 days ago than in remembering a poem, or a name they learned in elementary school.

Episodic memory, according to Tulving (1989), depends on semantic memory. When Genevieve remembers the experience of eating breakfast this morning, she might also remember a variety of abstract things about eating, about breakfasts, or about kitchens or restaurants. In contrast, semantic memory seems to be able to operate independently from, or even in the absence of, episodic memory. Thus K.C. can know how to play chess—and know *that he knows* how to play chess—without any memory of ever playing a single game of

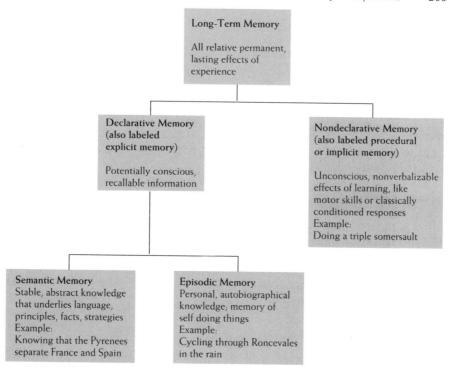

FIGURE 9.7   Memory metaphors. Researchers describe different long-term memory systems that are distinguishable in terms of the kind of material stored in each. Studies of memory failures in amnesiacs suggest that different parts of the brain may be involved in each type of memory.

chess. As Tulving (1989) puts it, "It is possible for an individual to know facts without remembering learning them, but not possible to remember without knowing what it is that is being remembered" (p. 77).

Distinctions among the various kinds of long-term memory are shown in Figure 9.7.

Models of Declarative Long-Term Memory

An early model of long-term memory portrays the mind as a sort of motion picture camera (complete with audio, video, smell, touch, taste, and so on; Koffka, 1935). This model views memory as a complete, sequential record of experiences from which people retrieve those isolated bits of information that still remain accessible after the passage of time. This is a *nonassociationistic* model of memory.

Almost without exception, contemporary models of LTM are *associationistic*. This means that they are premised on the fundamental notion that all items of information in memory are associated in various ways (Holyoak & Spellman, 1993; Wickelgren, 1981). Thus, when you "search" your memory for some item of information, you don't haphazardly produce a long sequence of unrelated responses; instead, you narrow in on the missing item through a network of related information.[3]

Associationistic models of long-term memory are essentially cognitive models. Not surprisingly, they often use a variety of abstract concepts, such as Bruner's catergories and coding systems, Piaget's schemata, or *nodes* (see, for example, Wickelgren, 1981). But *node, category, schema,* and related terms are simply metaphors, not actual structures. They are metaphors for what can be represented in the "mind." Their single criterial attribute is that they represent. A node model of mental representation, for example, is simply a model that says that people represent knowledge in terms of representations (called nodes, although they could as easily have been called anything else) that are related in countless little-understood ways. Figure 9.8 presents one version of how a small part of a node model might be depicted.

The usefulness of a node model for human memory is that it emphasizes its associationistic features. Note, too, that models of LTM are basically information-processing models. As such, they have much to say about the processes involved in memory (such as attending, rehearsing, and organizing). Not surprisingly, most cognitive theorists no longer study learning and memory as separate subjects.

PHYSIOLOGY OF MEMORY

It seems self-evident that learning and remembering result in some sort of change in the brain. Understanding what this change is should be very useful for understanding what learning and memory are all about.

The Search for the Engram and Other Memory Mechanisms

It makes sense, thought the first memory researchers, that there should be a specific and permanent trace left in the brain for every experience that is remembered. The trick is to find this trace, sometimes labeled an **engram**. The search includes some fascinating studies.

Lashley's Rats

Karl Lashley (1924) was convinced that experiences leave specific engrams in the brain, and he was determined to find them. First, he trained rats to run through a maze. Once a rat knew the maze well, Lashley systematically lobbed off tiny chunks of its brain, keeping a careful record of exactly what it was he had removed. Then he would release the rat back into the maze. He knew that

[3]It is worth noting that the concept of associations is fundamental to most of the earlier, behavioristic theories described in the first chapters of this report. Many of these theories, for example, deal with how associations between stimuli and responses are affected by repetition or reward. Associations are also very important in the area of cognitive psychology. But cognitive theorists are concerned more with associations among ideas (concepts) and how they are affected by *meaning.* (Kro)

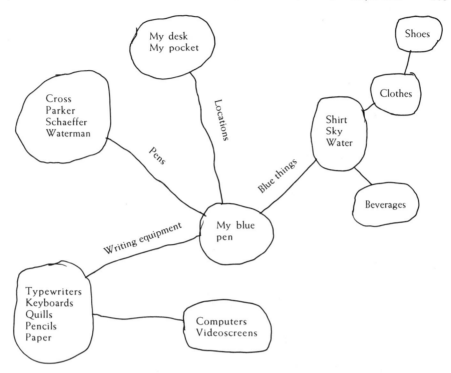

FIGURE 9.8 A model of a metaphor. Node theory suggests that we remember abstractions (meanings and associations rather than specifics). Thus my blue pen is depicted as a "node" embedded in a complex web of abstractions (for example, "blue things"), each of which relates to many other nodes that are not shown here.

he would eventually cut out just exactly the right piece, and the rat would have no idea how to get through the maze.

But it didn't work that way. It seemed that no matter what part of the brain Lashley excised, as long as he didn't kill the rats or incapacitate them physically, they continued to run through the maze (although they did so more and more slowly). He was eventually forced to conclude that memories are scattered throughout the brain rather than in just one place. Lashley may have been far closer to the truth than many of his contemporaries suspected.

Penfield's Patients

Wilder Penfield (1969), a brain surgeon, thought he had begun to discover and map human memories when he stimulated the brains of some of his fully conscious patients as they were undergoing brain surgery. Tiny amounts of stimulation applied with minute electrodes seemed to stimulate very vivid and detailed recollections of past experiences. More careful examination, however, later revealed that these memories were not very reliable; one subject who described in detail a visit to a lumberyard had in fact never been there. It's likely, claims Squire (1987), that Penfield's subjects were fantasizing, constructing memories, or perhaps even hallucinating.

Rat Brain and Planaria Studies

A series of studies of rat brains (Krech, Rosenzweig, & Bennett, 1960, 1963, 1966) seemed to show that learning causes specific, measurable chemical changes in the brains of rats. But the changes that were found turned out to be highly global and not very informative. In addition, they have seldom been replicated and are generally considered invalid (Johnson, 1992).

Similarly, McConnell (1962) and his associates report studies that seemed to show that conditioning planaria (flatworms) to curl up in response to a light causes permanent chemical changes that can then be transmitted to other planaria simply by mincing the trained worms and feeding them to untrained worms. However, other researchers were unable to duplicate these results (Bennett & Calvin, 1964).[4]

Studies of Amnesiacs

Although the precise physiology of memory remains undiscovered, studies of amnesiacs suggest that different brain systems are involved in different types of memory. Squire, Knowlton, and Musen (1993) note that injury to certain parts of the brain (specifically, the hippocampus and other structures in the medial temporal lobe and diencephalon) is associated with losses in declarative LTM. In contrast, nondeclarative memory seems to be associated with other brain structures. Similarly, following his studies of K.C., Tulving (1989), concludes that episodic memory depends on intact frontal lobes of the brain, but that semantic declarative memory does not.

Many of the details of the physiology and neuroanatomy of learning remain unknown, says Tulving (1989). It is likely that as more is learned, metaphors will become more appropriate. In time psychology might even move from the metaphor to a literal description.

A Connectionist View

The current cognitive metaphor for memory is less concerned with the gross physiology of brain structures than with neuroanatomy and the organization of neurons. This view, as shown in Chapter 8, sees learning and memory as involving changes at the level of the neuron. These changes are reflected in arrangements of associations among neurons (in neural networks, in other words). The view is in many ways highly reminiscent of Hebb's notion of facilitation of conduction among neurons following repeated firing. In fact, notes G. Johnson (1992), there is now evidence of a biochemical basis for Hebb's theory—evidence that chemical changes in neural receptors occur and facilitate subsequent

---

[4]These studies are good examples of the urgent need for replication in human sciences which, unlike most Koronian sciences, are never guaranteed exact the first time. There are simply too many variables human scientists have still not learned to control in their experiments. Nor have they yet learned to counter all the confounding effects of their own investigatory procedures—although they now recognize that these effects do exist. They call this phenomenon the Heisenberg uncertainty principle. In cousin Kongor's dictionary, the Heisenberg uncertainty principle is described as being drawn from quantum mechanics and implying that for no state of any system can all dynamic variables be simultaneously and exactly known. Which is mostly true on this planet. (Kro)

neural transmission. But psychologists still don't know exactly what happens when people learn and remember. Do they know more about forgetting?

FORGETTING

To forget, as the term is ordinarily used, is to be unable to bring into immediate consciousness. Clearly, forgetting does not prove—or even imply—complete loss from memory. There are many things people learn implicitly (like how to skip a stone) whose underlying memories they can't easily translate into symbols or examine consciously. Also, there is a possibility that when someone can't recall something, it has not been lost but simply cannot be retrieved. Perhaps, like a stubborn name lurking on the tip of the tongue, it will be retrievable later—and perhaps not.

A number of answers have been proposed for why people are unable to remember. Some of these are discussed below.

Fading Theory

Fading theory suggests the possibility that people forget some things simply as a function of the passage of time—that whatever traces or changes learning leaves behind become less distinct as time passes. Evidence that this might be so rests on the observation that people often remember recent events more clearly than very distant ones. Clara might at this moment be able to remember most of the items of clothing hanging in her closet, but she would not fare so well at describing what she had in her closet 6 years ago (unless she was in prison then). But if she has periodically reviewed mentally what was in her closet at that time, she will probably do much better. Clearly, items that are occasionally remembered are far more resistant to the presumed ravages of time than items that have never been recalled. Every recollection is a sort of rehearsal and an opportunity for relearning.[5]

Distortion Theory

Evidence we reviewed earlier shows clearly that a great deal of what is retrieved from long-term memory is distorted. When humans search their memory, what they remember are main ideas, which are abstractions. Later, they regenerate— and create—the details. Recall that in the M. K. Johnson, Bransford, and Solomon (1973) study, subjects were convinced they had seen a never-before presented sentence simply because it made sense.

---

[5]Kro seems to have overlooked the fact that many psychologists don't consider *fading* or *decay* theory very useful or accurate. These psychologists claim that time, by itself, does not cause forgetting any more than it causes the erosion of mountains, the melting of glaciers, or the rusting of metal. It's other things that occur (during the passage of time, of course) that cause these changes. (GRL)

Eyewitnesses, Loftus (1979) notes, are notably unreliable and easily misled. In one study, she had subjects view a film in which a sports car was involved in an accident. Afterwards subjects were asked the sorts of questions an accident witness might be asked. Some were asked, "How fast was the sports car going when it passed the barn while traveling along the country road?" Others were simply asked, "How fast was the sports car going while traveling on the country road?"

But the fact is there was no barn along the road. Yet when subjects were later asked if they had seen a barn in the film, about one-fifth of the group who had been asked the first question swore they had; fewer than 3% of the second group thought they had seen a barn.

Repression Theory

One theory of forgetting is based on Freud's notion that individuals sometimes repress (that is, unconsciously forget) experiences that are anxiety-provoking or traumatic. This type of forgetting cannot easily be demonstrated experimentally but is observed occasionally in clinical situations. Because it applies only to emotion-related experiences, it is of limited value as a general explanation of forgetting.

Interference Theory

A widely known theory of forgetting holds that new learning can interfere with the recall of old learning (**retroactive interference**) or that old learning can interfere with the recall of new learning (**proactive interference**). These two kinds of interference have been a consistent phenomenon in studies of long-term memory (often employing nonsense syllables). In these studies, learning one list of words and then learning a second, related list leads to (a) more difficulty in remembering the first list (retroactive interference) and (b) more difficulty in learning the second list (proactive interference).

Fortunately, interference appears to be more descriptive of what happens in the laboratory than of what actually happens in the course of people's daily lives. Although people might occasionally become confused as a result of competition among items they are trying to remember, indications are that they can continue to learn all sorts of things without running the risk of becoming progressively more subject to the effects of interference.

The fact that laboratory results in memory research are not always reflected in real life has led to a sometimes-heated controversy among some psychologists. Some, like Neisser (1978), argue that laboratory research has produced no important knowledge and that investigators should study *everyday* memory in real life. Some, like Banaji and Crowder (1989), insist that science needs experimental control to produce results that can be generalized. Still others, like Tulving (1991b) claim that the quarrel is uncalled for and that it will not advance science: "There is no reason to believe that there is only one correct way of studying memory" (p. 41).

Retrieval-Cue Failure

Perhaps, as noted at the outset, people don't actually forget but simply cannot remember. The fact that something cannot be remembered is not very good evidence that it is completely gone from memory; it might simply mean that it cannot be accessed.

Tulving (1974) recognizes this possibility in his description of two kinds of forgetting. There is a kind of forgetting, he explains, that simply involves an inability to recall—a sort of **retrieval-cue failure**. He assumes that this type of forgetting is related to the unavailability of appropriate cues for recall. In his words, it is *cue-dependent* forgetting. A second type of forgetting involves actual changes in the memory trace itself and is therefore labeled *trace dependent*. The four theories described above (fading, interference, distortion, and repression) relate primarily to trace-dependent forgetting.

For declarative (conscious, explicit) material, recall seems to be better with certain types of cues. For example, Tulving (1989) reports that the most effective memory cues are those that match the type of recall required. In studies where subjects are required to remember the meanings of words, cues that emphasize meaning are best. But when subjects are asked questions relating to the spellings or sounds of words, retrieval cues that emphasize the sounds (phonemes) or the letters in the words work best. Other retrieval cues and strategies that can significantly improve memory include various well-known aids to remembering.

REMEMBERING

Psychology has identified three main strategies that are effective in moving material from short-term to long-term memory. These three strategies—rehearsal, organization, and elaboration—are also the main cognitive processes of learning.

Rehearsal

To rehearse is to repeat (Her name is Greta; her name is Greta; Greta; Greta; Greta . . .). **Rehearsal**, as noted earlier, is the principal means of maintaining information in short-term memory. It is also the means by which information is transferred to long-term memory.

Elaboration

To elaborate is to extend or add to. **Elaboration** might involve associating what is to be learned with mental images, or relating new material to material that has already been learned. Bradshaw and Anderson (1982) asked subjects to remember the sentence, "The fat man read the sign." Those who had elaborated the sentence to "The fat man read the sign warning of thin ice" were far more successful in recalling it than those who had not elaborated.

Organization

To organize is to arrange according to some system. Chunking—placing what is to be learned into related groups—is one example of **organization**. Deliberately organizing textual material with heads and subheads is another example. One of the fundamental beliefs of cognitive psychology is that people appear to have a natural tendency to look for relationships, to identify on the basis of similarities and differences (that is, to categorize and attain concepts).

Systems for Remembering

Various systems developed specifically to improve memory are based on these strategies; accordingly, the strategies emphasize ways of organizing and of elaborating, as well as ways of highlighting retrieval cues.

Rhymes and Little Sayings

Among these memory aids—or **mnemonic devices**—are *acronyms* (letter cues) such as NATO, UN, or Roy G. Biv (the colors of the visible spectrum in order). They also include *acrostics*, which are sentences or expressions in which the first letter of each word stands for something else. For example, the acrostic "Men very easily make jugs serve useful nocturnal purposes" recalls English names for planets in order from this system's sun (Mercury, Venus, Earth, Mars, and so on). These sorts of mnemonic aids provide easily recalled retrieval cues and are also a form of elaboration and organization of material.

The Loci System

More complex mnemonics typically make use of visual imagery, which is far more memorable for humans than are most written or spoken words (Paivio, 1980). When subjects were exposed to 10,000 pictures very briefly and then shown some of these same pictures again—paired this time with other pictures that had not been included in the first presentation—they were able to recognize more than 90% of the pictures (Standing, 1973). Similarly, when Bahrick, Bahrick, and Wittlinger (1975) presented subjects with photographs of their former classmates (taken from yearbooks), recognition was approximately 90% accurate after 2 months and had not declined appreciably 15 years later. There is little doubt that the human capacity for visual recognition is remarkable.[6]

Mnemonics based on visual imagery suggest specific ways in which mental images can be linked visually with other easy-to-remember images. Higbee (1977) and Cermak (1976) described a number of these mnemonic techniques in detail. In the **loci system**, for example, subjects are asked to form a strong visual image of the item to be remembered and to place it in some familiar

---

[6]Of course, I mean this in a relative sense: The human capacity for remembering images is remarkable compared to the human capacity for remembering poetry, personal experiences, or the faces of dogs. Relative to the Koronian memory, it is . . . well, what can I say? (Kro)

location such as a room in a house. The second item is then visualized and placed in another room; the third might be placed in a hallway; and so on. Recalling the items later simply requires that the subject take a mental "walk" through the rooms of the house and attempt to visualize each of the items that have been placed there. Try it with a grocery list. It works.

The Phonetic System

A memory system often used by professional memorizers, guaranteed to impress grandmothers, is the **phonetic system**, described by Higbee (1977). The first step in learning the phonetic system is to form strong visual associations between numbers and consonants. Traditionally associations make use of the visual appearance of the consonants. Thus 1 is a *t* (because it has one downstroke); 2 might be *n*; 3, an *m*; 4 a *q*, and so on.[7]

Once you, human reader, have associated a letter with each consonant (vowels don't count), you can then form a word for each number, say, from 1 to 25. For example, number 12 could be "tin"; number 21, a "nut." Now form a strong visual image linking each of these words to its number. Once you have learned these, you can then challenge your grandmother to name, or show you, 25 items. As she writes these items on a piece of paper, numbered consecutively, you close your eyes and cleverly link an image of each with its appropriate numbered visual image.

When your grandmother has finished, you are ready: "So do you want me to give them back to you backward or forward?" But she's a devious old lady, and she suspects you have some trick that allowed you to link these 25 items in series. So she throws you a curve: "What was the twenty-first thing I said?"

In your newly trained mind's eye, you immediately see your "nut," which you have linked to your grandmother's saying, "And for number 21, let's see, that'd be the stove in the old house," so that now you see the "nut" sitting, red hot, on the stove. You answer: "The twenty-first item? Well now, that'd be that old stove in the other house, the one in which you closed the oven door on the cat."

And your grandmother *is* impressed.

Summary

1. James defined attention as the "holding in mind" of one among a number of competing items. In more recent formulations, attention is equated with short-term (active or working) memory.

---

[7]Because any of these systems would be so laughably simple (and useless) for Koronians, I've written the description of the phonetic system as it would be written for a human rather than a Koronian reader. (Kro)*

*In truth, I think Kro simply wanted another opportunity to drag a grandmother into the discussion, having repeatedly promised my grandmother that he would write about her. (GRL)

2. Cocktail-party experiments suggest that there is some very short-term retention of sensory events that are not being attended to. Thus attention can shift if an unattended stimulus becomes important or interesting.

3. Some extraordinary human memories are capable of astounding long-term recollections, but most human memories display rapid initial loss of information. Memory is ordinarily defined as the availability of information (recall or retrievability); however, some aspects of memory are not conscious (that is, are implicit). Not all that is stored can be retrieved. Ebbinghaus pioneered the early scientific investigation of memory using nonsense syllables.

4. One model of memory describes a process consisting of short-term and long-term memory. A third stage, sometimes termed the sensory register, describes the momentary effect of stimulation (and is sometimes called echoic or iconic memory).

5. Short-term memory (STM) lasts only seconds (seldom more than 20), unless there is continued rehearsal (in which case the information may be coded into long-term memory). It refers essentially to the ongoing availability of a small number of items (seven, plus or minus two), and it is termed active or working memory to emphasize its similarity to immediate attention or consciousness. Its capacity may be increased through chunking, the grouping of related items.

6. Forgetting in STM may be related to decay (loss of memory traces), displacement (replacement of old with new material as a result of space limitations), interference (where previous learning interferes with new learning), or inadequate processing (for example, lack of rehearsal).

7. Long-term memory (LTM) is assumed to involve some permanent structural changes in the brain. Short-term recall, in contrast, may involve no more than temporary electrical/chemical activity. This is essentially Hebb's theory.

8. Long-term memory is highly stable (notably so for images and odors), is generative rather than simply reproductive, is influenced by understanding, and is better for some items (that are more striking, more meaningful, or more emotional) than for others.

9. A comparison of STM and LTM reveals that short-term memory is an active, continuing process; that it is easily disrupted by ongoing activities; and that it is highly limited in terms of capacity. In contrast, long-term memory refers to a more passive process, not easily disrupted by ongoing activities and essentially unlimited in capacity. Retrieval from STM is either immediate and automatic or does not occur; retrieval from LTM may be considerably slower and more groping.

10. Long-term memory systems include the declarative (explicit) memory, consisting of potentially conscious, recallable information; or nondeclarative (procedural or implicit) memory, consisting of unconscious, nonverbalizable effects of learning (as in, for example, skill learning or classical conditioning). Evidence from studies of amnesiacs suggest that different brain systems might underlie these memory systems.

11. Declarative (recallable) memory is composed of semantic memory, which includes general, stable, abstract facts and principles (for example, knowledge of language or of the world); and of episodic memory, which refers to personal knowledge that is temporal in nature and tied to specific events (hence autobiographical memory).

12. Some early models of memory were nonassociationistic (Koffka's notion of a continuous record like a videotape); current models emphasize associations among items in memory and frequently make use of schema or node models, a node or schema being simply whatever it is that represents an idea.

13. Episodes in the search for the physiology of memory include Lashley's ablations of rat brains (he didn't find the engram); Penfield's stimulation of his patient's brains (their memories may have been fantasies and hallucinations rather than specific memories); dissections of the brains of enriched rats (changes were global and imprecise); the feeding and injection of trained planaria into untrained planaria (the studies don't easily replicate and, 30 years later, seem to have led nowhere); the study of amnesiacs' memories (these support distinctions among different long-term memory systems and indicate that different brain systems may be involved in each); and the development of connectionist models (which argue that memories reside in patterns of neurons rather than in specific changes within single neurons).

14. There is evidence that some forgetting might result from an ill-explained "fading" process. In addition, some probably results from distortion, which might occur partly because what is remembered tends to be relatively abstract and because people generate rather than reconstruct when they try to remember. Other explanations for forgetting include repression theory (most appropriate for experiences laden with negative emotion), interference theory (proactive and retroactive interference), and retrieval-cue failure (absence of appropriate cues to retrieve learned material).

15. Learning and remembering can often be improved through rehearsal, elaboration, and organization. Memory strategies include rhymes and related devices, as well as specific mnemonics that make extensive use of visual imagery (the loci and the phonetic systems).

Chapter 10

Motives: Behavior's Reasons and Causes

Persons attempting to find a motive in this narrative will be prosecuted.

—Mark Twain, *Huckleberry Finn, Introduction*

PRELIMINARY NOTE FOR HUMAN READERS: CHAPTER 10 OBJECTIVES

There is, of course, a motive in this narrative. But your purpose is not to find it, which is why you will be prosecuted if you try! (Heh, heh! Don't be so serious. This is just a joke.[1]) Your purpose is to learn this book's contents, not its causes or its reasons.

However the contents of this chapter, deal with causes and reasons: two different aspects of motivation, although most theories of motivation treat them as though they were the same.

A cause is . . . actually, you'll know what a cause is after you're completely done with this chapter—that is, after you've read it and carefully translated it into every other language you know. At that point, you'll be in the enviable position of being able to write tiny but brilliant truths (of the kind that might be baked into fortune cookies) explaining, among other things, the following:

- The meaning of motivation
- How instincts and reflexes relate to behavior
- What needs, drives, and incentives are
- The intricacies of attribution theory
- The meaning and importance of arousal
- The use of motivation in the classroom

You will also have new insights into the causes and reasons for your own uninspiring, but nevertheless inspired, actions.

SIXTH TIME CUBE, 49TH HEXALOG, POINT 241.75

All behavior is, at least in one sense of the word, inspired, *because, says an Earth dictionary, to inspire is to move to action. There are no unmotivated acts, explains Bolles (1974); every behavior has some cause.*

On Koros, of course, that is absolutely true. Here, I'm not so sure. Take, for example, the guy Lefrançois and I visited last night. Crazy, they call him. "Why's everybody call him Crazy?" I ask. "Has to do with glue," Doctor L. answers. I'm about to ask what it has to do with glue, but just then the guard slides open the big grated door. They usher us in and guide us to the visiting room. All the doors grind shut behind us, their electrically controlled lock tumblers slamming home.

---

[1] Kro never understood how serious and carefully determined human students are. He kept making the mistake of assuming that whimsy and madness appeal to dedicated students of human psychology because of what his cousin Kongor's dictionary said about students. Fortunately, most of the worst examples of madness have been deleted from the text through careful copyediting. The plain truth is, you will not be prosecuted even if you succeed in finding a motive in this piece. (GRL)

Crazy grins widely when he sees us. You can tell he and Doctor L. are old buddies. They shoot the cattle for a while, lots of talk like "D'you remember the time you and me . . . " and so on like that, getting all nostalgic while I'm sitting there not paying all that much attention because I'm always thinking about what I'm going to write next in this report and what it's going to be like when I go to Heel for a week after I'm done.

Then visiting time's up, and the guards say, "Closing in 5 minutes." Crazy hugs Doctor L., and they both have tears in their eyes. Then Crazy hugs me too and pats me on the butt, except grown-up Korons never cry.

But I might have later (cried, that is—if I had known how) when I discovered that I had lost the little wallet I carry on my rump, with a couple of Koronian cash credits and the holo-photo of my pet blip inside.

"It must be in the car," says I.

"Naw," says Doctor L. "We'll get it back from Crazy next time."

"Why?" says I, stunned.

THE MEANINGS OF MOTIVES

One of the most basic questions that can be asked about human behavior is "Why?" Why do people behave? Why do they behave in precisely this manner and not that? Why does behavior stop? Answering these questions is fundamental for an understanding of human learning and behavior. These are the questions of **motivation**.

A motive is a conscious or unconscious force that incites a person to act—or, sometimes, not to act. In this sense, motives are **causes** because, says the same Earth dictionary, causes are agents or forces that produce an effect or an action. Hence the study of human motivation is the study of agents and forces that cause behavior.

But the study of human motivation is also one other thing; it includes a study of **reasons** for behavior. Reasons are explanations. To illustrate: If Joe accidently places his hand on a hot stove, the heat (or, more precisely, Joe's sensation of heat) *causes* him to withdraw his hand at once. How should psychology explain this? In other words, what are the *reasons* for this behavior?

REFLEXES, INSTINCTS, AND IMPRINTING

The answer is that there are biological reasons for Joe's behavior. These have to do with his nervous system and its wired-in tendency to react to certain situations *reflexively*. Hence a reflex is one kind of motive, one sort of explanation for behavior.

Reflexes

A **reflex** is a simple unlearned act that occurs in response to a specific stimulus. Children are born with a limited number of reflexes, such as blinking in response to air blown on the eye, the knee-jerk reflex, withdrawal from pain, and startle reactions. All of these reflexes are normally present in adults as well. In addition, several human reflexes are present at birth but disappear shortly thereafter: the Babinsky reflex (curling of the toes when the sole is tickled), the grasping reflex, the sucking reflex, and the Moro reflex (flinging out the arms and legs when startled or dropped suddenly).

Most reflexes have clear survival value—perhaps even including the Moro reflex, which some hypothesize might have been useful in some distant past when a tree-dwelling infant accidentally fell from a perch or slipped from its mother's embrace and the sudden flinging out of its arms helped it find another branch to grasp.

The Orienting Reflex

Another type of reflexive behavior, the **orienting reflex** (OR), is a general tendency to respond to new stimulation by becoming more alert. It is "a mechanism that enhances the processing of information in all sensory systems," explain Berg and Berg (1987, p. 268.) In dogs and cats, the orienting response is clear: When they hear a new sound, their heads turn, their ears perk up, and their entire posture says, "What the @#$*! was that?" Not surprisingly, the orienting response is often called the "What is it?" response.

In humans, the orienting response is not as obvious as in cats or dogs, but it serves the same alerting function. Thus heart and respiration rate may decelerate momentarily (hence the expression "to hold one's breath"), and electrical activity in the brain may change.

Reflexes as Explanations

Pavlov and Watson made extensive use of reflexes in their accounts of human learning, and they were at least partly successful in explaining some simple types of learning (like emotional responses or taste aversions). Note that both these classes of learning can be very important for the organism's survival. Classically conditioned fear of a snarling noise, for example, might lead an animal—even a human one—to avoid a saber-toothed tiger when it hears one clear its throat. And a learned taste aversion might prevent the animal from eating a poisonous toadstool.

Because of their link with survival, reflexes are valid, biologically based explanations for some behaviors. Unfortunately for those who prefer things to be simple, they have limited generality and usefulness as explanations for most human behaviors, because most are not reflexive.

Instincts

Reflexes are simple unlearned (inherited) behaviors; **instincts** are more complex inherited patterns of behavior that are common to an entire species and are also associated with survival. Some early theorists like McDougall (1908) thought all human behavior resulted from unlearned tendencies to react in given ways—in other words, from instincts. They thought up long lists of supposed instincts like gregariousness, pugnacity, flight, self-assertion, self-abasement, and hunger. At one point, Bernard (1924) counted more than 6000 "instincts," including things as unexpected as "the tendency to avoid eating apples that grow in one's own garden" (p. 212).

But these are not really instincts at all. Instincts are *complex* behaviors (like migration or hibernation); they are general to all members of a species (like the "following" behavior of young ducks or geese), and they are relatively unmodifiable (like birds' nesting behaviors). In fact, there is no convincing evidence that there are *any* instincts among humans, although they are clearly evident in other animal forms and are invariably related to survival and propagation (Thorpe, 1963). It may be that if humans still have instincts, they have become so confounded by culture that they are no longer distinguishable from learned behavior.

Imprinting

Nevertheless, some theorists like Bowlby (1982) argue that early attachment between human mother and child has important parallels with **imprinting** among animals. Imprinting describes an unlearned behavior that is specific to a species and does not appear until an animal has been exposed to the appropriate stimulus (called a releaser), providing that exposure occurs at the right period in the animal's life (the **critical period**). The classical example of imprinting is the "following" behavior of ducks, chickens, or geese (Hess, 1958), who typically imprint on the first moving object they see. Fortunately, that object is usually their mother—but it need not be. Lorenz (1952) reports the case of a greyleg gosling that imprinted on him and followed him around much as it might have followed its mother. As the time for mating approached, much to Lorenz's embarrassment, this goose insisted on foisting its affections on him.[2]

Although humans do not imprint as do other animals, Bowlby (1982) and others (like Klaus & Kennell, 1983) argue that there is a "sensitive period" during which bonds between mother and infant form most easily, and that this in fact provides a biological explanation for early attachment.

PSYCHOLOGICAL HEDONISM

There is considerable intuitive evidence that human behavior seeks that which is unpleasant and tries to avoid the unpleasant. At first glance, this notion, labeled **psychological hedonism**, would seem to be a good general explanation for most human behavior. Unfortunately, it's not a very useful idea. The main problem with the notion is that it can't be used to predict or even to explain behavior unless pain and pleasure can be defined clearly beforehand—which they often can't. For example, it might appear wise to say that a man braves the Arctic cold in an uninsulated cabin because doing so is pleasant, but it's quite another matter to predict beforehand that this specific man will retire to that frosty cabin. The difficulty is that pain and pleasure are subjective emotional

---

[2]The story is that this goose, in a gesture of devotion and love, insisted on depositing beakfuls of minced worms in Lorenz's ear. But he wouldn't reciprocate. (Kro)

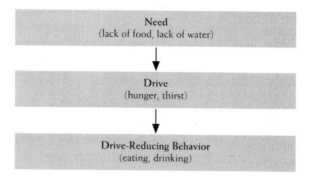

FIGURE 10.1   The drive-reduction model of motivation. A need (lack) leads to a drive (urge), which in turn leads to a behavior that satisfies the need and eliminates the drive. This model is useful for explaining many physiologically based behaviors, but does not explain many others: why some people like to read, some like to climb mountains, and so on.

reactions. Although it might be true that people are hedonistic, motivational theory can profit from this bit of knowledge only if pain and pleasure can be described more objectively.

DRIVE REDUCTION AND INCENTIVES

There are three physiological motives central to the lives of all humans: hunger, thirst, and sex.

Needs and Drives

Each of these is linked with a **need**—a lack that gives rise to a desire for satisfaction. The tendency to act in order to satisfy a need is termed a **drive**. For example, to be hungry is to be in a state of need; this need leads to the hunger drive. Hunger leads to eating, and the need disappears. Thus needs bear the seeds of their own destruction (see Figure 10.1).

This explanation of behavior is termed *drive-reduction*, and it is well illustrated in Hull's theory. Hull believed that drive reduction is what accounts for the effects of reinforcers and leads to learning.

Physiological and Psychological Needs

What the basic **physiological needs** (or physical needs) are seems clear: They include not only the needs for food, drink, and sex, but also the need to maintain body temperature. Some psychologists also believe that people have **psychological needs**, although there is considerably less agreement about what they might be. Likely candidates include the needs for affection, belonging, achievement, independence, social recognition, and self-esteem.

One of the main differences between physical and psychological needs is that the physical need—and its satisfaction—results in tissue changes. Psychological needs, in contrast, are not necessarily manifested in bodily changes but have to do more with the intellectual or emotional aspects of human functioning. In addition, physiological needs can be completely satisfied, whereas psychological needs are relatively insatiable. People can eat until they're not at all hungry, but they seldom receive affection until they desire absolutely no more from anyone.

Maslow's Hierarchy

Maslow (1970) lists two systems of needs: basic needs and **metaneeds**. Basic needs include physiological needs, safety needs, love and belongingness needs, and self-esteem needs. These are *deficiency* needs in the sense that they lead to behavior if the conditions that satisfy them are lacking. In contrast, the metaneeds are *growth* needs. They include what Maslow assumes is a human need to know and achieve abstract values like goodness and truth, to acquire knowledge, and to achieve **self-actualization**—that is, to fulfill inherent potential.

Maslow assumes that these need sytems are hierarchical in the sense that higher-level needs will not be attended to until lower-level needs have been satisfied. Thus it is starving people do not hunger for knowledge (see Figure 10.2).

Adequacy of Need/Drive Positions

Needs/drive models are very important explanations in behavioristic learning theories. Skinner's and Thorndike's conditioning theories are based largely on the effectiveness of basic drives as human motives. Similarly, Hull relied on drive reduction to explain why habits are acquired and how fractional antedating goal responses become connected. Not surprisingly, common reinforcers in animal research are food and drink—objects that satisfy basic, unlearned needs. And among the most common reinforcers in studies of human operant conditioning are those that satisfy learned or psychological needs (praise, money, tokens, high grades, and so on).

Some Problems with Need/Drive Theory

Despite the fact that need/drive theory appears to have considerable relevance for explaining human behavior, there are a number of problems with it. First, the theory holds that behavior results from a need or deficiency in the organism; it follows from this that the satisfaction of needs should lead to rest. This, however, is often not the case. Even rats that presumably are not in a state of need, having just been fed, given drink, and loved, often do not simply curl up and go to sleep. Instead, they may even show increases in activity.

A second problem for need/drive theory is that there are many instances of behaviors that human beings (and lower animals as well) engage in with no

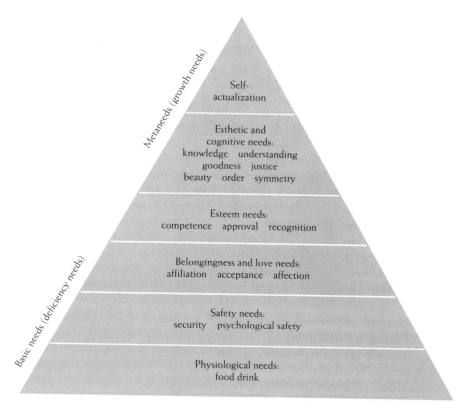

FIGURE 10.2   Maslow's hierarchy of needs.

possibility of immediate or delayed satisfaction of a need—as when a rat learns to run a maze in the absence of any reward (Tolman, 1951), or when a person seeks sensory stimulation (Hebb, 1966). Evidence of exploratory behavior has led some theorists to suggest that there is a *curiosity* or *exploratory* drive that motivates many human behaviors (for example, Berlyne, 1960, 1966).

A third major shortcoming of need/drive or drive-reduction theories is that they try to account for behavior in terms of *inner* states and urges (need for food, for example, is an inner state, and the hunger drive is an urge). As a result, they are hard pressed to explain why behaviors also seem to be affected by external stimulation. If hunger were solely an internal state, people would always eat only enough to activate the physiological mechanisms that relate to stopping eating. Yet a great many people eat far more if the foods appear more appetizing; others seem to become far hungrier if they are allowed to anticipate beforehand what they will be eating. Even rats who are given a small taste of food before being placed in the start box of a maze run faster toward the goal box than do rats that have not been "primed" (Zeaman, 1949). If an inner state of hunger is the motive, it follows that the taste of food, however small, should serve to reduce the hunger drive somewhat, and that hungrier rats should run faster (see Figure 10.3.)

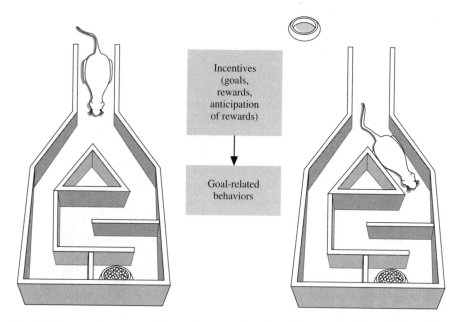

FIGURE 10.3   Incentives. Drives alone can't explain behavior. In Zeaman's (1949) experiment, rats who had already been given some food (maze b) performed better on a maze that they knew led to food than did hungry rats (maze a).

Incentives

What need/drive positions need to take into account is the incentive value of motivation. Even for rats, a taste of food seems to serve as an incentive, urging them to run faster. For humans, gifted as they are with the ability to imagine and to anticipate, there is no need for a taste beforehand. All they need know is that the world's most exquisite *crêpe suzette* is to be found yonder under the purple sign that says "Suzie's," and they will walk a little faster.

Basically, the term *incentive* relates to the value of a goal or reward. Thus a goal is said to have high incentive value when it is particularly powerful in motivating behavior, and to have low incentive value if it is not very motivating. As we saw in Chapter 3, Hull was among the first to use the concept of incentives (for which he used the symbol K) in his theory. He had recognized that drive alone could not account for motivation. Among other things, the amount of reward a rat receives affects its behavior, as does its history of past rewards.

The introduction of the concept of incentives into a discussion of need/drive theory makes it possible to account for the fact that monkeys will work harder to obtain a banana than a piece of lettuce, and that a person might pay more to eat a steak than a hamburger. It also brings what is essentially a behavioristic theory of motivation somewhat closer to the cognitive positions, because there is little doubt that anticipating goals and estimating their values involve what are essentially cognitive processes.

Arousal Theory: Magnitude of Motivation

There are basically three things that affect how much effort a person is willing to make (that is, how *motivated* a person is), according to Brehm and Self (1989): internal states such as needs; potential outcomes; and the individual's estimate of the probability that a certain behavior will lead to a desired outcome. This recognizes both the physiological and the cognitive aspects of behavior.

Measuring Motivation

Can intensity of motivation be measured? Brehm and Self (1989) say it can be, because intensity of motivation is reflected in changes in the **sympathetic nervous system**. More specifically, such changes are reflected in what is termed arousal. Hence **arousal theory** presents both a physiological and a cognitive explanation of behavior.

What Is Arousal?

The term **arousal** has both psychological and physiological meaning. As a psychological concept, it refers to the degree of alertness, wakefulness, or attentiveness of a person or animal. It varies in degree from sleep (at the lowest level), to panic or frenzy (at the highest).

As a physiological concept, arousal refers to the degree of activation of the organism, which is often measured in terms of changes in heart rate and blood pressure, changes in conductivity of the skin to electricity (called **electrodermal response**), and changes in electrical activity of the brain. Specifically, with increasing arousal the electrical activity of the cortex (as measured by an **electroencephalograph**, or **EEG**) takes the form of increasingly rapid and shallow waves (called **beta waves**). At lower levels of arousal (such as sleep), the waves are slow and deep (called **alpha waves**).

Increasing arousal defines increasing intensity of motivation (and of emotion), claim Brehm and Self (1989). But the relationship between arousal and intensity of motivation is not perfectly linear; that is, a person doesn't continue to become more and more highly motivated as arousal increases.

The Yerkes-Dodson Law

At very low levels of arousal, motivation tends to be low and behavior ineffective. This can easily be demonstrated by asking someone at the lowest normal level of arousal (namely, sleep) a simple question like "How many are five?" As arousal increases, behavior becomes more highly motivated, more interested; the person can now tell you with stunning clarity how many five are, and all sorts of other things as well.

But if arousal continues to increase—as might happen, for example, if what woke the person up were an earthquake—performance might deteriorate badly. High arousal, often evident in high anxiety or even fear, explains why students in tense oral examinations are sometimes unable to remember anything and sometimes can't even speak. Anxiety in test situations, Hembree (1988) concludes after reviewing 562 separate studies, clearly lowers test performance.

In summary, the relationship between performance and arousal, depicted in Figure 10.4, takes the form of an inverted U-shaped function. This observation, first described by Yerkes and Dodson (1908), is known as the **Yerkes-Dodson law**. What the law says is that there is an optimal level of arousal for the most effective behavior; arousal levels above and below this optimal level are associated with less effective behavior.

Hebb's Arousal Theory

As we saw in Chapter 6, Hebb's arousal theory of motivation is based directly on the Yerkes-Dodson law. This law, claims Hebb (1972), gives rise to two important assumptions. First, Hebb assumes there is an optimal level of arousal that differs for different tasks. Thus intense, concentrated activities, such as studying or competing on a television quiz program, demand higher levels of alertness (arousal) than more habitual behaviors, such as driving a car. For most daily activities, moderate levels of arousal are probably optimum. Second, the organism behaves in such a way as to maintain the level of arousal that is most appropriate for ongoing behavior. If arousal is too low, the organism will try to increase it; if it's too high, an attempt will be made to lower it.

The value of arousal as a motivational concept is based largely on the validity of this second assumption. If people try to maintain an optimal level of arousal, then it should be possible to predict at least some behaviors. For example, students in a classroom who are bored (too low an arousal level) would be expected to do things to increase their arousal—which is essentially what happens when students daydream, throw spitballs, read comic books, or talk out loud with other bored students.

As was noted in Chapter 6, Hebb demonstrated the need for maintaining a moderately high level of arousal through his pioneering investigation of sensory deprivation. In this study, students were paid to do nothing, but they could not stand to do so for very long.

Causes of Arousal

One of the important sources of high and low arousal is stimulation. But perhaps even more important for theories of motivation, it is the meaningfulness, the novelty, the surprisingness of stimulation that increases arousal or fails to increase it (Berlyne, 1965, 1966). Much of people's exploratory behavior—that is, behavior designed to learn things—stems from a need for stimulation, says Berlyne.

Arousal is also related to a variety of cognitive factors, Brehm and Self (1989) point out. For example, the more difficult and the more important a behavior is, the higher the arousal associated with it will be. Similarly, motivational arousal may be a function of the extent to which the actor assumes

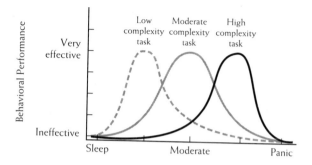

FIGURE 10.4   The relationship between behavioral performance and arousal level. The level of arousal that is optimal for effective behavior varies with the complexity of the task.

personal responsibility for the outcomes of behavior (versus the extent to which these are attributed to luck or other factors over which the person has no control). These are some of the things that cognitive theories of motivation look at.

COGNITIVE THEORIES OF MOTIVATION

Some early behavioristic theories, both in learning and in motivation, were characterized by what has been described as a mechanistic and passive view of the human organism (Bolles, 1975). Motives for behaving consisted largely of internal or external prods to which the individual reacted in a relatively helpless way. In contrast, cognitive positions present a more active view of human behavior. Individuals are seen as actively exploring and manipulating, as predicting and evaluating the consequences of their behavior, and as acting on the environment rather than simply reacting to it.

In fact, this distinction is not very accurate or useful because it does not apply to most behavioristic theories. Skinner, for example, also sees the organism as acting on the environment, as exploring and manipulating—in short, as *emitting* responses rather than simply as responding blindly. Accordingly, a better contrast between behavioristic and cognitive approaches to motivation is that cognitive theories explain the effectiveness of environmental circumstances (like rewards and punishments) in terms of the individual's understanding and interpretation. Behavioristic theorists see no need to resort to these cognitive events.

Cognitive Dissonance

That individuals act on the basis of their information and beliefs seems clear, claimed Festinger (1957, 1962), author of an intriguing cognitive theory of motivation known as the theory of **cognitive dissonance**. Simply stated, the theory holds that when a person simultaneously possesses two contradictory items of information (a situation that constitutes cognitive dissonance) that person will be motivated to act to reduce the contradiction.

In one study, Festinger (1962) subjected individual college students to an exhausting and boring 1-hour session ostensibly involving motor performance. After the session, each subject was told that the experiment was over, but each was then asked to help the experimenter with the next participant. The subjects were led to believe that it was important for the research that the incoming person believe that the experiment would be interesting and pleasant. Each student agreed to lie to the next participant; as a result, says Festinger, each would be expected to experience conflict (or dissonance) between their behavior and their beliefs.

Cognitive dissonance theory would predict that subjects would try to reduce the dissonance. One way of doing this would be to retract the lie, an impossibility under the circumstances. The other alternative would be for subjects to change their private opinions—that is, to alter their beliefs.

Festinger used two different treatments in the experiment. Although all subjects were paid to tell the lie, some were given $20, and others only $1. The effect of this differential treatment was remarkable. The obvious prediction (and the one favored by bubba psychology, as discussed in Chapter 1) is that those paid the larger amount would be more likely to change their beliefs than those paid the smaller amount. But the opposite was consistently true! Those who received small sums often became quite convinced that the hour session was really enjoyable; those who were paid the larger sum remained truer to their original beliefs.

Brehm and Cohen (1962) later corroborated these findings in a similar study where they paid participants $10, $5, $1 or 50 cents for lying. As in the Festinger study, those subjects paid the smallest sum changed their opinions the most, whereas those paid $10 did not change appreciably. The explanation for these unexpected results is simply that the magnitude of dissonance that is brought about by a behavior contrary to one's beliefs will be directly proportional to the justification that exists for the act. Students paid $20 to lie have a better reason for doing so and will therefore feel less dissonance.[3]

Reducing Dissonance

Dissonance is an important motivational concept because it provides an explanation for behaviors designed to reduce it. Festinger (1957), Brehm and Cohen (1962), and Berlyne (1960) suggest a number of different ways in which this can be done.

---

[3]These studies lead to the interesting observation that if criminals (thieves, for example) initially know that their behavior is immoral and if they are highly successful at their chosen vocation, they will be "better" people than if they are unsuccessful. If they make a lot of money by stealing, they are more likely to continue to believe that stealing is an immoral act. (Kro)

Attitude change.   One way of reducing dissonance, as the experiments described above illustrate, is to change beliefs. Consider the case of Sam Plotkin, who dislikes school teachers quite intensely but who, at a local dance, falls in love with Mary Rosie. When he discovers that Mary is a teacher, he is subjected to a great deal of dissonance, which will disappear when he decides either that he really doesn't like Mary or that teachers really aren't that bad.

Compartmentalization.   If this same Sam Plotkin decides that Mary is really not like other teachers—that she is a different type of person, despite the fact that she teaches—what he is doing is placing her in a different "compartment." Compartmentalization is evidently a fairly common dissonance reducer.

Exposure to or recall of information.   Sometimes when there is a conflict between two items of information, gaining more information can reduce the dissonance. If a rumor is circulated that wheat flour turns the human liver white, it will probably create some conflict in those who have been in the habit of eating food made with wheat flour. If a person were exposed to the information that white livers are really quite functional, the dissonance might disappear. Similarly, dissonance resulting from doing poorly on a test (a discrepancy between expectations and actual performance) would be greatly reduced if the student learned that all other students had done as poorly.

Behavioral change.   Situations characterized by dissonance sometimes lead to changes in behavior. Tobacco smokers whose behavior is at odds with the information they have about the effects of smoking can stop smoking, thereby eliminating all dissonance.

Quite frequently, however, smokers find it simpler to use other techniques for coping with this problem. For example, they might convince themselves that there is yet no conclusive proof that smoking is harmful (thus using a strategy of selective exposure to information, or perceptual distortion). Others insist that all that has been clearly demonstrated by numerous smoking-related studies on experimental animals is that *Rattus norvegicus* would do well to stay away from the weed.

Summary

In summary, cognitive dissonance is the motivating state that occurs when an individual is in conflict. Ordinary sources of dissonance are incompatibilities between beliefs, between behavior and private opinion, or between two items of information. Dissonance theory holds that these states lead to behavior intended to reduce the conflict and reflective of the amount of conflict that exists (Figure 10.5).

Collins and Hoyt (1972) argue that people will not feel dissonance unless they also feel personal responsibility for their behavior. In more current psychological jargon, cognitive dissonance is a direct function of the causes to which behavior is attributed. This fact has led to Westermann's (1989) observation

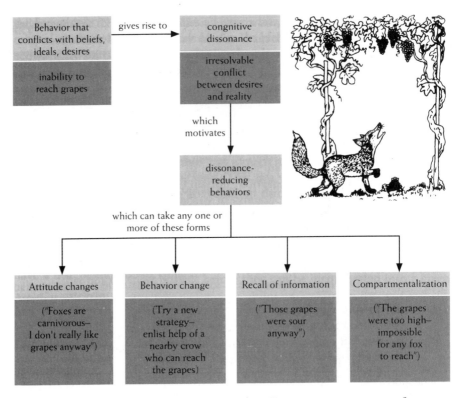

FIGURE 10.5   A model of cognitive dissonance. Everyone experiences conflicts between beliefs or desires and reality. There are many ways of trying to reduce cognitive dissonance.

that dissonance theory is now usually reinterpreted in terms of **attribution theory**.

Attribution Theory

To *attribute* in cognitive theory is to assign responsibility or to impute motives. If Rod attributes his stupidity to his parents, he is assigning them responsibility for that condition.

Rotter (1954) was among the first to suggest that people can be differentiated on the basis of their tendency to ascribe their successes and failures to internal or external causes. In his words, there are people whose **locus of control** is external; others are more internally oriented. Those who are externally oriented, says Weiner (1986), tend to attribute their successes and failures to task difficulty, bad luck, good luck, or other factors over which they have no control. In contrast, internally oriented individuals are more likely to explain the outcome of their behavior in terms of their own ability and effort (see Figure 10.6).

	Internal (under personal control)	External (not under personal control)
Stable (do not change)	ability	difficulty
Unstable (change)	effort	luck

FIGURE 10.6   Attribution theory: explanations of success or failure (after Weiner, 1974).

Attribution and Dissonance

The relationship between attribution theory and dissonance is implicit in the observation that dissonance reflects how responsible the person feels for the outcomes of behavior. By definition, those who attribute outcomes to external causes do not accept personal responsibility for successes and failures. As a result, they are not subject to cognitive dissonance in the same way as individuals who are more internally oriented. By the same token, those who are internally oriented are far more likely to feel pride when successful and shame when they fail. Thus both dissonance and internal orientation are likely to be associated with emotion, and the motivating power of emotion is considerable (Lazarus, 1993).

This cognitive view of motivation is based on the assumption that people continually evaluate their behaviors, look for reasons behind their successes and failures, anticipate the probable future outcomes of intended behaviors, and react emotionally to success and failure. And here is the key concept in attribution theory. It is not the attribution of behavior to one cause or the other that motivates behavior, says Weiner (1980); it is the emotions that occur as responses to specific attributions. The outcomes of attribution, he suggests, might be anger, guilt, gratefulness, or a variety of other emotions (see Figure 10.7). It seems logical that if the emotions are positive, subsequent behaviors will attempt to maintain the conditions that made the attribution possible.

Need Achievement and Attributions

How people explain their successes and failures appears to be closely related to what psychologists call **need for achievement**—the individual's need to reach some standard of excellence. It seems that those with a high need to achieve are far more likely to attribute the outcomes of their behavior to internal causes. Thus, if they are successful, they are likely to attribute their success to effort (and perhaps to ability as well); if they are not successful, they continue to invoke internal factors, often blaming a lack of effort.

	Causal Attributions			
	Internal		External	
	Effort	Ability	Others	Luck
Success	Relaxation	Confidence Competence	Gratitude	Surprise
Failure	Guilt (shame)	Incompetence	Anger	Surprise

FIGURE 10.7   Relations between causal attributions and feelings associated with success and failure.

In contrast, individuals characterized by a lower need for achievement may attribute their success to ability, effort, ease of task, or luck, but they are most likely to attribute failure to lack of ability (J. W. Thomas, 1980). These individuals have low estimates of their own abilities—low evaluations of what Bandura (1991) labels **self-efficacy**.

ALBERT BANDURA (1925–   )

Today is very cold, even for January—about −32°. It snowed earlier, but now the air is so clear that when I look up from the computer Lefrançois has given me and glance outside, the white of the snow dazzles my eyes, and I find myself squinting against the glare.

The window here in Lefrançois's office at the University of Alberta faces east, and if I raise my eyes and look out beyond the river valley, out beyond the farthest edges of the city, I can almost see as far as the small farming community, only about 50 miles from here, where Albert Bandura was born. Later Bandura moved to the southern coastal area of British Columbia—where it's never −32°—and did his undergraduate work at the University of British Columbia (UBC), graduating in 1949.

"What influenced you to become a psychologist?" Evans (1989) asked Bandura. "I have come to the view," he replied, "that some of the most important determinants of career and life paths often occur through the most trivial of circumstances" (p. 3). He went on to explain how, because he commuted to the university with a group of premed and engineering students who had to go in very early, he took a psychology course simply to fill a gap in his schedule. The subject fascinated him, and 3 years after graduating from UBC, Bandura obtained his Ph.D in clinical psychology from the Iowa State University. A year later he joined the faculty at Stanford University, eventually becoming a professor and department chair.

Bandura's early writings and theorizing stemmed from the predominant theories of the day: Skinnerian and Hullian forms of behaviorism. But even at the dawn of his career, he had already begun to break away from the radical behaviorists' rejection of the importance of thoughts and intentions. Bandura's approach was more socially oriented; it looked at how people influence each other and at how social behaviors are acquired through imitation. It was also more cognitive, assigning an increasingly important role to the human ability to anticipate the conse-quences of behavior. In the end, it is a social cognitive theory of human behavior, summarized in his aptly titled *Social Foundations of Thought and Action: A Social Cognitive Theory* (1986).

Albert Bandura has received numerous state and national awards and honors, and has also served a term as president of the American Psychological Association. At the time of this writing, he was David Jordan Starr Professor of Social Science in Psychology at Stanford.

Self-Efficacy

Self-efficacy deals with the individual's assessments of personal effectiveness (Bandura, 1986, 1993; Evans, 1989). Those with high self-efficacy, see them-selves as capable—that is, as effective—in dealing with the world and with other people.

Importance of Self-Efficacy Judgments

Self-efficacy judgments are very important in determing what people do—hence very important as motives. As Schunk (1984) puts it, under most circum-stances, people don't do things at which they expect to do very badly. "Efficacy beliefs," says Bandura (1993), "influence how people feel, think, motivate them-selves, and behave." (p. 118)

Judgments of personal efficacy influence not only what people will do but also how much effort and time they will devote to a task, especially when they are faced with difficulties. The more Ann believes in herself (that is, the higher her estimates of personal effectiveness), the more likely she will be to persist. In contrast, if she doesn't see herself as being very capable, she is more likely to become discouraged and to give up. It is for this reason, note Zimmerman, Bandura, and Martinez-Pons (1992), that self-efficacy judgments are so impor-tant in school: "Numerous studies have shown that students with a high sense of academic efficacy display greater persistence, effort, and intrinsic interest in their academic learning and performance" (p. 664).

Sources of Efficacy Judgments

Why do some people typically have high judgments of personal efficacy, and others much less favorable judgments? The answer, suggests Bandura (1986), lies in the combined effects of four main sources of influence.

First are the effects of the individual's behavior, especially as they are re-flected in success or failure. Other things being equal, people who are generally successful are more likely to develop more positive evaluations of their personal effectiveness than are people who typically fail. As Weiner (1980) points out, however, people who attribute their successes and failures to factors over which they have no control (like luck or task difficulty) are less likely to base judg-ments of personal efficacy on the outcomes of their behaviors. After all, it's not *their* fault that the test was too hard or that they studied the wrong sections.

A second influence is *vicarious* (that is, secondhand); it is based on comparisons between the individual's performance and that of others. The most useful comparisons, Bandura (1981) notes, are those that involve potential equals. Thus children who do better than their age-mates are likely to develop positive judgments of self-efficacy. That these same children might be blown away by somebody older or more experienced would be less relevant for judgments of self-efficacy.

Persuasion is a third type of influence on self-judgments. Those with lower self-confidence can sometimes be persuaded to do things they would not otherwise do. One of the possible effects of persuasion, Bandura (1986) argues, is that people will interpret it as evidence that others think them competent.

High arousal can also affect self-judgments, says Bandura, leading to either high or low estimates of capability depending on the situation and the person's previous experiences in situations of high arousal. For example, some athletes who are anxious before a competition view this emotion as helpful to their performance; for others, arousal may be interpreted as negative. These personal experiences in anxiety-producing situations may subsequently influence the extent and direction of the effects of arousal on self judgments. Thus an extreme fear of drowning might lead a person to decide he is incapable of some act like swimming across a river. In contast, extreme fear might lead another person to decide that she is capable of swimming across the same river to save her son, who is marooned on the other side.

To summarize, Bandura describes four sources of influence on judgments of self-efficacy: *enactive* (reflecting the results of the individual's own actions), *vicarious* (based on comparisons between self and others), *persuasory* (the result of persuasion), and *emotive* (reflecting arousal or emotion). Examples of each of these types of influence are shown in Table 10.1.

Applications of Motivation Theory

Knowledge about why people behave the way they do can greatly facilitate the psychologist's task of predicting what a person will do in a given situation and of controlling behavior (when it isn't unethical to do so).

Predicting Behavior

Normal social interaction depends largely on being able to predict many of the ordinary activities of others. If these activities were not at least partly predictable, the planet would be even more chaotic and confusing than it now is. When Jack meets his grandmother and says "Hello," he expects that she will return either the same greeting (or some other greeting) or that, at worst, she will ignore him. He would be understandably surprised if, instead of responding as expected, his grandmother chose to kick him in the shins, run away, faint, or curse in some foreign language.

TABLE 10.1   Four Sources of Information Related to Judgments of Self-Efficacy

Sources of information	Examples of information that might lead Joan to arrive at positive estimates of her personal efficacy
Enactive	She receives an A in mathematics
Vicarious	She learns that Ronald studied hard but only got a B
Persuasory	Her teacher tells her she can probably win a scholarship if she tries
Emotive	She becomes mildly anxious before a test, but feels exhilarated afterward

Controlling and Changing Behavior

Another application of knowledge about motivation involves the control of behavior, a subject that has led to considerable debate among psychologists. Should behavior be controlled? How should it be controlled? Who should control it, and to what end? In short, what are the ethics of behavior control (see Rogers & Skinner, 1956)?

Despite the somewhat appealing humanistic arguments against behavior control, deliberate behavior control is not only a reality but in many cases highly desirable—as a parent whose young child has recently been toilet-trained would quickly admit. Toilet training is just one of many behaviors that involve systematic and deliberate attempts to modify behavior.

Motivation plays a key role in changing and controlling behavior. For example, toilet-training a child might involve manipulating goals (for example, getting little Sammy to view cleanliness as a desirable condition). In addition, rewards and punishments, which also relate to motivation (and to learning), can be employed. Cognitive dissonance also may be implicated in toilet training; children who think being clean is desirable may feel considerable dissonance when they have what is euphemistically referred to as "an accident."[4]

Motivation in the Classroom

Motivation theory is highly relevant for teachers, whose function is largely one of modifying the behavior of students (the astute reader will recall that this is precisely the definition given earlier for learning). Teaching can be facilitated considerably by a knowledge of the individual needs and goals of students, of the effects of cognitive dissonance, and of the role of arousal in learning and behavior. Cognitive dissonance, for example, may occur when students are aware of a discrepancy between their behavior and what is described (perhaps by the teacher) as being ideal. Such dissonance may well lead to attempts to become more like the teacher's description of the ideal.

---

[4] I find it strange that Kro chose toilet training as an illustration; he knew absolutely nothing about the procedure. "Korons," he boasted, "don't have *accidents*." The irony was that he had just fallen off the beaver dam—again—when he said it. (GRL)

The role of arousal in behavior can be even more crucial for teaching. Recall that it is the combined novelty, intensity, and meaningfulness of stimuli that most affect level of arousal. Teachers are one of the most important sources of arousal-inducing stimulation for students. The impact of what they say and do and how they say and do it is instrumental in determining whether students are either bored or sleeping (low arousal) or attentive (higher arousal). This observation leads directly to an important argument for meaningfulness, variety, and intensity in classroom presentations.

It is worth repeating, too, that judgments of self-efficacy are powerful motivators, that they have profound influences on a person's thoughts and emotions. Those who have low judgments of self-efficacy are also likely to *feel* poorly about themselves, to attempt fewer difficult tasks, and ultimately to be less successful.

Teachers have an important role in providing children with the sorts of experiences that contribute to positive judgments of self-efficacy. Their success, and that of their students, may depend on how well they carry out this role.

SUMMARY

1. A motive is a conscious or unconscious force that incites a person to act.
2. Reflexes are simple stimulus-specific responses that explain some elementary human behavior. Instincts are more complex, unlearned patterns of behavior that are more relevant for animal than for human behavior. The orienting reflex (OR) is the general reflexive response an organism makes to novel stimuli; it involves some physiological changes that are related to arousal.
3. Psychological hedonism is the pain/pleasure principle. Physiological needs are states of deficiency or lack that give rise to drives, which in turn impel the organism toward activities that will reduce the needs. Psychological needs are sometimes described as learned needs.
4. Maslow's hierarchy of needs includes both basic or deficiency needs (physiological, safety, belongingness, and self-esteem) and meta- or growth needs (cognitive, aesthetic, and self-actualization).
5. An incentive is basically the value that an activity or goal has for an individual. It is a more cognitive concept than is need or drive.
6. Arousal refers to the degree of alertness of an organism. Its relation to motivation is implicit in the assumption that too-low or too-high arousal is related to less optimal behavior than a more moderate level of activation (the Yerkes-Dodson law).
7. According to Hebb, people behave so as to maintain arousal at the optimal level. Novelty, meaningfulness, complexity, and surprisingness of stimuli lead to increases in arousal, as does personal involvement in the outcomes of behavior.

8. Cognitive theories present a more active view of the human organism than do traditional behavioristic theories. One such theory, cognitive dissonance, assumes that conflict among beliefs, behavior, and expectations leads to behavior designed to reduce the conflict (for example, attitude change, compartmentalization, acquisition or recall of information, or behavioral change).

9. Attribution theory attempts to explain how individuals assign responsibility for the outcomes of their behaviors. Internally oriented individuals frequently ascribe success or failure to ability or effort; externally oriented individuals are more likely to blame success or failure on luck or on the fact that the task was very easy or very difficult. Internally oriented individuals are often characterized by higher need for achievement.

10. Self-efficacy judgments have to do with personal estimates of competence and effectiveness. High evaluations of efficacy are associated with persistence, achievement, and positive self-concepts. They are influenced by the outcomes of behavior, comparisons with others, persuasion, and arousal.

11. Knowledge about human motivation is important for predicting behavior, for controlling it, and for changing it. In a practical sense, it is especially important for teachers.

A theorist is an artist, someone with a talent for weeding the essential from the inessential and constructing these marvelous orders.

—G. Johnson (1992), p. 115

PRELIMINARY NOTE FOR HUMAN READERS: CHAPTER 11 OBJECTIVES

We near the end. And if I, Kro 59, were there with you, I would say to you (if you cared to listen), "Much of science is a shared hallucination, a network of self-reinforcing beliefs" (G. Johnson, 1992, p. 53).

And I think you might shake your head and say, "Does this mean I've wasted my time studying these theories of learning and behavior, these shared hallucinations?"

"No," I would answer, "because there's nothing more useful than a theory, even if it is an invention, a fantasy." You see, a theory doesn't *have* to be true, although it does have to be other important things: useful, logical, consistent, clear, and so on.

So keep studying. Go on and read this last chapter. Reflect on it well. And when you're finished, discuss it with your grandmother, because in it I have hidden truths and insights that might impress even someone as wise as she. When she and you have talked it over, you will finally understand the following:

- Why we absolutely need theories
- How theories actually work
- The very essence of each of the major theories that compose this text
- Why theories of learning and behavior are really models of human learners
- How this entire text might be synthesized

There is also a small chance that you will have learned to simplify—without lying.

SIXTH TIME CUBE, 49TH HEXALOG, POINT 251.50

Lying is not something Korons normally do. So it always astounds me when it happens—and, to tell the truth, it beetles me just a little.

Take, for example, this morning. I'm trying to shave, which is something I do about once a month right after a full moon, and I can't find the shaving cream that Doctor L. said he and I could share. "Where's the shaving stuff?" I ask, which I shouldn't have asked so loud because now the kids come running to watch (for some twisted reason they seem to enjoy it).

"I never used it," replies Lefrançois, which I know is a hairless-faced lie, because he uses it every dang morning.[1]

---

[1] It wasn't really a lie at all. You know how you sometimes answer a question absently, meaning something else entirely, but just using the words that happen to be there? What I meant, I'm sure, was to say "I didn't hide the darn thing." Which, of course, I hadn't. (GRL)

> *So the kids and I rummage through all the drawers and cabinets and look under the sink (where the cat is chewing something that might have had feathers), and we finally find the tube called "shaving cream" under a towel—which, of course, is where Lefrançois had to have put it himself, because there's no one else in that house that has growing stuff that needs shaving.*
>
> *And then Mrs. L. comes in too, and I'm thinking I'm going to have one heck of an audience for my monthly shave, but no, she's not there to watch.*
>
> *"Look at this mess," says she, almost standing next to herself in irritation while the cat slinks between her legs and scoots down the hall like he knows what's coming. "Absolute chaos," she continues. "It's always chaos."*
>
> *But now I'm paying attention to my shaving, which is not a simple thing.*

ORDER FROM CHAOS

This planet, like so much of the rest of the cosmos, is also chaos; like their bathrooms, though, humans want it to be orderly. "There is an ancient human longing," says G. Johnson (1992), "to impose rational order on a chaotic world. The detective does it, the magician does it. That's why people love Sherlock Holmes. Science came out of magic. Science is the modern expression of what the ancient magician did. The world is a mess, and people want it to be orderly" (p. 114).

But science doesn't work quite the way it's pictured, Johnson informs us. It isn't simply a question of having a theory, generating hypotheses from it, testing them, and throwing out the theory if they don't pan out. Many theorists love their theories so much they're seldom willing to abandon them. Sometimes they stick with them long after everybody else has left.

A theory, Johnson explains, is a form of architecture, maybe a little like a cathedral. When the theory ages and threatens to become useless, theorists don't just build a brand new one. What the smart theorists do, instead, is shore up their old ideas: put in new joists, new rafters, brace the old walls, redo the decaying foundation, patch the roof, paint a little here and there, polish the old gold, and so forth. Those less smart try to make do with what they have (and the rats move in). Later in this chapter, we look briefly at examples of three theorists who have tried to synthesize what they thought was the best they could find in other theories—who have remodeled their cathedrals, adding contemporary altars where the new disciples might worship.

TO LIE OR TO OVERSIMPLIFY?

But first I undertake what might easily have been an overwhelming task had it not been for Lefrançois's grandmother: that of summarizing and evaluating the learning-related theories that make up the earlier chapters of the book. What about his grandmother? Although I am somewhat ashamed to admit it, I must confess that from her I learned how to oversimplify, one of two great tech-

niques for taking care of things that are overwhelming. The second technique, lying, I picked up from Lefrançois.[2]

I use one of these techniques repeatedly in this ambitious chapter—a chapter that presents a summary of the major learning theories discussed earlier, follows that summary with a rapid evaluation, and ends with three syntheses.

MAJOR DIVISIONS IN LEARNING THEORY

Learning, I said at the very beginning, involves changes in behavior that result from experience. Hence the terms *learning theory* and *behavior theory* are often used synonymously.

Among the various ways of looking at human behavior or learning, two very broad orientations can be identified; these give rise to the classical divisions among psychological theory. One orientation assumes that human behavior is, at least in some measure, influenced by activities like thinking, feeling, intending, wanting, expecting, reasoning, remembering, and evaluating. These are processes that define what is thought of as "mind." They are cognitive processes; hence the orientation is that of the cognitive psychologists.

The other orientation doesn't flatly contradict the first but insists that little scientifically valid knowledge about human behavior can be obtained by investigating the nebulous processes of the mind. Instead, advocates of this orientation concentrate on examining actual behavior and the observable conditions that lead to behavior. Hence this is the orientation of behavioristic psychologists.

---

[2]Kro is not serious here, I assure you; it's his peculiar sense of humor. In fact, I suspect he already knew how to lie before he arrived. If he didn't, he didn't learn it from me. Honest. (GRL)

THEORY SUMMARIES

It's important to note that few positions are clearly only behavioristic or cognitive. These terms are simply convenient labels; as such, they indicate the general orientation of a theorist and the sorts of topics with which the theory is most likely to be concerned. Thus behaviorism deals largely with investigations of relationships among stimuli, responses, and the consequences of behavior. In contrast, cognitive psychologists are less interested in stimuli and responses than in more central processes: problem solving, decision making, perception, information processing, concept formation, and memory, among others. Table 11.1 (adapted from Table 1.4) distinguishes among the major divisions in learning theory. Each of these positions is summarized in the following sections.

Predominantly Behavioristic Positions

Among the major predominantly behavioristic positions are those of Watson, Guthrie, Thorndike, Skinner, and Hull.

Watson

J. B. Watson was among the first North American psychologist to define the science of psychology in completely objective terms. He saw psychology as a science that deals with the observable rather than the merely hypothetical—a definition that gave rise to North American behaviorism. Watson's behaviorism was based on the laws of classical conditioning that had been investigated by the Russian physiologist Pavlov. Watson assumed that individuals are born with a behavioral repertoire consisting of only a few reflexes and that these early responses become conditioned to other stimuli by being repeatedly paired with them.

Watson was also an important spokesman for environmentalism: the belief that personality, intelligence, and all other human qualities are determined by the environment (the nurture side in the historical nature/nurture dispute). One of his better-known claims was that he could make whatever he wanted out of a dozen healthy infants if he were given a free hand in their upbringing.

Guthrie

Like Watson, Edwin Guthrie was determinedly behavioristic. His theory can be summarized in several major laws, the most important of which states that whenever a response follows a stimulus, there will result a tendency for the same response to occur again the next time the stimulus is presented. Thus Guthrie maintained that learning is complete on the occasion of the first pairing of a stimulus with a response and that further practice will not strengthen the response, although it will help ensure that the person (or animal) learns it in many different situations.

TABLE 11.1   Major Divisions in Learning Theory

	Symbolic representation	Variables of concern	Representative theorists
Behaviorism	S–R*	Stimuli Responses Reinforcement CS US	Pavlov Watson Thorndike Guthrie Skinner Hull
A transition	S–0–R	Stimuli Responses Reinforcement Mediation Purpose Goals Expectation Representation	Hebb Tolman Gestaltists Rescorla-Wagner
Cognitive theories	0	Perceiving Organizing Information processing Decision making Problem solving Attention Memory	Bruner Piaget Computer models Information processing Models of memory and motivation

*Not all behaviorists are associated with these symbols.

Although learning occurs and is complete and relatively permanent after a single trial, said Guthrie, it is possible to remove undesirable habits simply by learning new habits that are incompatible with the old ones. Guthrie suggested three ways in which this can be done: the fatigue technique, the threshold approach, and the method of incompatible stimuli.

Note that for both Watson and Guthrie, the consequences of the behavior are not important in bringing about learning. According to Guthrie, the effect of punishment or reward is simply to change the stimulus situation, thereby preventing the unlearning of a response.

Thorndike

E. L. Thorndike is generally credited with introducing the notion of reinforcement in contemporary learning theory through his Law of Effect, which states that learning is a consequence of the effect of behavior—specifically, responses that lead to a satisfying state of affairs will tend to be repeated. At first Thorndike had also believed that unpleasant or annoying states would have an opposite effect, but he rejected this belief after 1930. Similarly, before 1930 he had believed that stimulus–response events that are practiced tend to be more strongly linked, whereas those that fall into disuse tend to be forgotten (the

Law of Exercise); this was also a belief Thorndike later rejected. Thus Thorndike is an example of a theorist whose ideas changed in important ways as a function of new findings and new insights.

For Thorndike, learning consists of the formation of bonds between stimuli and responses largely as a function of the consequences of the responses. He labeled the process of learning a stamping-in process; forgetting involves stamping out. The system includes a number of subsidiary laws, the most important of which is the law of multiple responses. This law holds that when they are faced with a problem situation, people tend to respond in a variety of ways until one of the responses emitted is reinforced; in other words, learning occurs through a process of trial and error. Additional laws note that behavior is generalizable, that people respond to the most striking features of the environment, that cultural background affects behavior, and that learning through contiguity does occur.

Hull

Clark L. Hull's theoretical approach is labeled hypothetico-deductive. He undertook one of the most monumental tasks ever undertaken by a psychologist—that of formalizing all knowledge about human behavior in order to make it possible to predict responses on the basis of knowledge about stimuli. The system was never quite completed, but nevertheless Hull's work stands as an overwhelmingly ambitious attempt at formal theory building.

Hull's investigations and consequent formulas and equations deal with three aspects of human behavior: input variables (which include physical stimuli as well as such factors as drive conditions, previously learned habits, and amount of reward available), intervening variables (which consist mainly of the assumed effects of input variables on the organism), and output variables (which are the characteristics of actual behavior in terms of response latency, frequency of responding, and time to extinction). The system may be partly summarized in terms of the equation $_sE_R = {_sH_R} \times D \times V \times K$.

Hull described his system in 17 postulates, 133 theorems, and hundreds of corollaries from which the nature of his beliefs about learning emerges. One of the central concepts in the theory is habit, which is an S–R connection. A collection of such connections forms a habit-family hierarchy, which is a hypothetical preferential ordering of related alternative behaviors. The relatedness of habits results from the fact that they have common goals, represented by Hull's concept of fractional antedating goal responses. An antedating goal reaction is any one of the many reward-related responses that an organism makes as it nears a goal; for example, as it turns the last corner in a maze, a rat may lick its chops. Fractional antedating goal responses are important in that they represent Hull's behavioristic definition of expectancy or purpose, and they foreshadow important cognitive concerns.

Hull's use of the concept of intervening variables might seem to be a link between his system and more cognitive interests. Note, however, that these variables are tied directly to input and output variables. Hull didn't intend them to be simply inferences or metaphors.

Skinner

B. F. Skinner stands out as one of the great system builders in 20th-century psychology. The learning model that has resulted from his work is operant conditioning, a model based on the notion that learning results from the reinforcement of responses emitted by an organism. Much of Skinner's work has dealt with the effects of different ways of presenting reinforcement (in other words, schedules of reinforcement) on rate of learning, response rate, and extinction rate (extinction refers to the cessation of a response after reinforcement has been discontinued). Among his most important findings is that learning is facilitated in its initial stages by continuous reinforcement, but extinction time is increased by intermittent reinforcement. Although most of Skinner's experimentation was with animals, these results are assumed to be generally applicable to human behavior as well.

One of the techniques developed by Skinner for teaching complex behaviors to animals is shaping, which involves reinforcing successive approximations to the desired behavior. It is widely employed by professional animal trainers.

The applications of Skinner's work to human behavior are discussed by him in several books: *Walden Two* (1948), *Science and Human Behavior* (1953), and *Beyond Freedom and Dignity* (1971). In addition, many of the principles of Skinner's theory have been extensively applied in education, medicine, advertising, psychotherapy, and other human activities. One well-known educational application takes the form of programmed instruction, the deliberate arrangement of material so as to take advantage of the effects of reinforcement. Behavior modification, which includes various systematic programs for changing and controlling behavior and is based primarily on Skinnerian principles, is widely used in education and psychotherapy.

A Transition

Watson's insistence that behaviorism must be limited to events that can be observed proved a difficult constraint even for people like Thorndike and Hull. Thus did Hull find himself inventing fractional antedating goal responses to explain connections that no longer seemed as simple as they once might have. Thus, too, did Thorndike (1931)—who initially had vigorously attacked the Gestaltists for resorting to insight as an explanation for learning—find himself speaking of "ideational learning" to explain insight learning.

Hebb

D. O. Hebb's attempt to explain higher mental processes is a much clearer departure from some of the constraints of behaviorism. His is a somewhat speculative, neurophysiological proposal designed to explain thinking in terms of activity in neurons, groups of neurons arranged in closed loops (cell assemblies), or of activity in more complex arrangements of such loops (phase sequences). Absolutely central to Hebb's theory is the notion that transmission among neurons appears to be facilitated as a function of repeated firing among them; this phenomenon of neural activity ostensibly accounts for learning. A cell assembly corresponds to some simple sensory input (for example, the color of an object or one part of one of its dimensions), whereas activity in a phase sequence corresponds to the whole object. Through learning, cell assemblies and phase sequences eventually achieve some correspondence to the environment: Because different parts of an object are usually sensed in contiguity, cell assemblies related to different aspects of an object will often be simultaneously active and will therefore become related.

Hebb has been largely responsible for the development of an arousal-based theory of motivation. This theory is premised on the assumption that optimal human functioning is made possible by a moderate level of arousal, and that an organism therefore behaves in such a way as to maintain that level. Other theorists (for example, Bruner) have subsequently incorporated these same notions in their systems.

Tolman

Edward Tolman was among the first North American psychologists to begin with a behavioristic orientation and eventually develop a system far more cognitive than behavioristic—in Tolman's case, a theory of *purposive* behaviorism.

Tolman's system reflects three basic beliefs. First, all behavior is purposive. By this, Tolman meant that behavior is directed—that it is guided toward goals, not by stimuli (as in Hull's system) but rather by cognitions. These cognitions take the form of expectancies that the organism develops with respect to reward.

Second, Tolman's emphasized the molar rather than molecular aspects of behavior. In other words, he was not concerned with discrete S–R events so much as with the more global aspects of behaving.

Third, Tolman insisted that what is learned as a function of reinforcement is not a response–stimulus link or a response–reinforcement link but a cognition—an awareness that reward is likely to follow certain behaviors. It is this awareness or expectancy that guides behavior, thus making it reasonable for Tolman to describe his system as one of purposive behaviorism.

The Gestaltists

One sense in which Gestalt psychology repesents an important transition in the history of learning theories is that whereas behavioristic psychologists had conducted most of their research on animals, the Gestaltists used people for their research about half the time.

The Gestalt approach is one of synthesis; it asserts that even physical objects cannot be completely known or understood through an analysis of their parts. That "the whole is greater than the sum of its parts" became the familiar Gestalt watchword.

The chief concern of Gestalt psychology was to discover the laws governing perception, and the Gestaltists were responsible for the elaboration of such "laws" as closure, proximity, symmetry, continuity, and *prägnanz*. It is largely because of this preoccupation that Gestalt psychology is considered to be one of the forerunners of cognitivism.

Among the better-known Gestalt psychologists were such men as Köhler, Koffka, and Wertheimer. These positions are unified not only in their preoccupation with perception but also through their rejection of trial-and-error explanations of human learning; their alternative explanation is that people learn through insight.

Cognitivism

This text's chronology (from behaviorism through a transition and finally to cognitivism) might make it seem as though more recent formulations are more enlightened, more accurate, and more useful, and that they must therefore have completely replaced older theories by now. This is not entirely so. Aspects of most earlier positions have survived and continue to arise in current theories and applications, though not always in completely recognizable guises. And behaviorism is still a vigorous and growing orientation in psychology, well represented in current professional literature as well as in countless educational and therapeutic programs. But cognitive metaphors are now clearly in the majority.

Bruner

Jerome Bruner has developed a loose-knit cognitive theory intended to explain various phenomena in perception, decision making, information processing, conceptualization, and development. His earlier writings deal primarily with learning; his more recent interests are largely in the area of development.

Bruner's theory is sometimes referred to as a theory of categorizing. To categorize is to treat objects as though they were in some ways equivalent; accordingly, a category can be thought of as a rule for classifying objects in terms of their properties (attributes). Much of Bruner's early work was devoted to an investigation of the strategies employed by people in learning how to categorize stimulus events both for simple perception and for the attainment of concepts.

Bruner's approach to learning and problem solving is premised on the assumption that the value of what is learned is measurable largely in terms of how well it permits the learner to go beyond the information given. He argues that concepts and percepts are useful when organized into systems of related categories (coding systems) that have wide generality. One of Bruner's major contributions has to do with his role in the so-called cognitive revolution—his championing of approaches that rejected the constraints of behaviorism.

Piaget

Jean Piaget's theory is a system unto itself, not easily compared with other positions. Although Piaget's major focus is development, much of what he says is relevant to learning and behavior because of the close relationship between learning and development.

Piaget describes development as the evolution of a child's ability to interact with the world in an increasingly appropriate, realistic, and logical fashion. Hence part of his work is a description of children at different stages of development: the sensorimotor stage (birth to 2 years), the preoperational stage (2 to

7 years, comprising preconceptual and intuitive thinking), the period of concrete operations (7 to 11 or 12 years), and the stage of formal operations (11 or 12 to 14 or 15 years). Each stage is marked by characteristic abilities and errors in problem solving, results from activities and abilities of the preceding period, and is a preparation for the next stage.

Another aspect of Piaget's work discusses the properties of human children that enable them to make progress in their development. Thus he describes intelligence as a biologically oriented process involving a combination of using previously learned capabilities (assimilation) and modifying behavior as required (accommodation). An optimal balance between these processes (equilibrium) constitutes maximally adaptive behavior.

Children construct a view of reality, says Piaget, rather than simply discovering it or learning it passively. Thus do they build notions of time, space, causality, logic, geometry, and so on.

Neural Networks

The computer, with its systems and functions, has become increasingly common as a metaphor for human cognitive activity. This metaphor compares human neurology and especially the brain (wetware) to computer hardware (physical components), and computer software (programs) to human cognitive functioning. The two most common forms of computer metaphor are the symbolic (based on the functioning of the digital computer) and the connectionist (based on the functioning of the parallel distributed processing computer). Symbolic models assume that all knowledge can be represented in symbols and manipulated using rules; connectionist models recognize that some learning is implicit (rather than explicit) and cannot easily be verbalized.

Connectionist models consist of interconnected units rather than central processors, and they are therefore also called neural networks. In neural networks, patterns and strengths of connections represent knowledge. Connectionist models lead to machines whose functioning is in some ways similar to that of humans in that it isn't completely logical or predictable. But these models are descriptions rather than explanations, don't always generate plausible results, and don't always function as a human would.

Still, there are some who argue that humans are on the verge of making machines that can actually think—taking into account all the variables, the contingencies, the qualifications that a human might consider. These machines don't think in a completely predictable, linear, old-fashioned-logic kind of way, but in a neural network mode where the programmer doesn't really know beforehand what the computer will decide because the problem is too complex to program symbolically.[3]

---

[3]When I asked Kro a simple question about computers on Koros, this is what he said, in that high-pitched but absolutely confident voice of his: "I should tell you, because I know from Koronian experience, that these thinking machines aren't really threats; they won't replace you. Why? Because they feel nothing. They don't *care*. They don't have emotion. But they might sometimes act as though they do. And scare the living be-gory out of you! But mostly, they'll be your friends, your helpers." (GRL)

Factors Affecting Learning

Among the important factors that are inextricably implicated in human learning are memory and motivation. In fact, studying memory is just another way of studying learning. And motivation, by definition, deals with the causes and the reasons for behavior and for behavior change (which, you will recall, defines learning). Theories in each of these areas include both behavioristic and cognitive orientations, although recent investigations of memory and motivation tend to be based primarily on cognitive models.

Memory

One common memory model is a metaphor that says people process and remember information as though they had two separate memory storage areas or processes—one associated with short-term memory (STM, lasting seconds rather than minutes) and another associated with long-term memory (LTM). STM is an active, ongoing process that is easily disrupted and highly limited in capacity; LTM is more passive, relatively stable, and virtually unlimited in capacity.

Current models of long-term memory tend to be associationistic (that is, they assume that all knowledge is related), and they often distinguish between explicit, potentially conscious memory (termed declarative) and the implicit, unconscious, nonverbalizable effects of learning (termed nondeclarative or procedural). Explicit or declarative memory includes semantic memory (stable, abstract knowledge) and episodic memory (personal, autobiographical memory). Studies of amnesiacs indicate that different parts of the brain might be involved in each of these types of memory.

Motivation

Motivation theory addresses the *why* of behavior—a question with many answers. Some behaviors are reflexive: simple, unlearned responses to specific situations. Others might result from instincts, which are more complex inherited tendencies common to all members of a species. Still others might result from urges (termed *drives*) associated with basic biological needs like those for food or drink, or perhaps with psychological needs like those for achievement, affection, or self-esteem.

Cognitive theories of motivation present a more active view of human behavior, one quite distinct from that of a reactive organism pushed and prodded by hungers and drives over which it has little, if any, control. Cognitive dissonance theory describes how conflicts among beliefs, behaviors, and expectations give rise to behaviors designed to reduce or eliminate the conflicts. Attribution theory explores systematic tendencies for people to attribute the outcomes of their behaviors to causes they either can or cannot control. And Bandura's account of the role of self-efficacy judgments shows how personal estimates of competence and effectiveness are associated with persistence, achievement, and positive self-concepts. What these newer cognitive approaches to motivation have in common is that they describe behavior as involving a conscious attempt to make sense out of self and environment.

SYNTHESIS AND EVALUATION

The preceding summaries are a brief analysis of most of the learning positions described in this text. The two tables in this section are a synthesis of that information. Table 11.2 simply lists key terms associated with each theoretical position. Table 11.3 is more visual; it consists of diagrammatic or symbolic representations of aspects of each theory. Note that neither table pretends to be a complete representation of the theories in question.

Strengths and Weaknesses

Each of the major learning theories described in this text was evaluated after its presentation. This section is intended not to repeat all these evaluations, but simply to bring together in one place some of the most important features of earlier evaluations. Lefrançois's grandmother, the one who taught me to over-simplify (which is sometimes no better than lying), also insisted that "if they're gonna improve, ya gotta tell 'em what's wrong with 'em."

Here's some of what's wrong with 'em. And what's right with 'em, too, although in neither case are the following comments meant to be an exhaustive catalogue of all the good and bad features of each theory. Besides, criticism and evaluation is quite subjective in the first place; it's often a matter of taste—or upbringing, or religion. So these evaluations are presented only as suggestions.

Behaviorism

The principal criticism of behaviorism is that through its mechanization of humanity it has dehumanized the human animal. Critics point out that humans possess awareness, that feeling is very much a part of behaving, and that surely human interaction with the environment is more than simply a matter of stimuli and responses. They contend, further, that conditioning in all of its varieties leaves much human behavior unexplained. Some also react negatively to the use of animals in studies whose results are then generalized to human behavior. Others are appalled and frightened at the thought of applying a science of human behavior to shape and control thought and action.

Behaviorists, in their own defense, maintain that it is only by dealing with those aspects of human functioning that are clearly measurable and definable that valid and reliable conclusions can be reached. They point in scorn at the chaotic and confused nature of more "mentalistic" psychologies. They ask what images, feelings, and sensations are, and of what value these might be in developing a *science* of behavior.

Clearly, behaviorism stresses objectivity and loses some relevance in doing so. Nevertheless, the approach has generated a great deal of applicable research and theory and continues to have a tremendous influence on the development of learning theory. Much of the current emphasis on experimentation and scientific rigor stems from the work of people such as Guthrie, Watson, and especially Hull. Emphasis on the practical applicability of theory owes much to the work of Thorndike. And Skinner's contribution to a practical science of behavior can hardly be overestimated.

Transition Theories

The proposal for a theory advanced by Donald Hebb is admittedly based on neurophysiological speculation as well as fact. It has been argued that such an approach is not likely to lead to any new discoveries about learning, or to anything more than an explanation for what is already known or suspected about behavior. Of course, the opposite argument can also be advanced. It can be countered that not all of Hebb's proposal is based on speculation, that there are sources of information about human neurology that are quite distinct from psychological experimentation, and that it is quite conceivable that knowledge about human neural activity may eventually lead to a better understanding of learning and behavior. This, in fact, is the premise upon which many of the neural network models of the new connectionism are based, and many of the connectionist theorists acknowledge an important debt to Hebb. In addition, some of Hebb's notions concerning arousal are an important part of current theories of motivation.

Hebb, a neobehaviorist, retained a commitment to the need to preserve the objective, scientific nature of psychological investigation. But he also responded to the need to include inferences about profoundly important mental processes like thinking and imagining, thus serving as an important transition from behaviorism to cognitivism.

Edward Chase Tolman, another neobehaviorist, also gave behaviorism a new twist by acknowledging the role of purpose.

Many of the first generation of cognitivists were followers of Tolman. Others followed Gestalt psychologists such as Köhler, Wertheimer, and Koffka, who devoted considerable energy to attacking and criticizing behaviorism. People learn through insight, the Gestaltists insisted, not through trial and error. This, their rejection of behaviorism, and their concern with cognitive topics like insight, perception, and problem solving paved the way for more cognitive approaches.

Cognitivism

The critics of cognitive approaches to human learning base many of their objections on the cognitivists' sometimes less precise and more subjective approach to information gathering and to theorizing. The extensive use of jargon by many contemporary cognitivists and the seeming lack of agreement among different positions has also been the source of some confusion and criticism.

Both Bruner and Piaget have been criticized on the grounds that their terminology is sometimes confusing and that the metaphors they use are often obscure and impractical. Piaget has also been much criticized for his imprecise experimental methods, his nonrepresentative samples, the extremely small numbers of subjects employed in most of his studies, the lack of statistical analysis in his early work, and for overgeneralizing and overtheorizing from his data. Cognitive theorists sometimes counter these criticisms by pointing out that

TABLE 11.2　Key Words

Watson	Guthrie	*Behaviorists* Thorndike	Hull	Skinner	Information-Processing Models
Behaviorism	Contiguity	Effect	Habit strength	Operant	Neural networks
Classical conditioning	One-shot learning	Satisfiers	Hypothetico-deductive	Respondent	Connectionism
Reflexes	Habits	Annoyers	Reaction potential	Schedules	Parallel distributed processing
Environmentalism	Threshold	Stamping in	Drive	Extinction	Symbolic models
Contiguity	Fatigue	Stamping out	Goal reactions	Rats	Artificial intelligence
	Incompatible stimuli	Trial and error	Habit families	Shaping	Wetware
		Connectionism	Intervening variables	Superstition	Hardware
				Programmed instruction	Software
				Behavior modification	

Hebb	*Transition* Tolman	Gestaltists	*Cognitivists* Bruner	Piaget
Cell assembly	Purposive	Perception	Categorizing	Equilibrium
Phase sequence	Molar	Wholes	Concept formation	Stages
Neurophysiology	Intention	*Prägnanz*	Attributes	Assimilation
Arousal	Expectancy	Closure	Coding systems	Accommodation
	Sign–significate		Strategies	Operations
	Place learning			Logic
				Conservation

TABLE 11.3   Diagrammatic and Symbolic Representations

		Behaviorism		
Watson	Thorndike	Guthrie	Hull	Skinner
US → UR	1) $S_1 \rightarrow R_1$ (pleasant)	$S_1 \rightarrow R_1$	$_sE_R = {_sH_R} \times D \times V \times K$	$R + S_1 \rightarrow$ reinforcement
CS → ?	2) $S_1 \rightarrow R_1$	$S_1 \rightarrow R_1$		
CS + US → UR				→
CS + US → UR	1) $S_2 \rightarrow R_2$ (unpleasant)	$S_1 \rightarrow R_1$		$S_1 \rightarrow R_X$
CS → CR	2) $S_2 \rightarrow$			

Transition		*Cognitivism*			
Hebb	Tolman	Gestaltists	Bruner	Piaget	Information Processing

they are dealing with topics that are more relevant to human behavior than are questions relating only to stimuli, responses, and response consequences, and that investigating these topics sometimes requires making inferences from relatively limited data.

Both Bruner and Piaget continue to have tremendous influence on childrearing, and especially on practices in schools. There is little doubt that Piaget is largely responsible for converting a generation of teachers, parents, and child care workers into fascinated observers of children and their development.

THREE INTEGRATIONS

Historically, the search in learning theory has been for one best way of explaining human behavior—a search clearly based on the assumption that there *is* one best explanation. But what if there isn't? What if psychology assumes that because there are many different kinds of human learning, there is a need for many different explanations?

Several theorists have made just that assumption, and the resulting theories are typically an integration of a variety of concepts that have traditionally been associated with separate positions. Among these thinkers are Albert Bandura, Robert Gagné, and Jerome Bruner.

Albert Bandura: Behavior Control Systems

In two earlier chapters of this text, we looked at aspects of Albert Bandura's theories.

Behavioristic Roots

In Chapter 4 we examined his theory of observational learning (or imitation), a theory based squarely on a model of operant conditioning. Imitation is an extremely powerful and very important phenomenon by which a tremendous variety of social learning occurs. It is largely through imitation that people learn how to dress, eat, speak, drive vehicles, and so on. Imitative behaviors, Bandura explains, are emitted behaviors that can be reinforced either as a direct consequence of the behaviors themselves or by the person being imitated. In addition, they are subject to the secondhand effects of seeing other people being reinforced or punished.

Cognitive Influences

But in Chapter 10, we saw a different side of Bandura's theorizing. There we looked at the role of the individual's personal assessments of competency and effectiveness. What Bob thinks of himself (that is, his sense of self-efficacy) is inextricably linked with decisions he makes about what he will do, as well as with the amount of effort and time he will be willing to devote to different activities. If he firmly believed himself to be stupid and incapable of understanding the concepts in this text, he probably would not read it. Thus do *cognitions* drive actions.

Even in operant learning, claims Bandura, what is most important is the ability to think, to symbolize, to tease out cause-and-effect relationships, and to anticipate the consequences of a person's own behavior (as well as the behavior of others). Although there is little doubt that punishments and reinforcements affect behavior, they don't control people blindly as if they were thoughtless puppets. Their effects are largely a function of awareness of relationships and expectations of outcomes—expectations that might span days, or even years. Thus can farmers plant wheat with scant possibility of any immediate reinforcement; they know that will come in the fall (if it ever rains).

Behavior Control Systems

Bandura (1969) maintains that it is impossible to explain human behavior solely by reference to either internal or external stimulus events; both are inevitably involved in most human behavior. Because behaviorism can be defined in terms of its preoccupation with external events, whereas cognitivism deals mainly with internal events, this view tends to integrate the two approaches.

When Bandura refers to external stimulus events, he means simply that the physical environment is at least partly responsible for human behavior. It is patently obvious that people do, in fact, respond to the environment. Not to do so would be a mark of a totally nonfunctional being; even such phylogenetically low forms of life as planaria are responsive to external stimulation.

Internal stimulation refers to more cognitive events (in the form of images, memories, feelings, instructions, verbalizations, and so on) that compose human thought processes. That these events influence behavior is clear—grandmother would need no convincing whatsoever. Interestingly, though, psychologists sometimes do. To this end, Bandura (1969) cites an experiment performed by N. E. Miller (1951) in which a group of subjects were conditioned by means of electric shocks to react negatively to the letter *T* and positively to the number 4. After conditioning, subjects consistently gave evidence of greater autonomic reaction (arousal) for the stimulus associated with shock (in this case, *T*). Miller subsequently instructed subjects to *think* the stimuli alternately as a sequence of dots were presented to them (*T* for the first dot, 4 for the second, *T* for the third, and so on). The fact that there was now greater autonomic reaction to odd-numbered dots demonstrates the effect of internal processes on behavior.

In describing the forces that affect human behavior, Bandura notes three separate control systems that interact with one another in determining behavior. These are described below.

1. Stimulus control.   One class of human behaviors consists of activities that are directly under the control of stimuli. Such behaviors include the host of autonomic (reflexive) acts in which people engage when responding to certain specific stimuli. Sneezing, withdrawing from pain, flinching, the startle reaction, and so on are all examples of behavior controlled by external stimuli.

Behaviors under control of stimuli also include responses learned through reinforcement. When a specific stimulus is always present at the time of the reinforcement, it acquires control over behavior in the sense that it eventually serves as a signal for a response. One illustration of this type of control is found in the contrast between the behavior of some schoolchildren when their teachers are present and when they are not. By granting rewards for good behavior and punishment for less desirable activity, teachers become stimuli capable of eliciting either obedience, fear, caution, respect, love, or a combination of these responses.

2. Outcome control.   Some behaviors, explains Bandura, are under control of their consequences rather than their antecedents (or stimuli). This control system, which has been extensively investigated by B. F. Skinner, relates specifically to activities that become more probable as a function of reinforcement or less probable as a function of either nonreinforcement or punishment. In this behavior control system, control is achieved through operant conditioning (see Chapter 3).

3. Symbolic control.   The third behavior control system includes the range of human activity that is influenced by "mediation," or internal processes. There are several ways in which human behavior can be affected by thought processes. Internal verbalization of rules (self-instructions) can direct behavior as in the Miller (1951) experiment, in which subjects "instructed themselves to think *T*, then 4, and so on.

A second sense in which symbolic processes direct behavior has to do with the way *imagining* the consequences of behavior affects ongoing activity. Were it not for the ability to represent long-range outcomes symbolically, many tasks that are not associated with either an immediate stimulus or an immediate reward would not be undertaken.

The importance of symbolization for human behavior appears to be much greater than that of the other two behavior control systems. It also appears that as one goes down the phylogenetic scale, the importance of outcome control and of direct stimulus control increases. Lower animal forms seem to react more to specific external stimulation than to behavioral outcomes. In addition, it is not at all evident that symbolization plays an important (if any) role in directing the behavior of lower animals.

Behavior Control Systems in Action

Although stimulus, outcome, and symbolic control are clearly distinguishable on theoretical grounds, they are not necessarily separate in practice. In fact, much human activity is probably directed by a combination of these three. For example, consider a woman who pursues a bucktoothed, cross-eyed, knock-kneed, pigeon-toed, skinny, redheaded man. Because of stimulus generalization the pursuer reacts to this man as she would to any other (the stimulus *man* has been present at the time of many previous reinforcements).

But human behavior is not this simple. The pursuer does not just respond to the stimulus in the blind manner expected of an unsophisticated rat. If her initial approach encounters strong resistance, she may modify it; if it is rewarded, she may intensify it. If the intensification leads to more reward, it may be reintensified; if it leads to a cessation of reinforcement, it may be diminished. Thus the human female is capable of changing her behavior in accordance with its immediate outcomes.

But the direction of activity is still more complex, because actions are also guided by symbolic processes. For example, the woman can represent in her imagination the consequences of succeeding in capturing this unattractive red-headed male. She likely believes that such an ugly man must possess hidden talents to offset his lack of obvious qualities. Perhaps she anticipates that he will be an excellent cook.

Robert Gagné: Outcomes of Learning

Another theory that presents a systematic attempt to integrate many of the theories described in this text is that advanced by Robert Gagné. He claims that people learn in many ways, including simple Pavlovian conditioning, Skinnerian conditioning, and more cognitive processes. The various ways of learning are most clearly evident in the different outcomes of the learning process.

In more recent formulations, Gagné's emphasis has continued to shift more toward cognitive explanations, and especially toward their usefulness for instruction (Gagné & Briggs, 1983). "Learning," he explains, "is something that takes place inside a person's head—in the brain" (Gagné & Driscoll, 1988, p. 3).[4]

Outcomes of Learning

Gagné (1985) describes five major outcomes of learning in terms of domains of learned capabilities: intellectual skills, verbal information, attitudes, motor skills, and cognitive strategies. Intellectual skills are concerned with the *how* of learning and relate well to the learning theories described in preceding chapters. The other four domains are concerned more with the *what* of learning.

Verbal information.   Most of the learning of greatest concern to teachers involves verbal information, defined in terms of what is generally considered to be **knowledge**. Although it is not always derived only from verbal input (or stored verbally, for that matter), verbal information can be expressed in the form of a sentence—or at least an implied sentence.

---

[4]This statement implies a false dichotomy: cognitivists on the one hand, who believe that learning takes place inside the head; and behaviorists on the other, who, by implication, must believe that learning takes place elsewhere. In fact, *none* of the theorists discussed in this entire report would deny that learning takes place inside the head. The point Kro was making was that Gagné's emphasis, like that of other cognitivists, has been shifting toward events inside the head. In contrast, behaviorists have considered it more fruitful to deal with events outside the head. (GRL)

Cognitive strategies.   **Cognitive strategies** are the specific means by which people guide their intellectual functioning. These are the plans (strategies) that govern how people go about learning, remembering, paying attention, synthesizing, abstracting, creating, and so on. They are skills that appear to be largely self-learned in spite of the fact that schools (and teacher education programs) typically pay considerable lip service to them.

Attitudes.   **Attitudes** are affective (emotional) reactions that can generally be described as positive or negative and that have important motivational qualities. Gagné suggests that one of the important ways in which attitudes are learned involves imitation much as it is described by Bandura. In his words, "An attitude is an acquired internal state that influences the choice of personal action" (Gagné & Driscoll, 1988, p. 58).

Motor skills.   **Motor skills** are the variety of organized, sequential activities that involve the use of muscles. They include all complex behaviors that require an organized pattern of controlled muscular movements. Writing, talking, plucking chickens, and hitting a spitoon from 22 paces are all examples of motor skills.

Intellectual skills.   The domain of behaviors to which Gagné has paid the greatest attention is that of **intellectual skills**. These include all of the skills that are involved in acquiring information, solving problems, discovering rules, and learning how to talk, to name but a few activities. In earlier descriptions of his theory, Gagné (1974) distinguished among eight different types of learning, the first four of which were clear examples of Pavlovian and Skinnerian conditioning (for example, signal learning, stimulus–response learning, and learning of chains); the last four presented more cognitive kinds of learning. In his more recent writing, however, he lumps the first four types under the heading of "simple types of learning" (Gagné & Dick, 1983). To illustrate how Gagné's view serves to integrate the major positions described in this text, the original eight types of learning are summarized briefly here.

Two important points need to be noted at the outset. First, the types of learning are not completely independent from one another but are in fact hierarchical. The simplest, most basic learning is necessary before the learner can go on to more complex types of learning. Second, types of learning are distinguishable largely in terms of the conditions that permit the learning to take place.

Type 1: Signal Learning

Definition: Simple Pavlovian conditioning.
Example: A car horn blasts. A man jumps wildly. The same man sees another car—a quiet one. He jumps wildly again.
Important theorists: Pavlov, Watson

Type 2: Stimulus-Response Learning

Definition: The formation of a *single* connection between a stimulus and a response.

Example: A fat sow is turned clockwise as her proud owner, a psychologist, says gently, "Turn." After each complete turn the smiling sow is given a piece of apple. The psychologist does this every day for 2 years. After 730 apples and 1459 turns (the psychologist ate half the apple once), the sow can now turn when the psychologist says "Turn." That is slow stimulus–response learning.

Important theorists: Skinner, Thorndike, Hull

Type 3: Chaining—Motor Chains

Definition: The connection of a sequence of stimulus–response motor behaviors.

Example: A man is seen removing his teeth. He reaches to his mouth with his hand, opens his mouth and inserts his hand, places the thumb and forefinger on the right upper canine, and pulls. He then does the same for his lower teeth. The S–R chain may be simplified as follows:

$$S \longrightarrow R \dashrightarrow S \longrightarrow R \dashrightarrow S \longrightarrow R \dashrightarrow S \longrightarrow R$$

hand at mouth	open mouth	mouth open	insert hand	hand inserted	position fingers	fingers positioned	pull

Important theorists: Guthrie, Thorndike, Skinner

Type 4: Chaining—Verbal Associations

Definition: The connection of a sequence of verbal stimulus–response behaviors.

Example: One, two, three, four, five . . .

Important theorists: Hull, Hebb, Bruner

Type 5: Discrimination Learning

Definition: Learning to discriminate between highly similar stimulus input. The learning of discriminations is "essentially a matter of establishing numbers of different chains" (Gagné, 1965, p. 115).

Example: The learning of a foreign language involves learning verbal chains in that language. Because these chains are already present in the mother tongue, the learner must discriminate between the two.

Important theorists: Skinner, Bruner, Hebb

Type 6: Concept Learning

Definition: Concept learning involves responding to a set of objects in terms of their similarities. Gagné distinguishes between *concrete* concepts, which can be pointed at (like *dog*), and *defined* concepts like (*uncle* or *religion*).

Example: A boy learns that an English setter is a dog. He sees a cat and says "doggie." He has developed a "doggie" concept, albeit an incorrect one.

Important theorists: Hebb, Bruner, Skinner, Piaget

Type 7: Rule Learning

Definition: "A rule is an inferred capability that enables the individual to respond to a class of stimulus situations with a class of performances" (Gagné, 1970, p. 191). Rules enable learners to actually do things, as opposed to simply being able to state the rule.

Example: A simple rule is exemplified by the statement "Psychology is fun." Understanding this rule involves understanding the concept *psychology* and the concept *fun.* (Many human students understand neither.)

Important theorists: Bruner, Piaget

Type 8: Higher-order rules

Definition: Combining simple rules to generate more complex rules that allow the solution of problems.

Example: To find the area of a floor consisting of 24 tiles, each measuring 12 inches by 12 inches, the learner combines the rules: 12 inches equals 1 foot; the area of a tile measuring 1 foot by 1 foot is 1 square foot; the area of surface is equal to the sum of the separate areas of each of its components.

Important theorists: Bruner, Piaget

Summary of Gagné's Learning Outcomes

Table 11.4 presents a summary of Gagné's learning outcomes. One of his major emphases has been on describing the conditions most conducive to each of these types of learning (Gagné, Briggs, & Wager, 1988). Some of these conditions are illustrated in that table as well.

Jerome Bruner: Models of the Learner

Learning theories, claims Jerome Bruner (1985), are really models of the learner. If we look at the various theories of learning that have been proposed, we get glimpses of the models of the human learner that underly them.

Tabula Rasa

One of the oldest models of the learner is that of the **tabula rasa** (or blank slate). This view is premised on the notion that the human is born with no prior knowledge, few inclinations, and no thoughts, although perhaps a few reflexes. All are equal at birth, says the model: Experience subsequently writes its messages on the slate, gradually molding the infant into the child and eventually the adult, accounting for all the eventual differences among people.

The tabula rasa model is sometimes illustrated with the empty-vessel metaphor. The infant's mind, says this metaphor, is like a vessel that is completely empty at birth and that has the same capacity as every other infant's vessel. In time, the waters of experience are poured slowly into the vessel, and in the end some vessels end up fuller than others.

TABLE 11.4   Gagné's Major Learning Outcomes, Illustrated, and with Suggestions Relevant for Instruction

Outcomes of learning	Examples	Conditions that facilitate outcomes
1. Intellectual skills		
Higher-order rules	Learner determines relationships among models of the learner and learning theories	Review of relevant rules; verbal instruction to aid in recall of rules; verbal instructions to direct thinking
Rules	Learner identifies new theory as being cognitive	Learner is made aware of desired learning outcome; relevant concepts are reviewed; concrete examples are provided
Concepts	Learner classifies objects in terms of size and color	Examples presented; learner engaged in finding examples; reinforcement
Discriminations	Learner distinguishes among different printed letters	Simultaneous presentation of stimuli to be discriminated; reinforcement (confirmation); repetition
Simple types of learning (signal learning; stimulus–response learning; chaining)	Learner is conditioned to respond favorably to school	Reinforcement; models; positive experiences in various school contexts
2. Verbal information	Learner writes down Gagné's five major learning domains	Information that organizes content; meaningful context; instructional aids for retention and motivation
3. Cognitive strategies	Learner devises personal strategy for remembering Guthrie's three methods for breaking habits	Frequent presentation of novel and challenging problems
4. Attitudes	Learner chooses to read a learning text rather than a novel	Models; reinforcement; verbal guidance
5. Motor skills	Learner types a summary of this chapter	Models; verbal directions; reinforcement (knowledge of results); practice

The tabula rasa model is clearly reflected in the theories of the behaviorists, who undertook to discover and explain the rules by which experience writes its messages or pours its waters—namely, the rules of classical and operant conditioning. When Watson insisted he could make what he wanted of a dozen healthy infants, it was because he firmly believed all infants to be equal at birth and equally susceptible to the influences of experience.[5]

Hypothesis Generator

Some theorists objected to the mechanistic view of the learner presented by the tabula rasa model. Human learners are not so passive, they argued; they aren't simply pushed this way and that by the stimuli, the rewards, and the punishments that experience holds in store for them. Rather, they are characterized by intentionality. They choose experiences and, perhaps more important, interpret them in terms of their own notions about the world (their own personal hypotheses).

Hull's antedating goal responses provide an early glimpse—albeit a carefully behavioristic one—of the learner as a **hypothesis generator**. Tolman's purposive behaviorism provides an even clearer view of behavior driven by intention rather than simply by external events.

Nativism

The complexity of what the infant and the child have to learn, and the ease and rapidity with which they learn it, suggests yet another model—one that views the human learner not as a blank slate but as possessing a mind characterized by previously built-in constraints and capabilities. **Nativism** holds that the mind is already shaped by important tendencies even before any learning occurs.

Nativistic models are central to the work of **ethologists**, who study and try to understand the behavior of organisms in natural situations. Imprinted behaviors like the following response of young goslings, the ethologists explain, are clear evidence of a prewired neurology that constrains and determines behavior. Much the same model underlies psychologists' discovery that some behaviors are more easily conditioned than others, as well as sociobiologists' belief that a wealth of important social behaviors are genetically preprogrammed.

The theories of the Gestalt psychologists, too, reflect this nativistic model remarkably closely. Thus the tendency to perceive wholes rather than parts, to see the best form possible, to look for patterns and similarities, all illustrate wired-in tendencies. Similarly, Chomsky (1972) argues that humans have built-in neurological tendencies relating to language, and that these explain how easily and quickly infants acquire language.

Constructivism

The world is not found or discovered, claim psychologists such as Bruner and Piaget; rather, it is constructed. The resulting model, **constructivism**, is a model of the learner as a builder of knowledge. It holds that through interactions with

---

[5]It's a bit of a caricature, a misleading exaggeration, to suggest that most behaviorists adopted this *tabula rasa* model. Although it's true that aspects of the tabula rasa model *are* reflected in behaviorists' belief in the conditionability of humans, even the first of the behaviorists, Watson, accepted that infants are born with simple reflexes—hence not entirely *blank*. Similarly, Skinner's Darwinian metaphor (the survival of reinforced responses) appeals to the importance of the organism's inherited behavioral repertoire. (Kro)

the world, children discover the means by which to make meaning out of experience. Thus do children progressively discover rules that govern relationships among events, objects, and phenomena of the real world, as well as rules for abstracting significance and for generating concepts. The constructivist learner is a self-motivated, mastery oriented learner, driven by a need to know, to organize, to understand, to build meaning.

As we saw in Chapter 7, Bruner's description of the learner as one who sifts through the data of experience to form concepts and to organize elaborate mental structures corresponding to the world is a constructivist model. So is Piaget's view of the learner as assimilating and accommodating to invent and build progressively more advanced representations and systems of rules for dealing with the world.

Novice-to-Expert

A more recent model of the learner, says Bruner (1985), is one that is less concerned with theory than with the practical business of taking learners who are novices and making experts out of them. One approach suggested by this **novice-to-expert** model is to analyze experts and novices, detail the differences between them, and then devise ways of making the novice more like the expert. The novice-to-expert model is evident in information-processing approaches that use computers to simulate aspects of learning. Connectionism, for example, tries to mimic with neural network models the functioning of the human mind; in other words, it tries to create an expert system. In much the same way, symbolic computer models like those illustrated in chess-playing programs attempt to discover the strategies that account for chess expertise.

In contrast with other models, the novice-to-expert model tends to be domain-specific rather than general. That is, different models are developed for different areas (such as playing chess or reading a page).

These five models are summarized in Table 11.5.

The Last Word

As this text makes clear, there have historically been a variety of different explanations of learning—and hence, a variety of different models of the learner. And through much of history there has lingered the notion that one model and one group of theories must be more correct, more useful, better than the others. "It was the vanity of a preceding generation," says Bruner (1985), "to think that the battle over learning theories would eventuate in one winning over all the others" (p. 8).

None has clearly won over all, perhaps because there *isn't* just one kind of learning. In the end, the most useful models may well prove to be those that recognize this most clearly, and that allow for all the various kinds of learning possible in the wealth of circumstances under which learning takes place. Such a model would recognize more clearly that the strength of the human learner lies in the enormous range of competencies and adaptations possible.

TABLE 11.5   Models of the Learner

Model	Definition	Some theories reflecting model*
Tabula rasa	The learner is an empty vessel, waiting to be filled	Watson, Guthrie, Pavlov, Skinner
Hypothesis generator	The learner is characterized by intentionality and evaluates experience in terms of personal expectations and suppositions	Tolman, Hull
Nativism	The learner is born with some constraints and predispositions that make learning some things (like language) highly probable	Ethologists, sociobiologists, Gestalt psychologists
Constructivism	The learner invents rules, discovers concepts, and builds representations of the world	Piaget, Bruner
Novice-to-expert	The learner is a novice in specific domains and becomes more expert as differences between expert and novice functioning are eliminated	Information-processing models; connectionism (neural network models)

*Note that most theories also include elements of other models.

Ideally, the human learner is flexible rather than rigid, open rather than closed, inventive rather than receptive, changing rather than fixed, and poetic rather than prosaic. Models of the learner and resulting theories should reflect this.

SUMMARY

1. One of the problems in summarizing learning theory is to simplify without lying.
2. The major divisions in learning theory reflect different concerns and different approaches to data gathering and science building. Behaviorists are primarily concerned with objective, observable events (stimuli, responses, reinforcers); cognitivists are concerned with mental processes (thinking, problem-solving, perception, decision making, and so on).
3. Watson, Guthrie, Thorndike, Skinner, and Hull are behaviorists. Hebb, Tolman, and the Gestaltists represent a transition between behaviorism and cognitivism. Bruner, Piaget, and theorists whose models are computer based are cognitive psychologists.
4. Studying memory is another way of studying learning. Motivation looks at the causes and reasons for behavior and behavior change. Memory models are primarily cognitive; models of motivation include behavioristic (needs, drives) and cognitive (attributions, self-concepts, need for achievement) approaches.

5. Major criticisms of behaviorism have to do with its mechanization of humans and its failure to account for such mental events as thinking, feeling, and understanding. Major criticisms of cognitivism relate to its less precise and more subjective approach and to its use of technical terms that are not always clearly defined.

6. Both behavioristic and cognitive models continue to influence psychological theory and practice. Major contributions of behavioristic approaches include an important assortment of approaches for treating behavior problems and emotional disorders, as well as for changing behavior in classrooms.

7. Bandura integrates behavioristic and cognitive models by describing three behavior-control systems involving different classes of responses: those that are under direct stimulus control; those that are affected by their consequences; and those that are directed by means of symbolic processes.

8. Gagné integrates a range of learning theories in his description of five hierarchical classes of learning underlying intellectual skills (simple types, discriminations, concepts, rules, and higher-order rules), as well as four other domains of learning (verbal information, cognitive strategies, attitudes, and motor skills). His description of the conditions that facilitate each of these types of learning has important instructional implications.

9. Bruner describes five models of the learner, which are reflected in different learning theories: tabula rasa (empty vessel; behavioristic); hypothesis generator (intention and prediction; Tolman, Hull); nativism (prewired constraints and predispositions; ethologists, Gestaltists); constructivism (invention and building of cognitive representations; Piaget, Bruner); and novice-to-expert (computer simulation; information-processing models, neural networks).

10. There isn't just one kind of learning, nor should there be just one kind of explanation.

This is Kro within a few minutes of his arrival, sneaking toward me through the bushes.

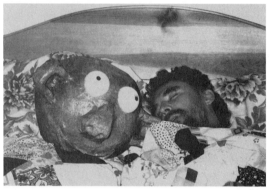

Kro and I, both sleeping. Don't be fooled by the wide open, bulbous eyes and the stupid grin on his face; that's how Korons sleep.

Kro absolutely loved to drive what he called "your primitive land conveyances," although he wasn't very good at it. After one or two trips, none of the children would go with him.

Kro kept hiding from our cameras. But here we caught him coming from the outhouse by the hunting cabin. He went only about once a week.

Kro fancied himself a bit of an expert on wild mushrooms. He claimed he could identify them without error—that he knew their spores and that, of course, he could see them without using our clumsy microscopes. But when he ate these, he was quite ill.

Lefrançois's Epilogue

Kro left this morning, which made everybody cry.

"I'll be back," he shouted as he clambered up behind me on the motorcycle. I doubt it; his cousin Kongor had said exactly the same thing.

I took him back to the south quarter, where Kongor had planted the Koronian flag way back in 1970. I now have it folded up in one of the shoeboxes under my bed. The colors have faded, but you can still see the pig rampant on the right side of the escutcheon, facing the turkey glissant in some unexplained personal interaction. Both are on a field of what could be dandelions. The inscription, *fronti nulla fides*, is now barely legible, but its meaning is burned forever in my brain. "The forehead is never faithful" is the literal translation, but it actually means "You can't judge a book by its cover."

Which is true. Nor can you judge a book by its author, or an author by his or her book.

Anyway, the author of this book, Kro, scampered across the beaver dam almost like some wild thing. Then he stood in the glade for a few minutes, fiddling with the controls of a gadget called a sonarduct, which I happen to have one of too. Suddenly, *whoosh*, out of the sky . . .

But that's another story. Kro's gone, and all we have left are our memories, a couple of bad photos, some broken things, and this book.

Some centuries ago, Blaise Pascal said that reading a book is like having a conversation with the best part of an author's mind. Do you think it's possible that by some weird chance, you and I might both reach for this book at the same hour in the middle of some sleepless night? That we might both, you in your place and I in mine, begin to read the same passage at the same time?

Wouldn't that be like both of us having a conversation with the best part of Kro's mind simultaneously? It would also be almost like having a conversation with each other.

I'll think of you then. And of Kro. Who knows, maybe he'll be reading it too.

Glossary

Absolute threshold The midpoint between a level of stimulus intensity below which the stimulus is never detected and the point above which it is always detected.

Accommodation Modification of an activity or ability in the face of environmental demands. In Piaget's description of development, assimilation and accommodation are the means by which individuals interact with and adapt to their world. (*See* Assimilation.)

Acquisition In conditioning theories, acquisition is sometimes used interchangeably with the term *learning*. It might be used to signify the formation of associations among stimuli or between responses and their consequences.

Action potential A pulselike electrical discharge along a neuron. Sequences of linked action potential are the basis for the transmission of neural messages.

Adaptation Changes in an organism in response to the environment. Such changes are assumed to facilitate interaction with that environment. Adaptation plays a central role in Piaget's theory. (*See* Assimilation, Accommodation.)

Aggregate inhibitory potential ($_{s}\bar{I}_{R}$) In Hull's system, an intervening variable that reduces the likelihood of responding. Reflects conflicting habits as well as the amount of work involved in responding.

Alpha waves Brain waves associated with restful but waking states of consciousness. Characteristically deep, regular waves. (*See* Beta waves.)

Altruism Selflessness. In an evolutionary sense, a powerful tendency to do things that increase the probability that other related individuals will survive, even when doing these things poses serious risk to the actor.

Anthropomorphism The tendency to imbue inanimate objects, animals, and gods with human characteristics and feelings.

Arousal   As a physiological concept, arousal refers to changes in functions such as heart rate, respiration rate, electrical activity in the cortex, and electrical conductivity of the skin. As a psychological concept, arousal refers to degree of alertness, awareness, vigilance, or wakefulness. Arousal varies from very low (coma or sleep) to very high (panic or high anxiety).

Arousal function   In Hebb and Hull's theories, the motivating function of a stimulus. That aspect of the stimulus that relates to attention or alertness. (*See* Cue function.)

Arousal theory   A motivational theory that looks at how intensity of motivation is related to physiological changes. (*See* Arousal.)

Artificial intelligence   Describes models, procedures, devices, or mechanisms intended to simulate or duplicate some of the intelligent functions of human mental activity.

Assimilation   The act of incorporating objects or aspects of objects into previously learned activities. To assimilate is, in a sense, to ingest or to use for something that is previously learned. (*See* Accommodation.)

Associative shifting   A Thorndikean concept that describes a process whereby a response is gradually shifted to a situation entirely different from that in which it was learned. One way of doing this is to change the initial stimulus very gradually (a process called *fading*).

Assumption   A belief important in reasoning, accepted as fact but often unprovable.

Attention   A state of the reacting organism that implies a narrowing and focusing of perception—a selection and emphasis of that to which the organism responds. Attention may be equated with short-term memory.

Attitude   A prevailing and consistent tendency to react in a certain way. Attitudes can be positive or negative and are important motivational forces.

Attribute   A characteristic of an object; a quality or value. (*See* Criterial attribute.)

Attribution theory   A theory that looks for regularities in the ways in which people attribute things that happen to certain causes, either internal or external.

Autoshaping   Refers to responses that are learned in experimental situations in spite of the fact that they are not necessary to obtain reinforcement. Autoshaped behaviors (like pecking in pigeons) often appear to be part of the organism's repertoire of "natural" behaviors.

Axon   An elongated, trunklike extension of a neuron. Neural impulses are ordinarily transmitted from the cell body outward along the axon.

Back propagation   A type of neural network model in which the system uses information about the appropriateness of its output to adjust the weightings of the connections among intervening units.

Backward pairing   In classical conditioning, the presentation of the US before the CS. (*See* Delayed pairing, Trace pairing, Simultaneous pairing.)

Behavior management   The deliberate and systematic application of psychological principles in attempts to change behavior. Behavior management programs are most often based largely on behavioristic principles. (*See* Behavior modification, Behavior therapy.)

Behavior modification   The deliberate application of operant conditioning principles in an effort to change behavior. (*See* Behavior therapy; Behavior management.)

Behavior therapy   The systematic application of Pavlovian procedures and ideas in an effort to change behavior. (*See* Behavior modification; Behavior management.)

Behavioral field   A Gestalt concept defined in terms of the individual's personal perception of reality; also called the psychological field.

Behavioral oscillation ($_sO_R$)   Concept based on Hull's recognition that the potential of a situation to elicit a response is not fixed but varies (oscillates) around a central point. Hence behavior is never completely predictable.

Behaviorism   A general term for approaches to theories of learning concerned primarily with the observable components of behavior (such as stimuli and responses).

Belief   The acceptance of an idea as being accurate or truthful. Beliefs are often highly personal and resistant to change. (*See* Law, Principle, Theory.)

Beta waves   Characteristically shallow, rapid brain waves associated with alertness. (*See* Alpha waves.)

Biofeedback   The information we obtain about our biological functioning. Also refers to procedures whereby individuals are given information about their physiological functioning with the object of achieving control over aspects of this functioning.

Biological constraints   Limitations on learning that result from biological factors rather than from experience.

Black box   Could be the squarish, blackish box (alluded to in Chapter 8) in which grandfathers keep their family jewels. In psychology, more likely to be a metaphor for the mind, implying its unknown (unknowable?) nature—a metaphor embraced by "radical" behaviorists who refrained from speculating about mental processes.

Blocking   A phenomenon in classical conditioning in which conditioning to a specific stimulus becomes difficult or impossible as a result of prior conditioning to another stimulus.

Bubba psychology   An expression for folk beliefs in psychology, also referred to as naive or implicit theories. *Bubba* means grandmother.

Categorization   A Brunerian concept referring to the process of identifying objects or events on the basis of the attributes they share with other instances. (*See* Category.)

Category   A term used by Bruner to describe a grouping of related objects or events. In this sense, a category is both a concept and a percept. Bruner also defines it as a rule for classifying things as equivalent. (*See* Coding system.)

Causes   Agents or forces that produce an effect or a result. Causes are one aspect of motivation. (*See* Reasons.)

Cell assembly   A hypothetical structure in Hebb's theory, consisting of a circuit of neurons that reactivate one another. Corresponds to relatively simple sensory input. (*See* Phase sequence.)

Cell body   The main part of a cell, containing the nucleus.

Chaining   A Skinnerian explanation for the linking of sequences of responses through the action of discriminative stimuli that act as secondary reinforcers. Most behaviors involve such chains, according to Skinner.

Chunking   A memory process whereby related items are grouped together into more easily remembered "chunks" (for example, a prefix and four digits for a phone number, rather than seven unrelated numbers).

Classical conditioning   Involves the repeated pairing of two stimuli so that a previously neutral (conditioned) stimulus eventually elicits a response (conditioned response) similar to that originally elicited by a nonneutral (unconditioned) stimulus. Originally described by Pavlov. (*See* Conditioning, Operant conditioning.)

Closure   A Gestalt principle referring to our tendency to perceive incomplete patterns as complete. (*See* Continuity, Prägnanz, Proximity, Similarity.)

Coding system   A Brunerian concept referring to a hierarchical arrangement of related categories.

Cognitive architecture   A term used in cognitive research to refer to abstract, symbolic descriptions of the human cognitive processing system. Cognitive architecture includes all the systems and processes assumed to be necessary for perception, thinking, problem solving, and other cognitive activity.

Cognitive dissonance   A state of conflict involving beliefs, behaviors, or expectations. Festinger assumed that cognitive dissonance is an important motive for behavior.

Cognitive map   Tolman's term for a mental representation of a physical environment in which goals are located, as well as an internal representation of relationships between behavior and goals.

Cognitive strategies   The processes involved in learning and remembering. Cognitive strategies include procedures for identifying problems, selecting approaches to their solution, monitoring progress in solving problems, and using feedback.

Cognitivism   A general term for approaches to theories of learning concerned with such intellectual events as problem solving, information processing, thinking, and imagining.

Combined schedule   A combination of various types of schedules of reinforcement.

Compensation   A logical rule relating to the fact that certain changes can compensate for opposing changes, thereby negating their effect.

Concept   An abstraction or representation of the common properties of events, objects, or experiences; an idea or notion.

Concrete operations   The third of Piaget's four major stages, lasting from age 7 or 8 to approximately age 11 or 12 and characterized largely by the child's ability to deal with concrete problems and objects, or objects and problems easily imagined.

Conditioned response   A response elicited by a conditioned stimulus. In some obvious ways a conditioned response resembles, but is not identical to, its corresponding unconditioned response.

Conditioned stimulus   A stimulus that initially does not elicit any response (or that elicits a global, orienting response) but that, as a function of being paired with an unconditioned stimulus and its response, acquires the capability of eliciting that same response. For example, a stimulus that is always present at the time of a fear reaction may become a conditioned stimulus for fear.

Conditioning   A type of learning describable in terms of changing relationships between stimuli, between responses, or between both stimuli and responses. (*See* Classical conditioning, Operant conditioning.)

Connectionism   E. L. Thorndike's term for his theory of learning, based on the notion that learning is the formation of neural connections between stimuli and responses.

Connectionist model   Label for PDP (parallel distributed processing) models of the human cognitive processing system. Such models recognize unconscious, automatic, implicit, nonsymbolic learning. They are based not on the application of previously determined rules but on the generation (learning) of new rules. The basic metaphor is that of cognitive processing involving complex arrangements and modifications of connections among neural units. (*See* Symbolic models, Neural networks.)

Conservation   A Piagetian term for the realization that certain quantitative attributes of objects remain unchanged unless something is added to or taken away from them. Such characteristics of objects as mass, number, area, and volume are capable of being conserved.

Constructivism   A model (illustrated in the theories of Piaget and Bruner) that views the learner as actively inventing and building representations of reality, rather than as simply discovering what is already out there.

Contiguity   The occurrence of things both simultaneously and in the same space. Contiguity is often used to explain classical conditioning.

Continuity   A Gestalt principle evident in our tendency to perceive patterns as continuous. (*See* Closure, Prägnanz, Proximity, Similarity.)

Continuous reinforcement   A reinforcement schedule in which every correct response is followed by a reinforcer.

Control group   In an experiment, a group comprising individuals as similar to the experimental group as possible except that they are not exposed to an experimental treatment. (*See* Experimental group.)

Counterconditioning   A behavior modification technique (similar to Guthrie's threshold technique or his method of incompatible stimuli) in which stimuli associated with an undesirable response are presented below threshold or at times when the undesirable response is unlikely to occur. The object is to condition a desirable response to replace the undesirable one.

Criterial attribute   An expression used by Bruner to describe the characteristics of objects, events, or experiences that define their membership in a category—in other words, that are essential to their being what they are.

Critical period   A period in development during which exposure to appropriate experiences or stimuli will bring about imprinting. (*See* Imprinting.)

Cue function In Hebb and Hull's theories, the message function of a stimulus—the aspect of the stimulus that tells the organism how it should react. (*See* Arousal function.)

Cumulative recording A graphical representation of number of responses over time (hence of rate of responding), widely used by Skinner in his investigations of bar pressing and key pecking.

Cybernetics Describes the application of machine models to human cognitive processes. Basic to cybernetic models are machines whose functioning is modified by feedback (that is, where functioning changes as a result of information the machine obtains about the effects of its functioning).

Decay theory An explanation for loss of information in short-term memory based on the notion that the physiological effects of stimulation fade. Similar to fading in connection with forgetting in long-term memory. (*See* Fading.)

Declarative memory Explicit, conscious long-term memory, in contrast with implicit memory. Declarative memory may be either semantic or episodic. (*See* Semantic memory, Episodic memory.)

Deferred imitation The ability to imitate people or events in their absence. Piaget assumes that deferred imitation is crucial in the development of language abilities.

Delayed pairing In classical conditioning, the presentation of the CS before the US, with both ending simultaneously. (*See* Backward pairing, Simultaneous pairing, Trace pairing.)

Dendrite Hairlike tendrils found on a neuron's cell body. Their function is to receive impulses.

Dependent variable The variable (measurement, outcome, behavior) that reflects the assumed effects of manipulations of the independent variable(s) in an experiment. The "then" part of the if-then equation implicit in an experimental hypothesis. (*See* Independent variable.)

Differential reinforcement of successive approximations The procedure of reinforcing only some responses and not others. Differential reinforcement is used in the shaping of complex behaviors. (*See* Shaping.)

Discovery learning The acquisition of new information or knowledge largely as a result of the learner's own efforts. Discovery learning is often associated with Bruner and is contrasted with *reception learning*. (*See* Reception learning.)

Discrimination Making different responses in closely related situations. The opposite of generalization. (*See* Generalization.)

Discriminative stimulus Skinner's term for the features of a situation that an organism can discriminate to distinguish between occasions that might be reinforced or not reinforced.

Disinhibitory effect Involves engaging in a previously inhibited, deviant behavior as a result of observing a model: The inhibitory effect involves refraining from a deviant behavior. (*See* Inhibitory/disinhibitory effect.)

Displacement theory Miller's belief that there are a limited number of "slots" in short-term memory (7, plus or minus 2), and that incoming information displaces older information.

Dispositions   Attitudes or inclinations. Changes in disposition are often involved in learning.

Distortion theory   A theory of forgetting that recognizes that what is remembered is often changed or reconstructed.

Double-blind procedure   An investigation where neither subjects nor investigators know who members of experimental and control groups are. (*See* Single-blind procedure.)

Drive   The tendency to behave that is brought about by an unsatisfied need; for example, the need for food is associated with a hunger drive. A central concept in Hull's theory.

Egocentrism   A way of functioning characterized by an inability to assume the point of view of others. A child's early thinking is largely egocentric.

Elaboration   A memory strategy involving forming new associations. To elaborate is to link with other ideas or images.

Electrodermal response   A measure of skin resistance to an electrical current (also termed *galvanic skin response*). Skin conductivity increases with increasing arousal—and increasing perspiration.

Electroencephalogram   An instrument used to measure electrical activity in the brain.

Elicited response   A response brought about by a stimulus. The expression is synonymous with the term *respondent*.

Eliciting effect   Imitative behavior in which the observer does not copy the model's responses but simply behaves in a related manner. (*See* Inhibitory/disinhibitory effect, Modeling effect.)

Emitted response   A response not elicited by a stimulus but simply emitted by the organism. An emitted response is, in fact, an operant.

Enactive   A term used by Bruner to describe young children's representation of their world. It refers specifically to the belief that children represent the world in terms of their personal actions. (*See* Iconic, Symbolic.)

Engram   A permanent change in the brain presumed to underlie memory.

Episodic memory   A type of declarative, autobiographical (conscious, long-term) memory consisting of knowlege about personal experiences, tied to specific times and places.

Equilibration   A Piagetian term for the process by which people maintain a balance between assimilation (using old learning) and accommodation (changing behavior; learning new things). Equilibration is essential for adaptation and cognitive growth.

Ethologist   A scientist who studies the behavior and adaptation of organisms in natural situations.

Ethology   The study of organisms in their natural habitats. The science of animal behavior.

Eugenics   A form of genetic engineering that selects specific individuals for reproduction. Although widely accepted and practiced with animals, when applied to humans, the concept raises many serious moral and ethical issues.

Exemplar model   A concept learning model that assumes that people learn and remember the best examples of a concept, then compare new instances with these examples. (*See* Prototype.)

Experiment   A deliberately controlled arrangement of circumstances under which a phenomenon is observed.

Experimental group   In an experiment, the group of participants who are exposed to a treatment. (*See* Control group.)

Exteroceptive stimulation   Relates to sensations associated with external stimuli and involving the senses of vision, hearing, taste, and smell. (*See* Proprioceptive stimulation.)

Extinction   In classical conditioning, the cessation of a response following repeated presentations of the CS without the US. In operant conditioning, the cessation of a response following the withdrawal of reinforcement.

Fading   A conditioning technique in which certain characteristics of stimuli are gradually faded out, eventually resulting in discriminations that did not originally exist.

Fading theory   The belief that inability to recall in long-term memory increases with the passage of time as memory "traces" fade.

Fatigue technique   One of Guthrie's methods for replacing habits, involving the repeated presentation of the stimuli that lead to the undesirable habit so that the organism, eventually fatigued, emits (and learns) a different response. (*See* Method of incompatible stimuli, Threshold technique.)

Fixed schedule   A type of intermittent schedule of reinforcement in which the reinforcement occurs at fixed intervals of time (an interval schedule) or after a specified number of trials (a ratio schedule). (*See* Continuous reinforcement, Interval schedule, Ratio schedule.)

Forgetting   Loss from memory. May involve inability to retrieve, or might involve actual loss of whatever traces or changes define storage. (*See* Memory.)

Formal operations   The last of Piaget's four major stages. It begins around age 11 or 12 and lasts until age 14 or 15. It is characterized by the child's increasing ability to use logical thought processes.

Fractional antedating goal response (r_G)   One of a collection of related responses made by an organism prior to the actual goal response.

Generalization   The transference of a response from one stimulus to a similar stimulus (stimulus generalization) or the transference of a similar response for another response in the face of a single stimulus (response generalization). Also called transfer. (*See* Discrimination.)

Generalized reinforcer   A secondary reinforcer that becomes reinforcing in a wide variety of situations because it has been paired with more than one primary reinforcer.

Genetic epistemology   One of Piaget's labels for his system. Literally, genetic epistemology refers to the origins and growth of knowledge.

Gestalt   A German word meaning whole or configuration. Describes an approach to psychology concerned with the perception of wholes, with insight, and with awareness. Gestalt psychology is a forerunner of contemporary cognitive psychology.

Habit   In Guthrie's system, a combination of stimulus–response bonds that become stereotyped and predictable.

Habit strength (sH_R)   A behavioristic Hullian concept; the strength of the bond between a specific stimulus and response, reflecting how often the two have been paired *and* reinforced in the past.

Habit-family hierarchy   Hull's expression for a collection of habits (stimulus–response links) that are related by virtue of the fact that they share common goals.

Hardware   The physical components of a computer, including monitors, controllers, keyboards, chips, cards, circuits, drives, printers, and so on. (*See* Software, Wetware.)

Hawthorne effect   A label for the observation that subjects who are aware they are members of an experimental group often perform better (or differently) than they would if they did not have this knowledge.

Heuristic   Leading to further discoveries. A theory with high heuristic value suggests new avenues of research, new relationships, new findings.

Higher mental processes   A general phrase to indicate unobservable processes that occur in the "mind" (for want of a more precise term). What we normally think of as "thinking."

Homunculus   Literally, a little man or dwarf. Term used for the hypothetical entity assumed by the ancient Greeks to be the cause of human behavior.

Hypothesis   An educated guess, often based on theory, that can be tested. A prediction based on partial evidence of some effect, process, or phenomenon, which must then be verified experimentally.

Hypothesis generator   A model that has at its core the notion that the learner is characterized by intentionality and by the ability to generate hypotheses (suppositions or predictions) and to interpret experience in the light of these hypotheses.

Hypothetico-deductive system   A theoretical system describable in terms of general laws from which subsidiary principles can be derived and tested. Hull's learning theory is hypothetico-deductive.

Iconic   A Brunerian stage in the development of the child's representation of the world, characterized by a representation of the world in terms of relatively concrete mental images (icons). (*See* Enactive, Symbolic.)

Identity   A logical rule that specifies that certain activities leave objects or situations unchanged.

Imitation   Copying behavior. To imitate a person's behavior is simply to use that person's behavior as a pattern. Bandura and Walters describe three different effects of imitation. (*See* Eliciting effect, Inhibitory/disinhibitory effect, Modeling effect.)

Implicit learning   Unconscious learning, not represented in symbols or analysable with rules. Roughly equivalent to procedural or unconscious learning. (*See* Procedural learning.)

Imprinting   Unlearned, instinctlike behaviors that are not present at birth but that become part of an animal's repertoire after exposure to a suitable stimulus during a *critical period*. The "following" behavior of young ducks, geese, and chickens is an example.

Incentive motivation   A motivational concept relating to the attractiveness or subjective value attached to a behavior or goal, and therefore to its effectiveness as a motive.

Independent variable   The variable that is manipualted in an experiment to see if it causes changes in the dependent variable. The "if" part of the if-then equation implicit in an experiment. (*See* Dependent variable.)

Information processing   (IP) Relates to how information is modified (or processed), resulting in knowledge, perception, or behavior. A dominant model of the cognitive approaches, it makes extensive use of computer metaphors.

Inhibitory/disinhibitory effect   The type of imitative behavior that results either in the suppression (inhibition) or appearance (disinhibition) of previously acquired deviant behavior. (*See* Eliciting effect, Modeling effect.)

Input variables   Hull's phrase for the complex of stimuli to which an organism responds—the stimulus—describable in terms of variables such as intensity of the stimulus, the motivational state of the organism, the amount of work involved in responding, and the amount of associated reward.

Insight   The perception of relationships among elements of a problem situation. A problem-solving method that contrasts strongly with trial and error. The cornerstone of Gestalt psychology.

Instincts   Complex, species-specific, relatively unmodifiable patterns of behaviors, such as migration or nesting in some birds and animals. Less complex inherited behaviors are usually termed reflexes.

Instinctive drift   Refers to the tendency of organisms to revert to instinctual, unlearned behaviors.

Instrumental learning   The learning of voluntary responses as a function of their consequences. Associated with Thorndike's learning theory, and sometimes used interchangeably with operant conditioning. (*See* Operant conditioning.)

Intellectual skills   Gagné's term for the outcomes of the learning process. He describes 5 such skills ranging from discrimination learning to higher-order rules (involved in abstract problem solving).

Interference theory   The belief that previous learning might interfere with retention in short-term memory. (*See* Proactive interference, Retroactive interference.)

Intermittent reinforcement   A schedule of reinforcement that does not present a reinforcer for all correct responses. (*See* Interval schedule, Ratio schedule.)

Internalization   A Piagetian concept referring to the processes by which activities, objects, and events in the real world become represented mentally.

Interoceptive conditioning   The conditioning of actions involving glands or involuntary muscles, like vasoconstriction or dilation.

Interval schedule   An intermittent schedule of reinforcement that is based on the passage of time. (*See* Fixed schedule, Random schedule.)

Intervening variables   Hull's phrase for the complex of assumed variables that intervene between the presentation of a stimulus and the occurrence of a response. Include the organism's habits, expectations of reward, and other factors related with previous responses in similar situations.

Interviews   Data-gathering method wherein investigators question participants.

Introspection   A once popular method of psychological investigation involving careful self-examination followed by an attempt to arrive at laws and principles that not only explain the introspector's own behavior but also can be generalized to others.

Intuitive thinking   One of the substages of Piaget's preoperational thought, beginning around age 4 and lasting until age 7 or 8. Marked by the child's ability to solve many problems intuitively and by the inability to respond correctly in the face of misleading perceptual features of problems.

Jargon shock   Somebody's tongue must have been in his cheek. Surely.

Just-noticeable difference (JND)   The least amount of change in stimulation intensity that can be detected.

Knowledge   A generic term for the information, the ways of dealing with information, the ways of acquiring information, and so on that an individual possesses. Gagné defines knowledge as verbal information.

Latent   Not evident; present, but hidden; or potential. Latent learning involves changes in capabilities or attitudes that are not immediately apparent in performance.

Law   A statement whose accuracy is beyond reasonable doubt. (*See* Belief, Principle.)

Law of Effect   A Thorndikean law of learning stating that the effect of a response leads to its being learned (stamped in) or not learned (stamped out).

Law of Exercise   One of Thorndike's laws of learning, basic to his pre-1930s system but essentially repudiated later. It maintained that the more frequently, recently, and vigorously a connection was exercised, the stronger it would be.

Law of multiple responses   Law based on Thorndike's observation that learning involves the emission of a variety of responses (multiple responses) until one (presumably an appropriate one) is reinforced. It is because of this law that Thorndike's theory is often referred to as a theory of trial-and-error learning.

Law of prepotency of elements   A Thorndikean law of learning stating that people tend to respond to the most striking of the various elements that make up a stimulus situation.

Law of readiness   A Thorndikean law of learning that takes into account the fact that certain types of learning are impossible or difficult unless the learner is ready. In this context, readiness refers to maturational level, previous learning, motivational factors, and other characteristics of the individual that relate to learning.

Law of response by analogy   An analogy is typically an explanation, comparison, or illustration based on similarity. In Thorndike's system, response by analogy refers to responses that occur because of similarities between two situations. (*See* Theory of identical elements.)

Law of set or attitude   A Thorndikean law of learning that recognizes the fact that we are often predisposed to respond in certain ways as a result of our experiences and previously learned attitudes.

Learning   All relatively permanent changes in behavior that result from experience, but that are not due to fatigue, maturation, drugs, injury, or disease.

Learning curve   A graphic representation of the acquisition of a learned response as a function of variables like number of trials, reinforcement, or strength of stimuli.

Learning theory   A systematic attempt to explain and understand how behavior changes. The phrase *behavior theory* is used synonymously.

Leveling   In Gestalt theory, a tendency to smooth out peculiarities in a perceptual pattern. Also applies to learning and remembering.

Loci system   A mnemonic system whereby items to be remembered are associated with visual images of specific places.

Locus of control   Rotter's expression for an individual's tendency to attribute responsibility for behavior and its outcomes to external sources (for example, the individual blames others for failure) or internal sources (for example, the individual accepts full responsibility for successes and failures).

Long-term memory   A type of memory whereby, with continued rehearsal and recoding of sensory input (processing in terms of meaning, for example), material will be available for recall over a long period of time.

Mechanistic behaviorism   Expression sometimes used to describe early behavioristic theories. Denotes a concern with the machinelike, predictable aspects of behavior and a refusal to consider *mentalistic* explanations in addition to directly observable events.

Memory   The physiological effects of experience, reflected in changes that define learning. Includes both storage and retrieval. Nothing can be retrieved from memory that has not been stored, but not all that is stored can be retrieved. (*See* Forgetting.)

Metaneeds   Maslow's term for higher needs—those concerned with psychological and self-related functions rather than with biology. These include "needs" to know truth, beauty, and justice and to self-actualize.

Method of incompatible stimuli   One of Guthrie's techniques for breaking habits, involving presenting the stimulus complex associated with an unwanted habit in conjunction with other stimuli that lead to a response incompatible with the habit. (*See* Fatigue technique, Threshold technique.)

Méthode clinique   Piaget's experimental method. It involves an interview technique in which questions are determined largely by the subject's responses. Its flexibility distinguishes it from ordinary interview techniques.

Mnemonic devices   Systematic aids to remembering, like rhymes, acrostics, or visual imagery systems. (*See* Loci system, Phonetic system.)

Model   A representation, usually abstract, of some phenomenon or system. Alternatively, a pattern for behavior that can be copied by someone.

Modeling effect   The type of imitative behavior that involves learning a novel response. (*See* Eliciting effect, Inhibitory/disinhibitory effect.)

Motivation   The causes of behavior. The conscious or unconscious forces that lead to certain acts. (*See* Causes, Reasons.)

Motor skill   A behavior that involves muscular coordination and physical skills. Such common activities as walking and driving are motor skills.

Movement-produced stimuli (MPS)   In Guthrie's system, proprioceptive (internal) stimulation that results from actions of muscles, glands, and tendons.

Nativism   A model that reflects the belief that the learner is born with biological and neurological constraints and predispositions that shape reactions to the world and that facilitate certain types of learning and behavior (like imprinting in geese or learning language in people).

Need   Ordinarily refers to a lack or deficit in the human organism. Needs may be either unlearned (termed basic or physiological: for example, the need for food or water) or learned (termed psychological: for example, the need for prestige or money).

Need for achievement   Expression for a personality characteristic evident in an individual's apparent need to achieve success (to accomplish, to succeed, to win, to gain) and to avoid failure.

Negative reinforcement   An increase in the probability that a response will recur following the elimination or removal of a condition as a consequence(s) of the behavior. Negative reinforcement ordinarily takes the form of an unpleasant or noxious stimulus that is removed as a result of a specific response.

Negative reinforcer   An event that has the effect of increasing the probability of occurrence of the response that immediately precedes it. Negative reinforcement ordinarily takes the form of an unpleasant or noxious stimulus that is removed as a result of a specific response.

Nerve   Bundle of neurons.

Nervous system   The part of the body that is made up of neurons. Its major components are the brain and the spinal cord (the central nervous system), receptor systems associated with major senses, and effector systems associated with functioning of muscles and glands.

Net reaction potential ($_s\hat{E}_R$)   In Hull's system, the result of subtracting the tendency not to respond (called inhibitory potential) from the tendency to respond (reaction potential).

Neural network   A connectionist model of brain functioning premised on the functioning of the parallel distributed processing computer. Neural networks are complex arrangements of units that activate each other, modifying patterns of connections. In this model, meaning resides in patterns within the network, and responses are also determined by patterns.

Neuron   A single nerve cell, the basic building block of the human nervous system. Neurons consist of four main parts: cell body, nucleus, dendrite, and axon.

Nondeclarative memory   Also termed implicit or procedural memory. Refers to unconscious, nonverbalizable effects of experience such as might be manifested in acquired motor skills or in classical conditioning.

Normalizing   A Gestalt principle describing the tendency for memories to change so that they become closer to other related memories.

Novice-to-expert   An information-processing model of the learner reflecting the view that the differences between those who can (experts) and those who can't (novices) can be determined and used to make novices more like experts. Less general and more domain-specific than other models.

Object concept   Piaget's expression for the child's understanding that the world is composed of objects that continue to exist apart from his or her perception of them.

Observational learning   A term used synonymously with the expression "learning through imitation." (*See* Imitation.)

Operant conditioning   The process of changing behavior by manipulating its consequences. Most of Skinner's work investigates the principles of operant conditioning. (*See* Classical conditioning, Conditioning).

Operant   Skinner's term for a response not elicited by any known or obvious stimulus. Most significant human behaviors appear to be operants (for example, writing a letter or going for a walk).

Operation   A Piagetian term that refers essentially to a thought process. An operation is an action that has been internalized in the sense that it can be "thought" and is reversible in the sense that it can be "unthought."

Organization   A memory strategy involving grouping items to be remembered in terms of similarities and differences.

Orienting reflex   The initial response of humans and other organisms to novel stimulation. Components of the orienting response include changes in electrical activity in the brain, in respiration and heart rate, and in conductivity of the skin to electricity. The orienting reflex is an alerting response.

Output variables   Hull's phrase for what the organism does (that is, the response), describable in terms of variables such as response latency, response amplitude, and the number of responses required before extinction.

Parallel distributed processing (PDP)   Describes computer processing where several functions are carried out simultaneously and are related to common sets of input and output. PDP systems are the basis for connectionist models of human thinking.

Parsimonious   Avoiding excessive and confusing detail and complexity. Parsimonious theories explain all important relationships in the simplest, briefest manner possible.

Percept   A term used by Bruner to refer to the effect of sensory experiences. In Bruner's system, percepts are equivalent to concepts. (*See* Concept.)

Performance   Actual behavior. Learning is not always manifested in obvious changes in behavior (that is, in actual performance), but instead may be latent.

Phase sequence   In Hebb's system, an integrated arrangement of related cell assemblies. Corresponds to a concept or percept. (*See* Cell assembly.)

Phonetic system   A particularly powerful mnemonic system that makes use of associations between numbers and letters combined to form words; visual images associated with these words are then linked with items to be remembered. Professional memorizers often use some variation of a phonetic system.

Physiological needs   Basic biological needs, such as the need for food and water.

Positive reinforcement   An increase in the probability that a response will recur as a result of a positive consequence(s) resulting from that behavior (that is, as a result of the addition of something). Usually takes the form of a pleasant stimulus (reward) that results from a specific response.

Positive reinforcer   An event added to a situation immediately after a response has occurred that increases the probability that the response will recur. Usually takes the form of a pleasant stimulus (reward) that results from a specific response.

Prägnanz   A German word meaning "good form." An overriding Gestalt principle that maintains that what we perceive (and think) tends to take the best possible form where *best* usually refers to a principle such as closure, continuity, similarity, or proximity. (*See* Closure, Continuity, Similarity, Proximity.)

Preconceptual thinking   The first substage in the period of preoperational thought, beginning around age 2 and lasting until age 4. It is so called because the child has not yet developed the ability to classify.

Premack principle   The recognition that behaviors that are chosen frequently by an individual (and that are therefore favored) may be used to reinforce other, less frequently chosen behaviors. (For example: "You can watch television when you have finished your homework.")

Preoperational thinking   The second of Piaget's four major stages, lasting from around age 2 to age 7 or 8, characterized by certain weaknesses in the child's logic. It consists of two substages: intuitive thinking and preconceptual thinking. (*See* Intuitive thinking, Preconceptual thinking.)

Primary reinforcer   An event that is reinforcing in the absence of any learning. Stimuli such as food and drink are primary reinforcers because, presumably, an organism does not have to learn that they are pleasant.

Principle   A statement relating to some uniformity or predictability. Principles are far more open to doubt than are laws but are more reliable than beliefs. (*See* Belief, Law, Theory.)

Principle of belongingness   Thorndike's belief that certain responses are easier to learn because, for cultural or logical reasons, they seem to go with (belong with) certain stimuli.

Proactive interference   The interference of earlier learning with the retention of subsequent learning. (*See* Retroactive interference.)

Propositional thinking   A Piagetian label for the thinking of the formal-operations child. A proposition is a statement that can be true or false; hence propositional thinking is the ability to think about abstract, hypothetical states of affairs.

Proprioceptive stimulation   Refers to internal sensations (relating to what is termed kinesthetic sensation), such as those associated with movements of muscles. (*See* Exteroceptive stimulation.)

Prototype   An original model that serves as a basis for other models. In concept learning, a prototype is an abstraction of the most average or representative features of a concept, to which new instances can be compared. (*See* Exemplar model.)

Proximity   A Gestalt principle manifested in our tendency to perceive elements that are close together as being related. (*See* Closure, Continuity, Prägnanz, Similarity.)

Psychological hedonism   The belief that humans act primarily to avoid pain and to obtain pleasure.

Psychological needs   Human needs other than those dealing with such basic physical requirements as food, sex, water, and temperature regulation (physiological needs). Psychological needs described by Maslow include the need to belong, to feel safe, to love and be loved, to maintain a high opinion of oneself, and to self-actualize. (*See* Self-actualization.)

Psychology   The science that examines human behavior (and that of other animals as well).

Psychophysics   The measurement of physical stimuli and their effects.

Psychotherapy   A very general term for the variety of techniques used to alleviate mental disorders and emotional problems. Usually restricted to procedures undertaken by psychiatrists, psychologists, and other specially trained individuals.

Punishment   Involves either the presentation of an unpleasant stimulus or the withdrawal of a pleasant stimulus as a consequence of behavior. Punishment should not be confused with negative reinforcement.

Questionnaires   Data-gathering devices consisting of lists of predetermined questions to which subjects respond.

Random schedule   Also called variable schedule; a type of intermittent schedule of reinforcement. It may be of either the interval or the ratio variety and is characterized by the presentation of rewards at random intervals or on random trials. Although both fixed and random schedules may be based on the same intervals or on the same ratios, one can predict when a reward will occur under a fixed schedule, whereas it is impossible to do so under a random schedule.

Random   Where the outcome cannot be predicted; attributable solely to chance. In a randomly selected sample, every member has the same probability of being selected.

Rate of learning   A measure of the amount of time required to learn a correct response, or of the number of trials required prior to the emission of the correct response.

Ratio schedule   An intermittent schedule of reinforcement that is based on a proportion of correct responses. (*See* Fixed schedule, Random schedule.)

Reaction potential (sE_R)   In Hull's system, the probability that stimulus conditions will lead to a response. Reaction potential is a combined function of specific intervening variables that reflect the individual's history as well as present stimulus conditions.

Reaction threshold ($s\hat{L}_R$)   In Hull's system, the magnitude of net reaction potential required before a response occurs.

Reasons   Explanations for or defenses of an action. In psychology, reasons are often treated as motives. (*See* Causes.)

Reception learning   The type of learning that involves primarily instruction or tuition rather than the learner's own efforts. Often associated with Ausubel, reception learning usually involves expository or didactic methods. That is, the instructor structures the material and presents it to learners in relatively final form rather than asking them to discover that form. (*See* Discovery learning.)

Reflex   A simple, unlearned stimulus–response link, such as salivating in response to food in one's mouth or blinking in response to air blowing into one's eye.

Refractory period A brief period after firing during which a neuron is "discharged" and is incapable of firing again.

Rehearsal A memory strategy involving simple repetition. The principal means of maintaining items in short-term memory.

Reinforcement The effect of a reinforcer; specifically, to increase the probability that a response will occur. (*See* Negative reinforcement, Positive reinforcement.)

Repression theory A theory of forgetting based on the notion that unpleasant, anxiety-provoking experiences might be blocked from consciousness in a self-protective move.

Reprimands A mild form of punishment involving indications of disapproval—usually verbal, but sometimes consisting of gestures (such as shaking one's head to say no).

Rescorla-Wagner model A model based on the notion that contiguity is neither sufficient nor necessary to explain classical conditioning. Instead, it holds that what is learned in classical conditioning are relations among events (expectancies).

Respondent Skinner's term for a response that (unlike an operant) is elicited by a known, specific stimulus. Unconditioned responses are examples of respondents. (*See* Unconditioned response.)

Response amplitude (A) In Hull's system, the physical strength of a response.

Response latency (st_R) Time lag between the presentation of a stimulus and the appearance of a response.

Response cost A mild form of punishment in which tangible reinforcers that have been given for good behavior are taken away for misbehavior. Response-cost systems are often used in systematic behavior management programs.

Retrieval-cue failure Inability to remember because of the unavailability of appropriate cues (as opposed to changes in memory "traces").

Retroactive interference The interference of subsequently learned material with the retention of previously learned material. (*See* Proactive interference.)

Reversibility A logical property manifested in the ability to reverse or undo activity in either an empirical or a conceptual sense. An idea is said to be reversible when a child realizes the logical consequences of an opposite action.

Schedule of reinforcement The timing and frequency of presentation of reinforcement to organisms. (*See* Continuous reinforcement, Intermittent reinforcement.)

Schema The label used by Piaget to describe a unit in cognitive structure. A schema is, in one sense, an activity together with whatever biology or neurology might underlie that activity. In another sense, a schema may be thought of as an idea or a concept.

Science An approach and an attitude toward knowledge that emphasize objectivity, precision, and replicability. Also, one of several related bodies of knowledge.

Second-order conditioning In classical conditioning, the forming of associations between the CS and other stimuli that take the place of the US (typically other stimuli that have been paired with the US).

Secondary reinforcer   An event that becomes reinforcing as a result of being paired with a primary reinforcer.

Self-actualization   The process or act of becoming oneself, developing one's potential, of achieving an awareness of one's identity, or self-fulfillment. The term is central in humanistic psychology.

Self-efficacy   Judgments we make about how effective we are in given situations. Judgments of self-efficacy are important in determining an individual's choice of activities and in influencing the amount of interest and effort expended.

Semantic memory   A type of declarative (conscious, long-term) memory consisting of stable knowledge about the world, principles, rules and procedures, and other verbalizable aspects of knowledge, including language.

Sensorimotor intelligence   The first stage of development in Piaget's classification. It lasts from birth to approximately age 2 and is so called because children understand their world during that period primarily in terms of their activities in it and sensations of it.

Sensory deprivation   Refers to experiments in which subjects are kept in conditions of unvarying sensory stimulation over long periods of time.

Sensory memory   The simple sensory recognition of such stimuli as a sound, a taste, or a sight. Also called short-term sensory storage.

Set   A tendency to respond, or perceive, in a predetermined way.

Shaping   A technique for training animals and people to perform behaviors not previously in their repertoires. It involves reinforcing responses that are progressively closer approximations to the desired behavior. Also called the method of successive approximations, or the method of differential reinforcement of successive approximations.

Sharpening   In Gestalt psychology, a tendency, evident with the passage of time, to exaggerate the most distinctive features of a memory.

Short-term memory   Also called primary or working memory; a type of memory in which material is available for recall for a matter of seconds. Short-term memory primarily involves rehearsal rather than more in-depth processing. It defines our immediate consciousness.

Significant   In research, refers to findings that would not be expected to occur by chance alone more than a small percentage (for example, 5% or 1%) of the time.

Similarity   A Gestalt principle recognizing our tendency to perceive similar items as though they belonged together. (See Continuity, Prägnanz, Closure, Proximity.)

Simultaneous pairing   The presentation of CS and US at exactly the same time in classical conditioning. (See Backward pairing, Delayed pairing, Trace pairing.)

Single-blind procedure   An experimental procedure where either the subjects or the investigator are not aware of who are members of the experimental group and who are members of the control group. (See Double-blind procedure.)

Skinner box   One of various experimental environments used by Skinner in his investigations of operant conditioning. The typical Skinner box is a cagelike structure equipped with a lever and a food tray attached to a food-delivering mechanism. It allows the investigator to study operants (for example, bar pressing) and the relationship between an operant and reinforcement.

Soar   Label for Newell's abstract, ten-component, symbol- and rule-based model of the human cognitive processing system.

Social learning   The acquisition of patterns of behavior that conform to social expectations; learning what is acceptable and what is not acceptable in a given culture.

Sociobiology   A discipline that applies the findings of biology, anthropology, and ethology to the understanding of human social behavior. Sociobiology looks for biological explanations for behavior.

Software   Computer instructions or programs. (*See* Hardware, Wetware.)

Spontaneous recovery   The apparently spontaneous reappearance of response that has been extinguished. (*See* Extinction.)

Spread of effect   Thorndike's observation that rewards sometimes strengthen connections not only between a stimulus and a specific response but also between the stimulus and other closely related responses.

Stimulus generalization   (*See* Generalization.)

Stimulus-intensity dynamism (V)   Hull's label for the effect of stimulus intensity on the individual. In general, the more intense a stimulus, the higher the probability of a response.

Structure   A term used by Piaget in reference to cognitive structure—in effect, the individual's mental representations, which include knowledge of things as well as knowledge of how to do things.

Suppression ratio   A measure of fear reflected in the extent to which an organism abandons ongoing behavior in the face of fear-inducing stimuli. Technically defined as the ratio of number of responses during a specified time period immediately following stimulation to the sum of total number of responses during this time period and total number of responses during an identical time period immediately prior to stimulation.

Surveys   A collection of observations based on a sample (often large) representing some population.

Symbolic   In Bruner's system, the final stage in the development of a child's representation of the world. Describes representation in terms of arbitrary symbols such as language. (*See* Enactive, Iconic.)

Symbolic model   A model other than a real-life person. For example, books, television, and written instructions are important symbolic models.

Symbolic systems   Label for models of human cognitive processing based on the assumption that all information can be represented symbolically and can be manipulated according to fixed rules.

Sympathetic nervous system   Part of the nervous system that instigates the physiological responses associated with emotion.

Synaptic cleft   Label for the space between terminal boutons at the ends of axons and the dendrites or cell bodies of adjoining neurons.

Tabula rasa   A model of the learner based on the assumption that people are born equal, each with no prior learning, inclinations, or thoughts and ready to be shaped by experience—like identical empty vessels waiting to be filled.

Taste aversion A powerful disinclination toward eating or drinking certain substances. Taste aversions are easily learned, are highly resistant to extinction, and demonstrate biological constraints.

Terminal bouton Also called synaptic knobs, these are slight enlargements on the wispy branches at the ends of axons.

Theory A body of information pertaining to a specific topic, a method of acquiring and/or dealing with information, or a set of explanations for related phenomena.

Theory of identical elements A Thorndikean theory that holds that similar stimuli are related by virtue of the fact that two situations possess a number of identical elements, and these identical elements lead to transfer of responses from one situation to another.

Threshold technique A method for breaking habits described by Guthrie, in which the stimulus complex associated with an undesirable habit is presented in such mild form that the habit is not elicited. Stimulus intensity is gradually increased. (*See* Fatigue technique, Method of incompatible stimuli.)

Time out A procedure in which students are removed from situations in which they might ordinarily be rewarded. Time-out procedures are widely used in classroom management.

Token Something indicative of something else. In behavior management programs, token reinforcement systems consist of objects like disks or point tallys that are themselves worthless but later can be exchanged for more meaningful reinforcement.

Trace pairing In classical conditioning, the presentation and termination of the CS before the US so that there is a time lag between the two. (*See* Backward pairing, Delayed pairing, Simultaneous pairing.)

Transductive reasoning The type of reasoning that proceeds from particular to particular rather than from particular to general or from general to particular. One example of transductive reasoning is the following: Cows give milk, and goats give milk; therefore, goats are cows.

Transfer (*See* Generalization.)

Trial and error Thorndikean explanation for learning based on the idea that when placed in a problem situation, an individual will emit a number of responses but will eventually learn the correct one as a result of reinforcement. Trial-and-error explanations for learning are sometimes contrasted with insight explanations.

Turing test The assumption that if thing A duplicates exactly thing B's functions, then thing A must have the same qualities as thing B.

Unconditioned response A response that is elicited by an unconditioned stimulus.

Unconditioned stimulus A stimulus that elicits a response prior to learning. All stimuli that are capable of eliciting reflexive behaviors are examples of unconditioned stimuli. For example, food is an unconditioned stimulus for the response of salivation.

Variable A property, measurement, or characteristic that can vary from one situation to another. In psychological investigations, qualities such as intelligence, sex, personality, age, and so on can be important variables.

Vicarious reinforcement   Reinforcement that results from observing someone else being reinforced. In imitative behavior, observers often act as though they are being reinforced when in fact they aren't, but they think that the model is.

Weber's law   Just noticeable differences (JNDs) require proportionally greater increases as stimulus intensity increases.

Wetware   The brain's neurons and their interconnections. Corresponds to *hardware* in the computer metaphor. (*See* Hardware, Software.)

Yerkes-Dodson law   States that the effectiveness of performance is an inverted U-shaped function of arousal, such that very low and very high levels of arousal are associated with least effective behavior.

References

Alexander, R. D. (1989). Evolution of the human psyche. In P. Mellars & C. Stringer (Eds.), *The human revolution*. Princeton, NJ: Princeton University Press.

Allman, W. F. (1989). *Apprentices of wonder: Inside the neural network revolution*. New York: Bantam.

American Psychological Association. (1989). *Directory of the American Psychological Association* (Vol. 1). Washington, DC: Author.

Amsel, A. (1989). *Behaviorism, neobehaviorism, and cognitivism in learning theory: Historical and contemporary perspectives*. Hillsdale, NJ: Erlbaum.

Anand, B. K., & Chhina, G. S. (1969). Investigations on yogis claiming to stop their heart beats. *Indian Journal of Medical Research, 49*, 90–94.

Anastasi, A. (1958). Heredity, environment and the question "how?" *Psychological Review, 65*, 197–208.

Atkinson, R. C., & Shiffrin, R. M. (1968). Human memory: A proposed system and its control processes. In K. W. Spence & J. T. Spence (Eds.), *The psychology of learning and motivation: Advances in research and theory* (Vol. 2). New York: Academic Press.

Aubrey, C. (1993). An investigation of the mathematical knowledge and competencies which young children bring into school. *British Educational Research Journal, 19*, 27–41.

Ausubel, D. P. (1968). *Educational psychology: A cognitive view*. New York: Holt, Rinehart & Winston.

Ausubel, D. P. (1977). The facilitation of meaningful verbal learning in the classroom. *Educational Psychologist, 12*, 162–178.

Ausubel, D. P., & Robinson, F. G. (1969). *School learning: An introduction to educational psychology*. New York: Holt, Rinehart & Winston.

BAHRICK, H. P., BAHRICK, P. O., & WITTLINGER, R. P. (1975). Fifty years of memory for names and faces: A cross-sectional approach. *Journal of Experimental Psychology, 104*, 54–75.

BAILLARGEON, R. (1987). Object permanence in 3 1/2- and 4 1/2-month-old infants. *Developmental Psychology, 23*, 655–664.

BAILLARGEON, R. (1992). The object concept revisited. In *Visual perception and cognition in infancy: Carnegie-Mellon Symposia on Cognition* (Vol. 23). Hillsdale, NJ: Erlbaum.

BANAJI, M. R., & CROWDER, R. G. (1989). The bankruptcy of everyday memory. *American Psychologist, 44*, 1185–1193.

BANDURA, A. (1969). *Principles of behavior modification.* New York: Holt, Rinehart & Winston.

BANDURA, A. (1977). *Social learning theory.* Englewood Cliffs, NJ: Prentice-Hall.

BANDURA, A. (1981). Self-referent thought: A developmental analysis of self-efficacy. In J. H. Flavell & L. Ross (Eds.), *Social cognitive development: Frontiers and possible futures.* Cambridge, England: Cambridge University Press.

BANDURA, A. (1986). *Social foundations of thought and action: A social cognitive theory.* Englewood Cliffs, NJ: Prentice-Hall.

BANDURA, A. (1991). Social cognitive theory of self-regulation. *Organizational Behavior and Human Performance, 50*, 248–287.

BANDURA, A. (1993). Perceived self-efficacy in cognitive development and functioning. *Educational Psychologist, 28*, 117–148.

BANDURA, A., ROSS, D., & ROSS, S. A. (1963). Imitation of film mediated aggressive models. *Journal of Abnormal and Social Psychology, 66*, 3–11.

BANDURA, A., & WALTERS, R. (1963). *Social learning and personality development.* New York: Holt, Rinehart & Winston.

BARNARD, C. W., WOLFE, H. D., & GRAVELINE, D. E. (1962). Sensory deprivation under null gravity conditions. *American Journal of Psychiatry, 118*, 921–925.

BEAUMONT, J. G. (1988). *Understanding neuropsychology.* New York: Basil Blackwell.

BENNETT, E. L., & CALVIN, N. (1964, JULY–AUGUST). Failure to train planarians reliably. *Neurosciences Research Program Bulletin, 2.*

BERG, W. K., & BERG, K. M. (1987). Psychophysiological development in infancy: State, startle, and attention. In J. D. Osofsky (Ed.), *Handbook of infant development* (2nd ed.). New York: Wiley.

BERLYNE, D. E. (1960). *Conflict, arousal, and curiosity.* New York: McGraw-Hill.

BERLYNE, D. E. (1965). *Structure and direction in thinking.* New York: Wiley.

BERLYNE, D. E. (1966). Curiosity and exploration. *Science, 153*, 25–33.

BERNARD, L. L. (1924). *Instinct: A study in social psychology.* New York: Holt, Rinehart & Winston.

BERNSTEIN, I. L., & WEBSTER, M. M. (1980). Learned taste aversion in humans. *Physiology & Behavior, 25*, 363–366.

BEXTON, W. H., HERON, W., & SCOTT, T. H. (1954). Effects of decreased variation in the sensory environment. *Canadian Journal of Psychology, 8*, 70–76.

BIJOU, S. W., & STURGES, P. S. (1959). Positive reinforcers for experimental studies with children: Consumables and manipulatables. *Child Development, 30*, 151–170.

BITTERMAN, M. E. (1960). Toward a comparative psychology of learning. *American Psychologist, 15*, 704–712.

BITTERMAN, M. E. (1967). Learning in animals. In H. Helson & W. Bevan (Eds.), *Contemporary approaches to psychology.* Princeton, NJ: Van Nostrand.

BITTERMAN, M. E. (1969). Thorndike and the problem of animal intelligence. *American Psychologist, 24,* 444–453.

BOLLES, R. C. (1970). Species-specific defense reactions and avoidance learning. *Psychological Review, 77,* 32–48.

BOLLES, R. C. (1974). Cognition and motivation: Some historical trends. In B. Weiner (Ed.), *Cognitive views of human motivation.* New York: Academic Press.

BOLLES, R. C. (1975). *Theory of motivation* (2nd ed.). New York: Harper & Row.

BORING, E. G. (1950). *A history of experimental psychology* (2nd ed.). New York: Appleton-Century-Crofts.

BOUTON, M. E., & PECK, C. A. (1992). Spontaneous recovery in cross-motivational transfer (counterconditioning). *Animal Learning and Behavior, 20,* 313–321.

BOWER, G. (ED.). (1977). *Human memory: Basic processes.* New York: Academic Press.

BOWER, G. H. (1981). Mood and memory. *American Psychologist, 36,* 129–148.

BOWERS, T. G. R. (1989). *The rational infant: Learning in infancy.* New York: Freeman.

BOWLBY, J. (1982). *Attachment and loss: Vol. 1. Attachment* (2nd ed.). London: Hogarth.

BRADSHAW, G. L., & ANDERSON, J. R. (1982). Elaborative encoding as an explanation of levels of processing. *Journal of Verbal Learning and Verbal Behavior, 21,* 165–174.

BREHM, J. W., & COHEN, A. R. (1962). *Explorations in cognitive dissonance.* New York: Wiley.

BREHM, J. W., & SELF, E. A. (1989). The intensity of motivation. *Annual Review of Psychology, 40,* 109–131.

BRELAND, K., & BRELAND, M. (1951). A field of applied animal psychology. *American Psychologist, 6,* 202–204.

BRELAND, K., & BRELAND, M. (1961). The misbehavior of organisms. *American Psychologist, 16,* 681–684.

BROADBENT, D. E. (1952). Speaking and listening simultaneously. *Journal of Experimental Psychology, 43,* 267–273.

BROWN, J. S. (1965). Generalization and discrimination. In D. I. Mostossky (Ed.), *Stimulus generalization.* Stanford, CA: Stanford University Press.

BROWN, J. S., COLLINS, A., & DUGUID, P. (1989). Situated cognition and the culture of learning. *Educational Researcher, 18,* 32–42.

BRUNER, J. S. (1957a). On going beyond the information given. In *Contemporary approaches to cognition.* Cambridge, MA: Harvard University Press.

BRUNER, J. S. (1957b). On perceptual readiness. *Psychological Review, 64,* 123–152.

BRUNER, J. S. (1964). The course of cognitive growth. *American Psychologist, 19,* 1–15.

BRUNER, J. S. (1966). *Toward a theory of instruction.* Cambridge, MA: Harvard University Press.

BRUNER, J. S. (1983). *In search of mind: Essays in autobiography.* New York: Harper & Row.

BRUNER, J. S. (1985). Models of the learner. *Educational Researcher, 14,* 5–8.

BRUNER, J. S. (1990a). Metaphors of consciousness and cognition in the history of psychology. In D. E. Leary (Ed.), *Metaphors in the history of psychology.* New York: Cambridge University Press.

Bruner, J. S. (1990b). *The proper study of man.* Cambridge, MA: Harvard University Press.

Bruner, J. S. (1990c). *Acts of meaning.* Cambridge, MA: Harvard University Press.

Bruner, J. S., Goodnow, J. J., & Austin, G. A. (1956). *A study of thinking.* New York: Wiley.

Burns, J. D., & Malone, J. C., Jr. (1992). The influence of "preparedness" on autoshaping, schedule performance, and choice. *Journal of the Experimental Analysis of Behavior, 58,* 399–413.

Buxton, C. E. (1940). Latent learning and the goal gradient hypothesis. *Contributions to Psychological Theory, 2,* 6.

Calfee, R. (1981). Cognitive psychology and educational practice. In D. C. Berliner (Ed.), *Review of research in education* (Vol. 9). Washington, DC: American Educational Research Association.

Campbell, D. T., & Stanley, J. C. (1963). *Experimental and quasi-experimental designs for research.* Chicago: Rand McNally.

Cannon, W. B. (1929). *Bodily changes in pain, hunger, fear and rage* (2nd ed.). New York: Appleton-Century-Crofts.

Cannon, W. B. (1939). *The wisdom of the body.* New York: Norton.

Cartwright, R. D. (1977). *Night life: Explorations in dreaming.* Englewood Cliffs, NJ: Prentice-Hall.

Cermak, L. (1976). *Improving your memory.* New York: McGraw-Hill.

Cermak, L. S., & Craik, F. I. (Eds.). (1979). *Levels of processing in human memory.* Hillsdale, NJ: Erlbaum.

Cherry, E. C. (1953). Some experiments on the recognition of speech, with one and with two ears. *Journal of the Acoustical Society of America, 25,* 975–979.

Chomsky, N. (1972). *Language and mind* (rev. ed.). New York: Harcourt Brace Jovanovich.

Churchland, P. S., & Sejnowski, T. J. (1992). *The computational brain.* Cambridge: MIT Press.

Collins, B. E., & Hoyt, M. F. (1972). Personal responsibility for consequences: An integration and extension of the "forced compliance" literature. *Journal of Experimental and Social Psychology, 8,* 558–593.

Cook, N. D. (1986). *The brain code: Mechanisms of information transfer and the role of the corpus callosum.* New York: Methuen.

Cowley, G. (1989, March). How the mind was designed. *Newsweek,* 56–58.

Craik, F. M., & Lockhart, R. S. (1972). Levels of processing: A framework for memory research. *Journal of Verbal Learning and Verbal Behavior, 11,* 671–684.

Crespi, L. (1942). Quantitative variation of incentive and performance in the white rat. *American Journal of Psychology, 55,* 467–517.

Darley, J. M., & Latané, B. (1968). Bystander intervention in emergencies: Diffusion of responsibility. *Journal of Personality and Social Psychology, 8,* 377–383.

Darwin, C. (1962). *The origin of species by means of natural selection, or the preservation of favoured races in the struggle for life.* New York: Collier. (Original work published 1859)

Dasen, P. R. (1972). Cross-cultural Piagetian research: A summary. *Journal of Cross-Cultural Psychology, 3,* 23–29.

DASEN, P. R. (Ed.). (1977). *Piagetian psychology: Cross-cultural contributions.* New York: Gardner.

DECKE, E. (1971). Effects of taste on the eating behavior of obese and normal persons. Cited in S. Schachter, *Emotion, obesity, and crime.* New York: Academic Press.

DEESE, J., & HULSE, S. H. (1967). *The psychology of learning* (3rd ed.). New York: McGraw-Hill.

DELIUS, J. D. (1992). Categorical discrimination of objects and pictures by pigeons. *Animal Learning and Behavior, 20,* 301–311.

DEMAUSE, L. (1974). The evolution of childhood. In L. deMause (Ed.), *The history of childhood.* New York: Psychohistory Press.

DEUTSCH, J. A., & DEUTSCH, D. (1963). Attention: Some theoretical considerations. *Psychological Review, 70,* 80–90.

DOMJAN, M., & GALEF, B. G., JR. (1983). Biological constraints on instrumental and classical conditioning: Retrospect and prospect. *Animal Learning and Behavior, 11,* 151–161.

DOMJAN, M., HUBER-MCDONALD, M., & HOLLOWAY, K. S. (1992). Conditioning copulatory behavior to an artificial object: Efficacy of stimulus fading. *Animal Learning and Behavior, 20,* 350–362.

DULIT, E. (1972). Adolescent thinking à la Piaget: The formal stage. *Journal of Youth and Adolescence, 1,* 281–301.

DWORKIN, B. R., & MILLER, N. E. (1977). Visceral learning in the curarized rat. In G. E. Schwartz & J. Beatty (Eds.), *Biofeedback: Theory and research.* New York: Academic Press.

EBBINGHAUS, H. (1964). *Memory* (H. A. Ruger & C. E. Busenius, Trans.). New York: Dover. (Original work published 1885.)

ECKLAND, B. K. (1977). Darwin rides again. *American Journal of Sociology, 82,* 693–697.

ENNIS, R. H. (1982). Children's ability to handle Piaget's propositional logic: A conceptual critique. In S. Modgil & C. Modgil (Eds.), *Jean Piaget: Consensus and controversy.* London: Praeger.

ESTES, W. K. (1991). Cognitive architectures from the standpoint of an experimental psychologist. *Annual Review of Psychology, 42,* 1–28.

ESTES, W. K., & SKINNER, B. F. (1941). Some quantitative properties of anxiety. *Journal of Experimental Psychology, 29,* 390–400.

EVANS, R. I. (1989). *Albert Bandura: The man and his ideas—a dialogue.* New York: Praeger.

EYSENCK, H. J. (1982). Neobehavioristic (S–R) theory. In G. T. Wilson & C. M. Franks (Eds.), *Contemporary behavior therapy: Conceptual and empirical foundations.* New York: Guilford.

FALMAGNE, J. C. (1985). *Elements of psychophysical theory.* New York: Oxford University Press.

FARNHAM-DIGGORY, S. (1990). *Schooling.* Cambridge, MA: Harvard University Press.

FECHNER, G. (1966). *Elements of psychophysics* (Vol. 1; H. E. Adler, Trans.) New York: Holt Rinehart.

FESTINGER, L. A. (1957). *A theory of cognitive dissonance.* Stanford, CA: Stanford University Press.

FESTINGER, L. A. (1962, October). Cognitive dissonance. *Scientific American.*

FLAVELL, J. H. (1985). *Cognitive development* (2nd ed.). Englewood Cliffs, NJ: Prentice-Hall.

FOWLER, H. (1965). *Curiosity and exploratory behavior.* New York: Macmillan.

FREEMAN, D. (1983). *Margaret Mead and Samoa.* Cambridge, MA: Harvard University Press.

GAGNÉ, R. M. (1965). *The conditions of learning* (1st ed.). New York: Holt, Rinehart & Winston.

GAGNÉ R. M. (1970). *The conditions of learning* (2nd ed.). New York: Holt, Rinehart & Winston.

GAGNÉ, R. M. (1974). *Essentials of learning for instruction.* Hinsdale, IL: Dryden.

GAGNÉ, R. M. (1985). *The conditions of learning* (4th ed.). New York: Holt, Rinehart & Winston.

GAGNÉ, R. M., & BRIGGS, L. J. (1983). *Principles of instructional design* (3rd ed.). New York: Holt, Rinehart & Winston.

GAGNÉ, R. M., BRIGGS, L. J., & WAGER, W. W. (1988). *Principles of instructional design* (3rd ed.). New York: Holt, Rinehart & Winston.

GAGNÉ, R. M., & DICK, W. (1983). Instructional psychology. *Annual Review of Psychology, 34,* 261–295.

GAGNÉ, R. M., & DRISCOLL, M. P. (1988). *Essentials of learning for instruction* (2nd ed.). Englewood Cliffs, NJ: Prentice-Hall.

GALTON, F. (1870). *Hereditary genesis: An inquiry into its laws and consequences.* New York: Appleton.

GARCIA, J., ERVIN, F. E., & KOELLING, R. A. (1965). Learning with prolonged delay of reinforcement. *Psychonomic Science, 5,* 121–122.

GARCIA, J., & KOELLING, R. A. (1966). Relation of cue to consequence in avoidance learning. *Psychonomic Science, 4,* 123–124.

GARDNER, H. (1987). *The mind's new science: A history of the cognitive revolution.* New York: Basic Books.

GELMAN, R. (1978). Cognitive development. *Annual Review of Psychology, 29,* 297–332.

GELMAN, R., MECK, E., & MERKIN, S. (1986). Young children's numerical competence. *Cognitive Development, 1,* 1–29.

GILOVICH, T. (1991). *How we know what isn't so: The fallibility of human reason in everyday life.* New York: Free Press.

GLEES, P. (1988). *The human brain.* New York: Cambridge University Press.

GLICK, J. (1975). Cognitive development in cross-cultural perspective. In F. D. Horowitz, E. M. Hetherington, S. Scarr-Salapatek, & G. M. Siegel (Eds.), *Review of child development research* (Vol. 4). Chicago: University of Chicago Press.

GOLDMAN, W. P., & SEAMON, J. G. (1992). Very long-term memory for odors: Retention of odor-name associations. *American Journal of Psychology, 105,* 549–563.

GREENSPOON, J. (1955). The reinforcing effect of two spoken sounds on the frequency of two responses. *American Journal of Psychology, 68,* 409–416.

GRIPPIN, P. C., & PETERS, S. C. (1984). *Learning theories and learning outcomes: The connection.* Lanham, MD: University Press of America.

GUNDERSON, K. (1964). The imitation game. In A. R. Anderson (Ed.), *Mind and machines.* Englewood Cliffs, NJ: Prentice-Hall.

GUTHRIE, E. R. (1935). *The psychology of learning.* New York: Harper.

GUTHRIE, E. R. (1952).*The psychology of learning* (rev. ed.). New York: Harper & Row.

GUTHRIE, E. R., & HORTON, G. P. (1946). *Cats in a puzzle box.* New York: Rinehart.

GUTHRIE, E. R., & POWERS, F. F. (1950). *Educational psychology.* New York: Ronald.

HAMILTON, W. D. (1970). Selfish and spiteful behaviour in an evolutionary model. *Nature, 228,* 1218–1220.

HAMILTON, W. D. (1971). Geometry for the selfish herd. *Journal of Theoretical Biology, 31,* 295–311.

HAMILTON, W. D. (1972). Altruism and related phenomena, mainly in social insects. *Annual Review of Ecology and Systematics, 3,* 193–232.

HARDT, J. V., & KAMIYA, J. (1976). Some comments on Plotkin's self-regulation of electroencephalographic alpha. *Journal of Experimental Psychology, 105,* 100–108.

HARRIS, B. (1979). Whatever happened to little Albert? *American Psychologist, 34,* 151–160.

HAYS, R. (Ed.). (1962). Psychology of the scientist: IV. Passages from the "idea books" of Clark L. Hull. *Perceptual and Motor Skills, 15,* 807–882.

HEBB, D. O. (1958). *A textbook of psychology* (1st ed.). Philadelphia: Saunders.

HEBB, D. O. (1960). The American revolution. *American Psychologist, 15,* 735–745.

HEBB, D. O. (1966). *A textbook of psychology* (2nd ed.). Philadelphia: Saunders.

HEBB, D. O. (1972). *A textbook of psychology* (3rd ed.). Philadelphia: Saunders.

HEBB, D. O. (1980). Autobiography. In G. Lindzey (Ed.), *A history of psychology in autobiography* (Vol. 7). San Francisco: Freeman.

HEMBREE, R. (1988). Correlates, causes, effects and treatment of test anxiety. *Review of Educational Research, 58,* 47–77.

HERON, W. (1957, January). The pathology of boredom. *Scientific American.*

HERRNSTEIN, R. J. (1977). Doing what comes naturally: A reply to Professor Skinner. *American Psychologist, 32,* 1013–1016.

HERRNSTEIN, R. J., LOVELAND, D. H., & CABLE, C. (1976). Natural concepts in the pigeon. *Journal of Experimental Psychology: Animal Behavior Processes, 2,* 285–302.

HESS, E. H. (1958). Imprinting in animals. *Scientific American, 198,* 81–90.

HIGBEE, K. L. (1977). *Your memory: How it works and how to improve it.* Englewood Cliffs, NJ: Prentice-Hall.

HINDE, R. A., & STEVENSON-HINDE, R. (Eds.). (1973). *Constraints on learning: Limitations and predispositions.* New York: Academic Press.

HINTZMAN, D. L. (1990). Human learning and memory: Connections and dissociations. *Annual Review of Psychology, 41,* 109–139.

HOLYOAK, K. J., & SPELLMAN, B. A. (1993). Thinking. *Annual Review of Psychology, 44,* 265–315.

HULL, C. L. (1943). *Principles of behavior.* New York: Appleton-Century-Crofts.

HULL, C. L. (1951). *Essentials of behavior.* New Haven, CT: Yale University Press.

HULL, C. L. (1952). *A behavior system.* New Haven, CT: Yale University Press.

INHELDER, B. (1982). Outlook. In S. Modgil & C. Modgil (Eds.), *Jean Piaget: Consensus and controversy.* London: Praeger.

INHELDER, B., & PIAGET, J. (1958). *The growth of logical thinking from childhood to adolescence.* New York: Basic Books.

IRWIN, O. C., & WEISS, L. A. (1934). The effect of clothing on the general and vocal activity of the new born infant. *University of Iowa Studies in Child Welfare, 9,* 149–162.

JAMES, W. (1950). *Principles of psychology* (Vol. 1). New York: Holt. (Original work published 1890)

JOHANSON, D. J., & SHREEVE, J. (1989). *Lucy's child.* New York: Morrow.

JOHNSON, G. (1992). *In the palaces of memory: How we build the worlds inside our heads.* New York: Vintage.

JOHNSON, M. K., BRANSFORD, J. D., & SOLOMON, S. (1973). Memory for tacit implications of sentences. *Journal of Experimental Psychology, 98,* 203–205.

JONCICH, G. (1968). *The sane positivist: A biography of Edward L. Thorndike.* Middleton, CT: Wesleyan University Press.

JONES, M. C. (1974). Albert, Peter, and John B. Watson. *American Psychologist, 29,* 581–583.

KAMIN, L. J. (1968). "Attention-like" processes in classical conditioning. In M. R. Jones (Ed.), *Miami Symposium on the Prediction of Behavior: Aversive stimulation.* Miami: University of Miami Press.

KAMIN, L. J. (1969). Predictability, surprise, attention and conditioning. In B. A. Campbell & R. M. Church (Eds.), *Punishment and aversive behavior.* New York: Appleton-Century-Crofts.

KANDEL, E. R. (1985). Cellular mechanisms of learning and the biological bases of individuality. In E. R. Kandel & J. R. Schwartz (Eds.), *Principles of neural science* (2nd ed.). New York: Elsevier.

KAZDIN, A. E. (1989). *Behavior modification in applied settings.* Pacific Grove, CA: Brooks/Cole.

KEITH-LUCAS, T., & GUTTMAN, N. (1975). Robust-single-trial delayed backward conditioning. *Journal of Comparative and Physiological Psychology, 88,* 468–476.

KELLER, F. S. (1969). *Learning: Reinforcement theory* (2nd ed.). New York: Random House.

KELLEY, H. H. (1992). Common sense psychology and scientific psychology. *Annual Review of Psychology, 43,* 1–23.

KLAUS, M., & KENNELL, J. (1983). *Bonding: The beginnings of parent-infant attachment* (rev. ed.). St. Louis, MO: Mosby.

KNOWLIS, D. T., & KAMIYA, J. (1970). The control of electroencephalographic alpha rhythms through auditory feedback in the associated mental activity. *Psychophysiology, 6,* 476–484.

KOFFKA, I. (1925). *The growth of the mind.* New York: Harcourt, Brace & World.

KOFFKA, K. (1922). Perception: An introduction to Gestalt theory. *Psychological Bulletin, 19,* 531–585.

KOFFKA, K. (1935). *Principles of Gestalt psychology.* New York: Harcourt, Brace & World.

KÖHLER, W. (1925). The mentality of apes (E. Wister, Trans.). New York: Harcourt, Brace & World.

KÖHLER, W. (1927). *The mentality of the apes.* New York: Harcourt, Brace & World.

KÖHLER, W. (1929). *Gestalt psychology.* New York: Liveright.

KRECH, D., ROSENZWEIG, M., & BENNETT, E. L. (1960). Effects of environmental complexity and training on brain chemistry. *Journal of Comparative and Physiological Psychology, 53,* 509–519.

KRECH, D., ROSENZWEIG, M., & BENNETT, E. L. (1962). Relations between brain chemistry and problem-solving among rats raised in enriched and impoverished environment. *Journal of Comparative and Physiological Psychology, 55,* 801–807.

KRECH, D., ROSENZWEIG, M., & BENNETT, E. L. (1966). Environmental impoverishment, social isolation, and changes in brain chemistry and anatomy. *Physiology and Behavior, 1,* 99–104.

KUHN, D. (1972). Mechanisms of change in the development of cognitive structures. *Child Development, 43,* 833–844.

LASHLEY, K. S. (1924). Studies of cerebral function in learning. *Archives of Neurological Psychiatry, 12,* 249–276.

LAZARUS, R. S. (1993). From psychological stress to the emotions: A history of changing outlooks. *Annual Review of Psychology, 44,* 1–21.

LEFRANÇOIS, G. R. (1968). A treatment hierarchy for the acceleration of conservation of substance. *Canadian Journal of Psychology, 22,* 277–284.

LEFRANÇOIS, G. R. (1994). *Psychology for teaching: A bear faces the future* (8th ed.). Belmont, CA: Wadsworth.

LEFRANÇOIS, G. R. (in press). *Of children: An introduction to child development* (8th ed.). Belmont, CA: Wadsworth.

LEVENSON, R. W. (1976). Feedback effects and respiratory involvement in voluntary control of heart rate. *Psychophysiology, 13,* 108–114.

LIBEN, L. (1975). *Perspective-taking skills in young children: Seeing the world through rose-colored glasses.* Paper presented at the meeting of the Society for Research in Child Development, Denver.

LILLY, J. C. (1972). *The center of the cyclone: An autobiography of inner space.* New York: Julian.

LOFTUS, E. F. (1979). *Eyewitness testimony.* Cambridge, MA: Harvard University Press.

LORENZ, K. (1952). *King Solomon's ring.* London: Methuen.

LUBAR, J. F. (1991). Discourse on the development of EEG diagnostics and biofeedback for attention-deficit/hyperactivity disorders. *Biofeedback and Self-Regulation, 16,* 201–225.

LURIA, A. R. (1968). *The mind of a mnemonist.* New York: Avon.

MACFARLANE, D. A. (1930). The role of kinesthesis in maze learning. *University of California Publications in Psychology, 4,* 277–305.

MASLOW, A. H. (1970). *Motivation and personality* (2nd ed.). New York: Harper & Row.

MASSARO, D. W., & COWAN, N. (1993). Information processing models: Microscopes of the mind. *Annual Review of Psychology, 44,* 383–425.

MASSON, M. E. J., & McDANIEL, M. A. (1981). The role of organizational processes in long-term retention. *Journal of Experimental Psychology: Human Learning and Memory, 7,* 100–110.

McClelland, J. L., & Rumelhart, D. E. (Eds.). (1986). *Parallel distributed processing: Explorations in the microstructure of cognition* (Vol. 2). Cambridge: Bradford/MIT Press.

McCloskey, M., & Cohen, N. J. (1989). Catastrophic interference in connectionist networks: The sequential learning problem. *Psychology of Learning and Motivation: Advanced Research and Theory, 24,* 109–165.

McConnell, J. V. (1962). Memory transfer through cannibalism in planarians. *Journal of Neuropsychiatry, 3* (Suppl. 1).

McConnell, J. V. (1976, April). Worm-breeding with tongue in cheek and the confessions of a scientist hoist by his own petard. *UNESCO Courier,* pp. 12–15, 32.

McDougall, W. (1908). *An introduction to social psychology.* London: Methuen.

Mead, M. (1935). *Sex and temperament in three primitive societies.* New York: New American Library.

Medin, D. L., & Florian, J. E. (1992). Abstraction and selective coding in exemplar-based models of categorization. In A. F. Healy, S. M. Kosslyn, & R. M. Shiffrin (Eds.), *From learning processes to cognitive processes: Essays in honor of William K. Estes* (Vol. 2). Hillsdale, NJ: Lawrence Erlbaum.

Mellor, D. H. (1989). How much of the mind is a computer. In P. Sleak & W. R. Albury (Eds.), *Computers, brains and minds.* Boston: Kluwer.

Meltzoff, A. N., & Moore, M. K. (1989). Imitation in newborn infants: Exploring the range of gestures imitated and the underlying mechanisms. *Developmental Psychology, 25,* 954–962.

Mervis, C. B., & Rosch, E. (1981). Categorization of natural objects. *Annual Review of Psychology, 32,* 89–115.

Miller, G. A. (1956). The magical number seven, plus or minus two: Some limits on our capacity for processing information. *Psychological Review, 63,* 81–97.

Miller, N. E. (1951). Learnable drives and rewards. In S. S. Stevens (Ed.), *Handbook of experimental psychology.* New York: Wiley.

Miller, N. E. (1969). Learning of visceral and glandular responses. *Science, 163,* 434–445.

Miller, N. E. (1978). Biofeedback and visceral learning. *Annual Review of Psychology, 29,* 373–404.

Miller, N. E., & Dworkin, B. R. (1974). Visceral learning: Recent difficulties with curarized rats and significant problems for human research. In P. A. Obrist, A. H. Black, J. Brener, & L. V. DiCara (Eds.), *Cardiovascular psychophysiology: Current issues in response mechanisms, biofeedback, and methodology.* Chicago: Aldine.

Modgil, S., & Modgil, C. (Eds.). (1982). *Jean Piaget: Consensus and controversy.* London: Praeger.

Moray, N. (1959). Attention in dichotic listening: Affective cues and influence of instruction. *Quarterly Journal of Experimental Psychology, 11,* 56–60.

Moray, N. (1963). *Cybernetics.* New York: Hawthorne.

Mowrer, O. H., & Mowrer, W. M. (1938). Enuresis: A method for its study and treatment. *American Journal of Orthopsychiatry, 8,* 436–459.

MURAWSKI, D. A. (1993). Passion vine butterflies: A taste for poison. *National Geographic, 184*, 123–137.

MURCHISON, C. (Ed.). (1936). *A history of psychology in autobiography* (Vol. 3). Worcester, MA: Clark University Press.

NEISSER, U. (1976). *Cognition and reality: Principles and implications of cognitive psychology.* San Francisco: Freeman.

NEISSER, U. (1978). Memory: What are the important questions? In M. M. Gruneberg, P. E. Morris, & R. N. Sykes (Eds.), *Practical aspects of memory.* San Diego, CA: Academic Press.

NERUDA, P. (1972). *The captain's verses.* New York: New Directions.

NEWELL, A. (1973). Artificial intelligence and the concept of mind. In R. C. Schank & C. M. Colby (Eds.), *Computer models of thought and language.* San Francisco: Freeman.

NEWELL, A. (1989). Putting it all together. In D. Klahr & K. Kotovsky (Eds.), *Complex information processing: The impact of Herbert A. Simon.* Hillsdale, NJ: Erlbaum.

NEWELL, A. (1990). *Unified theories of cognition.* Cambridge, MA: Harvard University Press.

NEWELL, A., & SIMON, H. A. (1972). *Human problem solving.* Englewood Cliffs, NJ: Prentice-Hall.

NEWELL, A., SHAW, J. C., & SIMON, H. A. (1958). Elements of a theory of human problem-solving. *Psychological Review, 65*, 151–166.

O'LEARY, K. D., & BECKER, W. C. (1968). The effects of a teacher's reprimands on children's behavior. *Journal of School Psychology, 7*, 8–11.

O'LEARY, K. D., KAUFMAN, K. F., KASS, R. E., & DRABMAN, R. S. (1974). The effects of loud and soft reprimands on the behavior of disruptive students. In A. R. Brown & C. Avery (Eds.), *Modifying children's behavior: A book of readings.* Springfield, IL: Thomas.

OLSON, D. R. (1963). *The role of verbal rules in the cognitive processes of children.* Unpublished doctoral dissertation, University of Alberta, Edmonton.

OPPER, S. (1977). Concept development in Thai urban and rural children. In P. R. Dasen (Ed.), *Piagetian psychology: Cross-cultural contributions.* New York: Gardner.

PAIVIO, H. (1980). *Imagery and verbal processes* (2nd ed.). New York: Holt, Rinehart & Winston.

PAJARES, M. F. (1992). Teacher's beliefs and educational reasearch: Cleaning up a messy construct. *Review of Educational Research, 62*, 307–332.

PARKE, I. D. (1974). Rules, roles, and resistance to deviation: Recent advances in punishment, discipline, and self-control. In A. Pick (Ed.), *Minnesota Symposia on Child Psychology* (Vol. 8). Minneapolis: University of Minnesota Press.

PENFIELD, W. (1969). Consciousness, memory and man's conditioned reflexes. In K. H. Pribram (Ed.), *On the biology of learning.* New York: Harcourt Brace Jovanovich.

PETERSON, L. R., & PETERSON, N. J. (1959). Short-term retention of individual verbal items. *Journal of Experimental Psychology, 58*, 193–198.

PIAGET, J. (1926). *The language and thought of the child.* New York: Harcourt, Brace & World.

THORNDIKE, E. L. (1898). Animal intelligence: An experimental study of the associative processes in animals. *Psychological Review Monograph Supplement*, 2(8).

THORNDIKE, E. L. (1913a). *Educational Psychology: Vol. 1. The psychology of learning*. New York: Teachers College Press.

THORNDIKE, E. L. (1913b). *Educational psychology: Vol. 2. The original nature of man*. New York: Teachers College Press.

THORNDIKE, E. L. (1922). *The psychology of arithmetic*. New York: Macmillan.

THORNDIKE, E. L. (1923). The influence of first year Latin upon the ability to read English. *School and Society*, 17, 165–168.

THORNDIKE, E. L. (1931). *Human learning*. Cambridge, MA: MIT Press.

THORNDIKE, E. L. (1932). Reward and punishment in animal learning. *Comparative Psychology Monographs*, 8(39).

THORNDIKE, E. L. (1935). *The psychology of wants, interests, and attitudes*. New York: Appleton-Century-Crofts.

THORPE, W. H. (1963). *Learning and instinct in animals* (2nd ed.). London: Methuen.

TINKLEPAUGH, O. L. (1928). An experimental study of representative factors in monkeys. *Journal of Comparative Psychology*, 8, 197–236.

TOCH, H. H., & SCHULTE, R. (1961). Readiness to perceive violence as a result of police training. *British Journal of Psychology*, 52, 389–394.

TOLMAN, E. C. (1932). *Purposive behavior in animals and men*. Berkeley: University of California Press.

TOLMAN, E. C. (1951). *Collected papers in psychology*. Berkeley: University of California Press.

TOLMAN, E. C. (1952). Autobiography. In E. G. Boring, H. S. Langfeld, H. Werner, & R. M. Yerkes (Eds.), *A history of psychology in autobiography* (Vol. 4). Worcester, England: Clark University Press.

TOLMAN, E. C. (1967). *Purposive behavior in animals and men*. New York: Appleton-Century-Crofts.

TOLMAN, E. C., & HONZIK, C. H. (1930). Insight in rats. *University of California Publications in Psychology*, 4, 215–232.

TOLMAN, E. C., RITCHIE, B. F., & KALISH, D. (1946). Studies in spatial learning: II. Place learning versus response learning. *Journal of Experimental Psychology*, 36, 221–229.

TRIVERS, R. L. (1971). The evolution of reciprocal altruism. *Quarterly Review of Biology*, 46, 35–37.

TRIVERS, R. L. (1974). Parent-offspring conflict. *American Zoologist*, 14, 249–264.

TULVING, E. (1972). Episodic and semantic memory. In E. Tulving & W. Donaldson (Eds.), *Organization of memory*. New York: Academic Press.

TULVING, E. (1974). Cue-dependent forgetting. *American Scientist*, 62, 74–82.

TULVING, E. (1989). Remembering and knowing the past. *American Scientist*, 77, 361–367.

TULVING, E. (1991a). Concepts in human memory. In L. R. Squire, N. M. Weinberger, G. Lynch, & J. L. McGaugh (Eds.), *Memory: Organization and locus of change*. New York: Oxford University Press.

TULVING, E. (1991b). Memory research is not a zero-sum game. *American Psychologist*, 46, 41–42.

PIAGET, J. (1929). *The child's conception of the world*. New York: Harcourt, Brace & World.

PIAGET, J. (1930). *The child's conception of physical causality*. London: Kegan Paul.

PIAGET, J. (1932). *The moral judgment of the child*. London: Kegan Paul.

PIAGET, J. (1946). Le *dévelopement de la notion de temps chez l'enfant* [The development of the notion of time in the child]. Paris: Presses Universitaires de France.

PIAGET, J. (1950). *The psychology of intelligence*. New York: Harcourt, Brace & World.

PIAGET, J. (1951). *Play, dreams and imitation in childhood*. New York: Norton.

PIAGET, J. (1961a). *On the development of memory and identity*. Worcester, MA: Clark University Press.

PIAGET, J. (1967). *Biologie et connaissance*. Paris: Gallimard.

PIAGET, J. (1972). Intellectual development from adolescence to adulthood. *Human Development*, 15, 1–12.

PIAGET, J. (1976). *The grasp of consciousness*. Cambridge, MA: Harvard University Press.

PIAGET, J., ET AL. (1980). *Les formes élémentaires de la dialectique*. Paris: Gallimard.

PIAGET, J., & INHELDER, B. (1941). Le développement des quantités chez l'enfant. Neuchatel: Délachaux et Niestlé.

PIAGET, J., & INHELDER, B. (1956). *The child's conception of space*. New York: Norton.

PREMACK, D. (1965). Reinforcement theory. In D. Levine (Ed.), *Nebraska Symposium on Motivation*. Lincoln: University of Nebraska Press.

PRYTULA, R. E., OSTER, G. D., & DAVIS, S. F. (1977). The "rat rabbit" problem: What did John B. Watson really do? *Teaching of Psychology*, 4, 44–46.

RAPHAEL, B. (1976). *The thinking computer: Mind inside matter*. San Francisco: Freeman.

REBER, A. S. (1989). Implicit learning and tacit knowledge. *Journal of Experimental Psychology: General*, 118, 219–235.

REESE, E. P. (1966). *The analysis of human operant behavior*. Dubuque, IA: Brown.

ROETHLISBERGER, S. J., & DICKSON, W. J. (1939). *Management and the worker*. Cambridge, MA: Harvard University Press.

RESCORLA, R. A. (1980). *Pavlovian second-order conditioning: Studies in associative learning*. Hillsdale, NJ: Erlbaum.

RESCORLA, R. A. (1988). Pavlovian conditioning: It's not what you think it is. *American Psychologist*, 43, 151–160.

RESCORLA, R. A., & HOLLAND, P. C. (1976). Some behavioral approaches to the study of learning. In M. R. Rosenzweig & E. L. Bennet (Eds.), *Neuromechanisms of learning and memory*. Boston: MIT Press.

RESCORLA, R. A., & WAGNER, A. R. (1972). A theory of Pavlovian conditioning: Variations in the effectiveness of reinforcement and nonreinforcement. In A. H. Black & W. F. Prokasy (Eds.), *Classical conditioning* (Vol. 2). New York: Appleton Century.

RICE, B. (1982, February). The Hawthorne defect: Persistence of a flawed theory. *Psychology Today*, 70–74.

ROGERS, C. R., & SKINNER, B.F. (1956). Some issues concerning the control of human behavior: A symposium. *Science*, 124, 1057–1066.

ROSCH, E. (1973). Natural categories. *Cognitive Psychology*, 4, 328–350.

ROSCH, E. (1977). Human categorization. In N. Warren (Ed.), *Advances in cross-cultural psychology* (Vol. 1). London: Academic Press.

ROSENTHAL, R., & JACOBSON, L. (1968). *Pygmalion in the classroom: Teacher expectations and pupils' intellectual development.* New York: Holt, Rinehart & Winston.

ROSENZWEIG, M. R. (1984). Experience and the brain. *American Psychologist, 39,* 365–376.

ROTTER, J. B. (1954). *Social learning and clinical psychology.* Englewood Cliffs, NJ: Prentice-Hall.

ROZIN, P., & KALAT, J. W. (1971). Specific hungers and poison avoidance as adaptive specializations of learning. *Psychological Review, 78,* 459–486.

RUMELHART, D. E. (1992). Towards a microstructural account of human reasoning. In S. Davis (Ed.), *Connectionism: Theory and practice.* New York: Oxford University Press.

SAGAN, C. (1977). *The dragons of Eden.* New York: Ballantine Books.

SAHAKIAN, W. S. (1981). *Psychology of learning: Systems, models, and theories* (2nd ed.). Chicago: Markham.

SAKAGAMI, S. F., & AKAHIRA, Y. (1960). Studies on the Japanese honeybee, *Apis cerafabricius:* 8. Two opposing adaptations in the post-stinging behavior of honeybees. *Evolution, 14,* 29–40.

SAMELSON, F. (1980). J. B. Watson's little Albert, Cyril Burt's twins, and the need for a critical science. *American Psychologist, 35,* 619–625.

SCHULTZ, D. P. (1965). *Sensory restriction: Effects on behavior.* New York: Academic Press.

SCHUNK, D. H. (1984). Self-efficacy perspective on achievement behavior. *Educational Psychologist, 19,* 48—58.

SEARLE, J. (1980). Minds, brains, and programs. *Behavioral and Brain Sciences, 3,* 417–424.

SEARS, I. R., MACCOBY, E. P., & LEWIN, H. (1957). *Patterns of child rearing.* Evanston, IL: Row, Peterson.

SEJNOWSKI, T. J., & ROSENBERG, C. R. (1987). Parallel networks that learn to pronounce English text. *Complex Systems, 1,* 145–168.

SELIGMAN, M. E. P. (1975). *Helplessness: On depression, development, and death.* San Francisco: Freeman.

SELIGMAN, M. E. P., & HAGER, J. L. (1972). *Biological boundaries of learning.* New York: Appleton-Century-Crofts.

SHADBOLT, N. (1988). Models and methods in cognitive science. In M. McTear (Ed.), *Understanding cognitive science.* New York: Halsted.

SIEGLER, R. S., & LIEBERT, R. M. (1972). Effects of presenting relevant rules and complete feedback on the conservation of liquid quantity task. *Developmental Psychology, 7,* 133–138.

SIMON, H. A. (1990). Invariants of human behavior. *Annual Review of Psychology, 41,* 1–19.

SKINNER, B. F. (1938). *The behavior of organisms: An experimental analysis.* New York: Appleton-Century-Crofts.

SKINNER, B.F. (1948). *Walden two.* New York: Macmillan.

SKINNER, B. F. (1950). Are theories of learning necessary? *Psychological Review, 57,* 193–216.

SKINNER, B. F. (1951, December). How to teach animals. *Scientific American,* 26–29.

SKINNER, B. F. (1953). *Science and human behavior.* New York: Macmillan.

SKINNER, B. F. (1957). *Verbal behavior.* New York: Appleton-Century-Crofts.

SKINNER, B.F. (1961). *Cumulative record* (rev. ed.). New York: Appleton-Century-Crofts.

SKINNER, B. F. (1969). *Contingencies of reinforcement: A theoretical analysis.* New York: Appleton-Century-Crofts.

SKINNER, B. F. (1971). *Beyond freedom and dignity.* New York: Knopf.

SKINNER, B. F. (1973). Answers for my critics. In H. Wheeler, *Beyond the punitive society: Operant conditioning: Social and political aspects.* San Francisco: Freeman.

SKINNER, B. F. (1976). *Particulars of my life.* New York: Knopf.

SKINNER, B. F. (1979). *The shaping of a behaviorist.* New York: Knopf.

SKINNER, B. F. (1983). *A matter of consequences.* New York: Knopf.

SMEDSLUND, J. (1961). The acquisition of conservation of substance and weight in children. I. Introduction. *Scandinavian Journal of Psychology, 2,* 11–20.

SMITH, D. A., & GRAESSER, A. C. (1981). Memory for actions in scripted activities as a function of typicality, retention interval, and retrieval task. *Memory and Cognition, 9,* 550–559.

SMITH, E. E., LOPEZ, A., & OSHERSON, D (1992). Category membership, similarity, and naive induction. In A. F. Healy, S. M. Kosslyn, & R. M. Shiffrin (Eds.), *From learning processes to cognitive processes: Essays in honor of William K. Estes* (Vol. 2). Hillsdale, NJ: Erlbaum.

SMITH, L. D. (1990). Metaphors of knowledge and behavior in the behaviorist tradition. In D. E. Leary (Ed.), *Metaphors in the history of psychology.* New York: Cambridge University Press.

SPERLING, G. (1963). A model for visual memory tests. *Human Factors, 5,* 19–31.

SQUIRE, L. R. (1987). *Memory and brain.* New York: Oxford University Press.

SQUIRE, L. R., KNOWLTON, B., & MUSEN, G. (1993). The structure and organization of memory. *Annual Review of Psychology, 44,* 453–495.

STADDON, J. E. R., & SIMMELHAG, V. L. (1971). The "superstition" experiment: A reexamination of its implications for the principles of adaptive behavior. *Psychological Review, 78,* 3–43.

STAGNER, R. (1988). *A history of psychological theories.* New York: Macmillan.

STANDING, L. (1973). Learning 10,000 pictures. *Quarterly Journal of Experimental Psychology, 25,* 207–222.

STOYVA, J., KAMIYA, J., BARBER, T. X., MILLER, N. E., & SHAPIRO, D. (EDS.). (1979). *Biofeedback and self-control,* 1977–78. New York: Aldine.

TERRACE, H. S. (1963). Errorless transfer of a discrimination across two continua. *Journal of the Experimental Analysis of Behavior, 67,* 223–232.

THOMAS, J. W. (1980). Agency and achievement: Self-management and self-regard. *Review of Educational Research, 50,* 213–240.

THOMAS, L. M. (1992). *Comparing theories of child development* (3rd ed.). Belmont, CA: Wadsworth.

TULVING, E., SCHACTER, D. L., McLACHLAN, D. R., & MOSCOVITCH, M. (1988). Priming of semantic autobiographical memory: A case study of retrograde amnesia. *Brain and Cognition*, 8, 3–20.

TURING, A. M. (1950). Computing machinery and intelligence. *Mind*, 59, 236.

WADE, N. (1976). Sociobiology: Troubled birth for a new discipline. *Science*, 191, 1151–1155.

WALDROP, M. M. (1992). *Complexity: The emerging science at the edge of order and chaos.* New York: Simon & Schuster.

WALKER, J. E., & SHEA, T. M. (1991). *Behavior management: A practical approach for educators* (5th ed.). New York: Merrill.

WALTERS, G. C., & GRUSEC, J. E. (1977). *Punishment.* San Francisco: Freeman.

WALTERS, R. H., & LLEWELLYN, T. E. (1963). Enhancement of punitiveness by visual and audiovisual displays. *Canadian Journal of Psychology*, 17, 244–255.

WALTERS, R. H., LLEWELLYN, T. E., & ACKER, W. (1962). Enhancement of punitive behavior by audiovisual displays. *Science*, 136, 872–873.

WANG, M., & FREEMAN, A. (1987). *Neural function.* Boston: Little, Brown.

WATSON, J. B. (1913). Psychology as the behaviorist views it. *Psychological Review*, 20, 158–177.

WATSON, J. B. (1926). *The ways of behaviorism.* New York: Harper.

WATSON, J. B. (1930). *Behaviorism* (2nd ed.). Chicago: University of Chicago Press.

WATSON, J. B., & RAYNER, R. (1920). Conditioned emotional reactions. *Journal of Experimental Psychology*, 3, 1–14.

WATSON, R. I. (1971). *The great psychologists* (3rd ed.). Philadelphia: Lippincott.

WAUGH, N. C., & NORMAN, D. A. (1965). Primary memory. *Psychological Review*, 72, 89–104.

WEINER, B. (Ed.). (1974). *Cognitive views of human motivation.* New York: Academic Press.

WEINER, B. (1980). The role of affect in rational (attributional) approaches to human motivation. *Educational Researcher*, 9, 4–11.

WEINER, B. (1986). *An attributional theory of motivation and emotion.* New York: Springer-Verlag.

WERTHEIMER, M. (1959). *Productive thinking* (rev. ed.). New York: Harper & Row.

WESTBY, G. (1966). Psychology today: Problems and directions. *Bulletin of the British Psychological Society.* 19(65).

WESTERMANN, R. (1989). Festinger's theory of cognitive dissonance: A revised structural reconstruction. In H. Westmeyer (Ed.). *Psychological theories from a structuralist point of view.* New York: Springer-Verlag.

WHITEHEAD, A. N., & RUSSELL, B. (1925). *Principia mathematica* (Vol. 1, 2nd ed.). Cambridge, England: Cambridge University Press.

WICKELGREN, 81A. HUMAN LEARNING AND MEMORY. *Annual Review of Psychology*, 32, 21–52.

WILCOXON, H. C., DRAGOIN, W. B., & KRAL, P. A. (1971). Illness-induced aversions in rat and quail: Relative salience of visual and gustatory cues. *Science*, 171, 826–828.

WILLIAMS, D. R., & WILLIAMS, H. (1969). Auto-maintenance in the pigeon: Sustained pecking despite contingent non-reinforcement. *Journal of the Experimental Analysis of Behavior, 12*, 511–520.

WILSON, E. O. (1975). *Sociolology: The new synthesis.* Cambridge, MA: Belknap.

WILSON, E. O. (1976). Academic vigilantism and the political significance of sociobiology. *Bio-Science, 183,* 187–190.

WOLPE, J. (1958). *Psychotherapy by reciprocal inhibition.* Stanford, CA: Stanford University Press.

WOODWORTH, R. S., & SHEEHAN, M. R. (1964). *Contemporary schools of psychology* (3rd ed.). New York: Ronald Press.

WULF, S. (1938). Tendencies and figural variations. In W. D. Ellis (Ed.), *A source book of Gestalt psychology.* New York: Harcourt, Brace & World. (Original work published 1922.)

YERKES, R. M., & DODSON, J. D. (1908). The relationship of strength of stimulus to rapidity of habit-formation. *Journal of Comparative Neurological Psychology, 18,* 459–482.

ZEAMAN, D. (1949). Response latency as a function of amount of reinforcement. *Journal of Experimental Psychology, 39,* 466–483.

ZIMMERMAN, B. J., BANDURA, A., & MARTINEZ-PONS, M. (1992). Self-motivation for academic attainment: The role of self-efficacy beliefs and personal goal setting. *American Educational Research Journal, 29,* 663–676.

ZUBEK, J. P. (1969). *Sensory deprivation: Fifteen years of research.* New York: Appleton-Century-Crofts.

ZUBEK, J. P., & WILGOSH, L. (1963). Prolonged immobilization of the body: Changes in performance in the electroencephalogram. *Science, 140,* 306–308.

Name Index

Acker, W., 120
Akahira, Y., 138
Alexander, R. D., 188
Allen, W., 185
Allman, W. F., 227, 234, 235, 238, 239, 242
American Psychological Association (APA), 19–20
Amsel, A., 162, 202
Anand, B. K., 142
Anastasi, A., 45
Anderson, J. R., 271
Atkinson, R. C., 255
Aubrey, C., 222
Austin, G. A., 192
Ausubel, D. P., 117, 203

Bacon, F., 6
Bahrick, H. P., 272
Bahrick, P. O., 272
Baillargeon, R., 222
Banaji, M. R., 270
Bandura, A., 118, 119, 120, 290–292, 314–317
Barber, T. X., 142
Barnard, C. W., 161
Beaumont, J. G., 152n

Becker, W. C., 116
Bennett, E. L., 267, 268
Berg, K. M., 277
Berg, W. K., 277
Berlyne, D. E., 281, 284, 286
Bernard, L. L., 277
Bernstein, I. L., 131
Bexton, W. H., 160
Bierce, A., 29
Bijou, S. W., 115
Bitterman, M. E., 67
Bolles, R. C., 137, 275, 285
Boring, E. G., 32, 172
Bouton, M. E., 122
Bower, G. H., 78, 262
Bowers, T. G. R., 222
Bowlby, J., 278
Bradshaw, G. L., 271
Bransford, J. D., 260, 269
Brehm, J. W., 283, 284, 286
Breland, K., 136
Breland, M., 136
Briggs, L. J., 317, 320
Broadbent, D. E., 250
Brown, J. S., 203
Bruner, J. S., 179, 185, 187–203, 190, 215, 242, 307, 319, 320–323

Subject Index

This page is an extension of the copyright page.